BALKAN FIREBRAND

This book has been designed in a Victory Format. Smaller type and margins produce fewer pages which permit a vital saving of paper and labor in the manufacture of a War-time book.

Balkan Firebrand

The Autobiography of a Rebel, Soldier and Statesman

by

KOSTA TODOROV

ZIFF-DAVIS PUBLISHING COMPANY

CHICAGO · NEW YORK

When General Sarrail told me he needed an emissary to carry the Allies' peace terms through the enemy lines to the Bulgarian General Staff, I answered that the man to be entrusted with that perilous mission was in the Foreign Legion on the Western Front—a Balkan firebrand named Kosta Todorov.

VLADIMIR LEBEDEV

I wish to express my appreciation to Suzanne La Follette for her splendid work as editor of the English text of my book. To a scrupulous care in verifying historical details she has added the innate elegance of a style whose clarity and precision bespeak her French origin. I would be ungrateful indeed if I did not say to her with all my heart, Thank you!

KOSTA TODOROV

CONTENTS

PART IV

E X I L E

1923–1943

PART I

TERRORIST

1889-1913

*You should never wear your
best trousers when you go out
to fight for freedom and truth.*

HENRIK IBSEN

CHAPTER 1

Born in Moscow. Russian, eh?"

"No, Bulgarian."

It was November, 1940, in a New York post office during Alien Registration.

"So, you're a Bulgarian subject," said the clerk. Then he lifted startled eyes from the questionnaire I had filled out.

"You fought in the *French* army?"

"Yes, during the first World War."

He read on: "Delegate to the League of Nations. . . . Present occupation, correspondent for the Yugoslav press. . . ." A light suddenly broke through his bewilderment.

"I get it. You're a Jew."

"No, I'm not."

He waved his hand in a friendly gesture of dismissal.

"I give up," he said.

It was all quite simple, really. Take, to begin with, my being born in Moscow. My father, a Bulgarian army captain, had found himself on the losing side of a coup d'état. In 1886 he had taken part in an abortive plot against the Bulgarian dictator, Stepan Stambulov, and had escaped execution by fleeing with other officers across the Russian border, accompanied by my loyal and intrepid mother. In Russia, he joined the crack Second Rostov Grenadier Regiment, with the same rank he had held in Bulgaria, and was stationed in Moscow. There I was born on July 13, 1889.

From babyhood I breathed the air of conspiracy. My earliest memories are of Bulgarian officers in Russian uniform, gathered around a steaming samovar in our Moscow home, exhaling clouds of tobacco smoke and planning assassination. Most often their plans concerned Stambulov; but sometimes the talk even veered to Ferdinand, the German Prince who occupied the Bulgarian throne.

Even more vividly I remember the imposing portrait of my grandfather Kosta on our parlor wall, his uniformed figure bristling with guns and his warlike countenance framed in a huge white beard. "A great hero," my mother would say proudly. "He killed more than a hundred Turks in the Balkan Mountains."

She had inherited her father's strong and independent spirit, and his hatred of oppression. She loved to tell about his exploits. For twenty years he had carried on guerrilla warfare in the mountains against the Turks, and he had sworn never to shave his beard until the day Bulgaria was free. It was never shaved; he died just a year too soon, leaving behind him a fame secured for posterity in legend and folk song, and a choice collection of gold and silver objects and precious stones, the spoils of his long war upon the Turkish landlords.

Early in life I understood that being a man meant bearing arms like my grandfather and father, and killing as many Turks as possible.

My father, a true soldier, lived by two immutable principles: duty and honor. He despised traders and lawyers, loved the peasants, was outraged by injustice, protested loudly against corruption, and never shook hands with a man he suspected of the slightest dishonesty. Father shook hands with few people.

"If you want to be respected," he told me when I was still very young, "never lie, never tolerate an insult, and behave so that you can always look every man squarely in the eye."

In 1894 King Ferdinand dropped his pilot Stambulov—the "Bismarck of the Balkans." In July, 1895, the indomitable ex-Premier was assassinated and his body mutilated in the streets of Sofia. With his removal from the Bulgarian scene, our family re-entered it. Perhaps Ferdinand himself was our benefactor—Stambulov's murderers not only escaped, but when brought to trial the next year got off with light sentences.

After Moscow, life in Varna seemed drab and provincial, even to a six-year-old. The streets were muddy, our house uncomfortable. When we were invited out, we were offered coffee instead of tea, and the jelly was doled out by the spoonful, not by the saucerful as in Russia. I was very unhappy.

In vain I longed to return to Moscow. I was placed in a school in Varna, where my chief occupations were fighting my schoolmates and reading. As soon as I discovered the stories of James Fenimore Cooper I knew what I wanted—to run away to America and become a redskin chief. Armed with a kitchen knife and carrying a sack of bread for food, I started on my journey. A few miles from Varna, some soldiers sent by my father overtook me. With the help of his belt, Father taught me that America was very far away.

At ten I was sent back to Russia, to the estate of General Minkov in the province of Grodno, where many Slav lads from the Balkans were prepared for entrance into the Russian Cadet Corps. My tutor, Andrey Krachina, a dour drunkard, drilled Russian grammar into me and with the assistance of his aide—a cat-o'-nine-tails—taught me respect for Pushkin and Lermontov. After passing the examinations for admission to the Cadet Corps, I returned to Bulgaria for my summer vacation and remained there, entering the Sofia Military Academy instead. The discipline was severe, the food excellent, the education good, the attitude of the officers contemptuous. I enjoyed the courses in literature and history, detested mathematics, and passionately loved military training. But I became less militaristic under the influence of the great Russian novelists and of the many Russian revolutionary pamphlets that fell into my hands.

When I was a sixth-term cadet, my military schooling ended abruptly. Captain Selveliev, my instructor, insulted me, whereupon I hurled an inkpot at him. Arrested, I escaped, went home, and told my father I no longer wished to be a soldier. Two days later, the academy dismissed me.

My father, now a colonel, was stationed in Sofia as assistant chief of the operations division of the general staff. He belonged to a circle of strong Russophiles, which included the man who was to influence me most—Colonel Radko Dmitriev, who defeated the Turks in 1912 and commanded a Russian army in the First World War. My elder brother, Kyril, who had completed his education in Russia and was now a second lieutenant in the first Sofia regiment, was also intensely pro-Russian. The Revolution of 1905, following the Russo-Japanese War, deeply agitated not only our family but Bulgarian society in general. The revolutionary current overflowed into neighboring Macedonia, where our blood brothers were smarting under the yoke of Abdul Hamid, Sultan of Turkey.

Directing the Macedonian revolutionary movement was the mysterious and powerful IMRO (Internal Macedonian Revolutionary Organization), founded in 1894 and organized in *chetas* (detachments). Macedonia was divided into eighty revolutionary districts, and in every village was a secret *cheta* which could be mobilized by the district *voivoda* (chieftain) in case of emergency. These village *chetas* formed a secret insurrectionary army always ready to answer the summons of the IMRO, whose decisions were made by an executive committee representing the four Macedonian provinces of Skoplje (Usküb), Salonika, Bitolj (Monastir), and Adrianople.

With its many sporadic raids and revolts against the Turks, the IMRO kept the Balkans in constant turmoil. And the IMRO itself was kept in turmoil by two clashing factions. One, entirely nationalistic, stuck close to Prince Ferdinand and the official Bulgarian policy. The other, socialistic, wanted an autonomous Macedonia within a general Balkan federation—which might have stabilized Europe and saved it.

The struggles for freedom in Russia and Macedonia stirred me deeply. Before long I became acquainted with young students who affected red shirts and flowing hair and read Gorki, Korolenko, Andreev, Kropotkin, Bakunin, Jean Grave, and Malatesta. These students belonged to a revo-

[5]

lutionary group directed by a Russian exile named Shapiro. Evenings, we gathered in his house and sat on benches, suitcases, and beds, listening to his passionate harangues about social revolution and the need for terror against the enemies of the people.

The hero of the group was handsome young Michel Ghirgikov, with his fiery black eyes, thick black beard, and pale face. At twenty-eight he had already won fame as the *voivoda* of a group of *chetas* which in 1903 had held out for several months in the Adrianople district against an entire Turkish division. Another member, Petko Penchev, although only twenty-four, belonged to the Central Committee of the IMRO. Once, when we were aroused to revolutionary pitch, a not infrequent occurrence, Petko commented ironically, "Before fighting for socialism in a country like Bulgaria, we need to build water closets." We regarded him as a reactionary, but tolerated him because of his common sense and proved valor. Three young girls also were members—Mary, Zina, and Olga.

Mary was a seventeen-year-old beauty with a halo of blond braids, pale ivory skin, soft brown eyes, a perfect Grecian nose, and a charming dimpled smile. Later she won an all-Bulgarian beauty contest and a rich husband. Of course I fell under her spell. All three girls adored Michel —and ignored me. Indeed the whole group ignored me, for, although well developed, I was not yet sixteen. It seemed unfair, even foolish, to be so young, and with no heroic past. Sitting on a suitcase in a corner I watched Mary furtively, but when the meeting broke up I never dared speak to her. Almost every day I waited near the entrance of the girls' school, hoping to see her. Twice we met, and I bowed timidly while she smiled sweetly. That smile seemed to me so important that for days it glowed in my memory. But at our meetings, she still stared at Michel. I felt hurt.

"I'll go to Macedonia to fight," I muttered to myself. "I'll do great deeds and return crowned with glory. She'll see what I can do. I'll return to her. Of course, I'll be wounded and she'll be sorry and love me. Then —only then—will I tell her of my love."

In May, 1905, our group made an excursion to the Dragalevsky Monastery on towering Mount Vitosha, whose highest pinnacle, Black Peak, rises more than seven thousand feet. From Sofia the mountain resembles an enormous reclining beast, its sides bristling with forests and in its hollows eternal mists. The beast lay warm and bright in the late spring sunlight. Leaving the road at the village of Boyana, we started along a forest path up the mountain. There were six of us—Michel, Petko, the three girls, and I. The path was tortuous and difficult, but I was happy—Mary walked beside me. She started off in good spirits but as we climbed she began to tire. At last I had the courage to offer her

[6]

my arm and led her slowly, conscious of her labored breathing and of the pressure of her firm, warm arm against mine. Often, on the twisting path, our companions disappeared from view and we were alone. The aroma of mint, fern and pine filled the air, and the white birch trees loomed up under the overarching green, like the marble pillars of an ancient temple.

"Look!" I suddenly exclaimed. We were standing on a flat stone in a clearing. Below us in the sun-drenched plateau gleamed the green and golden cupolas of Sofia.

"Yes," she almost whispered. Then, sitting down on the stone, "I'll have to rest for a moment, I'm so tired."

I wanted to say something beautiful, something tender and noble. But I was tongue-tied. Conscious of my embarrassment, she broke the awkward silence: "How are you getting along in school?"

How could she mention school? Was I a child?

"I'll be through in June," I replied, "and then—"

"To the university?"

"No . . . to Macedonia!" I blurted, to my own astonishment.

She looked at me in surprise. It was too late; I could not retreat, for I had practically taken an oath.

"I'll go to fight for the people and for freedom—like Michel."

"But you're still so young."

This seemed a terrible insult. I lied defiantly, "I'm seventeen."

We continued up the mountain path, but I was no longer happy. In Mary's eyes I was nothing. Now I had to go to Macedonia and prove to her how wrong she was, and in a confused way I knew that this bright May day had settled my fate.

We spent the evening in the forest near the monastery, roasted lamb over an open fire, sang the songs of the haiduks—the mountain guerrillas —slept in a cool, hay-scented barn, and started on our return trip before dawn, while the nightingales were still singing in the forest.

Back in Sofia, I told Michel my decision. He was not surprised.

"It would be better if you were to go to the university first," he said. "Then you'd be more valuable to us. For our future struggle we'll need educated men. You still have time."

Petko Penchev gave me the same advice. I dared not tell them why I could not wait.

From Michel and Petko I had learned that the *chetas* usually began crossing the Turkish frontier in June. During the winter and spring the warriors idled their time away in the Sofia cafés along Princess Marie Louise Street. The most notorious was the Miladinov Brothers Café, named in honor of two poets hanged by the Turks. I decided to seek my fortune among the Macedonian *voivodas*.

[7]

After luncheon one Sunday I slipped out quietly and went to the Miladinov Brothers Café, where I was greeted by powerful odors from the kitchen. Hundreds of flies swarmed around as a lanky young man in sandals and a filthy shirt swatted at them with a towel. There was no one else in sight. The young man stared at me through tiny, inflamed eyes, contemptuously took in my pressed trousers and polished shoes, and turned his back. I sat down near the window wondering what to order, while the towel continued to spank the walls and tables. Before I had decided what to have, the waiter came to my table and shouted through his discolored, broken teeth, "What'll it be?"

"Wine," I answered boldly.

Had I asked him to bring me the Sultan from Constantinople, he would have been less surprised.

"So it's wine you want! A liter or a barrel? Ha-ha-ha!"

He dropped his towel, held his hands on his hips, and roared with laughter. A fat, tousled head rose slowly from behind the bar, and a shrill voice cackled: "What're you laughing at, you fool? You woke me up."

"This 'gentleman'—ha-ha-ha—wants wine! Look at him."

The fat head rose a little higher and the sleepy eyes looked at me good-humoredly. "Enough, Giuro! If you don't stop baying like a dog at the moon, I'll break your head."

But Giuro's shoulders continued to shake with merriment as he went about swatting flies. The other man, apparently the proprietor, came to my table. "Why have you come here, son? What are you looking for?" he asked pleasantly.

"I've come to see the *komitajis*,"* I answered quickly, almost breathlessly.

"To see the *komitajis*? But what for?"

"I want—I want to go with them into the mountains to fight against the Turks."

He looked at me pityingly and shook his head. "What sort of business is that for you? Leave that to the bums. Who put that bug into your head? Better go home to your mother. What kind of *komitaji* would you be?"

"I'm not afraid of anything," I replied. "And I've decided to go. I want to speak to one of the *voivodas*. I'm still young, only eighteen," I added, blushing at the lie, "but I'm strong and I can fight."

"Well, as you wish. If you wait, they'll soon be coming in to play cards."

* The *komitajis* (committeemen) were so called by the Turks because they fought under orders of the IMRO Central Committee. The Bulgarian term was *chetnik* (member of a *cheta*.)

[8]

In an undertone, as if talking to himself, he muttered: "If you were my son, I'd beat the daylights out of you." Then he asked me, "Do you at least know what a *komitaji* looks like?" He pointed to Giuro. "He's a *komitaji;* that's the type. In winter and spring he works here and kills only flies; in summer he goes to the mountains and kills Turks. Well, what do you think of him?"

Could this creature really be a *komitaji* and were the others like him? I wondered, having seen them all in Michel's handsome image. I tried to convince myself that my first impression of Giuro was false, that I had judged him by his unattractive appearance only, that since he was a *komitaji* he couldn't really be a bad sort.

I hailed him to my table, shook his hand heartily, and said almost respectfully, "You're a *komitaji?*"

Giuro scratched the back of his head the way lousy apes do, spat, and posed himself impressively, if not pompously. "A *komitaji?* I've been fighting in Macedonia for four years. But to tell the truth, it's a tough job."

The word "job" grated on my ears. Could risking one's life in the struggle against tyranny be called a "job"?

"A tough job," Giuro repeated. "Hunger, lice, and perpetual flight."

"Flight?" That shocked me. In the songs and the newspaper accounts it was always the Turks who fled as the fearless *komitajis* swooped down from their mountain nests like eagles attacking a flock of ravens.

"Flight so fast you think your heart'll jump out of your body," Giuro replied. "When the Turks are after us, it's only a question of whose legs will hold out longest. For a *komitaji* the most important thing is to have strong legs. Nothing else matters. Legs, that's the thing! How are your legs?"

Completely abashed, I muttered, "Good."

Instead of wine, Giuro served me lemonade. I drank in downcast silence. Soon three bearded men in caps and without neckties came in.

"Here come the *voivodas*," said Giuro. "The tall fellow with a limp is Daiev. The blond one is Pesho Samardjiev. The third is Dusho Zheliev."

Daiev advised me to go home to my mother. Dusho didn't even bother to answer. But Pesho invited me to meet him that evening in the Armenian Café, opposite the public baths. His kind blue eyes twinkled with good humor and when he laughed his straight white teeth glistened. He was no Giuro. "I happen to need a secretary," he said. "You're young, but you may be useful. Come to the café at seven o'clock and we'll talk it over."

All the unrecognized geniuses of Sofia crowded together in the Armenian Café—actors without roles, poets without publishers, painters who did window posters, and sculptors who sold small plaster busts of

Tolstoy, Gorky, Ibsen, and Beethoven on street corners. In the Panakh Café near by, where a cup of coffee cost ten centimes, sat their acclaimed brethren; in the Armenian Café prices were much lower. These great men of the future milled about in filth, sneering at everyone who had already succeeded. When Pesho came in, they all greeted him affectionately, for he always listened patiently to them, believed everything told him, and treated everybody to coffee.

"Unhappy Bulgaria!" said Pesho. "So many talented men perish without work." Finally he took me aside and in a kindly manner tried to persuade me to give up my plan. I insisted, explaining that I could write well, speak a little French, and handle a rifle and revolver as well as anyone.

"Do you know what you're letting yourself in for?" he asked.

Triumphantly I echoed Giuro's words, "Hunger, lice, and perpetual flight!" Pesho roared with laughter. "Then you do know."

He gave me an address in Kustendil, the depot where the *chetas* assembled each year before going into Macedonia, and told me to meet him there four days later.

At home the next evening, I told my father that I wanted to go on a two-day trip and needed some money. We drank tea from the old samovar, my brother Kyril left for the Military Club, my younger brother went to sleep early, and my father retired to his study. My mother was busy knitting.

"Mother," I said, pointing to her father's picture, "I want to be like Grandfather Kosta."

"Those were other times, my son. Fighting was needed then. Now it's more important to study."

Mother little understood the tenderness with which I kissed her good night. At two in the morning I stole out of the house, taking with me my father's Nagan revolver and his field glasses. An hour later I hopped a freight train leaving Sofia for Radomir. The remaining thirty miles I covered on foot and in peasant carts when I could get a lift, and reached Kustendil by afternoon. Pesho had given me the address of Atse Dorev, commander of the Kustendil *cheta* headquarters. There, given a mattress, I fell asleep at once.

The next morning Pesho arrived and introduced me to the *chetniks*. "Here are the brothers Angel and Jordan, my comrades of 1903. And this is our sergeant and doctor, Vasili. He was a hospital orderly once. Treats all ailments with quinine and iodine. Here's your old friend, Giuro, and his pal Vasiliev, who has served two prison terms, and Bichakov, a crack shot who never misses and can stop a man at twenty paces with his knife. The rest of our members will be here tonight."

It was not a felicitous-looking company.

Early in June, armed with rifles, bombs, revolvers, and daggers—I felt like Grandfather's picture—we set out for Macedonia. At night, when heavy clouds shrouded the moon, we headed for the Turkish border and crossed the frontier, single file and crouching, under the noses of the Turkish border patrol.

The first days of the expedition proved strenuous for me. Arms, ammunition, knapsack, and goatskin cloak weighed heavily on my shoulders, and I found it hard to keep up with the veterans. Climbing through the pathless, rugged mountains so exhausted me that often I almost went to sleep on sentry duty. Pesho, so kind and easygoing in Sofia, now became a stern leader who tolerated no breach of discipline.

At the village of Russinovo, we were joined by the *voivoda* Dusho, whose *cheta* had been wiped out recently by the Turks. Dusho owed his life to his agility in leaping from rock to rock like a mountain goat. He led us into the dense, ancient forests of the Plachkovitza Mountain, where we joined another *voivoda*—Simeonov—and his band. We camped in a clearing near the edge of the forest. Simeonov's men butchered a suckling calf in our honor and prepared the meat in a huge copper vessel. About thirty of us surrounded the crackling campfire, with several men on sentry duty. Suddenly one of Simeonov's sentries, perched high in a tree, cried out, "Askers!"

Turkish troops! Quickly we smothered the campfire, hastily cut up and shared the half-cooked meat.

A company of Askers—regular Turkish troops—headed by a mounted officer and a bugler, was moving in column formation along a mountain ridge parallel to our line of march. We broke camp, eating as we went. In the forest we could travel more speedily than the column with its heavy packs. Soon we reached a cornfield; in the distance the Turkish column swayed against a background of low underbrush. Suddenly bullets whined over our heads. Panting and sweating, we leaped from rock to rock, tumbled down slopes, and scampered up mountain ridges. I thought my heart would burst. My eyes bulged and my teeth were tightly clenched. Finally came the whispered command, "Lie down!" I dropped in a heap.

"Well, they won't catch us now," Dusho said cheerfully.

Simeonov sent out couriers to get information from the neighboring peasants. Before sunrise they returned with alarming news. Both regular troops and gendarmes were after us. Strong patrols were prowling through the forest, guarding all the passes to the Strumitsa Valley. Moreover, armed Moslem peasants reinforced the Turkish regulars.

We passed the long day hidden in the forest, for nourishment gnawing the bones of yesterday's meat. Many times voices sounded not far off; we had to lie dead still. At nightfall we moved on. Pesho ordered that if our *cheta* should be forced to break up, each man was to keep toward the village of Nivichanje downstream. We slipped in silence through the green-vaulted aisles of the thick forest. To light our way we had to improvise torches of sticks tightly wound with rags dipped in fat—a dangerous expedient. The flickering torches cast fantastic shadows about us.

Our scouts discovered a Turkish detachment waiting to ambush us in a pass near by. It must have been about midnight. We crawled close to the Turks. My heart was thumping and a feeling of joyful dread and mystery seized me. Jordan pulled me by the sleeve. "Ready with your bomb," he whispered. "It's about to start."

"But where are the Turks?"

"Below, where those tiny lights are glimmering."

At a signal from Pesho an explosion rent the air. I ignited the short fuse of my bomb and hurled it as far as I could. The forest echoed and re-echoed with explosions and groans. We leaped from our positions against the Turks. Firing seemed to come from all sides at once. After a short skirmish with an enemy we never really saw, our band scattered in the forest.

I found myself alone; my stomach felt hollow. I remembered the *voivoda's* instructions to follow the stream to Nivichanje. Terrified, I groped through the darkness. The cartridge bandoliers cut my shoulders. The forest seemed filled with ominous sounds and shapeless specters. With trembling fingers I made certain that the small rubber pouch of strychnine was still in my pocket. In Kustendil, each *chetnik* had received this final safeguard against the shame and possible torture of capture. I stumbled on until I slumped to the ground, exhausted, and dozed off. When I awoke, dawn was breaking. The bells of a herd tinkled faintly in the distance. I looked around; the forest was deserted. Picking up my rifle, I advanced cautiously.

At the edge of the forest a sheep dog rushed toward me, barking angrily. I kept him at bay with my rifle until a boy yelled out, "Here, Sharko, here!"

"Where is Nivichanje?" I asked him.

"Down there in the valley," he replied. "You must belong to the *cheta*. They're all in the village. When I left at night with the sheep, I was told to keep a lookout for Turkish soldiers."

With a smile he offered me a chunk of bread and white cheese which I greedily devoured. Then he showed me the path to the village.

Every *chetnik* was there except Jordan. His brother Angel sat gloomily in a corner while the others smoked in silence. After three days in Nivichanje, we heard from the peasants that Jordan's severed head was being displayed on a pole in the market place of Strumitsa, where a Turkish crier beat his drum and proclaimed, "Such is the fate of all traitors to the Padishah. May Allah prolong his days!"

Angel silently swallowed his tears.

For the next three months we camped on the slopes of Mount Kojukh, never staying too long in one spot. Our food consisted mainly of bread, cheese, milk, and paprika; occasionally, when Pesho felt generous, lamb.

One morning the peasants warned us of the approach of Turkish soldiers. We took up a position on a hill two miles from Darlitza and waited. Twelve of us faced about thirty Turks—a platoon of Nizam in blue tunics and red fezzes. The Turks, trained for mountain fighting, climbed rapidly up the slope. They advanced in small groups, taking cover, then rising and darting forward again. When they halted about two hundred yards from us, Pesho cried, "Start firing the moment they rise. Each of you pick a target!"

A strange excitement coursed through me. My rifle sight bobbed up and down before my eye. Suddenly it seemed that all the Turks were advancing against me alone. Several heads rose on our left flank; I took careful aim and fired. Bullets whizzed back and forth. Several soldiers fell on their faces, dropping their rifles.

"Good," said Pesho, "I'll take the commander himself. Remember, leave him to me!"

The Turks continued to advance stubbornly, heedless of our fire. Suddenly their commander staggered, waved his arms, and fell. Several of his soldiers crawled over and dragged him to cover behind the rocks. We fired two more volleys and retired, using every rock and bush as cover. After this skirmish, we changed camp almost every night, bivouacking in inaccessible mountain gorges and remote villages.

The peasants of Macedonia lived in a state of semi-starvation. In addition to their heavy taxes, they were forced to pay exorbitant rents to the Turkish landlords—the beys. Pesho sent a circular letter to the beys of the district, commanding them to cut rents in half. If they refused, he wrote, the *komitajis* would act. Most of the beys hastened to comply, but one disregarded the letter. Lord of eight villages, he owned large herds of goats and sheep, two large creameries, and a fortified castle guarded by a dozen Albanians.

We retaliated by raiding and driving off one of his herds, which we distributed among the peasants in a distant village. Still he didn't yield. Then we set fire to his granary and threw several bombs into his courtyard. These did little damage but frightened the bey so thoroughly that the next day he summoned the mayors of his eight villages and announced a reduction in rents.

[13]

The new governor of Macedonia, Hilmi Pasha, appointed as *kaimakam* (chief) of the Tikvesh district an active young Albanian, Ibrahim Aga, who boasted that he would soon clean up the treasonable elements and hang *voivoda* Pesho. Mobilizing a detachment of gendarmes and armed Moslem Slavs *(Pomaks)*, he went through the villages, torturing the peasants in a search for hidden arms, and imprisoning many priests. One night his men raided a village near our camp, murdering eleven shepherds and stealing their herds.

We had long avoided camping in the villages, so as not to give the Turks a pretext for retaliating against the inhabitants. Therefore, when Pesho received word of the murders, he summoned me and dictated letters to all the local *chetas* of Tikvesh, asking for complete information about the movements of the brutal *kaimakam*. Toward the end of the month he received from the regional IMRO committee a letter which he read carefully and burned. Next he dictated letters to the *voivodas* of ten villages, asking each for three reliable armed men. On a night late in August we started on our special expedition, marching with light kits. Along the road, groups of armed men joined us, and by dawn our *cheta* numbered more than thirty. We rested during the day and marched by night, halting finally on the road from Tikvesh to Negotin. Now Pesho revealed that Ibrahim Aga had gone to Negotin and was returning that night, escorted by four mounted gendarmes. He produced a cardboard square and ordered me to write on it that in accordance with the verdict of the IMRO, *kaimakan* Ibrahim Aga, servant of the murderous Sultan Abdul Hamid, was sentenced to death by hanging for numerous assassinations, robberies, and other acts of violence against the inhabitants of the Tikvesh district. Pesho affixed the IMRO seal to the document and signed his name under the verdict, directing me to sign also as secretary of the *cheta*.

We lay in wait on both sides of the road. Soon after midnight the clatter of hoofs sounded in the distance. At Pesho's signal we opened fire, killing one gendarme and bringing down the horses. We dragged out the terrified riders. Ibrahim Aga, stunned by a blow from Angel's rifle butt, was held fast by two peasants. Pesho played his flashlight on the prisoner's lean face with its high cheekbones, and said in Turkish, "Effendi, I've been looking forward to this encounter. The time has come for you to pay for your crimes. Angel, proceed!"

The *kaimakam's* arms were tied behind his back and Angel slipped a noose around his neck. Seated on a stout branch of one of the mulberry trees flanking the road, a peasant caught the other end of the rope.

"Wait!" Pesho shouted, "I almost forgot the sentence." And he attached the inscribed cardboard to the top button of the *kaimakam's* uniform. In the meantime the condemned man's brain had cleared. He proudly raised his head and shouted, "I'll die a Moslem—without fear. You're a pack of infidel dogs!" He spat in the *voivoda's* face. Pesho wiped his face and smiled. "I like a brave man, Ibrahim. That's the way to die."

Shortly afterward we started home for the winter. The rains had begun, and the nights were damp and cold. As soon as we crossed the frontier from Macedonia to Bulgaria, our *cheta* was dispersed, each man receiving fifty leva for expenses.

When Pesho and I reached Sofia, we found that the news of Ibrahim Aga's hanging had traveled fast. The Turkish military court in Salonika had sentenced us to death because our names were affixed to the IMRO death warrant found on the hanged man's coat. Posters displayed in every Macedonian village offered a reward of five hundred Turkish lire ($2,500) for Pesho's head and two hundred lire ($1,000) for mine. Later, in my own country, I would be rated much higher. In 1924, the price reached two million leva—about $20,000—an encouraging sign.

GRANDFATHER HAD BEEN banished from the parlor wall as the instigator of my deviltry. The other members of the household rushed to greet me—mother weeping, my little brother, Vasili, lamenting that I hadn't brought back a single Turkish head, and father not quite concealing his pride. But to Mary, for whose sake I had gone to Macedonia, I was still no hero. When she opened her door and glanced at my *komitaji* outfit, caked with the authentic grime of the Macedonian mountains which I had so carefully preserved to impress her, all she said was, "How dirty you are!"

I had little time to brood over my failure. In a few days Pesho sent for me, to take me to Ivan Garvanov, the chief of the IMRO. Garvanov, a tall, powerful man who had lost an eye in battle, received us in his study littered with books and papers.

"This summer, as you know," he said, "we tried to assassinate Abdul Hamid. Unfortunately, the time bomb exploded too early, and though fifty men were killed, the Sultan escaped. We were lucky; lost only two men. But about two thousand Armenians were arrested and exiled to Diarbekr and Kurdistan. Now we've re-established contact with their Terrorist Committee and must prepare for another attempt against Abdul Hamid. We must strike at Yildiz Kiosk!"

His words bewildered me. I could hardly visualize myself breaking into the Sultan's palace in Constantinople. Garvanov must have perceived my doubts.

"You understand, of course, that all the technical details will be arranged by the Armenians. Your job will be to act as liaison between the Armenian Terrorist Committee and the IMRO. You'll report to me regularly from Constantinople. When everything is ready, you'll place yourself at the disposal of the terrorists—" He stopped short and smiled. "By the way, how old are you?"

"Eighteen," I replied, not batting an eye. Pesho, who knew I was under seventeen, did not betray me.

Garvanov shook his head. "Too young, too young . . . still, your *voivoda* recommends you highly. Will you go?"

By this time, I would have taken on the Yildiz Kiosk job single-handed. "Of course," I answered.

The organization provided me with a fashionable wardrobe, a false passport in the name of Nikolai Vasiliev, and a three-months allowance of eighteen-hundred francs. Ostensibly I was going to the Ottoman capital to study at the French School, Galata Sarail.

Constantinople in late autumn was languid and melancholy. Warm breezes wafted perfumes from the gardens along the Bosporus. The clear waters of the strait mirrored the white villas and stately cypresses of Buyoukdereh and Arnaoutkeui; sharp-nosed caïques cutting through the water rippled the images with glistening oars. From the balcony of my room in the Athene Palace Hotel, I looked out at the Golden Horn, where a solitary Turkish battleship lay anchored. It had only one gun turret; the others, I was told, had been in an arsenal for five years, awaiting repairs. The deserted ship, with a lone sentry pacing its deck, seemed to me a symbol of Ottoman decline.

The Athene Palace Hotel was in Pera, the bustling European quarter. In the Oriental sections the tempo was slower. On shaded café terraces, men in fezzes and turbans sipped thick black coffee and lazily smoked their narghiles, watched by inquisitive female eyes through shuttered windows. In the market place of Galata, booths and outspread carpets displayed rich wares: many-colored fabrics, vases, pistols and *yataghans* (curved swords) inlaid with silver and precious stones, amber-stemmed pipes, satin slippers brocaded in gold.

Each morning, in my hotel lobby, a smiling detective would greet me and follow wherever I went. After I had wasted several days trying to elude him by walking briskly to Galata, dodging in and out among the stalls, and hurrying back uphill to Pera, he approached me.

"It's a dog's life, effendi. Does the gentleman think I do this for fun? I have a wife and two children to support. My legs are worn out keeping up with you."

I suggested that in the future he take a cab.

"How can I afford a cab?" he lamented. "I'm a poor Greek. The stray dogs of Constantinople have an easier time than I. My wages aren't enough to feed my family."

I took the hint. For one medjidie (about $1) a week, he promised not to follow me. When I felt certain he was keeping his word—he was a Greek, after all—I went to the secret address in Taxim that Garvanov had given me.

At the door of a large villa set in a spacious garden, I gave the password, "Yildiz," and was admitted at once by an Armenian, Hadjian. He listened to me carefully, nodded his head and clicked his tongue several times, treated me to coffee and promised that I would soon meet the two leading Armenian terrorists.

"Be here Wednesday at two. Don't take a cab! This is a quiet street and any noise attracts attention."

When I returned to Hadjian's villa at the appointed time, I found two men seated with him on cushions, inhaling their narghiles. With their large, hooked noses and symmetrical black beards, they looked so much alike that I took them for twins. They were introduced to me as Garabet Bakladjian and Kirkor Aganian.

"We've already been informed of your arrival," said Bakladjian, "but you're so young!"

I blushed. "I'm secretary of the Tikvesh Revolutionary District of the IMRO. I'm not here by accident."

Bakladjian slapped me on the shoulder. "Well said, young man. Come here every Wednesday at this time. We'll keep you informed of every move we make."

They resumed their long pipes in silence, and fingered their amber rosaries. Quiet, self-satisfied smiles froze on their faces. That evening I sent my first report to Garvanov in Sofia.

Weeks passed in the same routine. My Armenian friends continued their mysterious silences and significant smiles. Everything was proceeding according to plan, they told me. In the meantime, I had nothing to do but amuse myself.

One morning at breakfast, I heard a girl behind me speaking Russian. Turning, I saw at the next table a Rubensesque blonde and a tall, long-faced gentleman with gray mutton-chop whiskers. They were having difficulty with the menu, and with a bow I offered my services as translator.

"How fortunate!" she smiled, while her escort nodded amiably. "Do sit at our table. My name is Eugenie. This is my uncle, Colonel Paul Cherepakhin. Are you from Odessa?"

When I explained that I was Bulgarian, the effect was even better, for the Colonel had fought for the liberation of Bulgaria, in 1877-78. Eugenie's healthy beauty, the rich texture of her fair skin, the deep vibrant tones of her voice, had a hypnotic effect on me. I became her slave and errand boy, fetching her gloves, her theatre tickets, her cabs. Although I soon discovered that she was twenty-eight, an actress in a St. Petersburg vaudeville theatre, and the mistress of her so-called "uncle," I continued to trail after her. My only reward was being allowed to remain in her room while she busied herself with her toilette.

Winter came. Every Wednesday afternoon my Armenian conspirators still performed their strange ritual, assuring me in whispers that the hour of retribution was drawing near. I kept Garvanov informed of the "developments" in this slow-motion mystery, and he advised me to be patient and trust the Armenians. Nevertheless, early in December I resolved to find out how matters really stood. Bakladjian and Aganian sat on their cushions, puffing away with Olympian serenity and drinking their thick black coffee.

"Will you tell me," I asked, exasperated, "when we begin real work?"

It was a warm day, and flies came buzzing through the open window. One dove into Bakladjian's cup. The Armenian plucked it out, squashed it between his plump fingers, and oracularly proclaimed: "The Padishah shall perish like this fly!"

He exchanged meaningful glances with Aganian and both, in perfect unison, expelled clouds of smoke through their monumental noses. "He'll perish like this fly!" they intoned in solemn chorus. And not another word out of them!

When things began to happen a few days later, I was more amazed than the Turks. First, a bomb was found in the Galata-Pera tram. Then a Turkish general, mistaken for the chief of the Secret Police, was shot dead in his carriage by two terrorists. My amenable Greek detective was replaced by a Turk. I warned Hadjian that from now on I would be closely watched. He became panicky and told me not to come again until I heard from him. He blamed Bakladjian for organizing the aimless terrorist acts in an effort to redeem himself in the eyes of the Armenian Central Committee.

"Under these circumstances, can anything come of our enterprise?" I asked.

"Don't worry. We'll go ahead with our plans," Hadjian declared. "Meanwhile, take this package with you. Bakladjian and Aganian left it here for you."

The package was heavy. When I opened it in my hotel room, three cylindrical bombs and a dozen revolvers of various calibers rolled out. I placed the arsenal in my trunk in the hotel cellar storeroom and spent a sleepless night trying to figure out what it all meant. Suddenly I understood; the Armenians, knowing that the police were closing in, had tricked me into taking the incriminating evidence off their hands. The attempt on Abdul Hamid's life obviously had been abandoned, if, indeed, it ever had been seriously intended.

Early the next morning I sent a complete report to Garvanov, asking for instructions. I was eager to leave Constantinople. During the next fortnight the Turkish detective shadowed me constantly, but did not search my trunk in the cellar. Life became dull.

The monotony was relieved by the appearance of a celebrated Russian explorer, Leontiev. He had become famous for his African travels, and Emperor Menelik II of Abyssinia had made him governor of the province of Tigre, a position which the Russian turned into a gold mine. Leontiev was tall, swarthy, about forty, with the manner of a man accustomed to power. He occupied a splendid suite in the Pera Palace Hotel, and when he emerged his Ethiopian attendant flung handfuls of silver to the expectant crowd of beggars. Once he bought up the whole house for a performance of the visiting Vienna Comic Opera and enjoyed it in solitary splendor. Another time he chartered a steamer for a solitary cruise on the Sea of Marmora. He wore enormous diamonds and had sets of sapphire, emerald, and ruby buttons for his white vests.

He began courting Eugenie the moment the Colonel introduced him. The first day he brought her a gigantic bronze box filled with choice candy; the next day an ermine cape; the next, a pearl necklace. Before the week was over, Eugenie ran off with him, leaving the Colonel and me to share our misery.

Meanwhile I had no instructions from Garvanov and no sign of the Armenians.

One evening, while strolling aimlessly through the streets, followed by the indefatigable Turkish detective, I was attracted by the lights of the Concordia Theatre. I entered, trailed by my faithful watchdog. Before the curtain went up, the gypsy orchestra struck up the hymn to the Sultan, *Hamidieh*. Instinctively I remained seated, arms crossed on my chest. Hisses spread through the theatre. One of my neighbors, a Greek, whispered, "Are you mad?"

When the lights dimmed and the curtain rose, I left my seat and made for the side exit, but the detective followed me and barred the way.

"Stop! You're my prisoner!" he cried.

It flashed through my mind that arrest meant search, the discovery of the bombs and revolvers in my trunk, and of my connection with the Armenian terrorists. I knocked him out with the butt of my revolver. Then I ran.

I knew that I had to leave Constantinople before a general alarm went out. Hailing a cab, I drove to the harbor, where I wandered along the water front, looking into the saloons. In one was a boisterous group of Russian sailors, the crew of the S. S. *Chihachov*. When I spoke Russian to them they invited me to their table. I ordered wine and shashlik for all, and soon we were embracing one another and bellowing drunken songs. At last the red-bearded mate rose and announced:

"The fun's over. Time to get going. We sail for Odessa at dawn."

At his command the Russians, although drunk to a man, obediently rose and followed. Arm in arm I trooped along with the stumbling, singing gang to their ship.

Two caïques brought us alongside the *Chihachov*, anchored midway in the Bosporus. No one noticed me when I climbed aboard. I found a spot on the deck between two coils of rope, huddled up in my coat and fell asleep. The sharp sting of icy water woke me up. The men were scrubbing the decks, and someone had spilled a pail of water over me. Jumping to my feet, I faced the red-bearded mate.

"Who the hell are you?" he asked gruffly.

I slipped him a gold coin and asked him to take me to the captain. He shrugged. "All right. Come on."

The captain, busy shaving, gave me a cold reception. But when I told him I was a Bulgarian fleeing the Turkish police, he brightened up and sent for the cook, a large, fat man in a spotless white apron.

"Denis," he said, "take this fellow below, dress him properly, and get him started on the dishes."

In a few minutes I was washing dishes like a veteran, while Denis gravely instructed me in the art of preparing a mushroom sauce made with sour cream. When the harbor police came aboard before we sailed, I worked industriously in the kitchen and no one paid any attention to me.

An hour later the Turkish shore receded. The Dolma Baghtcheh Palace with its gilded gates, the slender minarets, the cupolas of Aya Sofia glowing in the fire of the sunrise, a flock of pigeons dipping over the Genoese towers of Arnaoutkeui—all faded from view. Presently we passed the big guns of the Kavak battery guarding the eastern entrance to the Bosporus. Sea gulls wheeled above us. The ship throbbed and rolled gently in the swell. We were in the Black Sea.

At the Bulgarian port of Burgas I left the ship and went to Sofia.

RUSSIA WAS IN revolutionary ferment. In October, 1905, the Czar had been forced to grant a constitution and parliamentary government to the Russian people. Then came a general strike on the railways; then barricades and revolutionary warfare in the streets of Moscow. Russia, obviously, was the only safe place for me.

Late in January, 1906, with fifty rubles and my revolutionary ideals, I reached Odessa, having persuaded my family that I intended to study there. The city was at the crisis of its political fever. Several months earlier, the battleship *Potemkin,* manned by revolutionary mutineers, had fired upon it, and the workers had rushed to join the rebellion. Nicholas II suppressed the insurrection with violence and bloodshed. Pogroms, instigated by the police and carried out by harbor rats and hoodlums, succeeded the October Manifesto.

Now the people were excitedly awaiting the opening of the Imperial Duma in April. Despite the pretense of civil liberty, Odessa remained under martial law, with supreme authority vested in the commander of the military district, the arrogant General von Kaulbars, a Baltic German. The chief of police, Colonel von Gessberg, was also a Baltic German. The leading exponent of the third degree and instigator of anti-Jewish pogroms was Police Captain Panasiuk.

I became a "listener" at the University of Odessa. In my eyes, as a revolutionary socialist, my father was a "bourgeois" whose help I could no longer accept. And so, when my money was gone, I found employment in the harbor as a stevedore, loading two-hundred-pound sacks aboard vessels sailing for every port in the world. To save my kopecks, I lived in a cheap cellar dormitory for workers and ate in foul-smelling hash houses.

After a series of successful strikes by the stevedores' artel—a primitive sort of union—dockworkers' wages had risen sharply. We were paid from one and a half to two rubles a day. Living in a rathole, I could save more than half my earnings. Life would have been tolerable but for the hell of the cellar dormitory, where Vanka Zetz, a powerful drunkard whose surname came from a ribald water-front song, ruled as undisputed lord. Vanka the *gorlopan,* the "big shot," had slugged his way to power. About half the men in the dormitory worked; the others thieved, splitting their meager takings with the police for protection. Both workers and thieves bowed to Vanka's authority.

Each morning the same tribute awaited Vanka on the table beside his cot: a breakfast consisting of a bottle of vodka, a pound of sausage, a loaf of bread, and two cucumbers. In addition, he assessed each occupant one or two rubles a week. For several days he overlooked my presence, but late one evening he stopped before my cot.

"Hey, scholar," he growled, "do you know the law?"

"What law?"

"This law," he answered, bringing his huge bony fist to my nose. "Tomorrow evening you bring me two rubles. Understand?"

I spent a miserable night. The bold revolutionist who wanted to overthrow sultans and czars had been cowed by a red-nosed, pig-eyed tough.

When Vanka's hulking figure appeared in the doorway the next evening, I waited tensely, set to fight it out. Swaying slightly, he approached a group of men playing cards on the floor, but didn't molest them. Instead he shuffled to his cot, and was about to sit down when he remembered something. He turned and came toward me. I rose from my cot.

"The money," he said, yawned, looked past me, and stretched out his right hand. I stretched out my own in a resounding wallop to his jaw, followed by a rain of lefts and rights. The dazed *gorlopan* tottered from side to side, unable to regain his equilibrium for a return blow. Covering his face, he finally went down. I looked around. The men had formed a circle around us. "Hey you!" I shouted to one, "get a pail of water and splash it over this swine!"

He ran off without questioning my command. The men howled with laughter: "So that's what Vanka has come to!" "The *gorlopan* got his!" "He got what was coming to him, the lousy son of a bitch!"

Doused with a bucketful of water, Vanka choked and spluttered. He shook his head to clear it, stumbled to his cot, slowly and dazedly gathered together his belongings, and left.

The next morning the customary *gorlopan's* tribute rested on my table—vodka, sausage, bread, and cucumbers. I called the men together and told them that from now on we would have neither *gorlopan* nor tribute. They grinned sheepishly. Their unaccustomed freedom repelled them, and in a few days half of them had left.

After a couple of months on the docks, I rented a small room on Knyazheskaya Street and gave up my job, determined to devote all my time to study and to the revolutionary movement. I became acquainted with Sokolovsky, one of the editors of the Odessa *News*, the city's most influential newspaper. Eight years later, in 1914, I would become his correspondent in Sofia and Brussels. Although a radical, Sokolovsky belonged to no political party.

Through him I met several revolutionists, among them a law student, Yasha Fishman, who belonged to the Social Revolutionary Party. The Soviet authorities were to arrest Yasha in 1918 as a Left Social Revolutionary involved in the assassination of General Count von Mirbach, the German ambassador to Moscow. Granted amnesty, he later became a member of the Soviet embassy staff in Rome.

When I told Yasha I was eager to enter the party's Terrorist Brigade, he introduced me to the chief of the Odessa organization, a fair-haired, rather short, soft-spoken man of about twenty-five who questioned me about my background and my experience as a *komitaji*. Several days later I received word that I had been accepted into the Southern Flying Terrorist Brigade of the party.

The chief of the Odessa organization now revealed his name, Galka Shishmarev. That evening he took me to meet my new comrades at party headquarters, a cottage concealed in a garden on Lermontov Lane.

"Comrades," he said simply, "here is our new comrade who has fought in Macedonia. Accept him as a brother."

There were ten of us, including two girls. Galka, our leader, was a self-educated worker and a talented poet. We loved him for his humor and followed him for his intelligence and strength of character. When there was work to be done, none could have been more clearheaded and businesslike than Galka.

Our dynamite bombs and infernal machines were made by Herman, a timid, nearsighted little man, incapable of hurting a fly, who believed that his terrorist work would bring happiness to humanity. Vasya was cook, handyman, and coachman—his most important duty was to keep a light, rubber-tired carriage and a fast Orlov trotter ready for a quick getaway. Our best shot was Petya Sulimovsky, a Don Cossack who took no interest in theoretical discussions but prided himself on having killed seventeen stool pigeons. Nineteen-year-old Volodya Sharapov was Petya's closest friend. David and Syoma were from poor Jewish families; they had known both pogroms and starvation.

Tamara Prince, twenty-year-old daughter of the aristocrat, General Prince, who commanded an army division in Warsaw, was a symbol of the self-sacrifice, heroism, and beauty that we saw in the revolution. None of us thought of her as a mortal woman. With her huge gray eyes, transparent skin, and innate grace, she was ethereally beautiful, and we worshiped her as our spiritual leader. Tamara believed that through revolutionary terror she was expiating the sins of her class against the Russian people. Sometimes, before our meetings began, she would play the piano and sing a revolutionary song in her moving voice. The other girl, her schoolmate Celia, became a crack shot and an expert at handling bombs.

[24]

When the Imperial Duma convened in the spring of 1906, the Social Revolutionary Party suspended terrorism. But we were ordered to keep our powder dry, for no one believed the new era of parliamentary government was real or lasting. In Odessa we continued to arm the students and workers against the government-instigated Black Hundreds, the first storm troopers of Europe. "Strikers, Jews, and students" were defying the Czar, declared the official pronouncements calling upon patriots to "destroy sedition." Then drunken bands of Black Hundreds, wearing yellow shirts and armed with revolvers and clubs, would raid the poor Jewish sections of Odessa while the police looked on, inactive. Our brigade led many a street battle against these ruffians.

We needed dynamite. Galka established contact with workers in the quarries of Gnilyakovo, a village about ten miles from Odessa, who promised to steal and sell to us forty pounds of the dynamite used in blasting. Volodya, Petya, and I were sent to get it. Entering the village in high boots, old peasant coats and caps, and carrying gunnysacks, we applied for jobs at the employment office and were turned down, as we had expected. Then Volodya and I remained at the village inn while Petya went to speak to the quarry workers. He returned late at night.

The dynamite would not be ready until the next evening. So that night and all of the next day we stayed at the inn, our only company being two drunken peasants. The innkeeper eyed us suspiciously. At five o'clock we left, Petya muttering, "I don't like the looks of that innkeeper."

We looked back, but no one was following us. Children were playing in the street near the shack where we picked up the dynamite. We stowed it into our three gunnysacks, paid the workers, and went to the railway station to wait for the Odessa train. A fine drizzle of rain was falling. The station gendarme paid no attention to us. Ten minutes after our arrival, two rural policemen appeared, armed with rifles. They also seemed to ignore us as they talked to the gendarme.

"I smell trouble," whispered Petya. "Put down your bags and prepare for the worst."

The three police officers began moving toward us, still conversing casually. The train whistled in the distance. We arose, also pretending indifference. My heart was pounding.

Suddenly the gendarme brought up his revolver: "Hands up!"

In a flash we fired three volleys from our Brownings, and the gendarme and policemen fell. The train was now nearing the platform. We cut across the tracks, leaped over a ditch, and ran through plowed fields. Behind us we heard shouts and the shrill alarm signals of the locomotive. The rapidly increasing darkness and a sudden downpour saved us. A passing cart picked us up, and at about eleven that night we reached the suburbs of Odessa, drenched but safe. In the morning newspapers we read that the gendarme was dead and the two rural policemen wounded. Since the police had our three bags of dynamite, Herman was forced to make his own, out of nitroglycerin and fine sand—an extremely dangerous operation. At his insistence we kept away from Lermontov Lane for several days.

The armed truce between the regime and the revolutionists ended abruptly on July 20, 1906, when the Czar dissolved the Duma and appointed Piotr Stolypin Prime Minister. A new wave of police violence, riots, and strikes swept over Russia. Nicholas II preferred the known way of bayonets, gallows, prisons, and the twisted whips of the Cossacks to the uncharted course of constitutional monarchy. The Social Revolutionary Party reluctantly reverted to terrorism.

From Moscow, the party sent to us two tried terrorists, one of whom, the Bear, had fought bravely on the barricades during the December uprising. When they arrived at the Odessa railway station, they were arrested on suspicion and locked up in a precinct jail. Both carried "iron" passports—genuine, but belonging to other persons of similar description—and careful investigation by the police might reveal their identities and cost them their lives. We had to act quickly. Several schemes were proposed, including a mass assault on the jail, but Galka turned them all down as impracticable. At last my plan was adopted.

Two days later Celia and I, elegantly attired, drove up to the headquarters of Colonel von Gessberg, chief of police of Odessa. I handed a letter to the policeman stationed at von Gessberg's door and asked him to take it in at once.

"An important political matter," I added solemnly.

In the letter I described myself as Alexander Briansky, country squire and student at the Odessa University, and said that my sister and I had accidentally come upon the trail of a terrorist organization planning a series of political assassinations. We were afraid of reprisals, I wrote, if we went to the Okhrana—the secret police—and had decided to tell what we knew to a brave police officer, counting upon his taking the necessary steps to protect us.

A few minutes later we were in the office of von Gessberg, a tall trim man in a blue uniform, wearing the Order of St. Anne. With an air of anxiety, I asked him to keep the doors locked during our interview. The Colonel shut the door, turned the key, and benevolently invited us to sit down. As soon as he was back at his desk, I covered him with my Browning. Celia also drew her revolver and pointed it at the dismayed officer.

"Don't move," I said. "We are here by order of the terrorist section of the Social Revolutionary Party of South Russia. We demand the liberation of two prisoners now being held at the Bulvarny police station. In my brief case I have two bombs. If you make the slightest effort to raise an alarm, I'll blow you to bits."

Keeping him covered, I took his revolver. Von Gessberg tried to play for time. "How can I free the prisoners? It's against my oath of office."

"Colonel, let's not quibble. Telephone Captain Panasiuk. Here are the names of the prisoners." I handed him a slip of paper.

The telephone, which was attached to the wall, had two receivers. Von Gessberg raised one and I the other.

"Make it good," I warned.

The chief of police spoke with firm authority: "Captain Panasiuk? Von Gessberg speaking. You arrested two men at the railway station the day before yesterday. I have a favorable report on them. Release them at once."

"I can't, Your Honor," came the reply, "not without your written order."

Von Gessberg hesitated and grumbled, "Hmmm, we'll see," and hung up. He turned to me. "Well, you see for yourself, I can't do a thing."

"You damn well can," I answered. "Write an order for their release."

"Who'll deliver it?" smiled the Colonel.

"Write it and send for your orderly. Make sure he notices nothing. One false move and you'll both be blown to hell."

With a sigh the Colonel did as he was told. The order was sent to Captain Panasiuk, with instructions to telephone as soon as the men had been released. Now came the agonizing moment. The chief of police sat biting his mustache. Celia and I faced him across the desk. At last the telephone rang. Panasiuk's thunderous bass sounded like music. "I've released the prisoners! Somehow they look suspicious to me. But orders are orders—"

"It's none of your business," barked von Gessberg, and hung up.

"You see, Colonel," I said, "we haven't harmed you. Now we're leaving. Five of our friends are waiting outside in the street. Should you raise an alarm too soon, bombs will come crashing through your window."

Downstairs, Vasya was waiting for us in the carriage. As we drove off, we heard the crash of shattered glass. Later we learned that in his futile rage, von Gessberg had hurled a paperweight through the windowpane.

Soon after this, the party condemned to death General Baron von Kaulbars, commander of the Odessa Military District, and our Terrorist Brigade was ordered to carry out the verdict. Each of us volunteered, but Tamara Prince insisted upon doing it alone, because her father was a former messmate of von Kaulbars. After all our efforts to dissuade her had failed, Galka reluctantly gave his consent. Tamara had no difficulty in getting an appointment with the Baron. He wrote that he would be delighted to see his old friend's daughter at five o'clock. Galka stationed himself at a street corner not far from the Baron's palace. The rest of us gathered at Herman's apartment and waited in tense silence. It was seven o'clock when Galka returned.

"Tamara is dead," he said quietly.

No one spoke. Celia ran into the next room. Finally Petya asked, "What about von Kaulbars?"

"Alive."

Through the morning newspapers we learned how Tamara had died. While sitting in the General's reception room, she had fumbled nervously at her handbag. It dropped to the floor, and the bomb rolled out. The General's aide rushed up to seize her, but Tamara snatched her Browning, pressed the muzzle to her heart, and pulled the trigger.

Soon after her death, a new recruit joined us—Senka, a Bessarabian, who had been recommended as an experienced revolutionist. He had spent several years in prison and was suffering from tuberculosis. At once he asked Galka to give him an important assignment. "I'll die soon anyway," he said hoarsely.

Galka replied gently: "That is in store for all of us, but each must go in his turn."

We decided that our next job was to kill General Nishtenkov, presiding judge of the Odessa District Court-Martial. This court, which until Stolypin's advent had punished political crimes with short prison terms, was now meting out swiftly executed death sentences. Senka was assigned to shadow General Nishtenkov, and I was to carry out the sentence. From time to time Senka reported on the General's movements, but only vaguely. Vasya became suspicious and trailed Senka. One evening, outside the Café Robina, he found Senka in close conversation with an agent of the Okhrana. Senka handed the agent a slip of paper, which he read and thrust hastily into his pocket.

Vasya rushed over to Lermontov Lane. Galka was out.

"We must leave at once," said Vasya breathlessly, "sever all connections with Senka, move our bombs and dynamite, perhaps even leave Odessa."

We began packing. At about eleven o'clock there was a knock at the door. "Open up! It's I, Galka."

But the voice was not Galka's. Petya took command, "Follow me upstairs!" A volley rang through the door. Herman slumped dead in his chair near the piano. The police smashed in the door with their rifle butts. From the second floor, we began hurling our bombs. The house rocked with the explosions.

"Through the side window!" ordered Petya. One after another, we leaped from the second floor into the garden. Each of us had two revolvers and a bomb. The police, who could not see us, fired wildly. But we could see their figures against the light of the street lamp and continued firing as we retreated. In a little while we reached the shore. Petya ordered Vasya back to the city to warn the others. We arranged to meet him at eight in the morning at the Arcadia Restaurant near the sea.

Petya and I spent the night at Langeron, a summer resort near Odessa, in a vacant cottage we had used before. He summed up the situation simply, "Tomorrow we must kill Senka; after that, we'll see."

When Vasya joined us in the Arcadia we didn't recognize him. He had shaved off his beard and instead of his coachman's outfit wore a conservative business suit. He had passed on the warning to Volodya and Syoma, who would tell the others. He showed us the newspapers: four gendarmes killed and three wounded. Petya decided that Vasya and I should proceed at once to Kiev, where our party comrades would take care of us. He would join us the next day, "as soon as I finish the Senka business."

I insisted that that privilege belonged to me, because I had been chosen to kill General Nishtenkov. Petya admitted that I was right. We agreed to meet in Kiev after I had finished my work.

I went straight to Senka's house. A maid opened the door. Senka was sitting up in bed reading the morning papers.

"How glad I am to see you! I've just read the papers. It's horrible! Poor Herman. Someone must have betrayed us."

I closed the door and sat down, in a daze. It was my duty to fire point-blank at this traitor. But I couldn't move. Finally I said slowly and with deep emotion, "Yes, Senka, we've been betrayed. But you're the one who betrayed us. You're a treacherous scoundrel." With an effort I leveled my Browning at the sickly figure in the bed. Senka raised himself painfully.

"You accuse me—*me*—a sick and miserable victim of Czarism who has lost everything?" He bared his chest and cried, "Here, shoot! Shoot quickly!" A spasm of coughing racked his body, blood trickled from his mouth. "Well, kill me! I haven't much longer to live anyhow. I may as well die by the bullet of a comrade."

I lowered my revolver. What if he really were innocent? Perhaps the whole thing was a terrible mistake. I left without looking back at Senka, cursing myself for my weakness and knowing inwardly that he was guilty. I wandered through the streets, certain that this was my last day of freedom. I wanted to spend it differently from all other days.

I found myself on the Nikolaevsky Boulevard, before the palace of General von Kaulbars where Tamara had died so pathetically. Near by stood the London Hotel, in the heart of the fashionable section. Below, at the foot of the great stone stairway leading to the sea, lay the harbor. I descended the stone steps and went to my former comrades of the docks. Over a bottle of Jamaica rum they had pilfered from a British ship, we talked of old times. I left the harbor, following the beach. At a secluded spot between high rocks, I plunged into the sea, swam back, dozed on the sand until sunset and returned to the city. In the darkness of the summer evening, I felt a thousand eyes watching from every side, but saw no one.

After a hearty dinner, I bought the evening papers. They carried pictures of our wrecked cottage and of Herman slumped dead in his chair. A pang of shame passed through me at the thought that Senka, who was responsible for Herman's death, still lived. I had no right to escape.

Eugene Onegin was being performed that evening, and almost in a trance I bought an orchestra ticket and entered the opera house. A young girl sat next to me, listening ecstatically. Her excitement was contagious. While the music lasted, I did not feel so desperately alone. Then I was in the street again, walking slowly toward the house on Prokhorovskaya Street in which I had been living. A policeman on his beat passed me with a friendly nod.

I reached my house, opened the door. The hallway was dark. As I reached for the light, many hands seized me, twisting my arms behind me and forcing me to drop my revolver as I grasped it. Someone pressed my windpipe, and I lost consciousness. When I came to, my hands were tied behind my back and I was in my room surrounded by detectives and gendarmes. On my table were eight revolvers and four bombs. The janitor and two roomers stood terrified before Captain Panasiuk.

"Sign the search report!" growled Panasiuk. They hastily complied. Then he turned his heavy-lidded eyes to me. "Well, it's about time. Colonel von Gessberg will be delighted to know we've nabbed you. You're a lucky scoundrel. We've had instructions not to give you what you deserve." He held his Cossack whip taut, close to my face.

A coach arrived and, accompanied by three gendarmes and two carriages, I was driven off to the Odessa prison. It was dawn. Country wagons with their vegetables and dairy products were clattering through the streets; janitors were sweeping their sidewalks; from the bakeries came the aroma of freshly baked bread and rolls. The prison gates closed behind me. They did not open again until December, 1913, seven and a half years later.

The ODESSA PRISON, built in the form of a cross, was one of the most modern in Russia. The four-story wings converged into a rotunda from which the guards could observe all sides at once. Although built to accommodate only seven hundred and fifty, it housed more than two thousand inmates when I entered, three-fourths of them political prisoners. It was so overcrowded that Partenev, the warden, made scant effort to enforce strict discipline lest he provoke rebellion. Although freedom approaching anarchy prevailed in the prison, escape was virtually impossible. The building was surrounded by three high walls and guarded by two shifts of forty-four sentries each, as well as a company of soldiers on twenty-four-hour duty on the outer walls.

About a month after my arrest, Galka Shishmarev was brought in. He had been seized at the Odessa railway station, and was charged with having organized the attempt to assassinate Baron von Kaulbars. Galka assured me that most of my comrades were safe for the moment, and even eager to resume work.

The preliminary investigation of my case dragged on for months. The police who had survived the Lermontov Lane battle could not identify me because we had fought in darkness. Other witnesses, however, police and gendarmes, including the two rural policemen who had been wounded at Gnilyakovo, connected me with a number of other skirmishes in which I had taken part. The von Gessberg affair was not even touched upon, for the Colonel dreaded becoming the laughing-stock of Odessa.

In the fall of 1906, the so-called "Stolypin Necktie" went into effect. Prime Minister Stolypin met revolutionary terror with governmental terror. Field courts-martial tried, sentenced, and hanged revolutionists within twenty-four hours. Count Sergei Witte, who had drawn up the October Manifesto, said, "Capital punishment has become an act of assassination by the government authorities." During the autumn and winter of 1906 no fewer than thirty persons were executed in the courtyard of the Odessa prison alone; through spring of the next year the executions, for the whole country, reached almost seven hundred.

In November, Partenev was dismissed, and a new warden, Shafaruk, arrived from the provincial jail of Lutzk, where he had made a name for himself by his inventive brutality. With him came his assistant and six guards, all members of the Black Hundreds. His first "reforms" were to curtail our exercise periods, reduce our rations, and force us to spend our days in complete idleness. We rebelled, smashing chairs and tables. The Odessa district attorney was forced to investigate. In Shafaruk's presence he listened to our representatives, myself among them.

Pointing to the warden, I said, "I make no complaints, but wish to declare that this person will soon be dealt with by our friends outside."

Shortly afterward, while driving to the governor general's palace, Shafaruk was killed by a terrorist unknown to us, who was hanged the next day. My threat had been pure bravado, but the morning after the assassin's execution, the district attorney came to my cell.

"A few days ago," he said, "you threatened the warden in my presence. He has been assassinated. Under the circumstances, I must recommend that you be tried by field court-martial as an accomplice."

"Very well," I answered, "but you must realize that those same friends of ours outside know that you were the only official to hear my threat against Shafaruk. If anything happens to me, they'll kill you."

The district attorney did not turn me over to a field court-martial. Instead I was tried by a regular military court on December 29, 1906. The presiding judge was General Nishtenkov, the very man I had been assigned to kill, and whom Senka's treachery had saved. The single spectator admitted to the courtroom was Kissimov, the Bulgarian Consul General, an old friend of the family who had known me since early childhood.

"Your name?" asked General Nishtenkov. I gave it.

"Your religion?"

"I'm a Socialist."

The General frowned and the Bulgarian Consul lowered his head in shame.

"Your profession?"

"Terrorist."

The clerk reeled off the indictment: "A secret society seeking to overthrow the existing order by force and violence . . . Article 102, Paragraph 2 of the Penal Code . . . possessing arms and explosives . . . Statute of February 9, 1906 . . . armed resistance . . . organization of terrorist acts . . . Article 279. . . ."

When the clerk finished, my attorney, Joseph Pergament, an Odessa deputy to the Imperial Duma, spoke, "In view of the allegations in the indictment, I ask for the removal of the presiding judge. General Nishtenkov can not try a man charged with organizing an attempt on his life."

General Nishtenkov turned redder than a beet, but arose and declared, "The counsel for the defense is quite right. If the defendant so requests, I shall withdraw."

"No, I don't request it. It's all the same to me."

Pergament shrugged his shoulders, and General Nishtenkov remained on the bench. The testimony against me came from those policemen and gendarmes with whom I had at various times exchanged shots. Some identified me, others were not certain, but it was clear to the court that I had been an active terrorist.

Slowly, and articulating carefully, General Nishtenkov read the verdict: " . . . sentenced to suffer death by hanging."

Spontaneously, I gave the traditional response, "Long live the Revolution!"

The General paused a moment, then continued, "In view of the defendant's youth, however, the death sentence is commuted to eight years imprisonment."

I remained standing, open-mouthed in amazement. Pergament smiled; Kissimov pretended to blow his nose, and nodded reassuringly to me. Both happy and somewhat disappointed, I asked Pergament to assure my comrades that I had not sought clemency.

Back I went to my cell and joined my friends. All the revolutionary parties—Social Revolutionary, Anarchist, Menshevik, and Bolshevik—were fully represented in the Odessa prison. There were men of exceptional moral fiber and great intellectual gifts—scholars, authorities on Greek culture, specialists on Dante and Goethe, admirers of Poe and Baudelaire, devotees of the French symbolist school. Many were influenced by the philosophy of Vladimir Soloviev; others by the moral teachings of Leo Tolstoy. At that time the flower of Russian culture was blushing unseen in Czarist prisons.

In the summer of 1907 the political prisoners decided to attempt a mass escape. We began burrowing a long tunnel, starting under a large, movable bookcase in the library and extending through the dungeon almost 500 feet to the graveyard outside the prison wall. Ordinarily such an undertaking would have been impossible, but after Shafaruk's assassination prison discipline had once more been relaxed. We prisoners worked in shifts of six, emptying the excavated earth into the huge boiler of the heating system, unused during the summer. The prison librarian, a pockmarked Bolshevik named Steinfinkel, whose party name was Vladimirov, acted as our lookout. When I was in Moscow in 1924, I discovered that Steinfinkel-Vladimirov had become Vice-Commissar of Finance.

We had dug more than a hundred feet and had reached a stretch of soft earth, when Steinfinkel signaled trouble from the library. We got back to our cells not a minute too soon. A little later, a squad of guards went below. The warden had sent for an engineer to inspect the heating system with an eye to some improvements. The boilerful of earth betrayed our scheme.

Shortly thereafter Mishka Niemoy, a nondescript person whom we promptly nicknamed Mishka the Dope, arrived in prison. For three days he was kept in solitary. On the fourth, he emerged among us in the courtyard with tales of his revolutionary exploits in the Ekaterinoslav prison, from which he had come. Before the week was over, one of our leading anarchists received word from his organization that Mishka Niemoy was an *agent provocateur* in the service of the Okhrana and had sent twenty men to their death in Ekaterinoslav. There was only one answer to that.

After convincing him that we were duly impressed by his feats, we invited him to attend a secret meeting in an unoccupied third-floor cell. Mishka entered and we locked the door; our guards stood at both ends of the corridor. One of the anarchists flashed a paper in front of Mishka.

"We understand that you wrote this letter. It's addressed to the Okhrana!"

Mishka turned white, but since he never communicated with the secret police in writing, he regained his composure almost instantly. "Nonsense!" he laughed, "look at the handwriting!"

"Fine," I remarked. "If it's not yours, our suspicions are unfounded and we know we can trust you. Please write the words I dictate and we'll compare the writing."

Mishka, greatly relieved, did not realize the significance of the words I dictated: "Don't blame anyone. Mishka Niemoy."

"Now," he smiled, "compare the writing."

As I took the paper from his hand, one of the anarchists seized Mishka from behind, pressing against his windpipe so that he could not utter a sound. Another directed a well-aimed blow at his solar plexus, and Mishka lost consciousness. A noose was quickly slipped through the top bars of the cell window, and Mishka was suspended with his toes a few inches from the floor. Sickened by the spectacle, I ran to my cell and threw myself on my cot. I remembered the "execution" of Ibrahim Aga in Macedonia; but those circumstances had been quite different. That night I could not sleep.

The guards found the body the next morning. The note in Mishka's handwriting convinced the prison authorities, who did not know his real role, that he had committed suicide. The Okhrana naturally had its suspicions, but an autopsy revealed nothing more than death by strangulation, and the suicide version was accepted.

The "loose" regime in the prison came to an end that winter. Outside the prison walls, the revolutionary tide was ebbing fast. The insurrections in Sevastopol and Sveaborg ended in a complete rout of the revolutionists. Stolypin's machinery of repression was running full blast. It took heavy toll of my Lermontov Lane comrades. Galka, transferred to Kiev, was sentenced to fifteen years at hard labor. I learned that Syoma and David had been killed while resisting arrest. Petya Sulimovsky, the bold Don

Cossack, cornered by gendarmes at a rural railway station, held them off and blasted his way free. Although gravely wounded, he tried to escape by wading across a stream, but was seized. He was unconscious when they hanged him. Volodya was ambushed and captured. Celia was sent to Siberia. Of all my Lermontov Lane companions, not one remained in Odessa.

Although a steadfast revolutionist, implacably opposed to Czarist tyranny, I began to question the value of political terrorism. It led almost always, I thought, to the useless sacrifice of the best men. My last doubts were dissipated by the shocking revelation, early in 1909, that Azev, one of the leaders of the Terrorist Brigade of the Social Revolutionary Party, had been working as an agent of the Okhrana all the years he had enjoyed the full confidence and love of the party leaders.

Inside the prison, Pereleshin, the new warden, began clamping down hard, but more intelligently than had his ill-fated predecessor Shafaruk. The privileges political prisoners had won during the revolutionary period were gradually annulled. We were allowed few visitors and little correspondence; our rations were cut again, and many prisoners died of malnutrition; bedding was changed only twice a month; we were allowed only fifty minutes a day in the open, spending the rest of our time in the vermin-ridden cells. Only bacilli remained free to increase and plot death; tuberculosis, scurvy, and typhus took heavy toll of the undernourished men.

Again we planned a mass jail break, but this time we patterned our scheme on that of the amazing Sergei Nechayev, disciple of Mikhail Bakunin. We decided to convert the guards—mostly peasants who had completed their military service and did not own enough land to provide for themselves and their families. I began with Waldeck, a goodhearted Pole who frequently said to me, "I'm a prisoner here myself. Twelve hours a day in jail and the rest of the time in the barracks."

"Why don't you go back to your village?" I asked.

"All we have is three acres of poor land. My brother needs every bit of it to feed his family."

"How many acres has your landlord?"

"Count Zaletski? Oh, seventy-five thousand."

I explained that the principal objective of the Social Revolutionary Party was division of the land among the needy peasants. Many nights thereafter we talked together, and finally Waldeck agreed not only to join us but to recruit other guards as well.

By February, 1908, we had a secret organization of twenty prison guards and, concealed in our cells, a store of eight revolvers and twelve pounds of dynamite. Seven more revolvers, we decided, and we would be ready to strike, disarming the hostile guards and breaking out with our supporters.

[35]

But we had waited too long. One night a drunken guard boasted that big things would soon happen in the prison. Arrested, he confessed the plot, naming Waldeck as leader of the rebel guards. Our cells were thoroughly searched and our arsenal confiscated, except for two Browning revolvers which remained immured in my cell for two years. When they were finally discovered, I was in another cell. Waldeck got six years at hard labor, and all the suspected guards were dismissed.

That marked the end of my efforts to escape, though not of my longing. From time to time I rebelled—even unthinking animals balk at constant imprisonment—the only result being a stretch in solitary confinement. Then my revolutionary faith was put to a cruel test; freedom, just for the asking, was placed within my reach.

My mother's sister, one of the most beautiful women in Europe, occasionally came to see me on her frequent visits to Russia. She was the wife of a famous French doctor, Charles de Vaume, wealthy, and a constant traveler. When she came to see me, she would arrive at the prison gates in a carriage drawn by six horses; and her state, her beauty, and her great dignity so impressed the authorities that they permitted her to see me without witnesses. On each visit she left for me a generous sum of money which I was not permitted to use, but would receive upon my release. My aunt had influential friends in St. Petersburg who, in 1909, obtained the promise of a pardon for me upon my petition to the Czar. But the prescribed terms of such petitions were humiliating—"I fall at your feet and implore your pardon, Majesty. . . ." Badly as I wanted to be free, I could not, as a revolutionist, bring myself to sign anything so abject. I remained in prison, facing five more years of confinement.

Had it not been for the friendship and help of Professor Shchepkin of the Odessa University, I must eventually have given way to despair. An eminent historian and deputy to the Duma, Professor Shchepkin in 1908 served three months in our prison for having signed the Viborg Manifesto against the dissolution of the Duma.

From my first day in prison I had devoured every work of history I could lay my hands on. Shchepkin found that under the law my conviction had not deprived me of my civil rights because at that time I was too young to have any. He therefore promptly registered me as a student of history at Odessa University, "absent on leave." Throughout my years in prison, he supplied me with all the books and other materials I needed.

From time to time my father came to Odessa to see me. On his first visit he had asked for my trial record. "There is nothing dishonorable here," was his relieved comment. He brought me news of my mother and my brothers and sister, and of Balkan events.

The Turkish Revolution of 1908-9 had not produced the expected results. Abdul Hamid was deposed and interned in Salonika, but the

Ottoman policy of oppression against the Balkan people had not changed under the rule of the Young Turks. Instead of introducing political and economic reforms, the new Turkish regime concentrated on strengthening the army. This had one good effect—the threat to the precarious independence of the Balkan nations forced them to patch up their differences and unite.

The Macedonian Revolutionary Organization, which had suspended its war against the Turks during 1908 and 1909, resumed hostilities in 1910. Now, in addition to the *komitajis* from Bulgaria, *chetas* from Greece and Serbia appeared in Macedonia and the three guerrilla forces not only fought the Turks, but occasionally one another.

One day in September, 1911, while taking my brief daily walk in the prison courtyard, I picked up a torn piece of newspaper which a guard had dropped. The first thing I saw was a Salonika dispatch reporting that in the village of Darlitza my old *voivoda*, Pesho Samardjiev, had been killed in a battle with the Turks.

The Balkan volcano seethed and boiled and threatened to erupt at any moment. The Balkan countries began negotiating for an alliance against Turkey, and in March, 1912, Serbia and Bulgaria finally came to an understanding for the future division of Macedonia. Two months later Greece joined the pact, with Montenegro following. On September 30, 1912, the allies delivered an ultimatum to Turkey, demanding that Thrace, Macedonia, Old Serbia, part of Epirus, and the Greek islands in the Aegean be made autonomous provinces under European governors. Turkey rejected the ultimatum, and the First Balkan War began.

Once more I thought of escape. The struggle concerned me in more ways than one. My father and my brother Kyril were both mobilized. Kyril, who had been studying law in St. Petersburg, visited me in prison on his way home to Bulgaria and the war. Impatient to be in it too, I appealed to the St. Petersburg authorities for permission to enlist in the Bulgarian army, solemnly swearing that I would return to prison after the war if I came through alive. They did not answer. While I fretted on the sidelines, the Balkan allies won swift victories. The Bulgarian army under General Radko Dmitriev triumphed brilliantly in the battles of Kirk-Kilissa and Lüleburgaz. The Serbs triumphed at Kumanovo. The military power of Turkey was shattered.

But my joy was mingled with sorrow. My brother Kyril fell on March 13, 1913, during the siege of Adrianople.

The war ended in complete defeat for Turkey, and the liberation of Macedonia. By the Treaty of London, on May 30, 1913, Turkey in Europe was reduced to Constantinople and the territory immediately surrounding it.

A few weeks later I was shocked to learn that Bulgaria had attacked its former allies, who in retaliation joined with Rumania and Turkey. Bulgaria was swiftly overwhelmed and forced to sign peace terms at Bucharest in August, depriving it of nearly all its gains in the preceding war, as well as the Dobruja, which was ceded to Rumania. Most of Macedonia was divided between Serbia and Greece; and Adrianople, for which 10,000 Bulgarians had died, my brother among them, was returned to Turkey.

My father came to see me late in August, broken by Kyril's death and Bulgaria's humiliation. He blamed King Ferdinand for the catastrophe. The King had made a secret agreement with Austria to attack the Serbs and Greeks at the very moment when Russia was ready to settle their territorial dispute by arbitration. Father added that Ferdinand had named General Radko Dmitriev envoy to Russia, to forestall a possible coup d'état under Dmitriev's leadership.

For once Ferdinand's interest coincided with my own. As soon as the new Bulgarian envoy arrived in St. Petersburg he took advantage of his great popularity among the Russian army men to request my immediate liberation. Early in December, 1913, I walked out of the prison gates. My first night of freedom I spent in the Bulgarian Consulate, a splendid mansion on Dvorianskaya Street. But I could not sleep—the bed was soft, the room was warm, and no vermin crawled over me.

The next day I went to see Professor Shchepkin. As dean of the department of history at Odessa University, he promised to arrange a special meeting of his colleagues to examine me for my degree. More than seven years in prison had given me plenty of time to master my subject. I appeared before a board of nine professors, and although two of them were ultra-conservatives intent on confusing me with obscure questions, I passed without difficulty.

The day after my examination, the Bulgarian consul received notice from the authorities that I must leave the country within two weeks. I remained in Odessa only long enough to receive my diploma from the university. Late in December I left by ship for Varna on my way to Sofia.

PART II

SOLDIER

1913-1919

Tonnerre de Dieu! On est jamais content ...
MARCHING SONG OF THE FOREIGN LEGION

BACK HOME AGAIN, I soon found that I could spread almost as much terror with my pen as with my pistol. The humiliating Peace of Bucharest had divided the country into two camps. The chauvinists who supported Ferdinand dreamed of revenge, while the opposition blamed the King and maintained that Bulgaria would have to look for safety to Russia and her allies. I belonged to no Bulgarian party, but naturally I sympathized with the opposition. I began to contribute cartoons and articles against King Ferdinand and his Premier, Dr. Vasil Radoslavov, to a Sofia newspaper, the *Balkan Tribune*. My caricatures must have been good; I was indicted for *lèse-majesté*. Pending trial I was not imprisoned but the lawyers whom my father consulted said I could not escape a two-year prison term. After Odessa, that was too much. I decided to go abroad.

Mary, my first love, now one of the most fashionable young ladies of the Bulgarian capital, had married a rich young attorney and no longer had any interest in either revolution or revolutionists. Michel, my former hero, had left Sofia and married an unattractive, tubercular schoolteacher because she was in love with him and he wanted to make her last days happy. During the Balkan wars he had performed incredible exploits and had been thrice decorated for bravery. At the head of seventy *komitajis* he had harassed the rear of the Turkish army, blowing up bridges and trains, attacking supply depots, and always breaking through the nets spread for him by thousands of Turkish soldiers.

Petko Penchev I found completely disillusioned. The IMRO had degenerated into a mere band of terrorists doing King Ferdinand's dirty work. While true *voivodas* like Michel had fought honorably against the traditional enemy, the newer leaders had followed like jackals on the heels of the regular troops, exploited the occupation of Thrace for personal gain, and committed horrible outrages against the Turks, such as locking them in their mosques and burning them alive. Now, since there were no Turks left to fight in the Macedonian mountains, they supported Ferdinand's pro-German policy by blackmailing and threatening death to opposition leaders.

"The professional revolutionists have won a complete victory," said Petko disgustedly. "When it looked as if Macedonia would at last be free, they fell into a panic at the thought of losing their 'jobs.' Some of them became bandits during the wars and are now buying up our forest lands with the money they stole."

Obviously I could have no further dealings with the IMRO.

Mischa Mikhailov, a friend who was studying at the University of Brussels, persuaded me to go to Belgium with him. There, he said, life was carefree and gay. It sounded better than prison. So I wrote to my friend Sokolovsky, political editor of the Odessa News, who had first introduced me to the Russian revolutionists in 1906, that I intended to travel through Europe. I was already sending regular dispatches from Bulgaria to his paper and translating Bulgarian poetry into Russian for the Sunday edition. Sokolovsky answered that he would print my articles from Western Europe if they were interesting enough.

With my trial pending, I could leave Bulgaria only on a false passport. Petko Penchev arranged the matter. A friend of his, the painter Karagiozov, who was my age and resembled me, took out a passport. My photograph was substituted for his, and the missing portion of the seal was sketched in by Karagiozov himself. It was as simple as all that in the early part of 1914.

Before joining Mikhailov in Brussels I made a short visit to Italy. In my second-class compartment on the Rome-Naples train was a man of imposing appearance who at once began a conversation, shifting to broken French when he found that my Italian was inadequate. He was dark, with jet-black hair and upturned mustache à la Victor Emmanuel, and across his fat belly drooped a heavy gold chain. Learning that I was going to Naples, he cried, *"Bellissimo! Magnifico! Superbo!"* After a half-hour of this, he slapped me on the back, said he loved me, and invited me to the dining car for coffee. Before we parted he gave me his card, which I slipped into my pocket without looking at it.

In Naples everyone, from the bellboy to the barber who came to my room to shave me, offered me women. I declined. Once, when going through my pockets, I found the card of my companion on the Rome-Naples train. His first name was Giovanni and he lived on Garibaldi Street. Under his name was this singular legend:

Il Primo Ruffiano di Napoli

The word *ruffiano* reminded me of something. Straining my memory, I recalled the poem *Le Ruffian* by Jean Moréas. Giovanni was obviously engaged in the disreputable business of procuring women.

Curiosity prompted me to hire a carriage and drive to Garibaldi Street. Although it was winter, the day was warm. I climbed to the second floor of what appeared to be a very decent building. All the windows in my friend's office were open and he was sitting in his shirt sleeves in a deep armchair, smoking a slim Virginia cigar and drinking lemonade. He welcomed me with outstretched arms and nearly kissed me. A bespectacled girl sat busily typing. There were two plain, businesslike desks.

[42]

On the wall hung a picture showing the Italians with bayonets pursuing the fleeing Turks in Tripoli. I decided that I had mistaken Signor Giovanni's profession.

At that moment he sent the girl out for ice cream, and turned to me with a wink. "I know just what you need. All your life you'll remember the pleasure which Giovanni shall procure for you."

Without waiting for an answer, he went into the next room and returned with two thick volumes. He sat down, opened one, and said triumphantly, "Look!"

They were albums containing photographs of half- and completely naked women. Nearly all were pretty and looked young. I pointed to one who appeared to be a blonde. In the meantime, the typist had returned with the ice cream.

"What excellent taste!" exclaimed Giovanni delightedly. "You've picked the most splendid of my daughters."

"Daughters?"

"I call them my daughters because I love them all; they're so sweet." He smiled. "But she—" he rolled his eyes toward the ceiling, "—she is an angel!" And he whispered, "She has very strict morals. She only goes with men she likes."

"Well," I answered, "send for her."

He spoke over the telephone for some time. "In five minutes she'll be here," he announced at last.

After a long hour she appeared, wearing a gray suit with a slit in the left side of the skirt, in the prevailing style. Under a hat that flaunted an entire botanical garden, she was really pretty. But her eyes and smile betrayed a stereotyped dullness.

Giovanni tapped me on the shoulder. "Don't worry," he whispered, "I'll fix the price."

He turned to the girl. "How much?"

She shrugged her shoulders, tilted her head, and answered in a melodious voice, *"Due cente lire."*

Giovanni shook with indignation. Even his mustache trembled. *"Due cente lire!"* Raising his arms and eyes to heaven, *"Due cente lire!"* he cried. "For that money my friend could have a princess of the House of Savoy!"

The girl lowered her eyes bashfully.

Giovanni, striking the pose of Napoleon at Austerlitz, shouted, *"Cinquanta lire!"*

She murmured obediently, *"Si, signor."* Fifty lire was ten dollars. The whole performance had, of course, been enacted for my benefit.

In Brussels I rented, with Mikhailov, a suite in a large pension on the rue du Boulet near the Stock Exchange. It turned out to be mainly a boarding house for divorced women.

After years in prison, everything attracted and excited me—the Grande Place, the University of Brussels at which I registered, the great Ste. Gudule Cathedral, the picture galleries, the cafés, bars, restaurants, the gay crowds, and, of course, the women. But I soon tired of the divorcees —and the others too. These triumphs without glory left me with a sense of futility. I moved to the Avenue Louise, not far from the Bois de la Cambre, to the home of Mme. Jirot, a widow who rented out a single room as a protection against burglary, which was frequent.

Unexpectedly I received an offer from the newspaper *Djen*, of St. Petersburg. My articles in the Odessa *News* had interested the editors, and at their suggestion I traveled through the cities of Belgium and described for *Djen* my impressions of Belgian culture, historical monuments, and works of art. Despite the endless rain the general impression was one of gaiety and well-being, as if the perpetual moisture preserved the freshness of Belgium's fair people as well as the green of its landscape.

Mikhailov and I often went to Paris for week ends. We attended the sessions of the Chamber of Deputies in the Palais Bourbon and witnessed many an oratorical tournament led by Clemenceau, Guesde, Jaurès, and Briand. We heard Mayole sing at the Casino de Paris. We strolled along the arcades of the Palais Royal and through the corridors of the Louvre. Evenings we often went to the Lapin Agile, the noted Montmartre cabaret frequented by the young artists. There I saw Picasso, Utrillo, Francis Carco, Guillaume Apollinaire, and real as well as synthetic Apaches. The cabaret was near the Butte de Montmartre, where the Jacobins had once strolled before the old houses on the Place de Tertre and where traveling players and clowns now performed.

Mme. Jirot, my landlady, looked after me as if I were her son. I took little notice at first of her daughter Angèle, who was only sixteen. Each morning she would bring in my breakfast with the same words, "Monsieur, it's nine o'clock. Time to get up."

To which I would reply, half-asleep and slightly annoyed, "It's still early."

One morning she added, "You came home very late again. That's not good."

I thought I detected chagrin in her voice. Surprised, I sat up in bed. There must have been something disconcerting in my stare, for she quickly set down the tray and ran off. The next morning she did not appear. Perhaps because she didn't come. I awakened at nine o'clock sharp and waited anxiously for her usual greeting. Perhaps she was ill. Strangely disturbed, I dressed quickly, only to find mother and daughter in the dining room.

"Forgive me, please," said Mme. Jirot, "I told Angèle not to disturb you so early."

Angèle sat without saying a word. All my efforts to draw her into conversation failed, and her typically Belgian face, blonde, blue-eyed, and rosy, remained stubborn.

From that time on, the thought of Angèle would draw me home. Soon we were taking walks together, and although I don't know whether we really loved each other, the words we spoke followed the ageless formula of love. Had life continued its normal course, perhaps we would have married. But on June 28, 1914, a bomb exploded in Sarajevo.

The murder of an Austrian archduke seemed of little importance in Brussels. But in Paris, in early July, I could sense a general anxiety over the quarrel between Serbia and Austria. When two weeks had passed and nothing happened, this agitation subsided. After the deceptive calm, tension again mounted rapidly in the latter half of July. From St. Petersburg my newspaper wired me to interview the Belgian leaders. I obtained an audience with the Prime Minister, Comte de Broqueville, who confidently assured me, "We regret what's happening, but it doesn't concern us. Belgium is a neutral country."

On the evening of July 29, the Socialist International held a great peace meeting in the Brussels Winter Circus. On the platform before a crowd of about 20,000 sat the leaders of the European labor movement. Among them were small, thin, black-bearded Emile Vandervelde, who presided; the gray-haired Scotsman, James Keir Hardie; awkward, neurasthenic Hugo Haase, the German delegate; the Dutchman Pieter Troelsta; the Russian Rubanovich; and redheaded, broad-shouldered Jean Jaurès.

I sat at the press table. Of the speakers I knew personally only Vandervelde, whom I had heard lecture at the University. Jean Jaurès impressed me with his extraordinary eloquence. Eschewing the hackneyed phrases about proletariat and bourgeoisie, imperialism and capitalism, he gave a prophetic vision of the horrors of war—the coming destruction of cities, libraries, and museums, the danger to civilization, the senseless sacrifice of youth, the hunger and deprivation which would follow the war. His deep, impassioned voice resounded through the great auditorium and stirred every heart. This stout, ugly man projected such spiritual force that I understood the great power his name carried in France. The others spoke, some of them well, but only Jaurès swayed that vast crowd. When it rose as one man with the cry, "War against war!" and raised thousands of clenched fists I felt that if only there were a Jaurès in every country, war could never be. When the meeting ended, the crowd moved in a great procession through the streets of Brussels. I pushed my way to Jaurès, told him I represented a leftist Russian newspaper and, continuing along with the marchers, attempted to get his answers to several important questions.

"What do you think? Will the Germans attack?"

He shrugged his shoulders. "Haase says it's still possible to avert war."

"Your opinion?" I insisted.

"We must fight against war to the end!" he answered. "As far as France is concerned, I'm certain she will not attack."

"And still, suppose the Germans do strike?"

He stopped short for an instant, his large, blue eyes flashing.

"*Alors—Alors—*I will be the first to volunteer."

An hour later I sent a dispatch to St. Petersburg, ending, "The meeting against war was a big success. War is inevitable."

On July 31, Jean Jaurès was assassinated in Paris by a half-witted fanatic. The next day Germany declared war on Russia.

From the moment Archduke Francis Ferdinand was murdered, everyone who spoke of the prospect of war had an imposing array of arguments to prove it could not come. Those sensible people forgot that irrationality plays a bigger role in history than logic. Madness in Germany created the legend of *frische und lustige Krieg*. And, though madness, war came.

Austria's attack on Serbia, Germany's declaration of war against Russia and France shook me deeply. The war had begun in the Balkans, and I was a Balkan native. It involved Russia, the land of my birth. It had spread to Belgium and France, and I had come to love those two countries—their cathedrals, their art and spirit, the lust for life of the Belgians, the sacred soil of the French Revolution. I decided to volunteer. But I didn't tell Angèle of my decision. She would learn of it only when I was gone.

On August 2, I rushed from one Belgian military establishment to another—to the Ministry of War; to the army recruiting bureau on the rue de la Loi, where I succeeded after considerable effort in seeing an old captain.

"You're a volunteer? There are 40,000 men in Brussels who want to volunteer, but we have no arms for them."

A middle-aged woman, there with her son, begged with tears in her eyes, "I am the widow of an officer. My son is sixteen. I want him to take his father's place in defending Belgium."

The captain could only shrug his shoulders helplessly.

The crowds on the streets shouted, *"Mort aux Boches!"* On the rue Neuve, a large German department store was raided, and on Anspach Boulevard the Café Aux Augustins was wrecked.

I took a cab and drove to the university. The students, mostly foreigners, were standing around in crowds, hotly debating the latest news. On impulse, I jumped up on a bench and began an excited harangue.

"It's the duty of the foreign students, who owe so much to this country, to defend its liberty with their blood," I cried. "Let's go to France and join up. There aren't enough guns for us here."

"Long live Belgium! Long live France!" they shouted.

By four o'clock that afternoon seventy-five students—Russians, Poles, Greeks, Rumanians, Serbs, and, alas! only one Bulgarian—were ready to go. The Bulgarian students didn't volunteer because, with the Second Balkan War fresh in memory, they still hated Serbia. To me what seemed important was that the Bulgarian people should be on the side of Russia. Neither the Russian Czar nor the Russian regime mattered at a moment when Germany was setting out to subjugate the Slavs and make them helots for the greater glory of *Kultur.*

I took the names of the volunteers and rushed to the French Embassy. Because of my press card, the Minister, de Klobukowski, received me at once. I quickly explained why I had come, and requested visas for the entire group of seventy-five. Although de Klobukowski was kept incessantly busy at the telephone, by six o'clock he had arranged everything. The next day, at eleven in the morning, we would leave for France.

When I came home for supper, Mme. Jirot and Angèle bombarded me with questions. "Is it true that the Germans are moving on Liége and Namur?" "Is it true that Russian Cossacks have invaded East Prussia and taken 10,000 prisoners?" "Is it true that Italy has already joined the Allies and that the British fleet has attacked Hamburg?"

Mme. Jirot sighed. "Chicken and butter have already disappeared from the markets. Everyone is hoarding food, and prices are soaring. The speculators have already begun to profit by the war."

Angèle pressed close to me. "How lucky we are to have you with us when such frightful things are happening," she said quietly. "What would we do without you?"

I tried to jest, but emotion choked me. I kissed Angèle but told her nothing. In my room I left a letter for her.

Early the next morning I packed my bag, pocketed my revolver, and went out into the street. The morning was bright and fresh. Since I had four hours until train time, I went to the nearest café. After writing a letter to my mother, I walked to the station. When the train pulled out, our group of seventy-five student volunteers had dwindled to eighteen.

We presented ourselves at headquarters in Lille, which was already swarming with troops, and were shipped off to Paris to be placed at the disposal of General Joseph S. Galliéni, the military governor. In the French capital nobody knew what to do with us, for the problem of foreign volunteers had not yet been solved. At the Invalides, a clerk took our names and told us we would be called later. Except for the general nervousness and the great number of men in uniform on the streets, nothing in Paris indicated war. The street demonstrations of the first days had given way to strained expectation. I joined a group of eighty-six Russian revolutionary volunteers taking preliminary military training in a large garage on the rue Tolbiac, under Captain Osberg and Lieutenant Vladimir Lebedev, both former officers in the Russian army.

At last we were notified that foreign volunteers would be signed up at the Invalides. More than 30,000 men jammed the large inner court of the Invalides that day. When my turn for medical examination came, the army doctor measured my chest, stopped short, and looked at me in amazement.

"You'll do for three volunteers!" he exclaimed.

WE ENLISTED FOR the duration and were assigned to the Foreign Legion. It seemed as if all the nations of the world were represented in the Babel of languages that filled the court of the Invalides. There were Italians, who formed a separate Garibaldi regiment; Spaniards and Portuguese; Russians and Poles; Scandinavians; men from the Balkans; and even some whose native tongue was German—volunteers from the German cantons of Switzerland.

The Swiss formed a special unit, and as they marched through the streets to the Orléans station they sang in husky voices in their peculiar dialect, *"Wir wollen keine Schwauben sein!"* (We won't be "Swabians.")

On the Avenue La Motte-Picquet, one youngster asked another, "Who are they?"

"Don't you hear? Boches, of course!"

In Camp Cercotte, eight kilometers from Orléans, three thousand of us went into training. Legion regulars from Africa soon arrived to be combined with us into new regiments. Except for a few Algerians, all the colonial officers were French. Most of the soldiers and noncommissioned officers had served from five to fifteen years in the colonies. Many, although French, were classified as foreigners—"Belgians" or "Luxemburgers" with unmistakable Parisian accents, "Italians" who sounded strongly of the Marseille docks.

In the camp, two worlds mingled, each utterly strange to the other. It reminded me of the Odessa prison. Idealists who had come to defend the principles of the French Revolution marched in the same ranks with professional soldiers indifferent to all ideals and values save one—the honor of the Legion and its fighting prestige.

The African veterans eyed us incredulously. Why had these men rushed to volunteer? A hard-bitten sergeant asked, "What's the matter? Were you afraid of famine? Did you join up so you could eat at the expense of the army?"

An American with laughing blue eyes took out his checkbook.

"If this gentleman wishes it, I'll pay his wages for three years in advance."

"Shut your trap!" growled the sergeant. "I'm no 'gentleman' to you. I'm your sergeant."

Of the Russian writer, Stepan Sliotov, Corporal Bodet remarked, "He's a good fellow, but dumb. Holds his rifle like a broom."

Corporal Azria, an Algerian Jew, shook his head thoughtfully. "What learned people! Every one of them knows as much as a rabbi."

Sergeant Major Pontacier, a well-educated man but a hopeless drunkard, teased us contemptuously, drunk or sober. "Fools! So you've come to fight for freedom and civilization? Words, empty words!"

"Then why are you here?" I asked him.

"Orders, of course. We're professional soldiers. We don't give a damn what we fight for! It's our job. We've nothing else in life. No families, no ideals, no loves!"

Others, like Rouanet who was tattooed all over with obscene pictures, considered us rank amateurs who had no right to the glorious name of Legionnaire. To earn that, one had to live through the grueling African school of desert outposts, hunger, and thirst.

They all drank heavily, talked their own colonial slang, knew the field-service regulations by heart, were crack marksmen, bore up easily under prolonged marches, and had as much contempt for other regiments as for civilians. On their pre-Legion past they kept silent, but their military records could be read from their medals—China, Indo-China, Madagascar, Morocco. . . .

To Corporal Clots, geography was the comparative study of various local brands of liquor. "Tonkin? Nothing to drink except rice brandy called *shum-shum*. But Algeria—excellent wine and only twenty centimes a liter. Wonderful land!"

"How many years have you been in the service?" I asked.

"Seventeen. If I live I'll get a pension and a job as a forest warden somewhere in the south." He squinted thoughtfully. "My wages and pension should be worth about 200 liters of wine a month. I'll buy it by the barrel, lie on a couch, and drink all day."

Dufour growled, "I've just finished fifteen years of service, and now instead of a pension, it's war."

"And when it's over?"

"I'll try to get a tobacco concession in Sidi-bel-Abbès. That's a Legion post in Algeria; so I'll still be in the Legion, in a way."

Lemercier had three times earned his corporalcy and three times lost it through drunken brawling. Glaise's ambition was to become a sergeant. Tattooed Rouanet wanted only to be confined to a military prison for the duration.

The noncommissioned officers of the Legion were proud of their privileged position. During rest periods behind the front they had their own quarters and separate mess. Their pay was relatively good; their chance for promotion excellent. So high was their military rating that, if transferred to another regiment, they automatically became second lieutenants. But the hard African life had made them gruff martinets, and they had all the vices of the professional soldiers of a colonial army—drunkenness, homosexuality, gambling. And so, despite their ability and experience, they could seldom hold a higher post for long without some scandalous episode reducing them to the ranks again. The majority had served fifteen years before reaching the rank of sergeant. When one did become an officer, he was usually a bad one, remaining a sergeant at heart.

Marochini, a Corsican promoted to second lieutenant at the beginning of the war, was typical. He fussed over every detail, irritating the men with his pettiness. When he was killed a year later, it was not certain whether the bullet had come from the enemy or from one of his own men. On the other hand, there were some noncommissioned officers like Sergeant Vendame, who concealed under that fictitious name a scandalous affair in Paris. He became my friend, and we used to talk about the Renaissance and Eastern civilization. When he died at Souain, I sent his personal belongings to his father, Senator Delpech.

The trained officers were mostly of the best, both morally and professionally. The three of our company were Captain Tortel, Lieutenant Lebedev, and Lieutenant Leseur.

Tortel, well bred and educated, elegant in appearance and bearing, at first impressed one as cold and arrogant. His exquisite manners made him seem aloof. But this mask concealed a deep concern for the well-being of his men; the soldiers respected and loved him. When he fell in the Battle of Champagne, his fierce African wolves wiped their eyes with their sleeves.

Black-bearded, fiery-eyed Lieutenant Lebedev was one of us. When he joined the Legion he took the same rank he had held in the Russian army during the Russo-Japanese War. Army life held nothing new for him, and he obviously enjoyed it. Inexhaustible and experienced, he proved extremely valuable to the regiment. In the new trench warfare which began after the first battle of the Marne he was able, because of his Manchurian experience, to show us how to construct dugouts capable of withstanding shellfire. He organized patrols which continuously harassed the enemy. During the heaviest bombardments he kept in the midst of danger, his chest covered with four decorations. Often his daring moved our battalion commander to shout from the dugout, "Lebedev, you'll have the Boches at us again."

When Lebedev was wounded in a patrol action, he was succeeded by nagging Marochini.

Lieutenant Leseur was the hero of countless military and amorous adventures in Africa—also, in consequence, of Myriam Harry's famous poem, *La Divine Chanson*. Even the Arabs sang his courage in the African wars. Despite this reputation he had no trace of pose. Open-hearted, witty, he had a lot of fun in him. I can see him now, on our march from Epernay to the front, stopping before a signpost: VERTU, CINQ KILOMÈTRES.

"Well, well; for the first time in my life I'm on the road to virtue."

Later he was so severely wounded that we gave him up for dead. After the war, however, Lebedev met him, minus a leg and an arm, in Paris. Crippled as he was, he had finished the Sorbonne law course at the head of his class and had become a prominent attorney.

Judicelli, our battalion commander, hysterical, nervous under fire, always swearing, was liked by neither men nor officers. Once in the trenches on the Somme, with the Germans not far away, he was swearing loudly when suddenly from the enemy side a voice spoke out in French:

"That old fool Judicelli is still shouting. He hasn't changed a bit."

A German ex-Legionnaire had recognized the excited voice of his former commander.

But Judicelli had his moments of inspired courage. During the Battle of Champagne, when the battalion was moving in columns of sections against the second German defense line, a large enemy shell fell squarely in the midst of one section and wiped it out, killing about fifty men. The battalion was momentarily unnerved, but Judicelli did not lose control. He leaped to the forefront and shouted in a firm, clear voice, "Battalion, halt! On guard! In honor of our fallen comrades—present arms!"

With shells tearing up the ground all about us, we stood as smartly as on parade until we heard the command, *"L'arme à la bretelle!* Prepare to attack! Light your pipes!"

We lit our pipes, which we always carried suspended on chains, and, smoking, the entire battalion rushed into action. A General Staff colonel sent by General Noël Castelnau to observe the attack, leaped from the dugout and shouted, "Bravo, Legion!"

Colonel Passard, an austere old officer under whom I served early in the war as liaison between regiment headquarters and our battalion, inspired fear and respect in everyone. During the fighting on the Aisne, General Franchet d'Esperey, commander of the Fifth Army (known to the rank and file as "Franchement Désespéré"), dashed in unexpectedly. The Colonel's uniform was open at the collar.

"Colonel, how do you account for your disorderly appearance?" demanded the General.

Passard walked up to his car and said loudly, "I forbid you to shout at me in the presence of my soldiers!" His tone was so peremptory that the General drove off at once without a word. When Passard was made a General, he was succeeded by Colonel Lecomte-Denis.

The abyss between the professionalism of the veterans and the revolutionary idealism of the volunteers made it hard for the Russians in the Legion to adjust themselves to their new environment, and they remained isolated. The old legionnaires tried at first to bully them, but there my tough schooling in Macedonia and in prison stood me in good stead. Before all of them I declared that if they annoyed any of my Russian comrades, they would have to answer to me. The veterans laughed skeptically, but after I had cleaned up a couple of them, they let the Russians alone.

One of these private victories gained me my first promotion. An enormous old wolf tried to push me roughly out of line while we were waiting for water. I beat the living daylights out of him. Haled before Captain Tortel, I explained what had happened, expecting severe punishment. But Tortel was tired of the young soldiers' complaints of rough handling by the veterans. Winking at a fellow-officer he said, "A real Legionnaire must know how to defend himself. You have proved yourself worthy of the Legion."

He promoted me to first-class soldier of the Legion, and I received the small stripe of the rank.

Within two months I was a corporal commanding fifteen men, half of them veterans and half volunteers. My strength made me popular in the Legion, and I succeeded in maintaining harmony among my men.

Of our Paris unit of eighty Russians, all under Captain Tortel's command, only ten survived the war. Among those who fell was Sliotov, the Social Revolutionary writer, a frail man who suffered under the harsh routine of forced marches with full packs, night sentry duty, trench digging with pick and shovel, and stringing barbed wire. But he was always in good spirits and as one of the oldest among us (he was over forty) gave us wise counsel and cheered up those who faltered.

Alexander Yakovliev, a member of the Terrorist Brigade of the Social Revolutionary Party, typified that wonderful Russian intelligentsia which was capable of the most heroic sacrifice for an ideal. Such a pure spirit looked out through his blue eyes that no man dared utter an evil word in his presence. Even the tattooed Rouanet said, "When he looks at you, blasphemy sticks in your throat." Often at night, while artillery boomed and shells exploded, he would read Gogol aloud to us in our dugout.

Todoskov and Sapozhkov, two powerful, taciturn giants, went to sleep at every opportunity, but were my best comrades for patrol forays. Sapozhkov had been a Bolshevik, but when the war broke out he had joined the Legion.

"Todoskov, Sapozhkov, ready for patrol duty!"

From the depths of the trenches would come loud yawns and hoarse voices.

"You might have waited five minutes; we only just lay down."

"Why do you sleep so much?"

"To draw strength from the earth."

Victor Zelensky was a Jew and a fanatical Marxist. Although so frail he could hardly march, he was determined to die for liberty. Wherever he went, he carried with him a huge volume of Engels, almost as heavy as his pack. Twice he left the depot to which he had been sent and returned to the front. Once, in the lines near Rheims, with the German trenches some 200 yards away, Zelensky was on lookout duty when I came by at lunchtime on a tour of inspection.

"Sergeant," Zelensky reported, "I saw two Germans in the communication trench."

"Why didn't you shoot?"

"They seemed to be carrying food. How can one shoot men carrying food to their comrades?"

"Tonnerre de Dieu! On est jamais content!" The opening words of the Legion's marching song express the basic theme of the Legionnaire's life—perpetual discontent. Like Napoleon's *grognards*, he is forever grumbling. He does nothing without an order and never volunteers for special duty.

"Dufour, Lemercier, do you wish to do patrol duty?"

"If you order it."

Ask him how he likes the military life, and he will always answer, "It's a dog's life." Yet he wouldn't exchange it for any other.

When the Legion's song sounded from the distance, the village housewives would hastily collect their chickens, double-bolt their wine cellars, and with mingled curiosity and fear watch the lean, bearded men of the famous regiments march by. When we moved by night into a new position the other regiments, recognizing our distinctive broad blue belts, would say, "It's going to be hot in this sector. Here's the Legion; that means an attack." And as soon as the Germans discovered that the Legion faced them, the peaceful Saxon, Württemberg, and Rhenish regiments were at once replaced by fierce Bavarians, Pomeranians, and Prussians. Then we knew that our every attack would be met by counterattack.

We were the shock troops of the First Moroccan Division, under the command of General Godet, sent only to those sectors where there was action. Our thoughts, desires, and moods were defined by the present. The past seemed unreal and remote, and on those rare occasions when someone asked a question about the future, it took a strained effort to answer. For it was unimportant. What mattered was to eat well, to drink, to sleep. Rain, cold, the slime of the trenches, the stench of decaying corpses, the rancid odor of bursting shells, the zigzag of enemy trenches fading in the distance—in such a world, the commonplaces of normal life become ineffable joys, and the spectacle of death a commonplace. Horror repeated ceases to be horror. Unexpected pleasures acquire peculiar significance—an accidental bed, a table loaded with food, a smile.

The attack is a terrible and exciting leap into the unknown. A light, nervous tremor before it begins; then the signal, the subdued command, and everything else is forgotten. We hurtle forward, tight-lipped, with fixed stares, faces and bodies taut. Someone falls, groaning, someone cries plaintively for help; but all feelings are dulled, all will is directed to one goal—*to get to them*. If we succeed, we taste the bestial joy of crushing our prey.

Only later, as if in a dream, the blunt horror of what happened returns in memory: the expression in the eyes of that man you bayoneted; the ghastly white faces of the wounded; the trembling hands of those who surrendered. During the attack, our souls seem to revert to the savagery of our wild ancestors; the heritage of knowledge and feeling melts away to nothingness. Danger, reflection, horrors do not exist—except when we are face to face with a living enemy. For that flash of a second there is hesitation and a momentary surge of fear. But the instinct of battle conquers, and almost mechanically we perform the necessary killing motions—shoot, wallop with the butt of the gun, thrust with the bayonet. Afterward, when the battle is over, the scene emerges out of the haze as a terrible reality. We drink to forget it; we all drink, officers and men. We drink, we sing, we embrace women, pretty ones and ugly ones, and the joys of physical existence blot out the stains of remembrance.

A village on the banks of the Oise—clean, peaceful Verberie. Bivouac in a great barn; an excellent dinner. Fallen friends are forgotten. Glaise cleans his rifle and sings an old Legion song:

> "*Quand on a bouffé son pognon,*
> *Ou brisé d' un coup d' cochon*
> *Tout' sa carrière*
> *On prend ses souliers sur son dos*
> *Et on file au fond d' un paq'bot*
> *Aux légionnaires.*
> *Quinze ans on mène c' dur métier*
> *Au moins qu'une balle vienn' prendr' pitié*
> *De notr' misère ...*
> *Alors l'chacal apprête ses crocs,*
> *S'disant j'vais croquer les os*
> *D'un légionnaire.*
> *Mais ça c'est pas admis chez nous,*
> *Un copain vient dir' sur not' trou*
> *Quelqu' bout d' prière;*
> *Deux bouts d'bois en croix, p't'êtr' un nom;*
> *Ça n'fait rien si c'nom c'est pas l'bon*
> *C'est un légionnaire ...*"

(When you have eaten up your dough or wrecked your whole career with one swinish act, you sling your shoes over your back, file into the hold of a packet, and go to the Legion. For fifteen years you follow this hard trade, or at least until a bullet takes pity on your misery. . . . Then the jackal sharpens his tusks, saying to himself, "I'm going to crack the bones of a Legionnaire." But that we don't allow. A comrade comes to say some bit of a prayer over our last ditch. Two pieces of wood, crossed, maybe a name; if it's not the right one it doesn't matter. That's a Legionnaire.)

In another corner of the barn the Russians sing a revolutionary song:

> *"Smelo, druzya, ne teryaite*
> *Bodrost v neravnom boyu*
> *Rodinu—mat vyi spasaite*
> *Chyest i svobodu svoyu."*

(Be bold, friends, do not lose courage in the unequal struggle. Fight to save your country, your honor, and liberty.)

The two songs cross like sabers. In time we sing their old song and they stumble over the words of ours.

It is the spring of 1915. A warm day. The forest of Compiègne is filled with joyous murmurs. Through the sun-drenched streets of the village, groups of Legionnaires stroll. They have scraped the dirt of the trenches from their tunics, puttees and shoes. The inhabitants, who yesterday were still suspicious, now begin to emerge, the women first.

"Why, they're very nice, these 'terrible' Legionnaires," they whisper, nudging one another. Curiosity, acquaintance, flirtation—these stages pass quickly. The stores and cafés do a thriving business. Rapidly the money of the Legionnaires turns into wine. In the evening, drunken voices sound through the village. At night there are the words of love, the eternal vows. . . . Our squads collect the drunkards from the taverns and take them back to the barn, where they bury themselves in the hay and snore. Life has set apart one happy day. In our dreams there are no traces of the nightmare that was yesterday, and will be tomorrow.

News reached me that my brother Vasili, barely sixteen, had left the Kiev Cadet Corps and entered the Tenth Novogermanlanski Hussars Regiment of the Russian army as a volunteer. He wrote me proudly of his baptism of fire "in a cavalry charge in Galicia." My mother's letters did not quite conceal her suffering, but my father, pro-Russian and pro-Ally, was proud that both his sons were fighting for the cause in which he believed. He wrote to my regiment commander, Colonel Lecomte-Denis, but not to ask whether I was alive and well. "I beg you to inform me, Colonel, of my son's conduct at the front. Does he fulfill his military duty with honor?" The Colonel summoned me to his dugout and handed me the letter, which I read with emotion. He smiled and slapped me on the shoulder.

"Your father's a real soldier. I told him there was no better man in the regiment than you." Then he added sternly, "Try to live up to the reputation I've given you."

I was not a bad soldier. I liked army life and in time even acquired a certain passion for it. But it wasn't easy to live up to what the Colonel had said, for there were few opportunities to perform outstanding feats. We were all under fire together; we attacked together. The only way to distinguish one's self was through night patrol raids.

My first exploit of this kind resulted in the capture of a prisoner near the village of Craonnelle, in the region of the Chemin des Dames, early in 1915. Our positions were northeast of the village, near an apple orchard. The Germans occupied the heights about a half-mile away. Between the two lines stood haystacks, like pyramids. The seeds had fallen and rotted but the hay made good beds for the dugouts. At night, groups of soldiers of both sides would creep out to the stacks and drag sheaves back to their lines. At first this was done cautiously, then both sides became careless. I went to Captain Tortel.

"Sir," I said, "do you consider it right for the Germans to enjoy French property with impunity?"

"Of course not. What's up?"

"I'd like to set a trap near our haystacks."

He smiled. "Not a bad idea. You might try it."

That evening I chose three men, Dufour and those mighty sleepers, Sapozhkov and Todoskov. A cold, penetrating fog had settled over the countryside, and searchlights and rockets failed to pierce its thick, white wall. Such nights were best for raids, but it was also easy to get lost and stumble into the hands of the enemy. We should have to go very near his lines, for the Germans naturally took their sheaves from the ricks nearest them.

Our plan was, if there were many Germans, to shoot and dash back to our lines. If there were only a few, we would try to kill or capture them. One of them would have to climb onto the top of the rick. Dufour was to pick him off. One had to be below to catch the sheaves, and a third to stand guard. Todoskov and Sapozhkov were to seize the Boche who caught the sheaves. I was to take care of the sentry.

That night and the next we saw no one, although we lay in wait for hours on the damp ground. On the third, we saw three figures through the fog and heard the sound of German voices. We lay motionless, exerting every ounce of will power not to shoot. Everything happened

[57]

as we had foreseen. One German climbed aloft; a second stood below to catch the sheaves, with a heavy rope to bind them. These two dropped their guns. Only the sentry remained armed, but he smoked carelessly. Dufour had not boasted in vain that he never missed his man. He fired twice. The figure atop the haystack vanished. I aimed at the sentry, but apparently missed him, for he dropped his gun and disappeared into the fog. Meanwhile Todoskov and Sapozhkov pinioned the third German so firmly to the ground that he could hardly breathe. They bound him with his own rope and dragged him off as if he were a sack. From the German lines came a volley, but in a few minutes we were back in our trenches with our prisoner and three rifles.

Captain Tortel and Lieutenant Leseur awaited us in the flour mill which served as the Captain's headquarters. Tortel's eyes gleamed merrily through his spectacles as he poured wine. Leseur hugged us. We untied the prisoner, a Bavarian trembling with fright. When Tortel handed him a cup of wine he quickly calmed down and told Leseur, who spoke German, everything he knew about his detachment—the advance posts, the disposition of troops, and the mood of the soldiers. Leseur wrote it all down. Then he handed Dufour the sealed report, saying, "Take him to the battalion commander, and mind you don't beat him up on the way."

Dufour didn't budge. "Couldn't I have another cup of wine?"

Leseur poured it for him. Tortel turned to us. "What reward would you like? Decoration or leave? You have the right to choose."

Sapozhkov, Todoskov, and I chorused, "Leave."

But Dufour said bitterly, "I've no one to go to on leave, and I have enough medals. Couldn't I have double rations of wine for a month?"

Tortel had to repress a laugh, but he said sternly, "Impossible! You'll get the decoration."

Leseur winked at Dufour, whom he had known for many years. "Don't worry, old man. You'll get the wine from me personally."

We got our leave in February, the first granted in the regiment since the war began—eight days leave, two of which we would lose in travel. When we reached Paris, Todoskov went directly to his family. Since my Petrograd newspaper was publishing my "impressions of the front," I had accumulated a sizable sum of money in a Paris bank, and Sapozhkov and I took rooms on the rue Monsieur le Prince in the Latin Quarter.

We were engaged in a private conspiracy—to find and beat up Leon Trotsky for his campaign against the Russian volunteers, whom he constantly insulted as "mercenaries of French imperialism and capitalism."

Silent, unexcitable Sapozhkov raged. "Mercenaries! We get five centimes a day. We'll teach Trotsky a lesson!"

We spent our first evening strolling on the boulevards which, after seven months at the front, seemed unreal. The next morning we set out to find Trotsky at the office of his newspaper, *Nashe Slovo*. It was a small, one-story house in a deep court on the rue St-Jacques. The court-yard gates were open. As we approached the house we heard a woman's voice inside cry in French, "For whom are you looking?"

Sapozhkov answered, "Comrade Trotsky."

We knocked, but the door did not open. We hammered repeatedly. No reply. Infuriated, Sapozhkov kicked the door so hard that the windowpanes rattled. It opened a crack, and a thin, yellow-faced woman wearing glasses peered out.

"What do you want?" she asked in a trembling voice.

"We're looking for that son of a bitch Trotsky," said Sapozhkov.

"He's not here," the woman said querulously. "He's seldom in the office. Look for yourself."

There were two rooms and a kitchen. In one room a dark, stooped man was busily setting type. In the other an unfinished glass of tea stood on a table amid a pile of manuscripts, proofs, and newspapers. A rear exit through the kitchen led to another street. It looked as if someone had left in a great hurry.

"It's a pity," said Sapozhkov. "I was so anxious to give him what was coming to him."

As an outlet for his rage and disappointment, he smashed the manu-script-covered table and scattered the type. Then we left through the rear exit.

In Paris, our horizon-blue field uniforms made us heroes when we mingled with the crowds on the streets or in cafés, restaurants and shops. Soldiers on leave from the front, especially Legionnaires, were still a comparative novelty in February, 1915.

On the third day, I decided to visit my *marraine de poilu*—war god-mother. Those French women and girls who volunteered to act as "god-mothers" to lonely soldiers helped greatly to preserve the morale of the French army. They gave the lonely men the feeling that someone watched over their destiny. At the front, I had received a large package from an unknown woman and a letter saying she had learned that I was alone in France, and she wanted to be my *marraine*. The package contained warm underwear, chocolates, jelly, biscuit, soap, and many other things both useful and useless.

My godmother turned out to be a nineteen-year-old Baroness Léonino, of one of the richest families of France. But I didn't know this the day I called; her letters had been signed simply, "A. Léonino." When I reached the splendid mansion on the rue Euler between the Avenue Marceau and the Champs Élysées, I realized that I was among the very rich. For a moment I hesitated, but remembering that the Legion never retreats, I mustered enough courage to ring the doorbell.

A magnificent lackey with sideburns, who looked like a Russian general, examined me from head to foot. "What are you looking for?" he asked curtly.

"I wish to see my godmother, Mlle. Léonino."

"Your godmother?" His eyes popped. "Which of the two Mademoiselles? This must be a joke."

"Announce me," I insisted, "and tell them Corporal Todorov of the Foreign Legion wants to see one or both of them."

A little reluctantly, he admitted me to the library. In about ten minutes a smiling girl entered and held out her hand. She was not pretty, but charming and cultivated. Thereafter I had to visit her daily, to drive with her through the city in her automobile, to be exhibited to her friends as a "real *poilu*." Her mother was dead and her father, who was over forty-five, had been mobilized for home-guard duty. I spent the best part of several days in her beautifully furnished home, with its rare books and priceless works of art. But at last, heaped with gifts, I had to return with Sapozhkov and Todoskov to my regiment.

Things were going badly in Bulgaria. My father's letters, sent through the French diplomatic mail to escape censorship by the Bulgarian authorities, described the intrigues going on. The IMRO had gone over to the service of the Central Powers and was preparing for a guerrilla attack on the Serbian rear, to help the Austrians whom the Serbs had twice defeated. King Ferdinand and the Radoslavov government feigned neutrality while permitting arms to pass freely through Bulgaria to Germany's ally, Turkey. The Germans had bribed a large number of Bulgarian politicians and journalists to advocate an alliance with Germany and an attack on Serbia.

My father always ended his letter by blaming King Ferdinand for the past and present misfortunes of the Bulgarian people. Although these letters disturbed me greatly, I didn't want to believe that Bulgaria would join Germany. I tried to convince myself that my father was exaggerating because of his hatred of *der Schwabe,* as he called Ferdinand.

Our regiment was moved rapidly from one sector to another. In May I was promoted to the rank of sergeant and placed in command of the patrols for the entire battalion. Again my experience in Macedonia stood me in good stead. With picked men, I would crawl at night to the enemy lines, unseen and unheard, to cut barbed-wire entanglements and blast enemy outposts with hand grenades.

In June, when we were in the Rheims area, in Fort St. Thierry, I had to say good-by to my Russian comrades. The parting resulted from a tragic incident in the fourth battalion of our regiment. Several Russians, in protest against the brutality of an African sergeant, had refused to return from the village where they were on leave. Nine were court-martialed and shot. Whereupon War Minister Alexandre Millerand ordered Lieutenant Lebedev to investigate the situation of the Russian volunteers in the French army. Lebedev recommended that the Russians in the Legion be distributed among the French regiments—a change which the Russians themselves welcomed, for they could now fight beside the French people instead of the professional soldiers of the Legion.

Of the whole group of Russian revolutionists who had entered the French army together, I alone remained in the Legion, because I was Bulgarian. All my best friends left—Sliotov, Yakovliev, Sapozhkov, Todoskov, Shvetzov, Volzhin, Usikov, Neidman (who had been in prison with me in Odessa). All except Volzhin later died in action.

My own luck was incredible; I outlived nearly everyone I knew. Even while my comrades fell in battle around me, I felt a strange certainty that nothing could happen to me. In July, when we attacked the Germans around Fort Brimond, one of the Rheims fortified positions in enemy hands, only fifteen men in my platoon of sixty remained on their feet. Yet I was not touched by bullet or shrapnel. In the September fighting in Champagne, two Legion regiments numbering 8,000 men lost more than 6,000 effectives. Often I was drenched in other men's blood and covered with sticky bits of their flesh; but I didn't even get a scratch. More than once during that battle I hoped in vain for a small wound which would mean respite in a hospital. All the officers of my company were either killed or wounded, and I commanded its remnant, no more than seventy men. Dufour said, "You and I apparently lead charmed lives."

The soldiers in my platoon were always being replaced; new troops came from the depot and left directly for their graves or for the hospital. Over the mounded graves of our dead we placed wooden crosses with wreaths of empty rifle shells.

The officers, too, were constantly changing. In place of Colonel Lecomte-Denis came Colonel Cot, a brave and well-educated officer; in place of Tortel, Captain Jackson. I recall Captain Dubech, a noted royalist who used to say, "If we should suddenly catch Wilhelm, as a convinced royalist I should have to address him as Majesty and stand at attention before him." Captains Rousseau and Dumas. . . . How many of them are still alive? The four regiments with which the Foreign Legion entered the war were reduced to one after the bloody and futile Champagne offensive. And of the 46,000 men who passed through the

Legion in those four terrible years no more than 6,000 survived, including the disabled—the highest casualty rate of any detachment in the war.

Years later, when I traveled through what had once been the front, many bits of French soil had peculiar emotional significance for me. Here had been the dugout where the saintly Yakovliev read Gogol to us. Somewhere here in the forest the corpse of Captain Tortel was carried away. And there, on the bank of the Oise during a pause in the fighting under the sun of early autumn, Alan Seeger, the American poet, had read me his poem, *I Have a Rendezvous with Death*. He kept his rendezvous in July, 1916, when I was no longer on the Western Front.

After twenty-six years, when I see newsreels of the Legion and hear the strains of our march, *Tonnerre de Dieu*, a shudder passes through me. As I look at the bearded faces of the Legionnaires, I know that my memory and my love have fused together the idealist volunteers of 1914 and the professional soldiers with assumed names, who fell side by side on the battlefields of France.

W E MARCH ALONG an old Roman road paved with large, round cobblestones while night covers our movements. Our helmets reflect the glow of our pipes; our weapons clank. Horses' hoofs clatter amid the rumble of heavy trucks, tractors, and big guns. For more than a year now I have been fighting, smoking my pipe, drinking wine as if it were water, and never drinking water. I speak the pithy slang of the African troops, swear eloquently, read nothing, think of nothing. I have become a true Legionnaire.

Suddenly it seems to me that centuries ago I marched along this same road. It was night then too, and instead of tractors and artillery, Roman battering rams and catapults rolled over these cobblestones. I was a young centurion in the legions of Rome, crying "Ave!" to the man in the purple toga, the Emperor. Then I was a knight astride my war horse, passing with other knights along this road, bound for the Holy Land. On my helmet I wore a lock of my beloved's hair; on our banner fluttering ahead were the cross and the image of the Madonna. I was a musketeer in the company of some d'Artagnan, a *sans-culotte* marching to Valmy with the wrath of the Paris streets in my heart, a *grognard* of Napoleon. How many different banners! The golden eagles of Rome, the cross of the Crusaders, the white lilies of the Bourbons, the tricolor of the Republic, the eagles of the Empire. And always the same cry: Ave! Ave Caesar! Ave Maria! Ave Revolutia! . . . I marched with them all, in my soul the red flame of battle which shut out the sight of the dying.

My Legionnaires are grumbling. "We didn't get our coffee this morning. Tonight we had nothing but hardtack. Can we fight on empty stomachs? To hell with the command and to hell with the Republic! Didn't General Joffre have his coffee this morning? Didn't M. Poincaré dine in his palace?"

I pay no attention. I know my men. Legionnaires must grumble, but as soon as dawn breaks they'll sing their old battle song. And when we reach the front, I'll say, "Cut out the gaff; let's wallop the Boches!" And I'll hear the joyous response, "You bet we'll wallop 'em."

We pass through Suippes, in that part of Champagne called *Champagne Pouilleuse* (lousy Champagne). In the fertile section there are beautiful orchards and gardens and prosperous cities, but here the landscape is mournful, for only pine trees will grow in the barren soil and the villages are poor.

"An accursed land!" growls Corporal Clots. "If I'm not killed here, I'll find a better place to end my days. God was never the warden of this forest."

Lemercier, now my orderly, steals my wine and canned food, but in return brings me fresh game with the aid of a ferret brought with him from Africa. The animal lives in a wooden box tied to the back of the Legionnaire's knapsack. When released, he licks his master's hand and disappears. In a few minutes he runs back with a chicken, goose, or rabbit. He takes little of his prey for himself; only the liver which he rips out with his powerful teeth. The rest is for his master. An hour later, Lemercier has prepared an excellent dinner over the fire.

In Suippes, the rear services for several armies are concentrated—trucks, freight cars for horses, enormous covered stores of provisions, ammunition. Meanwhile, on the road to Sommepy countless batteries are directing hurricane fire at the German lines for the second successive day. We stop beyond Suippes to rest. The Colonel calls all officers and noncommissioned officers to his headquarters. We form a circle around him. His freshly shaved face is stern and thoughtful.

"Gentlemen," he says, "the decisive hour has come. I'll read you the brief order of General Joffre." The sheet of paper rustles in his hand.

"Officers, noncommissioned officers, corporals, and soldiers of the Republic! I order you to attack the enemy and expel him from the borders of France!"

We know that this means another attempt to break through.

It is September 25, 1915. Our big guns boom incessantly; thousands of exploding shells make the air an inferno of sound. Above us, in the morning mist, hang the sausagelike observation balloons. Troops clog the road. The officers of the Colonel's staff distribute among us maps on which are marked all the irregularities of the terrain in our sector, lying between the village of Souain and the Navarin farm. Joining us in the attack are the colonial troops of General Jean Baptiste Marchand. After the capture of the Navarin farm, we shall be assigned a further objective on the road to Sommepy.

By eight o'clock we are in our trenches. The Germans are not firing, and we sit carelessly on the parapets. Before us, not more than a hundred paces off, is the first German line, blanketed by a thick wall of smoke from the continuous explosions. Blasted by shellfire, barbed-wire barriers are ripped out of the ground and smashed to bits.

Dufour exults. "We'll take them like rabbits in their holes."

"Fix bayonets," the command runs along the trenches. Zero hour. The attack begins. We leap from the trenches and rush forward. Then for the first time the German artillery opens up and German guns rattle. A few men fall, but we press on. *En avant! En avant!*"

I chance to look about me and I don't recognize the faces of my comrades; they are so strangely tense, as immobile as masks. Our barrage thunders and we stumble on into the German trenches. Pale, frightened German soldiers begin to emerge, arms upraised. Many of them, fair-haired young recruits, fall on their knees and clasp our legs.

"*Kamerad*," they cry, "*Kamerad!*"

No one hurts them. Corporal Fournier, a native of German-occupied Tournai, has learned through the Red Cross in Geneva that one of his children died of hunger. He has sworn that at the first opportunity he will kill ten Germans. Now they are before him, and I watch to see that he doesn't carry out his threat. Instead, he takes out bread and gives it to the prisoners. He looks at me guiltily.

"They're swine, of course, but hungry," he mumbles.

Many soldiers follow his example. Even Dufour sacrifices a cup of his precious wine. Realizing that they are out of danger, the young Germans weep—a reaction natural enough after three days of incessant bombardment. We quickly mop up the trenches we have occupied. If no one from the inner trenches responds to our cry "*Geben Sie Sich!*" we hurl grenades into these underground passages.

Again the command, "*En avant! En avant!*" Again we rush to the attack, toward a new line of trenches. But the accurate, steady fire of the Germans proves too deadly, and we drop into the shell holes between the lines. On our left flank, beyond the hill of Souain, four full cavalry divisions, about 20,000 men on horseback, gallop to the attack, their white capes flying and their sabers flashing *à la* Murat. It is beautiful and inspiring, but the days of Borodino and Gravelotte have long since passed. The mounted squadrons of hussars, spahis, and dragoons trip over the hidden wire entanglements; simultaneously the Germans open up with shrapnel. The horses stumble and fall on top of one another. Frightened steeds gallop through riderless; riders lie wounded and dead.

Again our artillery blasts the German lines; again we hurl ourselves at the enemy trenches. Lieutenant Marochini is killed. Not far off lies his Corsican countryman, Spezza. (Later the rumor goes about that Spezza killed Marochini; they had old accounts from Corsica.) We leap into a German trench. An officer fires at me almost point-blank, but misses. I empty all six chambers of my revolver.

Again the Germans surrender. A soldier comes to me from the battalion staff. "You're ordered to mop up the trenches with your platoon."

It's a dirty, disgusting business, collecting prisoners and wounded and killing those who won't surrender. I send my soldiers through the trenches with orders to be back in fifteen minutes.

Not far off a wounded German groans, "*Mutter, Mutter.*" Exhausted, I pay no attention. I am curious to see the face of the German officer I killed. He has fallen forward, his cloth-covered helmet still on his head. I turn the corpse over on its back. Blood, congealed and sticky, moistens my hands. A shudder chills me, but my curiosity exceeds my revulsion.

His face is white and calm, but his eyes sparkle glassily. One bullet has passed through his helmet and forehead, from which a stream of blood trickles to his nose; another bullet through his chest. For the first time I face a man I have killed. Do I feel regret or aversion? "If he had hit me," I think, " I would be lying there, not more than two paces off, with my face to the ground." His hand still tightly grasps his revolver.

"Lemercier, Lemercier!" I shout. Lemercier comes and reports. He has found two wounded men and turned them over to Pontacier, the officer in charge of prisoners.

"Search this one," I say, pointing to the corpse. "And give me his binoculars; they're military spoils."

Lemercier goes about his business cold-bloodedly. He removes a leather pouch, unbuttons the coat, and searches the pockets: a gold watch, a notebook, a pen, a bundle of letters, a wallet containing money, a clean shirt.

"Is all that for me?" Lemercier asks slyly.

"No, we'll send it to Geneva to the Red Cross, for his family."

"Even the money?" sighs Lemercier.

"You fool, what good is German money to you?"

His face is so sad that I decide to give him something after all. "Take the pouch," I say, "it's yours."

He quickly makes a package of the remaining things. Among the papers I find the name of the dead man and the address of his family: Captain von Luetzendorff of the Fourteenth Brandenburg Infantry Regiment; Frau von Luetzendorff, Breslau—either his mother or his wife.

Several days later, we mailed the package.

When the fifteen minutes had ended, I blew my whistle for the men to return. The last to come, Corporal Cobet, the bugler, was an enormous, terrible-looking man, dark, sunburned, and heavily scarred. His hands and his uniform were smeared with blood.

"What have you been up to?" I shouted. "You've probably been killing prisoners."

"Not prisoners—spies." He smiled and drew out his curved Arabian sword.

"What kind of spies can there be here at the front?"

"Come with me, I'll show you."

About a hundred meters off, near a demolished dugout, lay seven German corpses, all with their throats slit. I shook with anger.

"I'll turn you over to court-martial for murder."

He laughed insolently, shrugged his shoulders.

"Court-martial? You ought to recommend me for a decoration. Look!"

The Boches lay outside an excellently camouflaged dugout. Cobet pulled out a concealed field telephone.

"They were inside, telephoning. When I passed I heard whispering—looked around and there seemed to be nothing. But when I came closer, I heard a German voice. I kicked, and there wasn't a sound. Then I began hammering with the butt of my gun and when the earth spilled I saw an opening. Through a hidden peephole in the rear they'd been observing the movement of our troops and telephoning to their headquarters. That's espionage, isn't it?"

I had to admit that according to military law he was probably right.

"But how did you do it? There were seven of them. Didn't they resist?"

Cobet laughed. "Germans are strange fellows. Under the command of officers, they're the best soldiers in the world. I know them from the Legion in Africa. But left to themselves they're sheep, not men. I took them out one at a time and slit their throats. All they did was to cower and whine, 'Mein Gott! mein Gott!'"

We overtook our company, which was slowly pushing against another German line. The German resistance was stiffening. Apparently our attack had not caught the enemy off guard. I found Tortel in a large shell hole and reported to him. He shook his head.

"The Germans have apparently succeeded in getting up their reserves. They occupy the whole line of forest, and fire incessantly. It'll be hard to drive them out."

"Where is the Navarin farm?" I asked him.

"It's still there—somewhere on the left," he laughed. "We've been shoved to the right by General Marchand's colonial troops. He's wounded and so is our Colonel, and Cot is our new regimental commander. Our battalion has lost contact with the others. Orders are to sit tight."

Corporal Cobet, the bugler, had stretched out and gone to sleep. Tortel looked at him and smiled.

"There's a man with a clear conscience! You said seven men, I believe, and all with a knife?" He shuddered. "Still, I'll cite him for a decoration. I must."

Night was falling. The forest before us turned dark blue, and the cannonade grew weaker. I climbed out of the shell hole to look over my platoon and fix the men up for the night. New soldiers arrived after dark, sent from the rear, looking wonderfully clean and fresh. Four were assigned to my platoon, all Italians from the Garibaldi regiment, which had been re-formed after the fighting in the Argonne. They chattered vivaciously in their native tongue and told how the grandsons of the immortal Garibaldi, Constantino and Bruno, had died in the Argonne. Bruno, mortally wounded by a bullet near his heart, had stood for more

[67]

than a minute on his feet and shouted, "See how a Garibaldi dies!"

Two friends, Feliciani and Corbella, who had left their little village in Italy to work in France, had volunteered together.

"Together we shall die," said Corbella. And he laughed.

He was not wrong. The next day they were buried by the same shell.

Three days of attack and counterattack. We are unshaved, hungry, exhausted. Mechanically we attack or repulse the enemy. We have emptied our last tins of food. We have plundered all the corpses, German and our own, looking for something to eat. We no longer count the killed and wounded. When we go forward, we go without excitement, without fear. When the Germans attack, they seem like mechanical toys, waving their arms strangely as they fall face forward—the way men usually fall in battle unless they are killed by an exploding shell. We remain checked in the spot to which we advanced the evening of September 25. On the twenty-sixth we tried to push farther, but with no success. On the twenty-seventh we withstood a counterattack, our temporary position became permanent, and we dug in.

For more than twenty-four hours we have eaten nothing, and the German artillery fire grows steadily heavier.

"If we don't get food tonight, I'll beat it back to Suippes. I'll eat and drink my fill there—even if I'm shot for it," muttered Dufour, staring through troubled, inflamed eyes into the darkness.

Corporal Clots swore. "You call this 'administration'? It stinks!"

Lemercier observed sadly, "I've searched all the dead Germans. Found some hardtack but couldn't swallow it. A dog wouldn't eat it!"

Later in the evening, news spread through the trenches that food was coming up at last. We ate ravenously, swallowed cold meat without chewing it, devoured the bread, and washed it down with wine and sugarless coffee.

Through the misty rain the yellowish rays of a searchlight crawled over the dead bodies in front of us, as if searching them as Lemercier had done. Rocket flares would soar up with a hiss and fall in sparks and sprays. The stench of putrefying flesh was growing stronger.

But we were no longer hungry. Life once more became tolerable.

Even here, in barren Champagne, in puddles churned up by the shells, my old Legionnaires, Clots, Dufour, and Lemercier were enjoying themselves, especially because rations had come for the whole platoon and nearly half the men were gone. Two extra gallons of wine!

They drank slowly, smacking their lips and chatting as if they sat in a comfortable inn. Their pipes glowed occasionally and lit up their faces.

"There's no army without wine," said Clots. "Napoleon lost his way in Russia because the wine gave out. In 1912 we took Taza, in Morocco, because the wine came in time—just before the attack."

The Moroccan war seemed to awaken pleasant memories.

"That was a real war—movement all the time—bugles, drums, fifes," Dufour sighed.

"And not so many casualties—only a dozen per company," added Glaise.

"Do you remember how the Moroccan women tried to hide from us? We caught 'em, though, young and old," roared Lemercier.

On the eve of the battle I had received a letter from my *marraine*. It was in the inner pocket of my tunic. I had not finished reading it. She mentioned our last walk in the Bois de Boulogne. Bois de Boulogne! Here the woods have different names. On the General Staff map they are called U 23, U 24. The wide field we crossed yesterday in platoon columns, under the bombardment of German heavy guns, was called the Place de l'Opéra.

Our company commander, Captain Tortel, has behaved splendidly. His trim, slender figure did not once waver under fire. Last night, when I quoted from Herédia's poem, *Après la Bataille,* he replied with Lecomte de Lisle's *Poèmes Barbares.*

Strange, that side by side with Tortel we have Clots and Lemercier, whose brightest memories are of raping a drove of Moroccan women!

But what good is Lecomte de Lisle; who needs him? Didn't we rejoice as much as Clots and Lemercier when food and wine finally arrived? We behave as they do, but they don't need our flowery phrases.

In the morning we occupied the fringe of the forest—U 22. Not a living soul left there—only a few dead Germans in their machine-gun nests. Tortel lay dead. His face was very placid, only paler than usual. In his kit was a woman's picture, with an unfinished letter. I gathered together his effects, made a package, and addressed it to his mother in Grenoble. Our stretcher-bearers carried him to the rear.

Later our battalion commander came and gave me the bit of gold stripe which meant I was an officer. He pinned it on my sleeve, made a little speech about heroism, and kissed me on both cheeks. I felt confused and embarrassed. I remembered nothing except that I had attacked together with the others, thrown myself into puddles, and advanced again with the rest. Still, the gold stripe pleased me.

At noon, the Germans began showering us with shells and shrapnel. Clots lost both legs. I gave him the little wine I had left. His eyes were strangely clear, and he whispered something, but I couldn't understand him. He was carried away. Glaise had a bit of real luck. A bullet passed through his thigh without touching the bone. He hobbled happily on one leg, leaning on his rifle, and winked.

"Now I'm in for a good long stay in the rear."

Conscious of my new dignity as platoon commander, I said something quite foolish: "Glaise, you've done your duty to the end."

He looked at me with ironical surprise. "Duty? Rubbish! I'm glad to be out of it."

In the evening we were ordered to retreat to our old position. We buried our dead in muddy graves and withdrew, loaded down by our loot of German knapsacks, helmets, and machine guns. Of the original sixty in our platoon, only twenty-eight remained.

The rain stopped at last, and I lay down for a nap. I covered myself with a German blanket and rested my head on a soft German goatskin knapsack.

Early in October we withdrew from the front lines and were relieved by a battalion of Senegalese. Poor African children! They trembled with cold and grumbled, *"Pas bon! Pas bon."*

"How are they as soldiers?" I asked their bearded French captain.

"Excellent! They're not afraid of death. Each one carries a talisman of chicken or goat bone, sewed into a leather pouch. He calls it his *'gri-gri.'* Their priest distributes these charms after pronouncing magic words over them, and the men believe their *gri-gris* make them invulnerable."

"But they see their comrades die."

The captain smiled. "That doesn't disillusion them. When one of their comrades falls, the others laugh. 'The priest fooled Bu-da-bu. He gave him a false charm. He didn't say the right prayer.' "

Thousands of these huge, good-natured, childlike men found their graves in France.

Our division also contained native Moroccan and Algerian sharpshooters. The Moroccans fought with great courage, but the Algerians often had to be driven to battle at the point of the bayonet.

On October 13, we were at last sent to the rear. Apparently the High Command had realized that a break-through was impossible. We rested in Camp de la Noblette for one day. On the next there was a general inspection. The remnants of the Legion marched before the reviewing general to the music of *Sambre et Meuse,* the march written in honor of the soldiers of the Year II of the First French Republic.

In the evening, at roll call, our names were barked out loudly. And often, too often, came the reply, *"Mort pour la France!"*

DURING THE CHAMPAGNE offensive I received a hasty note from my father:

> "Ferdinand has finally sold out Bulgaria to the Germans. He is sending us to fight against Russia, our liberator. Remain at your post, for the overwhelming majority of the Bulgarian people are against Germany and against the King."

Bulgaria in the war on Germany's side! My whole inner being rocked. Bulgaria was fighting Russia, which had freed her from the Turks, fighting the Slavic world which expected this war to liberate it from German hegemony and the Hapsburgs.

I continued to perform my duties but felt I could not go on as before. I needed someone to talk to, but most of my men were newcomers. Of my old soldiers, Dufour alone remained, and he could never understand. I gave him wine and tried to speak to him. He drank the wine and looked at me with uncomprehending eyes.

"This doesn't concern the Legion," was all the comfort he could give.

I racked my brains for a solution but could find none. I communicated with Lieutenant Lebedev, who answered that he was leaving for Salonika and the Balkan front. I wrote to General Radko Dmitriev, who now commanded the Third Russian army, in Galicia, asking his advice. I also wrote to my brother on the Polish front and, having no one closer in France, to my *marraine* in Paris.

In November I went on leave, but Paris no longer gave me any pleasure, and Baroness Léonino received me coldly. She was a passionate French patriot; I was a Bulgarian. She tried to be gracious, but it was a studied effort, and I did not visit her again. Before my leave was up I returned to my regiment.

Our ranks were being re-formed in the Vosges Mountains, about six miles from the town of Giromagny. It was foggy and rainy, but the inhabitants were hospitable and our men were in excellent spirits. The battalion was billeted in a small village, and a number of our men married village girls while we were stationed there. My own spirits, however, remained downcast. In vain did Philomène, a lovely girl, shower me with attentions, cook for me, and wash my clothes. In my free time I went alone into the forest, smoked my pipe, and drank more than ever.

A month swiftly passed, and again we were at the front, our new ties completely severed. Once more we knew only attack and counterattack:

Mikelbach in Alsace; Sailly-Saillisel on the Somme. It was 1916 now. Our company was commanded by Lieutenant Delanourienne, a Breton with an eagle's beak and cold blue eyes. Of the old soldiers, only Dufour and Lemercier, back from the hospital, remained. Both were now soldiers of the first class, but I couldn't make them corporals because they drank too much.

They suffered from that peculiar spleen which the Legion calls *cafard* and, in extreme stages, *bourdon*. It sometimes takes a very violent form. When in this state, Dufour and Lemercier could not be approached. They would pick fights, insult the command, and smash bottles in the taverns. If Dufour met a soldier or an officer of another regiment, he would force him to admit that the Legion was the best regiment in the world. At such times, I was the only one who could manage him. In the heat of his drunken brawls, he would calm down when he saw me, smile affectionately, and invite me to have a drink. With the aid of elaborate stratagems, I would get him to bed.

Sometimes I asked Dufour about his past, but no matter how drunk he was, he would shut up like a clam at the first question. When he finally did speak he was sober.

For a long time he had refused to accept leave from the regiment. "Where can I go?" he asked. "I haven't a single friend or relative." But in March, 1916, orders came through granting bonuses to veterans who had served more than fifteen years. Dufour received a lump sum of more than 200 francs. We were at Ribecourt, a ruined village on the Oise. The entire population had deserted it, leaving neither taverns, cafés, nor stores. We lived in gaping cellars and set up our posts along a canal. There was not a place to spend a centime.

Dufour groaned, "How can I drink up my money in this stupid place?"

"Well, why don't you go to Paname?" (Paname was Legion slang for Paris.)

"To Paname?" He thought for a moment and then with a sudden gesture of determination, "I'm going."

Three days later, before his leave was up, he returned completely sober. I was astonished.

"Why are you back so soon?"

"Now I can tell you all about myself. There's no longer any reason to conceal it." His eyes were brooding and sad as he began his story.

As soon as he reached Paris, memories of his past returned. He had left the city seventeen years before. His real name was Raoul Denis. He had been a foundling, brought up in an orphanage where he learned to steal. He was sent to a house of correction, and when he left it he was an accomplished Apache. For more serious jobs, for daring burglaries and gun play, he was trained by an elegant pimp and dope peddler named

Julot. Under Julot's tutelage he robbed many apartments and villas but was never caught.

He fell in love with red-haired Janet, a bold and merry girl who loved him and was true to him. Julot began to annoy her. When she repulsed his advances he threatened to turn her lover over to the police. Janet warned Dufour, who lay in wait for Julot and stabbed him to death on the Boulevard des Batignolles.

"Julot dropped like a sack. Didn't even grunt. I beat it. Thought it over all night, and knowing I couldn't escape the 'widow' [the guillotine] if I remained in Paris, I went to Marseille and joined the Legion under the name of Dufour.

"And now after seventeen years I was back in Paris. I walked through the same streets and stopped at the same taverns and thought of the days when I was young. But I had a strange feeling. Am I Dufour or Raoul Denis? I'm not Raoul. I wouldn't rob or kill anyone. I kill only in battle. Dufour is no longer an alias. I'm first-class Legionnaire Dufour, with the War Cross and four medals for distinction in colonial campaigns. Twelve campaigns and four wounds. I've marched through half the world with my gun and spade. I've defended advance posts, taken cities, built roads. I'm a drunkard and a rascal but not a thief or a murderer. I earn my money with blood and sweat and pay for everything. No, I'm not Raoul Denis. I'm Dufour.

"It seemed to me that everyone in Paris knew it. In the cafés people wouldn't let me pay for my drinks because of my medals. I forced everyone to drink in honor of the Legion. Women asked me about the front, and clung to me. I liked one of them. We were together until late at night and drank a good deal. In the Legion I'm accustomed to hold my tongue between my teeth. But the new atmosphere and the memories of the past made me talkative. I think I told her about Julot. She left the hotel early next morning, and I remained alone.

"When I went out later, a detective grabbed me by the arm and said, 'Raoul Denis, come with me.' A car with two policemen waited at the curb. I went quietly, cursing myself for having come to Paris. After spending an hour in the police station, I was taken to the captain. I didn't look at him and answered his questions angrily. Suddenly I heard him laugh, 'Dufour, old man, don't you know me?'

"I raised my head and saw a familiar face. It was my old Sergeant, Jean Lemer. We had taken Taza under him in 1912, and he'd been wounded in both legs by the Arabs.

"'Sergeant Lemer,' I said, 'why are you laughing? Arrest me and send me to hard labor or the guillotine; but I'm Dufour, not Raoul Denis. I've earned that name by sixteen years of service, and well you know it.'

"He stood up and slapped me on the back.

" 'Calm down. Let's go have a drink. It happened so many years ago you can't be tried for it. And anyhow, could a brave soldier of France be sacrificed because of a pimp?'

"We drank coffee with rum, reminisced about our old friends and commanders, and parted. I strolled aimlessly through the city. Suddenly I felt terribly bored. What was I doing in Paris? My regiment was my home. And so here I am, back before my leave is up."

My own affairs were not so fortunate. I sent a report through official channels to the Commander in Chief, General Joffre, expressing my love for France, but explaining that I found it difficult to remain in the ranks of Bulgaria's enemies, and asking to be discharged. I received no answer. The attitude of my superiors was no longer friendly. What could I do? I didn't want to desert. I loved my regiment and France. I desired two apparently irreconcilable things—victory for France and salvation for Bulgaria. And there was not a single person with whom I could share my loneliness.

Finally Lebedev wrote from Salonika that he had taken certain steps in my behalf, without revealing details. Almost at the same time I received a reply from General Dmitriev, advising me to remain in France and adding that my brother Vasili had disappeared and in all probability had been taken prisoner by the Austrians. That was in March, 1916. Late in April, when we were in a small village in Picardy, Colonel Cot sent for me.

He asked me to dine with him, questioned me politely about Bulgaria, and at the end of the dinner informed me that he had been ordered to send me to the depot of the Foreign Legion in Lyon. The order was brief, clear, and contained no explanation. Somewhat embarrassed, Cot added, "I think we're parting for good. I'm very sorry. Say good-bye to your friends, and be ready to leave tomorrow morning."

Battalion Commander Judicelli bade me farewell with considerable warmth. Delanourienne, who had just been promoted to the rank of captain, was coldly cordial. But my soldiers expressed themselves with such sincerity that it brought tears to my eyes. Dufour and Lemercier took advantage of the occasion to go on another spree.

Another phase of my life had come to a close. Ruined villages, blasted and charred forests, scenes of heroism, death, and horror, faces of comrades and strangers passed before my mind's eye as if on a motion-picture film. My Russian comrades; my old African warriors; the Englishmen on the Somme and in Artois who shaved before each battle and went into the attack like football teams; the Arabs with their vulture-like faces; the bearded French reservists; all belonged already to the past.

I was in Lyon only two weeks, doing garrison duty and training new recruits. By some irony of fate the Foreign Legion depot was on the rue Ste-Vièrge in what had once been a boarding school for young girls.

At the end of the second week I was ordered to Salonika, to the headquarters of General Maurice Sarrail, Commander in Chief of the Allied Armies in the Near East. I received a sealed envelope addressed to the General, and money for the trip, and left at once for Marseille to await a transport.

Marseille was then an enormous base through which passed all the colonial troops as well as supplies coming from every port of the world. The streets teemed with soldiers and civilians of every nationality. The garrison consisted of Senegalese and of Annamites from Indo-China. In old fort St.-Jean on the sea were quartered Legionnaires, Arab sharp-shooters, and marines. The British were billeted at a depot called the American Park. From the Far East arrived a brigade of Siberian sharp-shooters who marched proudly though Marseille in parade formation. In the evening, on leave, they all got drunk, wrecked several brothels, and staggered through the streets arm in arm with Senegalese soldiers. These Siberian giants immediately fell in love with the grinning sons of the African forests. They communicated with gestures. The French stared with open-mouthed astonishment at the quantities of cognac the Russians absorbed.

Serbians were in Marseille buying horses for the troops evacuated to the island of Corfu after the occupation of their country in November by Austro-German and Bulgarian troops. These forces were being reorganized for the coming fight in the Balkans.

On May 16, I embarked on the British military transport *Vanloo*, which was filled with soldiers and officers for the Army of the East. We slept in our life belts because Austrian submarines were operating in the Mediterranean. On May 25 we reached Salonika.

In Salonika, the largest seaport on the Aegean, Europe and the East mingled without fusing. This was the community to whose early Christians St. Paul addressed two of his epistles. The commercial section along the shore resembled Marseille and all the other large ports of the Mediterranean. Inland were Oriental streets, narrow and winding, of small two-story houses with latticed windows. Along the shore, away from the harbor, were sumptuous villas with gardens in which tulips, roses, lilies, and lilacs bloomed. Here were the homes of rich Europeans, Greeks, and Jews, and the foreign consulates. Where the common people lived, rivulets of sewage ran through the streets, hungry dogs roamed, and fish, cheap oil, and fried meat stank. Tables and chairs stood outside cheap taverns, and the meat was roasted in the open in the form of tremendous *shashliks*. Turks drank coffee, Greeks sipped anisette, the French drank sweet green wines, and the British angrily demanded unobtainable whisky. In the distance cloud-wreathed Mount Olympus, home of the ancient gods, was visible on clear afternoons.

The presence of the Army of the East made trade very brisk. Hermes, the sly god of commerce, followed closely in the footsteps of Ares, the war god, and rifled his pockets. The war god, expecting to enter the kingdom of Hades at any moment, spent his money lavishly. After a good stroll through the city, the soldiers no longer had even the obol to pay Charon to ferry them across the Styx.

Hermes assumed the most varied shapes. He sat as a stern, bearded merchant in a large shop; he ran through the city streets in the form of a boy, offering the soldiers combs and razor blades. He traded in drinks, obscene post cards, and shoes of scorched leather which fell apart in a few days. In conspiracy with Aphrodite, he enticed soldiers into blind alleys where, disguised as mysterious, veiled *hanums,* lived the experienced women of Montmartre and the brothels of Marseille. The French were cursing Pierre Loti for his fables of Eastern romance, and, ironically enough, Pierre Loti himself was now in Salonika as a naval officer. With comic solemnity he replied to the sarcastic quips of the officers, "It's all because the Turks have left and the Greeks now run the city."

The Army of the East had been created by Aristide Briand and Winston Churchill. It began with the unsuccessful attempt to seize the Dardanelles. In October, 1915, on the eve of Bulgaria's attack on Serbia, French and British troops under the command of General Sarrail landed in Salonika, despite protests of the Greek King Constantine, and advanced to the Vardar River. They marched to the aid of Serbia, attacked the Bulgarians at Krivolak, Macedonia, were repulsed, and retired to defensive positions, organizing a line on the northeastern frontier of Greece. At first this army had only four divisions. By the spring of 1916 there were eight.

The British occupied the eastern sector, between the sea and the Belasitza Mountains. The northern sector, from Belasitz to Albania, was held by four French divisions and one cavalry brigade. In addition, there were considerable artillery and technical detachments, and an aviation squadron based in the Vardar Valley. In Camp Zeitenlik six Serbian divisions had arrived from Corfu, numbering almost 100,000 men salvaged from the original Serbian army of 400,000. The position of General Sarrail's army was endangered by the official attitude of Greece. King Constantine, the Kaiser's brother-in-law, had dismissed the pro-Ally government of Eleutherios Venizelos in October, 1915, and installed a pro-German regime under Skouloudis. The Greek command also was hostile to the Allies. Chief among these pro-German Greek officers was

Colonel John Metaxas, a graduate of the Potsdam General Staff Academy.

The Army of the East had to reckon not only with a hostile Greek force in its rear, but also with as many Greeks engaged in German espionage. Moreover, there was strong opposition to the Near East Expedition in London and Paris. Nearly all the military and political authorities except Briand, Churchill, and Lloyd George considered it a useless expenditure of strength and insisted that the war would be decided on the western front.

General Sarrail himself strongly believed that the Balkan front would be decisive in the outcome of the war. In addition to his military task, he was obliged to carry on delicate political negotiations with the Greeks and to humor the obstinate General Milne, commander of the British troops. Technically, Sarrail was in command, but so confused was the situation that he was in perpetual conflict with the High Command, which persistently refused to send reinforcements.

General Sarrail, then about fifty-eight, was the handsomest man I have ever seen, very tall and straight, with a thick white mustache and snow-white hair. On horseback he looked like the god of war himself. He was loved and respected by all who served under him, but the reactionaries and Jesuits—and there were many in the French High Command—hated him because he was a Freemason and a Socialist sympathizer. After the war he joined the Socialist Party. His admirers called him the General of the Fourth Republic—the republic of the future.

The day after my arrival I reported to General Sarrail, who received me in his private office at headquarters, a large building near the sea. He shook hands warmly and his clear blue eyes smiled at me.

"I sent for you because I know you are an excellent soldier who has proved his love for France. I'm sure you also love your fatherland, Bulgaria."

"Even more than I love France."

Again he smiled. "That's as it should be. You may know, perhaps, that I have a soft spot in my heart for your country. And now"—he made a helpless gesture—"we have to fight your people."

Bulgaria had been very popular in the Parisian salon of Mme. Ménard-Dorian, which General Sarrail frequented. There political leaders such as Justin Godard and Francis de Pressancé and such illustrious professors as Seignobos and Aulard defended Bulgaria and remained her friends.

General Sarrail continued, "At the moment our problem is to save Bulgaria if possible and, at the same time, to simplify our task in the Balkans. We shall win in the end, of course." His voice was firm. "We'll reach the Danube and deliver a shattering blow to the already shaken Hapsburg structure. Our resources are steadily increasing, while those of the Central Powers are becoming exhausted. But Bulgaria blocks our way. I want to try to come to terms with your country and, if possible, induce it to make a separate peace. I can promise Bulgaria considerable territorial gains if we get a free road to the Danube."

He turned to a large map on the wall. A warm sea breeze drifted through the open windows. Below lay the Gulf of Salonika, dotted with merchant vessels and Allied warships.

He pointed to the map. "The war will be won on this front," he continued. "On the western front the chances of a shift from trench warfare to a war of movement are very slight. In France the smallest offensive means enormous sacrifices, while here we have before us a great field for maneuvering—if and when Bulgaria lays down her arms. If she won't we shall have to crush her in order to break through and end the war. If Bulgaria joins us, she'll get Turkish Thrace, the major part of Greek Macedonia, the Dobruja, and perhaps part of Serbian Macedonia. That depends on how much Serbia gets from Austria. The heroic Serbs deserve to be well compensated for their enormous sacrifices."

General Sarrail's offer opened attractive opportunities to my country; it impressed me deeply. I was as firmly convinced as he that the Allies would win, but I couldn't see a part for myself in his plans. He guessed my thoughts.

"You can be of great service," he said earnestly. "I am prepared to offer you an important mission. I want you to get to Bulgarian headquarters and propose a separate peace to the General Staff in my name. This isn't an order. You may accept or reject the proposal. It involves grave risk."

For months I had been tortured by the thought that my country was heading for disaster while I was fighting on the side of its enemies. General Sarrail's proposal offered not only my own salvation, but possibly that of Bulgaria as well. I accepted joyfully.

The General nodded. "Very well. The next step is to work out a plan. That I leave to you, because the risk is wholly yours."

We shook hands, and I left.

The esplanade swarmed with soldiers. The French could be singled out by their brisk, gay stride. They sang, flirted with passing women, and laughed. The British were still vainly searching for whisky. The Serbs strolled along slowly and sadly. Negro, Hindu, and Annamite troops mingled with the Europeans. Swarthy Greek hawkers peddled their wares in a strange jargon of all tongues and offered to guide the soldiers to the best brothels. Salonika resembled one vast carnival. I spent the evening on the terrace of the Biaz Kule Café with Lieutenant Lebedev and Jean José Frappa, the French writer.

The only way to reach Bulgarian headquarters, I decided, was by airplane. With this in mind, I had myself detailed, toward the end of June, to the Ninety-third Squadron of the French air force, billeted in the village of Topchi in the Vardar Valley, about forty miles from Salonika. I wore the uniform of a Russian officer and used the name Vasiliev. The squadron was commanded by Captain Potin, son of Félix Potin, famous canned-goods manufacturer, and so we ate everything that French gastronomical genius could devise. Among the other officers were Jacques and Tirko Richepin, sons of the poet; the celebrated playwright, Henri Bernstein; and Chaumet, who had won fame for his Paris-Rouen flight in 1909.

The squadron used Nieuport planes which were then the last word in aviation, attaining a record speed of eighty miles an hour and carrying sixty-liter gasoline tanks, barely enough for a two-hour flight. I trained in an Antoinette, a relic of wood, tin, and canvas. Twice I went up to an altitude of two hundred meters and twice I dived nose-first to the ground, turned over my machine, and climbed out with minor bruises. Captain Potin decided that I never would make a pilot.

Five days later I changed to the gray-green uniform of a Bulgarian officer, though with several flaws in my dress. The cap made in Salonika was not perfect, and the epaulets were taken from a Serbian uniform. Forged papers certified that I was Lieutenant Popov, on leave. I climbed into a Nieuport, with Sergeant Fetu at the controls, and headed for the Bulgarian lines. A German Fokker spotted us over Bulgarian territory and chased us back. I held him off with a machine gun, but couldn't hit him. We returned to Topchi. Three further attempts were equally unsuccessful.

I then transferred to another squadron. Sergeant Cabanne was assigned to pilot me, and one morning at about four we took off from Lake Ostrovo. We crossed high mountains far west of the Vardar Valley without meeting any German planes. On the road from Bitolj to Prilep we spotted cavalry, wagons, and trucks. Swerving away from the road, Cabanne picked out a small, flat-topped hill. He circled in a descending curve and, signaling to me, taxied over the grass, burned crisp by the July sun. I rose in the cockpit and leaped from the moving plane as it skimmed along the ground. I jumped forward, fell on my hands and knees, got up, and dusted myself off. The Nieuport, already high above me, headed back for Lake Ostrovo. It was now about five o'clock and already light.

Not far off stood two armed Bulgarian soldiers, watching the airplane disappear. I strode briskly up to them.

"Why are you standing there like sheep looking into the water?" I shouted. "Didn't you see that it was an enemy plane? Why didn't you shoot? Your regiment! Company! Names!"

The soldiers blinked guiltily and stood stiffly at attention.

I jotted down their replies and asked sternly, "What village is that?"

"Erekovtzi, Sir."

I was well inside the Bulgarian lines, in western Macedonia.

I HAD LANDED IN the rear sector of the Third Balkan Division, and the papers I carried described me as an officer of the Twenty-ninth Yambol Regiment of that division. On the face of my documents, therefore, my presence in this sector would arouse no suspicion. But the Bulgarian army headquarters, my destination, were in Kustendil, more than two hundred miles away.

As soon as the two soldiers disappeared from my sight, I walked rapidly toward the highway I had observed from the air, reaching it in an hour. It was jammed with Bulgarian and German army trucks, and heavy supply wagons drawn by plodding buffalo and oxen.

I stopped a cart loaded with hay, climbed aboard, and asked the driver to wake me up when we came to Prilep. I had had very little rest during the past few days and was far too tired to think about what lay ahead. In no time I fell sound asleep, but by midmorning I was awakened by the pesky flies and the baking heat. Parched fields stretched out on both sides of the road to distant mountain ridges. The driver told me it would be at least another two hours before we reached Prilep. Now my sense of danger became acute. If I were caught before reaching Kustendil I was lost. No elaborate explanation of my presence behind the lines, wearing a Bulgarian uniform and carrying forged papers, would help. I would be shot as a spy.

I wanted very badly to smoke but naturally had brought no Greek cigarettes with me. My driver had nothing to smoke or even to eat, and we did not pass a single army canteen. Soon a Benz truck overtook us. I leaped from the cart and hailed the driver, a German soldier in a fatigue cap. He hesitated for an instant, then signaled me to jump aboard. I sat down on a bale of wool, and the truck rolled on at about twenty-five miles an hour, churning up a good deal of dust. We soon reached Prilep, the depot for the rear services of several armies, and found the town swarming with officers and soldiers. I bought cigarettes and newspapers and finally found a place to eat, but all I could get was an omelet and coffee made of roasted barley. Everywhere I heard the same complaint, "No bread, no meat; 'they' take everything." "They" meant the Germans.

About noon I left Prilep in another Benz driven by a Bulgarian, which headed northeast through occupied Serbian territory. Two Bulgarian soldiers seated in the back of the truck snapped to attention and asked my permission to remain aboard. Accustomed to the democratic French army, I replied automatically, "Why not?" But I quickly recalled Bulgarian military etiquette and added severely, "Permission granted!"

I changed trucks frequently. Now and then I snatched something to eat at an army canteen. Twice the military police stopped me and examined my documents; they noticed nothing untoward. With the soldiers I met I felt quite at ease, but avoided conversation with the officers. Complaints of the rank and file always followed the same pattern. The Germans seemed universally hated, not only because they requisitioned food, but even more because of their arrogance and contempt for their Bulgarian allies.

As we drove into Kustendil the next morning, I thought of my *komitaji* days and of Pesho. Eleven years ago I had come to Kustendil to join his *cheta*. Now he was dead; so was Jordan and probably his brother Angel as well.

Hunger brought me back to the present. At an inn on the outskirts of the city, I had soup and a miserable portion of boiled meat. As I walked toward headquarters afterwards, memories of the past again disturbed me. I thought of my brother Kyril, who had died in Adrianople; of Vasili, either in an Austrian prison camp or dead; of my father, and wondered what he was doing. At that very moment, I learned later, he was in Kustendil, commanding a service of supply. Despite his known hostility to the Germans, he had been called up out of retirement.

Half an hour later I stood in the anteroom of General Jostov, Chief of Staff of the Bulgarian army, and told his aide-de-camp that I carried an urgent message from General Boyadjiev, commander of the First Bulgarian Army, with instructions to deliver it in person. The aide tried to persuade me to transmit it through him, but I insisted that I had no authority to do so. Finally I was ushered into General Jostov's office.

"What's all this talk about an important message?" asked the General impatiently. "Couldn't General Boyadjiev telephone me?"

I saluted and replied, "Sir, I have the honor to inform you that I come from General Sarrail, Commander of the Allied army in Salonika."

"What? What?" he spluttered. "What's that—from General Sarrail—who are you—aren't you a Bulgarian officer?"

"I am Kosta Todorov. I enlisted in the French army as soon as the war broke out. General Sarrail has sent me to propose a separate peace for Bulgaria. I accepted the mission in the hope of serving our country."

General Jostov sat down slowly, mopped his brow, and stroked his sharp little beard.

"But how on earth did you get here?"

"I landed by plane in Macedonia."

"And where's your plane?"

When I explained that the pilot had flown back across the lines, the General looked at me incredulously, then motioned me to be seated. Before doing so, I removed my belt and holster.

"Now that I am here as General Sarrail's emissary, I divest myself of my arms and place myself at your disposal."

Then I sat down, realizing that the first part of my mission had been accomplished. I could no longer be accused of espionage—or so I thought. General Jostov had calmed down. He offered me a cigarette, lit one himself, and scrutinized me keenly through his pince-nez.

"Now tell me what this is all about," he said.

I stated the terms of General Sarrail's proposal. Jostov smiled sardonically. "Our army holds more than that now."

"But consider, Your Excellency, that Bulgaria would receive eastern Thrace from the Turks and southern Dobruja from Rumania, and what is more important, escape the débâcle in which she stands to lose everything."

"Débâcle?" The General's eyes blazed with anger. "We're going to win this war!"

I tried to convince him that in the end Germany had to lose. He was not impresssed. I added that Rumania would soon join the Allies.

"Excellent!" he answered. "The Rumanians won't last long. Our army will have little trouble with them, especially now that Russia is on her last legs."

My mission had failed, I felt, but still I continued to do my best to convince him. I pointed out the probability of American intervention, and told him that fresh British and French troops were pouring steadily into Salonika. General Jostov listened carefully, but finally changed the subject, asking me what I expected to do next. I answered that as a Bulgarian I was ready to share the fate of my country. The General sent for food, and during the meal questioned me good-humoredly about my experiences on the Western Front. When it was over, he arose.

"Please go into the next room," he said. "You'll find paper and pen there. Be good enough to write a memorandum on the subject of your mission. When you've finished, we'll see!"

While completing my report, I heard someone enter the room. I glanced up from my paper. A trim, close-cropped German in a captain's uniform smiled pleasantly at me and said in precise French, "I have been told of your exploit. Remarkable! Worthy, I should say, even of a German officer."

With a smart bow he held out his hand, but I ignored it. He winced slightly, compressed his lips, and sat down, crossing his legs. Then he said imperiously, "And now be kind enough to tell me about the state of the Allied forces in Salonika."

"I am accustomed to talk to German officers with a rifle across barbed wire. I haven't returned to my country to be questioned by a German."

"Very well. We shall see!" And he slammed the door behind him.

Five minutes later a squad of Bulgarian soldiers entered. Their officer addressed me in a cool, incisive voice, "You're under arrest. Charged with high treason. Come with me!"

After being thoroughly searched, I was questioned for more than two hours by a Bulgarian colonel, who alternately tried kindness and threats to induce me to speak. I refused to answer any question concerning the Allied army in Salonika. Each time I gave the same reply: "I know nothing regarding the questions which interest you."

When the grilling finally ended, I was led through the city to the guardhouse of the Thirteenth Regiment and thrown into a room dimly lighted by a small, square window high in the wall. I soon fell into a deep sleep. At night I was awakened, given bread and water, and led into the open air. Outside the gates of the barracks a truck was waiting, its motor running. Six soldiers stood beside it.

A noncommissioned officer pointed at me. "Bind his arms and legs," he ordered.

Alarm flashed through my brain; I was to be taken before a firing squad. My arms were bound close to my sides and my legs were tightly tied together. Then I was lifted up and dropped onto a pile of straw in the truck. The soldiers sat down around me, and we jounced off over the rough road. The rope cut my muscles, causing me great pain and thirst. I asked the noncommissioned officer where we were going.

"Where ordered!"

We continued to bump along. My pain was steadily increasing. The soldiers smoked, ate bread and cheese, and talked among themselves. From their conversation I gathered that we were going to the headquarters of some division. Several times during the night we stopped, probably for gasoline. But lying on the bottom of the truck, I could see nothing.

I don't know how many hours my anguish lasted, but it was daylight and frightfully hot when I was carried into a small wooden hut, thrown on a bed, and untied. I could not move a muscle without intense pain. Only with great effort did I manage to retain consciousness and to ask, "Where are we?"

The officer answered, "With the staff of the Seventh Division at the Rupel Pass."

A little later another officer entered and tried to start a conversation, but I could not speak. He left and returned with a medical orderly, who undressed me carefully, felt the sore spots where the rope had cut in, and began slowly to massage me with a mixture which smelled like turpentine. For a short time the agony became even more acute, but I soon felt the blood circulating once more in my veins. About an hour later, when food was brought, I felt well enough to sit up.

When the officer appeared again, I recognized him as Major Bogdanov, who had attended the Sofia Military School with me. We used to call him Donna Sol, because in a school dramatic performance he had played that part in Victor Hugo's tragedy, *Hernani*. He was still plump and effeminate.

"I've come from the staff of the Second Army to question you."

"I said all I had to say in Kustendil."

He answered dryly, "You told us nothing except what General Sarrail offers us. And what does he offer? Less than what we hold right now. And at the price of betraying Germany, our ally!"

Bogdanov predicted that Verdun would soon fall and that the Germans would then take Paris. I replied that the Germans would be defeated.

He flared up. "I'm not asking for your opinion. You tried to deceive the Bulgarian Command, and you'll get what's coming to you. Try to understand your position. Only complete frankness can save you from the firing squad."

"The firing squad?" I asked. "What for?"

He grimaced. "What for? Treason, of course!"

I controlled myself and remained silent.

"Tomorrow," he said, on leaving, "when you're led out to be shot, you may wish you'd talked."

From my hut, guarded by a squad of soldiers, I could hear officers say loudly, "He'll probably be shot tomorrow."

There seemed little reason for bringing me so far from headquarters merely to shoot me. Naturally I had no inkling of what was going on behind the scenes. I lay down wearily, half closing my eyes. At night two soldiers with fixed bayonets stood guard at my window. They asked me to sit near the window and tell them what was going on in Salonika among the "Anglo-Frenchmen."

"Is it true that they have less to eat than we?" "Is it true that the Russians have joined them at the front?" "Is it true that there's been a mutiny among the troops in Salonika?"

Instead of answering, I asked them about the situation in Bulgaria. They complained bitterly.

"All the supplies in the villages are collected for the Germans. We get thin bean soup and bread mixed with straw, while the Germans devour our meat and good white bread."

No one disturbed me on the morrow. Other days came and passed with nothing new but books and cigarettes sent from the local staff headquarters (by my father's friend Colonel Sirmanov, I learned later). I seemed to have been forgotten.

Not until after the war, when I visited General Sarrail in Paris, did I learn what had happened during those days.

A few hours after my conversation with General Jostov, the Bulgarian High Command sentenced me to death. But a French secret agent in Kustendil, whom General Sarrail had notified of my mission in advance, managed to get word through at once to the French command in Salonika.

In his Paris apartment three years later, General Sarrail went to his files and took out a dossier. "July 7, 1916," he read.

I recalled the date vividly; on the morning of that day I had spoken to General Jostov. That same evening General Sarrail had been informed of my arrest. He read me the radio message which he had sent out that night from Salonika:

> To the Commander in Chief of the Bulgarian army, General Yekov:
>
> In the event of the execution or accidental death of Lieutenant Constantine Todorov, sent as my representative to negotiate with the Bulgarian Command, regarding such an act as contrary to international law, military ethics, and the usage of war, I will shoot fifty Bulgarian officers who are prisoners in Salonika.
>
> GENERAL SARRAIL,
> *Commander in Chief of the Allied Army in Salonika.*

I had known nothing of this at the time. Neither had I known that General von Mackensen, chief of the German forces in the Balkans, vehemently demanded that I be shot; that the Bulgarian command, frightened by possible repercussions—many of General Sarrail's prisoners belonged to leading Sofia families—refused to comply with von Mackensen's demand and decided instead to turn me over to field court-martial. I was sent to the Seventh Division because it was at the front, making trial by field court-martial possible under Bulgarian law.

For a full month nothing happened, but it became clearer every day that delivering me to a firing squad was not so simple.

I became quite friendly with my guards, all of them peasants and all opposed to the war. Quietly they cursed the High Command, King Ferdinand, and the Germans. Although they belonged to the divisional military police, a relatively privileged position, they longed to return to their villages, their families, and their land. Above all, they hated the Germans.

"They're a bad people. They steal everything we have, and treat us like cattle. In Nish, they commandeer the carloads of food intended for our people and ship them back to Germany."

Bulgarian peasants, they told me, often seized and killed Germans requisitioning supplies and buried them in secret places. Not one of these common soldiers believed in the possibility of German victory.

Literate enough to read the newspapers, which continued to proclaim the imminent fall of Verdun, they commented with malicious joy: "The Germans'll never take Verdun. They'll break their heads on it."

These simple peasants sized up events more clearly than many General Staff officers. They kept me informed of the latest news. The Rupel Pass, which the Seventh Division occupied, had great strategic importance. It was in Greek territory, not far from Demir Hissar. In August, the Germans reached an understanding with King Constantine. The Greek Third Army Corps surrendered to the Germans on the King's order, and was sent to Germany. Then Bulgarian troops moved in and occupied the entire area to the Struma River, establishing contact with the British and French forces.

The officers passing my window continued to speak of my impending execution, but the soldiers of my guard laughed.

"We do things simply. If someone's sentenced to be shot, it's done the same day."

In any event, I wrote my father a letter, explaining everything I had done and asking that after the war he make the truth known to the people. I asked one of the soldiers to deliver it if I were shot.

Suddenly, on August 15, staff headquarters bustled with unprecedented activity. Baggage was hastily packed into wagons and trucks, and the following day we moved through the Rupel Pass. I rode in a cart surrounded by a cavalry escort. Four hours later we reached the village of Savyak, on a mountain from which we could look down on the Struma River, a silver ribbon in the distance, winding through its sun-parched valley toward the Aegean. On the other side rose Mount Krusha, held by the British. From the window of my cell I saw a battle raging.

British artillery on the heights was shelling Bulgarian infantry which advanced in waves across open terrain without cover—a senseless operation with no chance of success. The shells spouted up geysers of brown earth, and the shrapnel kicked up little clouds like balls of cotton. More acutely than ever I felt the cruelty and stupidity of war. This time the men on both sides were my comrades, my fellow Bulgarians and the British beside whom I had fought for twenty months in the Legion. In France, Germans had faced me across the battlefield, but here I had no enemies. For the first time I saw war as fratricide.

But these emotions did not affect my critical capacity as a professional soldier. I would have camouflaged my batteries and placed them elsewhere on those heights. I would not have attacked Mount Krusha, but would have attempted to cross the Struma lower down, near the Orliak Bridge, barely visible toward the south. (Only much later did I realize how war deforms the human spirit. It was many years before I could look upon a landscape, however beautiful, without appraising it in terms of

[87]

military strategy—here I would place a nest of machine guns; there, on that ridge, would be a wonderful place for artillery. . . .)

For more than two weeks the battle continued without decisive results. The nights grew cold in early September, and I shivered in my summer uniform. Often my guards permitted me to warm up outside in the sun. One morning, as I sat on a pile of logs smoking, an officer came up to me, handed me an envelope, and left without a word. Opening it, I found an indictment signed by the prosecutor of the field court-martial of the Seventh Division. This remarkable document charged me with treason, espionage, and attempting to deceive and seduce the Bulgarian High Command; all set down in tedious legal style. Under military law each of these crimes was punishable by death. An accompanying letter informed me that I might reply in writing to the indictment and that my trial would begin the next day, September 16, 1916, in the Savyak town hall. I penciled my answer and gave it to a soldier who delivered it.

At nine o'clock the next morning I was led into the courtroom. Behind a large table sat three military judges. At another, on the right, sat a handsome young lieutenant who was apparently the prosecutor. At a small desk beside him was the military stenographer. Four soldiers with bared swords stood guard behind my bench.

A few minutes later I was astonished to see my father enter, accompanied by General Mititelev, former chief of the Military Justice Section of the War Ministry. Both were in civilian dress. My father embraced me with tears in his eyes. His beard had become much grayer. General Mititelev, an old family friend, had known me since I was a child. A well-known Russophile and a close friend of General Radko Dmitriev, he had resigned his post as soon as Bulgaria entered the war.

"I'm here as your attorney," he said.

He turned to the presiding judge, Lieutenant Colonel Ionchev.

"I should like to speak freely with the accused before the trial begins."

The Colonel stood up, shook hands with his former chief, and bowed. "If you please."

I told General Mititelev everything I had done from the day Bulgaria entered the war until I reached Kustendil. My father whispered to me that my brother Vasili lived, a prisoner of war in Hungary.

At ten o'clock the trial began. After the prosecutor had read the indictment, the presiding judge called for the witnesses. The first was my old schoolmate, Major Bogdanov, who tried to prove that I had come to Bulgaria to deceive the High Command, to undermine morale, and thereby facilitate the military operations of the Allies against Bulgaria. Bogdanov spoke so long that he finally grew tiresome and the judge motioned with his hand, "Enough!"

Several soldiers then took the stand. I remembered riding with them on the road from Prilep to Kustendil. They all repeated an obviously well-rehearsed account of how I had tried to persuade them to desert to the French. During cross-examination General Mititelev asked one of them point-blank, "Who ordered you to say that?"

"The company commander, Your Excellency!" he answered, blinking.

The judges laughed and Lieutenant Boyadjiev, the prosecutor, shrugged his shoulders. Just then a colonel wearing the insignia of a military judge on his epaulets, tiptoed in and sat down at the back of the room. Following General Mititelev's advice, I told my story without unnecessary details. Then Lieutenant Boyadjiev, to everyone's amazement, rose and demanded my complete acquittal.

"The accused honestly performed his duty to Bulgaria. Not a single charge has been substantiated. This is all a misunderstanding, and it is morally impossible for me to demand his conviction."

The judges were confused. The colonel who had been sitting in the back of the room approached the presiding judge and excitedly whispered something in his ear. Whereupon Lieutenant Colonel Ionchev spread his arms in a gesture of helplessness, and called upon my attorney to speak.

General Mititelev smiled ironically.

"In view of the fact that the prosecutor has himself repudiated the charges and demands my client's acquittal, I can do no more than agree with him."

The judges did not even retire to deliberate. After each had written something on a slip of paper, everyone in the courtroom rose, and the presiding judge read the verdict. I was acquitted of all the capital charges in the indictment, but sentenced to three and a half years imprisonment for having failed to report for mobilization when Bulgaria entered the war! It was a two-to-one verdict. One judge, Lieutenant Volchev, voted for my complete exoneration. The court unanimously recommended that the execution of my sentence be stayed until after the war.

Two days later, I was haled before the court again to hear an order from headquarters nullifying the verdict and ordering a new trial. I was permitted to telegraph this news to my father. Because of General Mititelev's influence, the new trial never took place, but headquarters continued to weigh my fate for several weeks, with the Germans insisting that I be shot.

About two months after the trial, the verdict was finally confirmed, but General Yekov denied the court's recommendation that my sentence be stayed, and ordered that I be sent on foot to the Sofia prison, a distance of almost 250 miles. Since it was now late November, with cold fog and icy rains in the mountains, I suspected that I was not meant to reach Sofia alive.

On November 20, accompanied by a sergeant and a soldier, I left Demir Hissar. The sergeant constantly stared at me. We had gone only a short distance when he asked, "Which Todorov are you?"

The question didn't surprise me, for Todorov is a common name in Bulgaria.

"My father is Colonel Todorov."

He stopped short and looked at me closely.

"Your father isn't Colonel Vasili Todorov, is he?"

"Yes."

"My God! Then you are Kosta—the same little Kosta whom I knew in Stara Zagora when I served as your father's orderly."

In the bearded, sunburned face my memory slowly picked out the features of Ivan, the kindly soldier with whom I had hunted birds in the woods near Stara Zagora, when I was a lad.

"So that's what it's come to!" he groaned. "I lead you off to prison like a bandit." He shook his head, stopped short, and turned to the soldier. "I'll escort the prisoner myself. Go back to town. I'll be responsible for him."

When we were alone on the soggy road, Ivan told me why I was being sent to Sofia on foot. The night before, he had been summoned by an officer of the Second Army, who ordered him to shoot me in the back at the first secluded spot in the woods, "for attempting to escape." His reward was to be ten thousand leva—about a thousand dollars. When he hesitated, the officer had told him I was a French spy and traitor.

"And you accepted?"

"Ten thousand is big money," Ivan replied wistfully. "But to think that I might have killed the son of my beloved colonel! The scoundrels! Think what they've invented! Colonel Todorov's son a traitor!"

He spat with disgust.

"If you were some Anglo-Frenchman, Serb, or Greek . . . but the son of my chief—no! That shall never happen! And you're not going to walk either. We'll wait for a truck."

A cold rain was falling, soaking me to the bone. Shivering, I began to feel quite ill. Although a number of German trucks passed, none stopped. It was impossible to stand still, so we trudged slowly along in the mud, hoping for a Bulgarian truck.

About an hour and a half later we finally climbed aboard a tarpaulin-covered truck. I lay down on a pile of empty sacks. I felt feverish. Luckily the truck went through to Kustendil without a stop. We reached the city that evening. Ivan filled me with tea and biscuit and found quarters for me in a wretched inn. The next morning, after I had had tea, bread, and cheese, I felt much better.

From Kustendil to Sofia we traveled by train, over a line which had not existed when I was a *komitaji*. At Sofia, Ivan allowed me to visit my home before taking me to prison. I spent the evening with my father and mother and slept in a clean bed. The next morning Ivan called for me in a carriage, received a hundred leva from my father, and drove me off to the Sofia prison. After delivering me to the warden, he embraced me and departed mumbling:

"When you think what might have happened! Still, ten thousand leva is big money."

W HEN I ENTERED the Sofia prison, I found myself
in freedom's last refuge in Bulgaria. With a large suitcase of clothing, I
moved into one of the clean, spacious cells in the political section, which
I shared with a journalist convicted of Russian espionage. Later that
day my bed, linen and books arrived from home and I settled down quite
comfortably. We prisoners could walk about freely, visit one another,
and see our friends—for oddly enough the cells remained unlocked day
and night. We cursed Germany and King Ferdinand openly, read not
only Bulgarian but also French newspapers, and were even permitted to
go in custody to the city twice a week "to visit the dentist." Naturally we
spent these days at our own homes, meeting our guards in the evening at
some convenient tavern and returning to prison with them.

This extraordinary state of affairs reflected no generosity on King
Ferdinand's part. The entire prison staff, from the warden down, received
good pay from the political prisoners for these privileges. Moreover, they
realized that with the outcome of the war in doubt, today's prisoners
might well be tomorrow's Cabinet Ministers.

They reasoned shrewdly. For the man who dominated the prison,
Alexander Stamboliski, later dominated Bulgarian politics. He was only
thirty-six years old, powerfully built, with a full, round face, piercing
black eyes, and a thin mustache curving up at the ends. Stamboliski had
landed in prison for talking back to King Ferdinand.

When the King allied Bulgaria with Germany and Austria, Stamboliski, as head of the powerful Peasant Party, protested. On September 4,
1915, as spokesman for the forty-eight Peasant Party delegates, he had
an audience with the King. Other opposition chiefs had spoken mildly
and deferentially to Ferdinand, but Stamboliski was blunt.

"The people have no confidence in your ability to rule," he declared.
"Once before, in 1913, you brought the country to catastrophe. Now
you're planning to set yourself once more against the wishes and interests
of the Bulgarian people. If you involve this country in war on the side
of Germany and Austria, you'll answer with your head!"

Enraged by Stamboliski's strong language and his reminder of the
humiliating Second Balkan War, Ferdinand shouted, "Don't worry about
my head—I'm old. Think of your own!"

Convinced that the King meant to enter the war against the Allies,
Stamboliski lost no time in publishing this interview in pamphlet form.

"Defy the mobilization decree!" he urged the people. Ferdinand had him arrested. In protest, the Twenty-second Infantry Regiment in Samokov mutinied, and twenty soldiers were shot. Two weeks later, Bulgaria entered the war on the side of the Central Powers, and Stamboliski was sentenced to life imprisonment.

Another important prisoner, Dr. Nikola Ghenadiev, was in jail for being too good at prognosis. Highly cultured, fluent in almost every European language, Ghenadiev, a former foreign minister, had entree into the leading intellectual and political circles of Europe. Early in 1915, King Ferdinand had sent him through western Europe to study probable developments. When he returned, Ghenadiev delivered a written report predicting the imminent intervention of Italy, the eventual American intervention, and the ultimate victory of the Allies. (This amazing document was published in Bulgaria and France after the war.) When Bulgaria entered the war on Germany's side Ferdinand was placed in a rather embarrassing position vis-à-vis Ghenadiev, who was a leader of the influential Liberal Party. But he soon found a convenient way out. Ghenadiev and a number of his followers, Liberal and Peasant deputies, were accused of buying up grain for the benefit of the British and French "with the object of sabotaging defense." They joined our élite group under sentence of from eight to ten years imprisonment.

Another outstanding prisoner was Dr. Raiko Daskalov, thirty-year-old head of the great co-operative organizations of the Peasant Party. Two years later he would play a leading part in overthrowing King Ferdinand.

Captain Prutkin,* adventurous but somewhat erratic master of a merchant vessel, had been convicted of "Russian espionage"—the stock government definition of opposition to Bulgaria's alliance with Germany. It was Prutkin who engineered one of the most famous prison breaks of the war.

Patriotic Bulgarians could not forget Russia's help in liberating them from the Turkish yoke, and in the Sofia prison alone were more than three hundred soldiers who had refused to fight the Russians or had incited their comrades to desert to them. Two of these soldiers were sentenced to death.

One, a noncommissioned officer, had told his men, "It's a sin to fight the Russians who set us free." Since he was popular with the troops at the front, the military authorities were afraid to condemn him there, so they sent him to Sofia, where the district court pronounced the death sentence. In the depths of the prison dungeon he awaited execution the next morning, while a sentry stood guard before the door of his cell.

But Captain Prutkin made other plans, which he carried out with our

*Captain Antun Prutkin was sentenced to death and shot in January, 1942, in Varna, Bulgaria, under accusation of sabotage and conspiracy.

help. That evening, we all decided to bathe—the showers were in the dungeon. Two criminals whom we had let in on our plan went below with us. One had a skeleton key; the other brought along vodka, a big chunk of ham, and a huge loaf of fresh white bread. While gulping down his vodka and greedily eating his bread, he started talking to the sentry on duty before the condemned man's cell. The soldiers, whose bread was made of miserable substitutes, were always hungry. The sentry eyed the prisoner jealously.

"It's better to be in prison than the army," he mumbled.

"How about joining me? Come on, sit down."

The sentry frowned. "I can't leave my post."

The prisoner laughed. "The cell door's locked, isn't it?"

No longer able to resist, the sentry led the prisoner to an empty cell with a table, where he ravenously joined in the feast. The other prisoner immediately opened the cell door with his skeleton key, released the condemned man, pushed him into the shower room, and relocked the cell. We covered ourselves with sheets and went upstairs, the condemned man with us. The rest of the plan worked smoothly. From the political section it was easy to get to the prison office, where the windows were unbarred. Prutkin eased the condemned man out of the office window into the courtyard. It was dark, the sky starless. The prisoner reached the wall, climbed a waiting ladder and leaped to freedom. Not until he was on the wall did the guards see him, and their bullets went astray. The prison authorities never unraveled the mystery of his flight.

The other soldier sentenced to death escaped without Prutkin's aid. It was December, and the weather was freezing. On the morning set for the execution we were ordered to remain in our cells. Our windows overlooked the gallows in the prison courtyard.

At eight o'clock the condemned man was led out, his hands bound behind his back. He stood still, not uttering a word, staring vacantly into distance as the priest blessed him. Handed a glass of cognac, he gulped it down quickly. No cigarette. The military prosecutor read the sentence. Only the guards, the prison wardens, the military prosecutor, the priest, a doctor, and a noted Sofia executioner, Djemal, a gypsy, were to witness the hanging. Djemal covered the condemned man's head with a white hood, lifted him onto a stool beneath the rope, slipped the noose around his neck, and kicked the stool out from under his feet.

Several minutes passed. The doctor felt the hanged man's pulse. Djemal jumped onto the stool, cut down the body, and laid it on the snow. Two guards then placed it on a stretcher, covered it with a sheet, and trudged off with it toward the cemetery.

We remained in our cells, gloomy and silent. Half an hour later the prison rocked with laughter.

[94]

"Have you heard the news? The dead man has arisen! On the way to the cemetery he suddenly sat up on the stretcher, scaring hell out of the guards. They dropped him and ran. When the police arrived and pulled off the hood, they found him speechless but still alive. And now they've brought him back."

Ghenadiev laughed. "The government is so incompetent it can't even hang a man properly."

Nothing supernatural had happened. The rope, as always, had been well greased with soap and water to make certain that it would slip into a tight noose. The extreme cold, however, had caused the soap and water to form a coating of ice. When the noose closed, it grasped the condemned man's jaw, but did not grip his neck. His spinal column did not snap; only fear made him lose consciousness. Slowly he recovered, but for six months could not utter a word and never could remember the details of his execution. Under Bulgarian law, he could not be hanged again.

News of these two miraculous escapes from execution spread to the army and the people. A legend grew up that those refusing to bear arms against the Russians could not die by the noose or the bullet.

While I had been under arrest at the Southern front, the battles of August and September had ended in Bulgarian defeat. Late in September, the First Bulgarian Army, commanded by General Boyadjiev, in an attempt to encircle General Sarrail's left flank had started an offensive aimed at the Greek cities of Florina and Kastoria. But the French and Serbs speedily counterattacked and after fierce and bloody fighting occupied Mt. Kaimakchalan in Serbian Macedonia. Threatened with being cut off and annihilated, the First Army retreated to the Cherna River, and the enemy occupied strategic Bitolj, the third largest city in Macedonia. Although this defeat depressed both the people and the army, it was counterbalanced by Bulgarian victories over Rumania.

For once King Ferdinand had declared a popular war. Three years earlier, Rumania had taken advantage of Bulgaria's reverses in the Second Balkan War to occupy the Dobruja, its richest province, without firing a shot. Just before Rumania joined the Allies its envoy in Sofia, with Allied consent, had offered to return southern Dobruja as the price of peace with Bulgaria. At the same time the Allies again attempted to induce Bulgaria to sign a separate peace, renewing the offer I had conveyed to the General Staff a year before. The head of the Democratic Party, Alexander Malinov, urged acceptance of these terms, but Ferdinand and Radoslavov refused. When Rumania finally declared war on Austria-Hungary, Bulgaria, with Germany and Turkey, declared war on Rumania. Aided by the Germans and the Turks, the Bulgarian army invaded the

Dobruja, defeated a combined Russo-Rumanian force, and occupied the province all the way to the Danube Delta.

The occupation of the Dobruja aroused great enthusiasm in Bulgaria, for the people had deeply resented the Rumanian treachery. By the beginning of 1917, however, the victories over Rumania were recognized as Pyrrhic; rejoicing had given way to disillusionment, poverty, and hunger. The Turks were demanding territorial concessions in return for their help in winning back the Dobruja. The Germans had established themselves in northern Dobruja and set up a so-called condominium of powers to rule the province, with Bulgaria a reluctantly silent partner.

The food shortage was acute. At the front the soldiers were clamoring for bread. The army had lost heart. Many soldiers posing as relatives visited us in prison during leave. They told us of hardships at the front, of the disheartened mood of the army, of the crimes of Bulgarian officials in occupied Serbian territory, of wholesale murders, robberies, and rape committed by Macedonian *komitajis,* who were now no more than bandits in German pay.

Things were no better on the home front. In the villages, the peasants managed to hide their supplies from the thieving Germans, and they supplied Stamboliski and all of us with such quantities of provisions that we were soon sending food from prison to our families. But in the cities the food crisis became daily more serious, with the Germans siphoning off everything. The people grumbled openly, blaming the government. Amid the general poverty the ministers, deputies, and high officials— all waxing fat through speculation—lived resplendently. Trade with Germany, both import and export, was monopolized by government supporters who amassed huge fortunes while unwilling soldiers died, tradesmen went bankrupt, and the people starved.

Everyone wanted peace, but it seemed farther away than ever. The Pope had tried vainly to mediate in December, 1916. Two months later, in February, 1917, the United States severed diplomatic relations with Germany, and it needed no foresight to predict its intervention on the side of the Allies. Then suddenly, in March, came the Russian Revolution, and hope surged up once more within us. Now, we felt, the Allies would gain a swift victory, and Russia—the new, democratic Russia— would save Slavic Bulgaria from the disaster of a dictated peace. We believed that the Russian people, fighting with the zeal of liberated slaves, would carry on the war with renewed vigor.

Within Bulgaria, we expected, the Revolution would strengthen the democratic opposition to King Ferdinand and make possible his overthrow. Stamboliski, Ghenadiev, Daskalov and I began a feverish search for army support of a coup d'état to oust Ferdinand and switch Bulgaria to the side of the Allies. The Allied Army of the East, then 700,000 strong, would thus gain an additional half million men—enough to deal a fatal blow to Austria and Turkey. Bulgaria would be freed from the ruinous German hegemony and could count on regaining the territory lost in the Second Balkan War.

We worked out a plan of action. German forces in the Balkans—except in Rumania, where several divisions faced the Russians on the Moldavian front—numbered no more than 20,000 in all. These were technical units, scattered throughout Bulgaria, Serbia, and Macedonia. Necessarily, we had to avoid an uprising at the front. If our troops deserted, Bulgaria would quickly be defeated and would be treated as a conquered nation. In Sofia, however, and in the large cities generally, many troops still remained garrisoned—reserve detachments, wounded men once more fit for battle, and soldiers stationed there to keep the peace. If these were to revolt, if Ferdinand were seized, his government arrested and supplanted by a new government of popular opposition leaders, then it would be possible to maintain the morale of the army and keep it intact at the front during negotiations with the Allies.

We could save Bulgaria.

To our trusted friends in the army we divulged our plans. My own role was modest. It was to sound out two of my comrades from military-school days, who were now captains in the army. One commanded a squadron of the Royal Cavalry Guard, the other a battery of twelve heavy fortress guns. I cannot mention their names, for they are now in Sofia.

I sought out my friends, cautiously unfolded our plan, and found them sympathetic. It was decided that they were to organize a nucleus of officers for the coup d'état. Daskalov succeeded in winning over three young officers, all members of the Peasant Party. Ghenadiev informed us that a friend of his, a General Staff colonel on leave, had agreed to take command of the Sofia uprising at the crucial moment.

In May we began mobilizing our forces, and by July our men told us that we could rely on half the garrison. We set our uprising for September 15, because by then the harvest would be gathered and the peasants free to help us.

To this day I don't know what went wrong; how word of the brewing plot reached the government. On September 1, my two friends in Sofia were ordered to the front. Five days later the warden received orders to send me to Shumen, a city of about 20,000 inhabitants in northern Bulgaria. Stamboliski and Prutkin were transferred to the fortress of Vidin on the Danube. Other prisoners were scattered among the provincial jails. But the government never uncovered the details of our plot.

After a twelve-hour journey, I arrived in Shumen, a fortified city in a cluster of hills. My new prison was no Sofia, but a foul-smelling, vermin-ridden hole. Luckily for me, I was the only political prisoner, and so was not quartered with the others—the jail had no separate cells—but was assigned a fairly comfortable room in the warden's section. Like most semi-literates, he fancied himself an authority on public affairs, and bored me with his incessant stream of chatter on high politics. To gain his good graces (and freedom of movement for myself), I listened to his babbling, paid for his wine, and shared with him the food I ordered from outside. Fall and winter passed in a monotonous routine. I dined with my philosopher, read the censored Bulgarian newspapers, and occasionally strolled through the town in the company of a tottering old guard called "Uncle Peter."

After this winter of idleness and discontent, I was sent out daily in the spring to work with the other prisoners on the government's model farm about a mile and a half from the prison. I welcomed the change. Work refreshed me as much as the warden's profound speeches had deadened me. Pruning fruit trees and cleaning out caterpillar cocoons helped to restore my interest in life. Then suddenly, on June 21, 1918, a messenger from the warden interrupted my farmwork. He handed me a telegram:

RADOSLAVOV GOVERNMENT FALLEN STOP MALINOV PREMIER STOP RETURNING TO SOFIA WHERE WE SHALL SOON SEE ONE ANOTHER

STAMBOLISKI

Nот Sofia, but the Sofia prison, now became the pivotal point of Bulgarian politics. Two days after Stamboliski's wire, a telegram from Fadenhecht, the new Minister of Justice, ordered my return to the Sofia prison. I knew that Stamboliski had managed this. By June 25, I was back in my old quarters in the midst of the political turmoil. Deputies came at all hours of the night to confer with Stamboliski and Ghenadiev, for the Malinov government lacked a parliamentary majority and needed the support of the Peasant and Liberal Parties.

Stamboliski, offered a cabinet post on attractive terms, laid down a single condition on which he would take office: immediate negotiation for a separate peace with the Allies. Ferdinand had not the slightest intention of accepting such a proposal. He had parted with Radoslavov only under duress—the General Staff had warned that under a regime so unpopular with the soldiers and the people it could no longer assume responsibility for holding the front. The King had appointed Malinov merely to bolster the morale of the army, and Malinov was pledged to prosecute the war "until victory."

Ferdinand's "until victory" meant of course a German victory. Yet at this very moment Germany's position was becoming hopeless. Ludendorff's last supreme effort on the western front, the July 15 offensive, ended in failure. On July 18, the Allied counteroffensive began on a twenty-mile front from a point west of Soissons to Château-Thierry, and within two weeks 40,000 Germans were captured. More than a million American troops had landed in France, and the German tide was ebbing fast. Even the most optimistic pro-German in Bulgaria knew at last that Germany could not win. Only Ferdinand remained obdurate. He would sign no separate peace. He would remain loyal to Germany, the land of his birth, to the end. Naturally, Stamboliski refused to join the Malinov cabinet.

The new regime stubbornly sent its ministers and orators to the front to exhort the troops to keep fighting, for the military situation was deteriorating rapidly. Greece had joined the Allies on July 2, 1917, after the dethronement of King Constantine and Venizelos' return to power. Throughout the rest of that year the Allies had steadily strengthened their positions on the Macedonian front. A mighty Allied army of more than twenty-eight divisions, equipped with powerful artillery and aviation, confronted the battered, disheartened Bulgarian troops. The combined British, French, Italian, Serbian, and Greek forces were massed along a broad front extending for more than 200 miles from Lake Okhrida on the Albanian frontier to the mouth of the Struma River on the Aegean. The harried Germans could now furnish only a few battalions to the tired Bulgarian army.

From prison, Stamboliski and Ghenadiev vainly pleaded with the government to ask an immediate armistice, as the only way to save Bulgaria. "In a few weeks," they urged, "it will be too late, and instead of a negotiated peace, Bulgaria will be compelled to sign a new Treaty of Bucharest."

In August, the Malinov government not only suspended its negotiations with Stamboliski; it adopted repressive measures against political prisoners. Friends were not allowed to see us without permits from the prosecutor, and we were no longer allowed our visits to the "dentist." With our political and military ties virtually cut off, we could not organize a coup d'état. But we knew that in the discontent of the army lurked great danger of revolution at the front. Thousands of our soldiers joined the French. Other thousands deserted and in organized bands raided the mountain villages of the interior, pillaging, raping, and murdering. The authorities were powerless to restore order. Troops too demoralized to resist the enemy could scarcely be expected to fight their brothers.

Early in September the rumor spread through the army that Bulgaria's alliance with Austria and Germany was for three years only, and that "in a few weeks we all go home." On September 16, my old friend Petko Penchev, now general secretary of the cabinet, came to the Sofia prison, pale and agitated. I asked him what was wrong.

"Catastrophe! The front has been broken and the soldiers put to flight. Take me to Stamboliski and Ghenadiev at once."

In Ghenadiev's cell, Penchev told us what had happened. On September 14, the Bulgarian lines were subjected to devastating artillery fire. Then the Allied troops attacked, their main force striking at the sector held by the Third Balkan Division. The Bulgarian lines cracked and the Allies stormed into the breach, cutting off three Bulgarian divisions. The rout was complete.

"Our soldiers are retreating in disorder, crying 'Kill Ferdinand!' " Penchev explained. "The High Command has completely lost its head and Kustendil is in a state of panic. It's all over."

We listened gloomily, knowing that it was now too late to hope for a negotiated peace. Heavy punishment and sorrow lay in store for Bulgaria.

The next few days were a nightmare. The Allied offensive rolled rapidly forward. Only on the Struma front, near Lake Doiran, did the Second and Fourth Bulgarian Armies continue to resist fiercely, capturing 2,000 Greek and 800 British soldiers. On the morning of September 21, King Ferdinand summoned Stamboliski, who returned from the palace at noon, sent for Ghenadiev and me and told us how matters stood. Ferdinand wanted him to accompany the Minister of War to the front to address the soldiers in a last hope of checking the retreat and saving the country. In return Stamboliski had demanded that the King at once release all political prisoners. Ferdinand had agreed, with several exceptions. I was one of the exceptions.

"Why won't you release Todorov?" asked Stamboliski.

"Because I have information—I know that he intends to kill me the minute he is free."

I had no such intention, but apparently King Ferdinand had found out about my terrorist past.

"While I am King," he said, "Todorov does not go free."

Naturally I could not permit the question of my status to affect Stamboliski's decision. I urged him to accept the King's terms. At four o'clock that afternoon he returned once more, bringing the royal decree which released the political prisoners.

Stamboliski, Ghenadiev, and I held a final conference.

"We must organize an immediate armed uprising," said Stamboliski, "to rally the mutinous troops, lead them to Sofia, and force the government to sue for peace. We must salvage whatever we can. Raiko Daskalov will take command of the troops which will march on Sofia from Kustendil. If we get you out in time, join the Second Army at Samokov; it will move on Sofia from the southeast. That army is intact and disciplined and can assure order in the country."

I didn't remain quite alone in prison. A Socialist deputy arrested recently for his antiwar speeches was still there. He was a large, rather handsome man, with thick black hair and a black beard which he later removed. When he spoke, there was always a note of contempt in his voice. All of us were his enemies; Stamboliski as "the representative of the *petit bourgeoisie*," Ghenadiev and I as "defenders of Anglo-French imperialism." This man came from a poor family, had worked as a printer and was suffering from tuberculosis. His education, I gathered, had come entirely from newspapers and orthodox Marxist texts which he seemed to know by heart—Marx's *Das Kapital*, Engel's *Anti-Dühring*, Kautsky's *Erfuhrt Program*, and the Russian Marxist brochures. In 1914, the Sofia workers had elected him to the Sobranje as a Socialist, and he had at once joined the extreme left wing of the party, distinguishing himself by his oratorical talents. After Lenin seized power in Russia he proclaimed himself a Bolshevik. He was Georgi Dimitrov—later hero of the Reichstag-fire trial and present Secretary of the Communist International.

"How do you believe the war will end?" I asked.

Dimitrov replied firmly, "When the soldiers of the contending armies shake hands with one another and overthrow their governments. The war must end in world revolution."

"But suppose the revolution starts in France? Don't you think the German army would move in and impose its peace terms? On the other hand, if the Germans revolt, won't Clemenceau dictate the terms of peace?"

Dimitrov stuck to his guns, refusing to admit that the harsh peace terms the Germans had imposed on the Bolsheviks at Brest-Litovsk challenged the soundness of his position.

On September 24, the report reached our prison that the retreating Bulgarian troops had attacked and wrecked headquarters at Kustendil and that in the town of Radomir, southeast of Sofia, Raiko Daskalov, leading 15,000 soldiers, had proclaimed a republic. Next day we learned that Daskalov was advancing from Radomir on Sofia with a revolutionary army. On September 27, at Kniazhevo, a village six miles from Sofia, the revolutionary troops clashed with those units of the Sofia garrison remaining loyal to King Ferdinand.

Daskalov had hoped to occupy Sofia without firing a shot, but a trainload of his troops coming in from Radomir was machine-gunned at the Sofia station by the command of General Protoguerov, chief of the Sofia garrison. From their train the mutinous troops returned the fire. When news of this skirmish reached Daskalov, he was sorely tried. Although his army now numbered about 20,000 soldiers, most of them were unarmed and demoralized. Their chief ambition was to get home as quickly as possible. Still, Daskalov had no alternative—he attacked Sofia.

From the fourth floor of the prison, facing south, Dimitrov and I watched the battle, and I longed to be in the midst of it. One battery near Pavlovo, less than four miles from Sofia, shelled the advancing insurrectionary forces with shrapnel. Daskalov's soldiers attacked this position and stormed the battery with a bayonet charge. By sunset his advance patrols neared the sugar factory on the outskirts of the city. Daskalov could have occupied the capital that night, but fearing that his unruly followers might pillage the city, he decided to wait until sunrise.

It was a fatal mistake. During the night the government found new strength. As early as September 20, Ferdinand had appealed to the Germans to send artillery and several infantry battalions for his personal protection. They arrived in Sofia while Daskalov's troops lay outside the city, and occupied the important strategic centers. The next morning, when the revolutionary forces attacked, German artillery and machine-gun fire answered. The fight raged fiercely. One German infantry battalion was wiped out by units of the Fifth Bulgarian Regiment, but the main revolutionary forces were defeated by the Sofia garrison, supported by thirty-six German field guns. Daskalov's poorly armed soldiers fled to the mountains, leaving behind more than 3,000 dead. Daskalov himself was wounded and took refuge in southern Bulgaria. Stamboliski, charged with having organized the uprising, also was forced to flee.

Daskalov's rebellion had failed, but its main purpose was achieved. On the very day it was crushed, Malinov sent a delegation to Salonika to ask for an armistice, and persuaded King Ferdinand to abdicate.

The King left Sofia on the last Orient Express for Vienna, taking with him all the treasures of the royal palace—the carpets, the Gobelin tapestries, the paintings, vases, and silverware. Arriving in Vienna, he announced insolently, "For thirty years I tried to unite Bulgaria to Austria-Hungary and Germany. I did not succeed. My mission is ended."

On September 30 came the armistice, demobilizing the Bulgarian army and placing all transport facilities at the disposal of the Allies. On October 3, Ferdinand's son, twenty-four-year-old Prince Boris of Trnovo, took the throne as Boris III, Czar of all the Bulgars.

General Sarrail's prediction that an Allied victory on the Balkan front would cause Turkey and Austria-Hungary to collapse was coming true. The march of the Allied armies to the Danube broke the fragile ties of Hapsburg hegemony. On October 18, the Czech interim government in Paris proclaimed Czech independence, and ten days later the Austrian governor fled from Prague when the Czechoslovak National Council there promulgated an independent republic. On October 26, the Croat Sabor in Zagreb renounced Croatia's allegiance to Emperor Charles and the kingdom of Hungary. On October 31, Hungary rose in revolt. On November 5, her empire gone, Austria laid down her arms. On November 13, Count Karolyi, the new Hungarian Premier, announced that the Magyars were no longer bound by their oath of fealty to the Hapsburg throne.

Meanwhile, on October 30, the Turks capitulated and signed an armistice at Moudros, on the Aegean island of Lemnos, giving the Allies control of the Dardanelles and the Bosporus. Germany was left alone, with its armies in retreat on the western front. Six weeks after Bulgaria stopped fighting, Germany capitulated.

The Army of the East had been under the command of General Franchet d'Esperey since July, 1918, and the victor's laurels went to him. But later, in Paris, the saying went about that Franchet d'Esperey had merely "put on the boots which Sarrail made."

Under the terms of the Salonika armistice, Bulgaria was occupied only by French, British, and Italian troops, to avoid possible Serbian and

Greek reprisals against the civilian population. The Serbs marched through Nish to Belgrade, their capital, while the French moved into Rumania through Bulgarian territory. In March Rumania had been forced by the Germans to sign the brutal Treaty of Bucharest, but the Allied victory over Bulgaria had enabled her to mobilize once more and re-enter the war.

The Allied troops in Bulgaria did not requisition supplies or adopt repressive measures. Indeed, they behaved so much better than Bulgaria's late allies, the Germans, that the people welcomed their conquerors as friends.

As the first French columns were entering Sofia, on October 7, I was released from prison. Stamboliski and Daskalov were still outlaws because of their part in the insurrection and the short-lived republic. Ghenadiev remained under police surveillance. On the other hand, most of Radoslavov's former ministers and supporters, and all the speculators who had fleeced the country in partnership with the Germans during the war, could be seen promenading the streets of Sofia or lounging comfortably in the cafés as if nothing had happened.

With several friends I launched a weekly magazine called *Sila* (Strength) with which we set out to fight these people. We demanded that those responsible for the national catastrophe be brought to trial. "The Peasant leader, Alexander Stamboliski," I wrote, "is forced to live in hiding, although he fought heroically against King Ferdinand and Radoslavov's ministers, who ruined the country, sold it out to the Germans, and still continue to live on their loot under the very eyes of the plundered. If this scandal continues, the outraged people will find its own way to settle accounts with the enemy."

Stamboliski, in hiding, nevertheless was carrying on the same campaign in his paper, *The Peasant Banner*. He signed his articles, "Alexander Stamboliski, Hideout Number —." Daskalov had succeeded in escaping to Salonika.

In the not-distant future all three of us were destined to unite once more, not in prison, but in the government.

THE ARMISTICE ENDED the war, but not my military career. Since the French had not yet demobilized their volunteers, I could be considered a deserter if I did not report to the command in Salonika. I consulted the new Bulgarian Chief of Staff, General Loukov, who had commanded the unbeaten Second Army during the war. It was common knowledge in Sofia that General Loukov had always opposed the German alliance.

"You ask my advice?" he said. "Report at once to General Chrétien, commander of the Allied forces of occupation."

"But if I do, I may find myself back in the French army."

"So much the better!" the General laughed. "As a French officer you'd be in a position to do Bulgaria great service."

I went directly to the sumptuous Turkish legation, now serving as headquarters for the army of occupation. General Chrétien was a tactful, kindly old man. When I told him my story he was so deeply moved that he embraced me. He promised to write to General Franchet d'Esperey, recommending that I be relieved at once of further military duties, and asked me to visit him whenever I found time. Taking advantage of his friendliness, I asked him whether he could help Bulgaria. He shrugged his shoulders.

"I've only been here a month, but I've already learned to love your honest and courageous people. In all my reports I stress the importance of treating Bulgaria with the greatest leniency. But our Balkan allies demand stern punishment for your country. I don't know what will happen."

No one else knew either. The Sofia press wishfully emphasized Wilson's Fourteen Points as the basis for a just peace which would fix the Balkan borders along ethnological lines. Thus Bulgaria not only would lose no territory, but would even gain predominately Bulgarian provinces in Macedonia, Thrace, and Dobruja. For this very reason the Allies must be convinced that Bulgaria had broken completely with the past and wished to become a loyal collaborator in a new order for the Balkans. In my paper I continually stressed this as the only course which could save the country and demanded, therefore, the resignation of the Malinov cabinet—an unwelcome reminder of King Ferdinand's rule.

My parents were now happier than in many years. But it was not to last. My younger brother Vasili, who had been captured on the Carpathian front in 1916, had escaped from a Hungarian prison camp and returned to Russia in the spring of 1918. His passionate nature would not permit him to remain neutral in the Russian Civil War. Enraged by the Brest-Litovsk Treaty, he had entered General Markov's officers' regiment of the Volunteer Army, then fighting in south Russia. A brief note came to my father from Kuban:

> "We have found your address on the body of your son, Second Lieutenant Vasili Todorov. He was killed instantly by a bullet through his head."

Vasili, only eighteen years old, was dead. My mother never really recovered from this blow, and my father lost much of his spirit. Two sons had died in battle; I alone remained.

The struggle against the Malinov government rapidly gained strength. Peasants gathered at stormy mass meetings, threatening to withhold tax payments unless Malinov resigned and Stamboliski was granted amnesty. King Boris, sensing danger, asked for Malinov's resignation and late in December formed a new government with Theodore Theodorov as Premier and Stamboliski as Minister of Public Works. All the parties which had opposed the German alliance entered the cabinet—Russophiles, Peasants, Radicals, and Socialists. The Russophiles, a powerful force until the Bolshevik Revolution, now rapidly lost influence. The opposition to the Theodorov government came from Malinov's Democrat's, Radoslavov's Liberals, and the Communist Party. The Communists were demanding the immediate organization of a Soviet regime and the creation of a Balkan Soviet Federation, but the presence of the Allied army of occupation made them cautious for the time being, and there were no disorders.

On Christmas Day I received an order to report to the French Command in Salonika. General Chrétien obligingly furnished me with an automobile and driver, and I left on the twenty-ninth. In the picturesque Kresna defile of the Perin Mountains in Macedonia a deep snow delayed us, and we did not reach Salonika until New Year's Eve.

Not a soul remained at headquarters; all the officers were out celebrating the New Year. Salonika that night wasn't so fascinating a spectacle as in 1916. Soldiers of every nationality roamed through the city in drunken groups, often shouting, "We want to go home!" The fights between these groups and the military police raged almost as fiercely as those on the now deserted battlefields. The MP's rounded up the drunkards when they could and dragged them off to the barracks.

When I presented myself at staff headquarters again on January 2, I was received by officers whom I did not know and who never had heard of me. General Sarrail's staff had left with him—Colonel Michaud, Captain Lucien, and Captain Jean José Frappa. I referred to General Chrétien's report. A captain promised to dig it out and took my address, but didn't forget to add, "Since you're still in the French army, be good enough to get back into uniform."

A week later, again summoned to staff headquarters, I appeared in uniform, wearing the Croix de Guerre. This time I was received by a police official named Benoit. He came to the point at once.

"You told General Chrétien a number of things which we have checked. They proved to be inaccurate. You're under arrest."

I was astonished, but controlled myself.

"Your informants are probably fools."

"What do you mean?" flared Benoit. "Here in your account you say you were in a camp for prisoners of war in Shumen. Our investigation proves that you weren't."

"You're quite right. I was never in a camp for prisoners of war in Shumen."

"There, you see!" he said triumphantly. "Furthermore, we find that on the staff of the First Bulgarian Army there was a Captain Todorov. That's you!"

I laughed. "There are as many Todorovs in Bulgaria as Benoits in France. And if you'll read General Chrétien's report carefully, you'll find I was in the Shumen prison, not in the camp."

Benoit went through his papers again with a puzzled expression. At last he muttered, "Yes, yes, I understand. What idiots our agents are! Please forgive me."

I remained in Salonika with nothing to do. About a week later, I was summoned once more—this time by an elderly major.

"I think you speak Russian?" he said.

"Yes."

"Would you agree to go to Russia with an expeditionary force?"

"Is this an order?"

The Major hemmed and hawed.

"I don't wish to go as a volunteer. I entered the French army to fight the Germans. I've no desire to become involved in the Russian War."

The Major sighed. "Yes, yes. The soldiers don't want to go either, for that matter, and those we send won't fight. But we're ordered to find as many volunteers as possible. . . . So you decline?"

"Yes."

"Too bad. In your dossier we found General Sarrail's recommendation to the Commander in Chief that you be awarded the Legion of Honor for the mission to Bulgaria which you carried out so courageously. But since you refuse to go to Russia, you won't get it. I'm sorry."

I removed my Croix de Guerre. "Perhaps you'd like me to return this too?"

The Major laughed but said nothing.

I was forced to spend two more weeks in Salonika. One day I ran into Colonel Joseph Petrov of the Bulgarian General Staff, who had been sent there to petition for the release of Bulgarian prisoners of war. He was making little progress.

"Where are the prisoners?" I asked.

"In camps outside the city. During the day many of them work in the harbor as longshoremen."

"Do Bulgarian ships put in at Salonika?"

"Yes, quite a few. Right now the *Varna,* under Captain Prutkin, is in port."

I recalled that my old prison mate, Prutkin, had asked me to request General Chrétien to appoint him captain of a Bulgarian ship. Under the terms of the armistice, Bulgarian ships had to sail under the French flag, with their captains subject to the control of a French naval commissioner. A plan to get some of the prisoners home took shape in my mind.

My French uniform permitted me to board the *Varna* without difficulty. I found Prutkin asleep and woke him. At first he didn't recognize me in uniform. When he did, he was overjoyed.

"Here's a piece of luck! I won't let you go. You'll stay with me. I'm here for two days."

"Where then?"

"Then home through the Black Sea."

He told me he had already made a small fortune carrying contraband from Salonika to the Bulgarian Port of Varna.

"I have business for you," I said, and told him my plan. He was delighted.

"This is the real thing! There are at least 5,000 Bulgarian soldiers working in the harbor. I can get 500 on board. I'll send my sailors to choose men with families and tell them to be aboard by tomorrow night."

Before nightfall the next day the Bulgarian prisoners who were loading the *Varna* disappeared one by one into the hold. Prutkin, meanwhile, kept the French naval inspector entertained over a bottle.

"Don't worry about him," he said. "I'll feed him so much liquor he won't wake up until all our soldiers have been unloaded at Varna."

When the ship sailed, it carried 485 Bulgarian prisoners of war. No one ever noticed their absence, for more than 60,000 remained in the Salonika area.

At the end of January, I was assigned to General Chrétien's staff and returned to Sofia. When I reported to the General he said, "You've been attached to my staff at my request. Now you can get back into civilian clothes, and while technically you're on my staff, consider yourself completely free. Come when you wish to chat with me."

Shortly thereafter I was presented to Premier Theodorov, who advised me how to talk with General Chrétien in the interests of Bulgaria. Back I swam into the political current. Stamboliski urged me to join the Peasant Party, but although I supported its political and economic program, I didn't want to join at a time when it was represented in the cabinet and many of Radoslavov's late followers were therefore clamoring for admission. Jesting, yet half in earnest, I told Stamboliski I would join the party only when it was back in the opposition.

Conditions in Sofia were beginning to improve somewhat. In January, 1919, in response to the government's urgent plea to United States Consul General Murphy, a large shipment of American grain arrived, for which Bulgaria paid in gold. As a sign of the return to normal, the political friends of the new regime engaged in wild speculation. After three years of war and German looting the country was starved for everything, especially consumers' goods. Stringent tariff regulations encouraged smuggling, and with normal means of communication completely disrupted, Allied military trucks carried on most of this commerce.

In Salonika, through which all trade had to pass, the British, French, and Italians quickly learned the Oriental custom of palm greasing. In Sofia, many officers of the army of occupation engaged in contraband trade with Bulgarians whom they protected from arrest. Later this practice would reach scandalous proportions. In other respects the behavior of the Allied troops was exemplary. From Salonika they received ample supplies with which they set up soup kitchens to feed the undernourished Bulgarian children in the poorer districts. During the entire period of occupation I did not hear of a single act of violence or robbery on the part of the Allied forces.

There was a marked difference between the attitude of the British and French and that of the Italians. General Franchet d'Esperey ordered his men to remain politely aloof from Bulgarian society, and the British did likewise. On the other hand, General Monbelli, commander of the Thirty-fifth Italian Division, advised his officers to mingle in the influential circles of Sofia and to attend the receptions and balls. As a result, many Italian officers married Bulgarian girls.

The political motive for this policy would become clear soon enough, but even at this time it was no secret that the relations between Italians and Serbs had begun to cool. Italy claimed the eastern shore of the Adriatic, which was populated almost entirely by Slavs, mainly Croats. Seeking a Balkan counterpoise to Serbia, the Italians already had begun to woo defeated Bulgaria. For the moment, the Italian officers merely tried to make themselves popular at the social gatherings of Sofia, and no one

—themselves included—could dream that they were harbingers of Balkan ruin.

One spring evening in 1919 I attended a recital at the Military Club by a young violinist, Nadejda Ouzounova. Both her playing and her beauty captivated me, and after the recital I went backstage and introduced myself. A quick courtship followed. Her father, a colonel, had died in the war. Her mother was shocked when I asked for Nadejda's hand less than two weeks after our first meeting. Nevertheless, on June 23 we were married at Nadejda's home in the presence of Stamboliski, Ghenadiev, Daskalov, and the officers of General Chrétien's staff.

Several days before my marriage, Premier Theodorov had appointed me to take charge of Bulgarian propaganda in Paris during the forthcoming peace negotiations. The Versailles Conference was ending; on our wedding day the Weimar National Assembly ratified the Treaty of Versailles. But peace terms with Germany's former allies—Bulgaria, Austria, Hungary, and Turkey—were yet to be fixed. I naturally accepted Premier Theodorov's appointment, but I had to get General Chrétien's permission to leave Sofia.

When I explained the situation, the General thought for a moment. "I have it!" he said with a twinkle. "How long is it since you had leave?"

"Since the spring of 1916."

"Very well. You shall receive the accumulated leave to which you are entitled, and all the necessary papers to go to Paris with your bride."

I found that 119 days of leave were due me, within which time I could reasonably expect to be demobilized. Besides leave, I received my full back pay for almost three years—23,000 francs (nearly $4,000). I had not been paid from the moment I left Salonika in 1916.

Three days after our marriage, Nadejda and I left Bulgaria for Constantinople, there to take ship for Marseille.

PART III

STATESMAN

1919-1923

*The results of political changes
are hardly ever those which their
friends hope or their foes fear.*

THOMAS HENRY HUXLEY

On July 13, the eve of Bastille Day, we arrived in Paris, then preparing to celebrate its great national holiday, the first since the victory—that victory for which I had fought and which meant the defeat of my country. We were out at seven in the morning to watch French and Allied troops parade by, but already an enormous crowd had massed on both sides of the Champs-Élysées. The entire city was gay with flags, and flanking the parade route stood German guns captured on the western front. When the first columns of troops appeared and the bands boomed the stirring old war marches, I shared the contagious rapture of the crowd, yet I was saddened by the fate of Bulgaria.

Then suddenly through the crowd passed the roar, *"Légion! Légion!"* and I heard the swelling rhythm of the *Tonnerre de Dieu*. My regiment! The men marched in easy step, their bearded faces grave. Many of them were familiar to me. Behind Captain Delanourienne came Dufour. He was alive! I wanted to rush out and embrace him and in so doing embrace all my comrades of the Legion, living and dead.

Before that fatal August of 1914 there had been much grace and spontaneous joy in Paris life. During the war the city was calm and brave. But now a bacchanal of bad taste reigned. From every victory, I suppose, something arrogant and coarse arises—an outburst of long-restrained appetites. The soldiers had won the war, but they were not the victors. Back to their ruined homes they went, back to a drab existence where everything must be started anew. Exhausted, broken in health, nerves shattered, bodies crippled or eyes blinded—they had little enough left to build with.

Ghenadiev had given me letters of introduction to his friends in Paris, and I called on them at once. Senator Justin Godard received me cordially in his apartement in an ancient house on the Quai Voltaire, but confessed he could do nothing for Bulgaria. Professor Victor Bérard gave me a cold reception and argued that Greece was entitled not only to all of Thrace, but also to Constantinople and Asia Minor. But in Alice Ménard-Dorian's salon I made many useful contacts.

Mme. Ménard-Dorian was the widow of a minister in Waldeck-Rousseau's cabinet. She was related to Victor Hugo, belonged to the Socialist Party, and had a fortune of some 300 million francs. All the French politicians of the left, leading journalists, writers, and prominent artists attended her Thursday afternoon receptions. Gobelin tapestries and countless paintings by Watteau, Delacroix, Courbet, Carrière and Corot adorned the walls. Tea was served in gold teapots, we sat on Louis Quatorze and Louis Quinze chairs, and the heavy silver platters and dishes made the antique tables creak.

Mme. Ménard-Dorian introduced me to all her guests and arranged several dinners at which I spoke for my country, stressing the complete break with the past and our honest desire to co-operate with the rest of Europe toward a stable peace. In her salon I also found an opportunity to speak privately to leading French politicians—Briand, Painlevé, Berthelot. Briand was attentive and pleasant, but said in his melodious voice, "It all depends on Clemenceau."

His hair was almost entirely gray, his thick Gallic mustache yellowish from excessive smoking. His eyes, blue and slightly bulging, smiled at me. In his tone he was familiar from the start, slapped me on the back and called me *"mon vieux."* During our conversation, he continually drew crumpled cigarettes out of his pocket. As far as I could make out, he didn't keep them in a package and his supply was unlimited. He was always carelessly dressed in a rumpled suit and a badly made necktie, and his slight stoop emphasized his untidiness. Only when he spoke on a favorite subject did he straighten up—then his bearing took on strength and great dignity.

Paul Painlevé, who had been Premier in 1917, was, like Briand, only a Deputy now, but was considered the head of the Republican Socialist Party. He spoke little, walked through the salon with head high and eyes staring at the ceiling. One heard many anecdotes about his absent-mindedness. His lapses were attributed to his preoccupation with science; he was a remarkable mathematician and had made a number of important discoveries in the basic principles of aeronautics. Painlevé was not indifferent to my plea that he help Bulgaria, and even gave me letters to a number of journalists, which later proved useful.

Philippe Berthelot, General Secretary of the Foreign Office, impressed me at once with the brilliance of his mind, the precision with which he expressed his thoughts, and his understanding of European problems. He knew every problem facing Bulgaria down to the smallest detail.

"Of course, it's difficult with Clemenceau," he said. "He's very angry at Bulgaria. But it's even more difficult with our Balkan allies. For such small countries they have enormous appetites, and that complicates matters. The trouble with our victory is that we have far too many victors. Pashich, Venizelos, and Jonescu are here, and I have to talk with them often. I assure you our task isn't easy. The Serbs, for example, really fought heroically and suffered great losses, while the Rumanians concluded a separate peace with Germany. Yet Jonescu is demanding Bessarabia, the Bulgarian Dobruja, and half of Hungary for Rumania."

"What about Venizelos?" I asked. "He usually seems conciliatory."

Berthelot dismisssed this with a wave of his hand.

"He's suffering from delusions of Byzantium. I'm afraid some day he'll demand Marseille."

The noted professors Seignobos and Aulard also visited the salon. Both very old men, they took little interest in contemporary affairs. Only some obscure problem of the French Revolution could stir Aulard to life. Then his small beard would tremble with pleasure as he muttered in an almost unintelligible voice, "That was in the Year III of the Republic!" And he would plunge into a dissertation on some long-forgotten member of the National Convention. Seignobos' interest was more catholic: he'd even heard of the nineteenth century.

One Thursday afternoon at Mme. Ménard-Dorian's I was pleasantly surprised to find General Sarrail in the drawing room. He excitedly grasped my hand and, although everyone present knew me, loudly introduced me to the guests—"One of the bravest men I ever knew." He asked me to call on him the next day.

On the walls of his modest apartment were a number of photographs, including one of the Yugoslav Regent, Prince Alexander, and, to my astonishment, one of the former Crown Prince of Germany, with the inscription:

> *A mon adversaire chevaleresque, le Général Sarrail*
> *Wilhelm, Kronprinz*
> *1 Janvier, 1915*

"Does this surprise you?" laughed the General. "After we had beaten back the first German attack on Verdun, the Crown Prince sent me this under a flag of truce on New Year's Day, 1915. I'm keeping it as a souvenir for my children."

After showing me the documents concerning my mission to Bulgaria, he explained why he had been removed from the command of the Allied Army of the East. All the reactionaries had intrigued for his downfall. In the army he was attacked by the graduates of the Jesuit schools, particularly by the Chief of Staff, General Castelnau, and General Pétain. Also in the intrigue was the British General Milne, who demanded the power to operate independently of Sarrail.

"They charged me with a great many 'crimes.' They said I was supporting the Freemasons; that I was more of a politician than a general. They even reproached me with my second marriage, although I was a widower. I might have received another command, but after Clemenceau became Premier that was impossible. The old man dislikes me heartily."

Then General Sarrail suddenly asked me, "Did you receive the Legion of Honor?"

"No, General."

He reddened with anger.

"I cannot permit this injustice. I'll protest."

"No, I beg you not to. I returned to my country and am now involved in its politics. Bulgaria is a defeated country, and France is the victor. Under such circumstances the decoration might cause gossip."

The General understood.

During August, the delegations of the defeated small nations began to arrive. The Bulgarians were assigned to the Château de Madrid in Neuilly-sur-Seine, a suburb of Paris. The representatives of Austria, Hungary, Bulgaria, and Turkey were now treated as the Germans had been. They could not sit at the conference tables with the victors, and they could communicate only in writing. Virtual prisoners, they were accompanied by detectives whenever they went into the city. The victors handed them the text of the treaty and permitted them to state their objections in writing. But in the end no substantial changes were made; only unconditional acceptance was allowed. The terms which were to settle Europe's destiny and "preserve" its peace thus resulted not from free discussion but from superior force. All the agreements were patterned after the Treaty of Versailles.

Unlike the members of the Bulgarian delegation, I could move about freely, but conferring with them was another matter. When I met them at the station in Paris, I managed to whisper to Stamboliski, "Ask for permission to attend the Russian church on the rue Daru on Sunday. I'll be there."

He came, with a number of other Bulgarian delegates. The detective remained outside, and during services I spoke freely with my colleagues.

Later we set another meeting place. The Château de Madrid is at the very end of the Bois de Boulogne, near a number of lakes on which the members of the delegation could go boating. The central lake is quite long. With a French friend, I took one boat; Stamboliski another. We met midway on the lake while the detectives loitered on the shore. Thus I received all the necessary instructions and reports of the delegation.

In running from one newspaper office to another, trying to get the Bulgarian cause before the public, I learned something about the morals of the French press. Nearly every paper demanded money—not the writers, but the owners and managers. Of the highly respected Le Temps, looked upon as the mouthpiece of the Foreign Office, only Herbette, the editorial writer, was independent of the management. He took his instructions direct from the Quai d'Orsay and did not interest himself in the commerce conducted on the second and third pages by the business manager and virtual boss, M. Rolls, a Frenchified Dutchman who lived in a fine mansion on the Avenue Foch. Virtually all foreign news and articles on international affairs came under Rolls' supervision, and the space allotted depended entirely upon the amount paid by the interested government.

"In Paris," M. Rolls told me with cynical frankness, "real estate costs so much per square meter; in my paper, space so much per square centimeter."

Incidentally, he did not state the price. His writers on Balkan matters, Charles Rivet and Edouard Tavernier, both owned elegant villas. Rivet also had a château near Geneva. I later learned that they didn't even get salaries, but only a percentage of the profits from foreign propaganda. To understand Rivet's wealth it was necessary to know that before the war he had been *Le Temps* correspondent in St. Petersburg. Both he and Tavernier argued that all I had to do was to pay the paper a million francs and it would stanchly defend Bulgarian interests. The Greeks, Serbs, and Rumanians were paying, they said, and the Austrians and Hungarians had already contribluted a million each. I saw that it would be a waste of money to pay *Le Temps*; it was impossible to defend the interests of both Bulgaria and its rivals. But I told them I would agree on one condition: if they could guarantee several *editorials* in favor of Bulgaria. Only editorials were taken seriously, for they reflected the position of the Foreign Office. Although they could not promise this, M. Rolls made me what he no doubt thought a generous offer:

"Ask your government for a million and keep 300,000 for yourself."

I reported all this to Premier Theodorov, including my own opinion that giving a million francs to *Le Temps* would be an utter waste of money.

Le Matin, to my great surprise, not only accepted an article I wrote under a French pseudonym, but also asked for two more. Later I found out why only the first appeared. The paper had made a tremendous sum of money on it, for no sooner had it been published than the Serbs, Greeks, and Rumanians appeared in the editorial office, demanding that the pro-Bulgarian campaign cease. At the end of my article an editorial note had announced that others would follow. The editor showed them the two additional articles, ready for publication. To stop the campaign, each of the three delegations paid 100,000 francs.

Oddly enough I managed, without paying bribes, to get several articles into *L'Oeuvre, L'Ere nouvelle, L'Europe nouvelle,* and *Le Monde illustré,* the big weekly of my friend Jean José Frappa—all considered, quite a feat.

Despite my report, Premier Theodorov decided to pay Rolls the million francs. Rolls brazenly enough gave the government a receipt which I later saw in Sofia. Of the million, he got 500,000 francs, Tavernier 300,000, and Rivet 200,000.

My own experience proved that despite the corruption of the French press, results were possible without great financial resources if one only knew how to convince the honest people who, after all, were in the majority. A certain amount of money was needed, but not for bribery. In the afterglow of a good dinner with excellent wine, the French mind is amenable to argument. One had only to cultivate what Lord Chesterfield called the *leniores virtutes,* to know how warm the feelings of others. Gifts, too, were important, but one had to know how to give. Seneca wrote a whole essay on the art of giving. In Paris and throughout my diplomatic career I remembered his wise advice; I approached each individual in a different way, depending upon his tastes and temperament. One I treated to good food and wine, to another I gave a Japanese vase or a picture, to a third a rare book. Thus I created ties which were not only useful but lasting.

The peace negotiations dragged on and for purely technical reasons. Stamboliski and I met often, either in the Russian church or on the lake. In church one day an elegantly dressed man with a pockmarked face came up and addressed Stamboliski in the peasant dialect of western Bulgaria, offering to furnish him free of charge with an advance copy of the peace terms which Bulgaria would be asked to sign.

"But where can you get it?" asked Stamboliski.

"It's very simple," he said, smiling slyly. "I'm in the Italian delegation." He handed Stamboliski a large package of papers. I looked hard at his homely but energetic face, trying to remember where I had seen him before. At last I remembered. In Salonika, in 1916, I was sitting on the terrace of the Café Floka with Jean José Frappa and a Serbian captain, Milan Georgevich, when a tall, erect Serbian officer wearing a decoration entered. Georgevich said to me, "That's your compatriot, Captain Ivanov."

He invited the man to join us and presented him, "The son of the Bulgarian General Ivanov."

When Captain Ivanov learned that I was Bulgarian, he became confused, but sat down with us and ate ice cream. Then I asked him to take a walk with me. When we were out of earshot I said, "I know General Ivanov. He has no sons. What's this all about?"

He told me everything quite frankly. During the Second Balkan War he had been a noncommissioned officer in the Bulgarian artillery and was captured by the Greeks. After the war the Greeks continued to hold many Bulgarian prisoners. Ivanov didn't get out of Greece until July, 1914, and landed in Serbia just when that country was mobilizing. He told the Serbs he was the son of General Ivanov, that he was a lieutenant, and that he had escaped from the Greeks to join the Serbian army as a volunteer. In the confusion of mobilization no one had time to investigate, and he was accepted as an officer in the Serbian army. He distinguished himself in fighting the Austrians, rose to the rank of captain, and was decorated.

When I reminded Captain Ivanov of this meeting in Salonika, he was equally frank about all that had happened to him since then.

"The Serbs told the French I was General Ivanov's son, and they sent for me. I told them I didn't want to fight against Bulgaria and that I wanted to go to the Western Front. They sent me to France, where I was assigned to the Foreign Legion. But I never reached the Legion. They became interested in me in Paris. I was presented to Professor Victor Bérard, who liked me very much and introduced me into Paris society. In Bulgaria I had only finished elementary school, but I soon learned how to chatter in French and I appealed to the ladies. One of them"
—he mentioned her name—"fell in love with me, began to give me money, and interested the Deuxième Bureau in me. Here was a chance to earn big money. I told them my father was very popular in Bulgaria and so powerful in the army that if he took it upon himself, he could swing Bulgaria to the side of the Allies."

" 'Could you get in contact with your father?' they asked me.

" 'Of course!' I told them. I explained, however, that it would be necessary for me to go to Switzerland and organize a secret courier service consisting of Bulgarian merchants and students.

"Several days later, I was introduced to an important representative of the British Intelligence Service and my plan was accepted. The two intelligence services gave me 400,000 francs and sent me to Switzerland. Unfortunately the woman went with me. She's old, you know. I traveled a good deal 'on business,' so as to see her as little as possible."

"What did you do in Switzerland?" I asked.

"It was a regal existence—from palace to palace, from one resort to another. What did I do? I had a good time. To show my employers I was hot on the job, I hired a Bulgarian student to write me letters, supposedly from my father, demanding money for the organization of an uprising in Bulgaria. I carried these letters in my shoes to give them the appearance of having been smuggled out of Bulgaria. I translated them into French and sent them to the Deuxième Bureau. When I met Bulgarian merchants in Switzerland, I did talk with them and gave them letters, so that if anyone was watching I was on the job. But the letters were to my real family in my village. My father's a peasant and a drunkard.

[119]

"Sometimes I went to Paris by automobile. I got more than a million Swiss gold francs out of it and I'd probably still be on the pay roll if it hadn't been for a silly incident. In Paris I went about in uniform, but my Serbian decoration meant nothing to people. So I bought a collection of French medals—the Legion of Honor, the Médaille Militaire, and the Croix de Guerre—and my success with women was amazing. But suddenly the police arrested me because of those damned medals. Madame might have saved me from unpleasantness, but that bastard Clemenceau was in power. He demanded to see my dossier, turned down all petitions, kept me in jail for two months, and ordered me thrown out of France.

"But my old lady looked out for me. Somehow she got permission for me to go to Italy, and presented me to the important people there. They took me into their Intelligence Service to look after the Serbs. They paid me little, but with the help of my old woman and what was left of my Swiss money, I still lived very well. I spoke Serbian fluently and mixed with the Serbs, who told me everything frankly, but it wasn't much. They merely cursed the Italians and called them cowards.

"Now my prospects are good. Through the same woman, I was taken into the Italian delegation as an expert on Balkan affairs. I have access to all the documents concerning Bulgaria. I don't want money from my own people. But I expect to earn a lot from the Italians."

"How?" I asked, surprised. "The war's over."

"You don't understand. The Italians have differences with the Serbs over Dalmatia and Fiume. I've promised them that as soon as a conflict starts I will begin an uprising in Serbian Macedonia with the help of my father, the General. I've already collected 70,000 lire as a down payment."

I looked at him almost with rapture. The man was a genius!

"May God grant General Ivanov another hundred years!" I said. "But how does it happen no one ever thought of checking whether you're really his son?"

"God help me if they do. So far no one has."

I had no reason to expose him, and he proved useful to us. The documents he stole from the Italians were authentic; he didn't deceive his own countrymen.

Events in Bulgaria were rushing toward a crisis. The Theodorov government could not solve the vital internal problems. The old conservatives who were still influential in the cabinet did not understand that after the catastrophe of war and defeat the people expected fundamental changes, both economic and political. Bulgarians had lost faith not only in the Crown but in the leadership of the parties identified with Ferdinand's regime. The peasants were demanding radical agrarian reforms, and only the prestige of the Peasant Party and the popularity of Alexander Stamboliski stood as a barrier against Communist uprisings such as were taking place in Germany, Austria, and Hungary. The Peasant Party turned most of the unrest into the channel of democratic political action.

The workers and the minor government employees, on the other hand, began joining the Communist Party in great numbers. The leadership of the Bulgarian Communist Party was already in the hands of Vasili Kolarov and Georgi Dimitrov, both of whom were later to play key roles in the Communist International.

Within the Peasant Party, dissatisfaction continued to mount as the Theodorov regime vacillated and temporized, failing to punish those responsible for Bulgaria's defeat. Stamboliski demanded a general election, and on August 17, 1919, the Peasant Party won a great victory, increasing its strength in the Sobranje from forty-eight to eighty-eight seats out of a total of two hundred sixteen. The Communists and Social Democrats also gained ground, electing forty-seven and twenty-eight deputies respectively, while the so-called bourgeois parties suffered a decisive defeat. Radoslavov's Liberals, who had held one hundred ten seats in the preceding parliament, kept only two. For the moment, however, the Theodorov cabinet remained in office because of the delicate international situation.

A<small>T LAST THE</small> Bulgarian people were to know the price of King Ferdinand's treason. The final text of the peace treaty was submitted to the Bulgarian delegation, and Theodorov and Stamboliski left Paris for Sofia to present it to the cabinet and the parliamentary leaders. Like its predecessors of Versailles and St.-Germain, it bore no trace of the Fourteen Points on which we had based our hopes of a tolerable peace. The terms were harsh. Bulgaria lost the Dobruja to Rumania. All of western Thrace with its rich pasture lands and tobacco fields was ceded jointly to Great Britain, France, and Italy rather than to Greece outright, as a sop to Bulgarian pride. But the great powers were authorized to transfer it as they saw fit, and ultimately, of course, it would go to Greece. Bulgaria was thus cut off from the Aegean.

To the newly organized Kingdom of Serbs, Croats, and Slovenes (not officially named Yugoslavia until 1929) went a strip of frontier territory including Bosiljgrad, Tsaribrod and Strumitsa, an area of 2,430 square kilometers, with 92,000 inhabitants. Strategically this narrow strip was expected to possess great value should Bulgaria attack Serbia. When the test came, in April, 1941, and the Germans struck at Skoplje through Bulgaria, possession of this territory proved of no value to the Yugoslav army. Naturally those who drew the strategic map of 1919 couldn't foresee the German war machine of 1941.

The treaty forbade military conscription and limited the Bulgarian army to a volunteer force of 20,000 soldiers, 3,000 border guards, and no more than 10,000 gendarmes for internal security.

In the matter of reparations I had been fortunate enough to be of some service. Reparations, in the preliminary draft of the treaty, had been based on the official balance sheet of the Bulgarian National Bank. This strange document showed one hundred million Russian rubles and several hundred million German marks and Austrian crowns as part of the Bulgarian gold reserve. According to the balance sheet, Bulgaria's gold reserve was almost nine hundred million francs ($225,000,000), whereas in reality it did not exceed thirty-seven million. The rest had been wiped out by the Russian Revolution and the German-Austrian collapse.

I went to see Sergeant, chief secretary of the French Ministry of Finance, who had been assigned to work out the text of Bulgarian reparations. After a three-day discussion, reparations were fixed at two and a quarter billion francs instead of five billion, to be paid over a period of thirty-seven years. What was even more important, the reparation payments were made conditional on ability to pay. The Interallied Reparations Commission in Bulgaria was authorized to ask the Reparations Commission in Paris for the postponement, reduction, or even cancellation of reparations if Bulgaria could not pay.

But financial reparations were not all Bulgaria faced. It had to turn over to its Balkan neighbors a substantial number of cattle and a large quantity of coal. The Bulgarian government also obligated itself to punish those who had committed crimes of violence in occupied territory, mainly in Serbia. This meant certain leaders of the IMRO and a number of army men who had worked with them.

The peace terms were too much for Premier Theodorov. He resigned, and King Boris asked Stamboliski to form a government. On October 5, 1919, the Peasant leader presented his new Cabinet to the King—ten ministers, seven of whom were Peasants. The new Minister of Foreign Affairs, Madjarov, a member of the Popular Party, had been envoy to London and St. Petersburg. From the Russian capital in August, 1915, he had pleaded with Ferdinand to keep Bulgaria out of war. On the margin of Madjarov's report the King had written: *"Chant du cygne"* (swan song) .

Early in the morning of November 27, 1919, in the square before the City Hall of Neuilly-sur-Seine, a company of French soldiers presented arms while a band played the French and Bulgarian national anthems. Inside, Clemenceau, looking like the evil dwarf in a fairy tale beside the enormous figure of Stamboliski, signed the peace treaty with a quick flourish and handed him the pen. Stamboliski told the journalists who besieged him on the steps of the City Hall, "I have signed the treaty, but I believe that sooner or later it will be revised. My policy aims at peace and the brotherhood of peoples. We intend to live up to our obligations, but we shall not cease appealing to the conscience of the world for justice to defeated Bulgaria."

The next day Stamboliski, with my help, drafted letters to the Premiers of the three important Balkan Powers: the Kingdom of the Serbs, Croats, and Slovenes; Greece; and Rumania, proposing that the past be forgotten and that all Balkan governments collaborate for the common security and economic welfare of the Balkans. Not one of them answered. They could not understand that only this policy could save us all from tragedy.

Stamboliski went to Sofia, leaving me in Paris as general secretary of the delegation. The most important question still pending was that of 110,000 Bulgarian soldiers still held captive in Greece, Serbia, and Corsica. The Treaty of Neuilly would not take effect until ratified by the parliaments of the signatory powers. Meanwhile, the detention of these prisoners more than a year after Bulgaria had laid down its arms was not only causing needless sorrow but also meant a serious shortage of agricultural man power.

A note to Clemenceau as President of the Interallied Council brought no response. I brought up the matter several times with Philippe Berthelot, who only repeated what I had heard so often, "It all depends on the Tiger. I've spoken to him, but I can't persuade him to act." Finally I asked Berthelot to arrange an audience for me. At eleven A.M. on December 5, a wet, gloomy day, I was ushered into the reception room of Clemenceau's home on the rue François Premier. There I sat, nervously fingering the Croix de Guerre in my pocket, until I was shown into the study.

The blinds were drawn and the room, filled with books, was lighted by a single desk lamp. Behind the desk sat Clemenceau, wearing a black silk skullcap which made his face seem even rounder than it was. Sharp, dark eyes peered from under his bushy gray brows. His nose was small and round, and his enormous white mustache concealed his chin as well as his mouth. He wore the happy expression of a bulldog about to bite.

Suddenly I heard his crackling, angry voice, "What do you want?" Neither by word nor gesture did he invite me to be seated. I stood, ill at ease, in the middle of the room, feeling completely lost and mumbling words even I could not understand.

"Well?" snapped Clemenceau. "Talk! I'm busy."

I pulled myself together. "In the name of the Bulgarian delegation I appeal to your generosity for the liberation of the Bulgarian prisoners, who long to see their homes."

"Generosity!" His eyes flashed with rage. "Now you appeal to my generosity! Have you forgotten all the evil Bulgaria did during the war?"

This riled my Balkan blood. My timidity and confusion vanished.

"Mr. President, you seem to forget that Bulgaria is now ruled by men who spent the war in prison because they opposed it. As I listen to you, I begin to regret that I fought as a volunteer in the ranks of the French army."

"What's this?" he asked in an entirely new voice. "You fought for France?"

"Yes. In the Foreign Legion, in Artois and Champagne, on the Somme and in Alsace."

The ogre before me suddenly turned into a benevolent old gentleman. His face crinkled in a smile which ran down from his eyes and hid in his white mustache.

"In the Legion? A splendid regiment! The glory of the French army!"

He bounded from his chair, came up to me quickly, took my hands, and seated me in an armchair close to him. Then he rang for a lackey and shouted, "Jean! A bottle of Burgundy at once, and coffee—coffee for me."

He sat down and slapped me on the knee. "Why in the name of God didn't Philippe tell me?" he asked. "Well, tell me about yourself, about the regiment, and how you came to be in the Bulgarian delegation."

I told him my story briefly, while he smiled and nodded his head. Only when I mentioned General Sarrail did he frown slightly. I had not yet finished when the wine and coffee were brought.

"Excellent wine! But unfortunately I don't drink—and don't use sugar," he added. "As a doctor I have put myself on a diet. One egg in the morning, a little coffee in the afternoon, and a broiled cutlet in the evening."

At the end of my story, Clemenceau said, "Well, tell me, how can I make you happy?"

"Mr. President, I ask you to help us rebuild Bulgaria. We wish to destroy all traces of Ferdinand's rule and to bring our country to the side of the peoples who long for peace."

Clemenceau again frowned. "While there are Germans there will be no peace."

"But, Mr. President, the Bulgarian peasants love their peaceful labor and their land. Bring them joy by this gift for Christmas. Give us the opportunity to tell the Bulgarian people that France is generous in victory."

"Very well, very well, I'll do it." Clemenceau smiled. "I'll do it because you love France. Only for you—I wouldn't do it for anyone else."

Then, returning to the stubborn thought which seemed always to revolve in his brain, he added almost in a whisper, "But the Germans must be destroyed to the finish—of course not as a people, but as a force. Many people still don't understand this—neither the English, the Americans, nor many of our own Frenchmen."

I listened only through politeness, too excited by his promise of release for the Bulgarian soldiers to worry about the Germans. After a second glass of Burgundy, still almost unable to believe I had understood him correctly, I asked:

"May I inform my government of the good news?"

"You may. I'll issue the order today."

Half an hour earlier I had hated Clemenceau. Now I was ready to hug him. There were tears in my eyes as I pressed the old man's hand and stammered my thanks.

He escorted me to the door of his study, slapped me affectionately on the back, and said, "I'm supposed to be very evil." He laughed—an almost childlike laugh that lighted up his eyes. "Tell your people I'm not so bad."

S EVERAL DAYS BEFORE Christmas, Nadejda and I were in a Paris cinema when suddenly the film was interrupted and a news report was flashed across the screen:

REVOLUTION IN BULGARIA. COMMUNISTS ATTEMPT TO SEIZE POWER!

I rushed from the theater to our legation and sent a ciphered telegram to Sofia, asking for information. Back came the terse reply: "Return to Sofia at once." No explanation, no news. I left for Bulgaria on the Orient Express, then running once more as far as Belgrade. Nadejda remained in Paris because I feared what lay ahead. The newspapers I bought at every stop en route carried contradictory reports. It was not clear whether the Stamboliski government was still in power.

I had to remain overnight in Belgrade because railway schedules were badly snarled. The city was still in a wretched state. The streets near the docks of the Danube and Sava Rivers, torn up by Austrian shells, had not yet been repaired. But the city's inhabitants were filled with pride—little Serbia had become a big country and its capital one of the important political centers of Europe.

When I finally left Belgrade it was in a dilapidated and unheated coach, moving at a snail's pace. Three times I had to change trains before reaching the Bulgarian frontier at Tsaribrod the following day. My traveling companions were three French officers, a Bulgarian woman who had been living in Switzerland, a Frenchwoman on her way to join her Bulgarian husband, and two merchants of uncertain nationality bound for Constantinople. At the frontier we were informed that because of the general strike no trains were running to Sofia.

I went into the chilly station office and put through a call to Stamboliski. Briefly he explained the situation. The Communists' attempts to seize power had thus far failed. The Sofia railway terminal, post office, and telephone exchange were held firmly by the government despite Communist efforts to capture them. On the other hand, the Communist-organized general strike had the country paralyzed and had completely tied up transportation.

Stamboliski offered to send an automobile for me, but snowdrifts made the highways almost impassable. Instead, I suggested that, as Minister of War, he call out the Tsaribrod garrison and place it at my disposal.

"Why?" he asked.

"I'll force the railway workers to run through a train to Sofia."

"Very well," laughed Stamboliski. "It's worth the try."

In the waiting room I found my fellow-passengers gloomy. They had given up all hope of reaching Sofia, and the prospect of being stranded in a town which had neither hotel nor restaurant did not appeal to them.

"Ladies and gentlemen," I said, "bear with me for no more than two hours. I promise to have a train for you."

They exchanged skeptical glances. Half an hour later the stationmaster informed me that Lieutenant Colonel Popov, commander of the local garrison, awaited me in the station office. Rather sullenly, Popov told me he had just received Stamboliski's instruction to obey my orders.

"What is your pleasure?" he added coldly.

Curtly I replied, "In fifteen minutes I want a platoon of soldiers here, fully equipped and ready for action."

"With loaded rifles?" he asked in surprise.

"Yes, and with fixed bayonets."

Within the quarter hour the platoon arrived, and I led them to the barracks of the striking railway workers. After ordering the young lieutenant in command to bring in his men at the first signal from me, I entered alone. About fifty men were lounging about in an overheated dormitory, foul with tobacco and soft coal fumes. They were playing cards, drinking *raki*, eating, and talking loudly. No one paid any attention to me. I planted myself in the center of the room.

"Attention!" I shouted.

The voices died down and heads turned in surprise.

"What's up?" someone asked.

"In the name of the Prime Minister of Bulgaria, Alexander Stamboliski, I command you to proceed to the station at once and make ready a locomotive and one coach for Sofia."

They laughed raucously. "To hell with you and your Prime Minister!" shouted a large man who seemed to be their leader.

When the jeers had died down, I repeated my command. The man swaggered up to me, raised his coal-black fist to my nose and sneered, "Beat it if you want to stay in one piece."

I stepped back two paces and drew my revolver. It had an immediate sobering effect upon him. But the men shouted, "We take orders only from our committee in Sofia."

"This time you'll obey my order," I replied. "I prefer that you do so voluntarily, but if you refuse I'll use force."

They remained silent. No one moved. I went to the door and signaled, and the platoon of soldiers double-timed into the room. No violence occurred, and everything ended well. Within the time I had promised a locomotive drawing one car steamed out of Tsaribrod. We pulled into

Sofia, seventy kilometers away, at two o'clock in the afternoon.

Stamboliski received me at once, although he was in the midst of a conference with Raiko Daskalov and Minister of the Interior Alexander Dimitrov. The Minister of the Interior, no relative of his Communist namesake, was a man of inexhaustible energy. A self-educated peasant with a great deal of common sense, he was fanatically loyal to Stamboliski.

I now heard the whole story of the disturbances. At noon on December 20, the Communists had served the government an ultimatum demanding big increases in the wages of all government workers. Despite the difficult financial situation Stamboliski was prepared to double wages, because living expenses had risen greatly. But the Communists wanted no agreement with Stamboliski; they wanted power. Without awaiting the government's answer, they proclaimed a general strike at ten o'clock that same night. During the next few days they strove vigorously to turn the strike into a revolutionary insurrection, but the shrewd Minister of the Interior blocked all their efforts.

Thus far there had been no serious fighting or real bloodshed, but the fuse of revolution sizzled dangerously. Raiko Daskalov had mobilized the peasants who had done emergency railway work during the war, and with their help had restored a limited train service. None the less, the strike still paralyzed the economic life of the country. Unless the government acted soon, it would cease to exist.

"What about the army?" I asked.

"The reactionary officers are delighted with the strike," said Dimitrov. "They think it will force Stamboliski out and bring in the extreme right. We can't count on them. But we have a force of 5,000 armed peasants in Sofia who will back us to the hilt. We want you to take command."

With the Minister of the Interior I went to the barracks of the First Sofia Regiment, where the peasant volunteers were amassed. Dimitrov asked their temporary commander, Major Dobrovolsky, a Peasant Party member, to order the men out into the courtyard. When the 5,000 peasants, carrying rifles and various other weapons, had assembled outside, Dimitrov presented me as their new commander in a brief speech. Then he left. After dismissing the men, I asked Major Dobrovolsky to report on the condition of this volunteer army. The men were divided into four battalions, each commanded by a reserve second lieutenant. There were no other officers. Discipline was excellent, however, Dobrovolsky assured me. The men were in the best of spirits and eager to fight for Stamboliski.

"What have the men been doing?"

"Nothing so far. We sit in the barracks and await orders."

I told Dobrovolsky to have the men ready to march with full equipment in the morning, and ordered that the battalion commanders be mounted. I also asked him to borrow the services of the First Regiment's military band.

At eleven o'clock the next morning, December 27, the 5,000 peasant volunteers marched out of their barracks, preceded by a military band and several officers on horseback. In semi-military attire improvised for the occasion, I rode at the head of the procession. The peasants wore their national costume, but their military caps, rifles, and the hand grenades suspended from their belts gave them a sufficiently warlike appearance. Most of them were veterans of the three recent wars, and they marched in vigorous, even step. We headed for Iutch-Bunar, the working-class district of Sofia and the stronghold of the Communist Party.

As we moved through the prosperous section of town, a few bystanders cheered; others looked on sullenly. This army of peasants which frightened the rich might expect an even more hostile reception from the proletariat. Nevertheless, the men were in high spirits and sang as they marched.

As we neared the working-class district we split up, and each battalion took a different route, with the understanding that in an hour the entire force would meet in the outskirts of the city near my old home, the prison. The first battalion proceeded down Nishka Street, the main artery of Iutch-Bunar, with myself at the head. Rumors of the approach of a peasant guard had already reached the section. Doors were closed and the streets almost deserted. A handful of youngsters ran after us and swung into step with the music.

To demonstrate our peaceful intentions, I allowed a ten-year-old urchin to climb up on the saddle with me. He shouted with glee. Then I ordered the men to sing their songs in chorus. From time to time I checked my horse and moved aside, allowing the battalion to pass in review before me, then galloped to the head of the column. This gave me an opportunity to observe what was going on among the people. Doors and windows opened cautiously and bewildered faces peeped out as the troops passed by.

The four columns converged at the appointed spot, an open field within sight of the prison, where I ordered the men to break ranks. They stacked their rifles in pyramids and stood around in small groups. Meanwhile a crowd of curious workers had begun to gather. I approached a railway fireman and offered him a cigarette.

"Are you striking?"

"Yes, Colonel."

"I'm not a colonel, I'm a civilian like yourself. Tell me the truth; why are you on strike?"

"For better pay. We don't get enough to live on."

"Why didn't your organization ask the government for wage increases instead of striking without warning?"

"That's not my affair; it's up to the committee."

The crowd grew rapidly. When about two thousand spectators had gathered, I ordered my men to assemble in formation and addressed them. Although I spoke to the peasant soldiers, my words were really intended for the workers. I said that the government stood ready to double the wages of its employees on the railways and in the postal service, but that it would not permit the Communists to exploit labor grievances for their own purposes. Every attempt to use force, I warned, would be met by force, and until the strike ended the government would consider no demands. The crowd reacted in various ways. Some listened in silence; many muttered and grumbled; others shouted, "Down with the Communists! They've been deceiving us!" The Communists realized that Stamboliski had the peasants behind him, and the people saw that his authority did not depend upon gendarmes and police.

The government had not only the Communists to contend with. On the night of December 24 it had arrested several hundred persons, including all members of the Radoslavov cabinet still in Bulgaria, more than a hundred former deputies who had supported King Ferdinand, a number of war speculators, and many Macedonians who had been on the German pay roll. The Sobranje by an almost unanimous vote had adopted a special law to try these persons for their actions during the war.

The arrests were made by Captain Prutkin, now chief of the Sofia Police. Prutkin, a strange man, combined great abilities with equally great faults. The money he had made on contraband trade between Salonika and Varna he had lost by gambling in Russian rubles. Later we discovered that patriotism alone did not motivate his zeal as police chief. Most of those arrested were wealthy people from whom Prutkin extorted money by promising to set them free. For the moment, however, Stamboliski trusted him and gave him a free hand, making him virtual master of Sofia.

The general strike was petering out. Stamboliski ordered the arrest of the leading members of the Communist Central Committee—Kolarov, Georgi Dimitrov, Muletarov, and Lukanov—but only Muletarov was found and arrested. The others were in hiding. The strikers lost heart. Railway and post-office workers began to plead for their jobs. The government rehired them but only on an individual basis. By the end of January about half of them were back at work, and the others were returning as fast as they were accepted.

The failure of the strike dealt a severe blow to the Communist Party, especially because we had succeeded in restoring order without using violence.

Stamboliski said at the time, "A democratic government which derives its authority from the people has the right to defend the people's liberty by extreme measures. But it must never employ such measures except in case of absolute necessity."

The danger over, I sent for Nadejda, and we took an apartment in Sofia. One evening a woman of uncertain age knocked at our door and presented herself as Liuba Dimitrov.

"I'm the wife of Deputy Georgi Dimitrov," she began in a choked voice. "My husband suffers from tuberculosis. If he is arrested, his condition will become worse. He's now forced to remain in hiding and almost never gets out into the fresh air."

"What can I do?"

"Ask the government to cancel the order for his arrest. You've won; you don't need him."

Stamboliski smiled when I told him of Mme. Dimitrov's visit, but promised that the order would be rescinded. "Don't tell that to his wife," he added. "Tell her Dimitrov must call on you in person before the charges against him are dropped."

I followed the Prime Minister's instructions. Liuba Dimitrov suspected a trap. "You promise that he won't be arrested when he leaves your house?"

"Yes."

The next evening Georgi Dimitrov came with his wife. She remained with Nadejda in the living room while he and I had coffee in my study.

"Well, I've come," he said after an awkward pause.

"To ask that the order for your arrest be rescinded?"

He flushed. "I ask for nothing. I'm a deputy and as such I'm immune. Only parliament can—"

"So you want nothing? That's fine. We can chat a bit. After all, the defeated deserve mercy."

Dimitrov smiled sardonically. "This is only the first skirmish."

"If there is to be a second, so much the worse for you," I answered. "In the meantime we shall be generous; all the more so because you have failed so completely. We don't consider you dangerous. Tomorrow the government will issue the necessary decree."

"Why did you force me to come to you?"

"Because you sent your wife in your place."

"I didn't send her; she came without my knowledge," he said angrily.

I felt embarrassed. "Well, let's not quarrel about it. In any case, you're free."

He showed no sign of pleasure, rose, and called his wife, who was tense with anxiety as she entered the room.

"Your husband is free," I said.

[131]

Her face lighted up with joy, but her husband's glance restrained her from expressing her thanks.

As he coldly extended his hand, I said, "I know that if you had won, our fate would have been quite different."

Dimitrov smiled wryly.

I N RECOGNITION OF my services in Paris during the peace negotiations, Foreign Minister Madjarov informed me, I had been designated a plenipotentiary minister. With the appointment went a doubtful pleasure—the next morning, March 3, 1920, I would meet King Boris. I looked forward with some misgiving to an audience with the son of Ferdinand of Saxe-Coburg-Gotha; but Stamboliski reassured me.

"Boris is all right," he said. "He sympathizes with our ideas, loves Bulgaria, and is a very lonely and unhappy boy."

Much as I loved and respected Stamboliski, I knew that he often judged people far too charitably. Besides, I already knew a great deal about the King's "loneliness."

When he mounted the throne, Boris was a neglected and embittered young man of twenty-four, nursing resentful childhood memories of beatings by his stern father. Freed at last from paternal restraint, he began a career of dissipation. From his father he had inherited a passion for drink, but while Ferdinand drank cognac alone in the style of a *grand seigneur,* his son surrounded himself with sybaritic boon companions and a swiftly changing bevy of pretty women. The palace became the scene of bacchanals attended by all sorts of women—wives of prominent industrialists, actresses, artists' models. None of these affairs led to an enduring attachment, and the King remained a lonely young man.

King Boris received me in the Red Salon, so called because its walls were hung with red silk. He was in civilian dress and seemed modest, even shy. He greeted me cordially, and said he hoped we could collaborate for many years. In accordance with Bulgarian custom, coffee and jelly were served. The King questioned me at some length about my work in Paris, in a manner which showed surprising knowledge. Later I was to learn that Boris had mastered a technique all his own of appearing well informed on any subject he expected to discuss. Several times during the audience he spoke of his great affection for Stamboliski.

It was not easy to fathom this young man. His smile was warm, ingratiating, and Italian—from his mother, Princess Marie Louise of Bourbon-Parma. But he had cold, blue, lusterless German eyes, and his voice was nasal and insinuating. I left with the feeling that, as the French say, he was "too polite to be honest," and that he could be trusted least of all by the leader of the Peasant Party. When I told Stamboliski this, he accused me of permitting my dislike for King Ferdinand to prejudice me against Ferdinand's son.

As a plenipotentiary minister attached to the Foreign Office, I had not only a multitude of duties, but also a host of friends and relatives whose very existence I had not previously suspected. They all sought favors, usually of a kind I would not have granted even had I been able to. From morning until night petitioners besieged my home and office. Unless I took extreme measures, I soon realized, I would be unable to do any work. I therefore made it a rule to receive only written petitions, through my secretary, who passed on to me the handful meriting attention.

I also found new enemies. In a Communist weekly an article by one Harlakov appeared:

> Kosta Todorov was seized behind the Bulgarian front in 1916 as a French spy. He was saved from the firing squad because his father was a colonel with enough money to influence the military authorities. But that outrage was not enough. Now . . . as a reward for his espionage activities he receives the title of plenipotentiary minister of the King."

One of my duties in the Foreign Office was to handle the press censorship which still survived from war days. I summoned the Sofia editors and journalists and announced:

"As long as I'm in charge of censorship there won't be any. I ask only one thing: In your articles on foreign affairs, be careful not to irritate the Allies. Remember that Bulgaria is still on probation."

Nevertheless, one of my subordinates sent me the proofs of Harlakov's next attack on me, with the recommendation that it be banned. I ordered him to let it pass. But my father was less tolerant. Meeting Harlakov on the street, he slapped his face.

The Peasant Party had come to power solidly backed by the peasant masses but with the support of very few intellectuals. Stamboliski was besieged by a horde of hungry and ambitious office seekers—semi-intellectuals without scruples or political convictions, distinguished only by vulgarity and greed. They took over the thousands of minor administrative positions and formed a bureaucracy no better than the one they had succeeded.

What Stamboliski wanted was a real democracy, not only political but economic. That meant liberating the peasants from the control of the middlemen and usurers who had been robbing them for years. Through the co-operatives he expected to free them permanently from their dependence on speculators in farm products. He was also eager to teach them to fill administrative posts. But his generous nature handicapped him; he was the last to discover who was an adventurer and who a charlatan. And our comrade of the Sofia prison, Captain Prutkin, was one of the worst. As chief of the Sofia police, he continued to extort bribes from prisoners by promising to get them released. Stamboliski received many complaints, but as long as no one produced conclusive proof he refused to act. At last Muraviev, chief of the political police, made a thorough investigation and compiled documentary evidence of Prutkin's malfeasance. The inquiry revealed that Prutkin had even gone so far as to plant a time bomb in the Odeon Theatre in an effort to kill a number of his political enemies. Fortunately the bomb did not go off. When evidence of this attempt was laid before Stamboliski, he at last dismissed Prutkin.

In the new elections of April 12, 1920, the Peasant Party elected 110 deputies, a narrow majority but enough to govern alone. Flushed with success, it then resorted to the old Bulgarian custom of cutting down the total of opposition seats by finding technical violations of the election law. A few seats were lopped off each opposition party in turn, from the Communists to the extreme right, leaving Stamboliski with a more comfortable majority but impairing the moral prestige of the Peasant movement.

In the new cabinet, Premier Stamboliski succeeded Madjarov as Foreign Minister and I became Undersecretary of Foreign Affairs. Stamboliski, occupied with directing the general political course of the country, left me with almost unhampered authority in conducting the business of the Foreign Office. In my new position I understood for the first time the full implications of Bulgaria's defeat. Several governments had reopened their legations in Sofia; others still had temporary missions there. Almost every day, Allied diplomats came to me with impossible demands, usually presented as ultimatums.

They interfered scandalously with internal affairs and intervened in behalf of Bulgarian subjects engaged with them in contraband trade and speculation. The army of occupation had behaved with utmost decorum; the diplomatic representatives acted like proconsuls. They demanded the privilege of importing luxuries duty free and even issued their own passports to protect Bulgarian subjects. I fought these practices with all my might, and got myself thoroughly disliked by the diplomatic corps.

When they applied pressure, I reminded them that although Bulgaria had signed severe peace terms, it had not granted the Allies extraterritorial rights. When three freight cars loaded with champagne arrived at the Sofia station, earmarked for the "private use" of the French legation, I seized the shipment as contraband. Even the French Minister, M. Georges Picot, couldn't argue with a straight face that his staff could consume three carloads of champagne.

I told Stamboliski that I found it hard to handle these people tactfully and suggested that it might be better to find someone else for my job before I really lost my temper. He smiled good-naturedly and said, "Put up with them a little longer. I'll soon send you abroad."

Meanwhile the government was itself engaged in what might be called patriotic contraband trade. An Interallied Military Commission in Sofia, headed by the French General de Fourtou, had charge of locating, dismantling, and selling as scrap the war material Bulgaria was required to surrender under the peace treaty. Much of this material, especially artillery, was never dismantled. Businessmen acting as dummies bought it in sound condition and turned it over to the army. Within a short time enough equipment to put eight divisions on a war footing was cached in mountain shelters. But General de Fourtou had his price. He pocketed several million leva and reported to Paris that Bulgaria was completely disarmed. It took the French government until 1934 to catch up with him; he was arrested for his part in the Stavisky swindle.

The French representatives in Sofia not only permitted the Bulgarian army to buy back its own guns; they also closed their eyes to the close collaboration of former Bulgarian army officers with Kemal Pasha. The reduction of the army under the Treaty of Neuilly had thrown out of their jobs thousands of ambitious officers who had been accustomed to an important place in the life of the country. The treaty thus created a dangerous source of internal infection, for these men, deprived of their profession and status, bitterly opposed the government's efforts to fulfill its obligations and especially its conciliatory attitude toward Yugoslavia. For the moment, the struggle of the Turks against the Greeks afforded an outlet for their discontent. Many of them took part in the rebellion headed by Taiar Bey in eastern Thrace, after the transfer of that territory from Turkey to Greece.

The French government was backing Kemal Pasha against the Greeks and sending him guns through Syria. In this case French interest coincided with Bulgarian sentiment—Greek intransigence toward both Bulgaria and Turkey had ranged Bulgarian public opinion on the side of the Turks. The British, on the other hand, were supporting the Greeks. In the Interallied Commission was a Major of the British Intelligence Service, who spoke Russian and Bulgarian and had been a British agent in Russia under the Czarist regime. His chief concern, however, was not our artillery, but our relations with the Turks. Having large sums of money at his disposal and a network of agents throughout the country, he obtained accurate information on the movements of Kemal's representatives who came to Bulgaria to confer with Bulgarian officers. Often he gave their names and addresses to the police and demanded their arrest. The police were never able to "find" them.

His continual interference in our affairs so irritated everyone that we hired an attractive Russian refugee to engage in counterespionage at the Major's expense. Within a short time she became his mistress and supplied us with reports on all his activities. On one occasion we learned that he was going to Plovdiv in southern Bulgaria to force the local police to arrest certain members of Kemal's staff whom his agents had tracked down. We ordered the Plovdiv chief of police to arrange a proper reception. When the Major, in civilian clothes, arrived in Plovdiv and went to the local café, a pleasant young man who spoke English began a conversation, had several drinks with him, and then picked a fight. During the scuffle he stole the Major's identification papers. At the right moment the police broke in and arrested both men. Protests were vain; the Major couldn't establish his identity. He was beaten up and kept in jail overnight. Returning to Sofia, he protested against his outrageous treatment in Plovdiv. The government expressed regret and promised to punish the culprits.

About two weeks later, his Russian mistress appeared with a suitcaseful of documents and announced she had enough. Her final haul included virtually the complete files of the unfortunate Major. He left the country in a few days, not stopping to bid us farewell.

The third of the Allied Powers, Italy, had not forgotten the motive prompting the order to its officers to make friends with the Bulgarians during the military occupation. One day Baron Aliotti, the Italian envoy, called on me for a confidential talk. He began by explaining that Italy felt dissatisfied with the conduct of the Kingdom of Serbs, Croats, and Slovenes and with the special favors which Great Britain, France, and the United States were granting the Serbs. He expatiated at length on Italy's right to the province of Dalmatia and added that Bulgarian and Italian interests now coincided. The Italian government, he said, recognized the justice of Bulgaria's claim to Macedonia. I expressed surprise at this, reminding him that at the peace conference Italy had agreed to Bulgaria's being shorn not only of Macedonia but also of Thrace and the Dobruja.

"Italy was in no position to resist the will of Clemenceau," explained Aliotti. "Now we must look ahead. An understanding between Italy and Bulgaria would serve the interests of both."

"What do you suggest?"

The Baron rose. "In the name of my government," he intoned, "I propose a secret military alliance for the purpose of returning to Italy the Adriatic provinces which are historically hers and for the return of Macedonia to Bulgaria."

After a brief silence I answered, "You understand, of course, that I can't give an immediate reply to such an important proposal. I must place it before the Prime Minister."

"I understand," replied Aliotti. "For that reason I should like an audience with M. Stamboliski."

That evening I reported the conversation to Stamboliski. The Peasant leader had a clearly defined foreign policy, the keystone of which was the closest possible understanding with the Kingdom of Serbs, Croats, and Slovenes, with a view to ultimate Balkan solidarity. His aim was a Yugoslav-Bulgarian union within a free Balkan federation. Baron Aliotti's proposal was repugnant to everything in which he believed, but diplomatic courtesy demanded that he grant the audience.

Two days later, when the Prime Minister received the Italian envoy, I acted as interpreter. When Aliotti repeated his offer of a secret military alliance, Stamboliski said, "Tell this Italian musician that because of similar seductive melodies, Bulgaria entered the war in 1915 and lost everything."

I translated: "The Premier is deeply touched by the proposals of the Italian government, but inasmuch as Bulgaria is bound by a treaty which forbids all secret commitments, we unfortunately cannot avail ourselves of this gracious offer."

Aliotti frowned. "Is this a rejection?"

"Certainly!" Stamboliski answered in Bulgarian.

I translated: "To our great regret, yes."

Baron Aliotti rose and departed. Three weeks later he left for Rome.

This Italian offer, made in June, 1920, more than two years before Mussolini came to power, was the first clear indication of an anti-Yugoslav policy on the part of Italy. Whether it reflected the official line of the Nitti government, however, was open to some doubt. When I met Nitti as an exile in Paris, he assured me that for years a permanent clique inside the Italian Foreign Office had been pursuing its own objectives with little regard to government policy.

Seeing that diplomacy was futile in trying to cope with abuses by the foreign representatives, I decided to call for a showdown. On my wedding anniversary I invited the members of the diplomatic corps, with their wives, to a dinner in the salon of the Ministry of Foreign Affairs. The meal was lavish, with wine from the private cellars of King Boris. At the table were Baron Aliotti; Collins, the British chargé d'affaires; Romero y Dusmet, Spanish envoy and dean of the Sofia diplomatic corps; Picot, the French minister, and a number of others. Of the leading diplomats, only Collins and Wilson, the American Minister, could dine with clear consciences. They had no hand in contraband trade.

Before dessert was served, I rose to propose a toast. In the name of the government I extended my good wishes to all the nations represented at the table and spoke of the solidarity of the new Europe in its determination to preserve peace and promote mutual understanding. Then I said:

"I hope I shall not occupy my present post much longer, and in all probability I shall soon part with you. But as long as I am here, I wish to make clear what I conceive to be the correct relations between us. Bulgaria is a defeated country. We have signed a severe peace treaty and we intend to live up to it faithfully. Therefore, I can repeat here what I have several times told each of you separately.

"Every lawful demand will meet with my full co-operation. Lately, however, a practice has arisen which degrades not only Bulgaria but also those countries whose representatives engage in it. Contraband trade has been conducted under cover of diplomatic immunity, and foreign passports have been illegally issued to Bulgarian subjects. I take advantage of this occasion to announce that in the future all contraband will be confiscated. Yesterday, with the consent of the Prime Minister, I ordered the arrest of all Bulgarian subjects carrying foreign passports. Furthermore, I have instructed the Bulgarian delegate in Paris to transmit a note of protest to the Conference of Ambassadors of the great powers—a note pointing out a number of deplorable facts which complicate the friendly relations between Bulgaria and the Allies."

I sat down amid the stony silence of my guests.

When dessert was served, M. Picot looked at the excellent fruit pastry and asked, "Is this to sweeten the bitter pill?"

The next day, Romero y Dusmet, as dean of the diplomatic corps, called on Stamboliski to protest against the insult, adding that his colleagues would find it difficult to work with me in the future.

"It's very hard to handle Todorov," apologized Stamboliski. "He doesn't always obey me. But he'll soon be sent abroad."

Romero y Dusmet raised his hands imploringly.

"Please don't send him to Spain!"

S PAIN WAS SPARED. In September, 1920, Stamboliski sent me abroad on an unofficial mission. On the pretext of inspecting our legations, I was to visit Vienna, Budapest, and Berlin and sound out the defeated governments on their methods of seeking legal changes in the peace terms. But when I reached Vienna, I received a telegram ordering me to return to Sofia; Stamboliski had become fearful lest my mission arouse Allied suspicions. In Vienna I had only time to learn that the Reparations Commission, after receiving enormous gifts of money and rare works of art, had reported that Austria was in no position to pay.

Meanwhile Stamboliski had proposed me as Minister to Yugoslavia, and Belgrade had signified its approval. So, on October 3, once more I left Sofia, this time for the Yugoslav capital. My instructions were to work persistently for close relations between the two countries.

The Yugoslav Prime Minister, Milenko Vesnich, and the Minister of Foreign Affairs, Dr. Ante Trumbich, a Croat from Dalmatia, received me cordially. But the press was hostile. Articles dealing with my arrival rehashed all the crimes committed by the Radoslavov government and the *komitajis* during the occupation of eastern Serbia. Moreover, when the Yugoslav parliament ratified the peace treaty with Bulgaria, not long after my arrival, Toma Popovich, a deputy from the Serbian provinces Bulgaria had occupied during the war, turned toward the diplomatic gallery where I sat, and shouted:

"The presence of a representative of the people who were murdering Serbian citizens a short time ago is an insult to this House. I think he should be shot down in the street."

Premier Vesnich at once arose and angrily replied, "Such views are a disgrace to the Serbian people. I ask the Bulgarian Minister to accept my sincere apologies."

In this stormy atmosphere I had to work for an alliance between my country and Yugoslavia. I had also to contend with the whole course of Belgrade's foreign policy. In August of that year Yugoslavia and Czechoslovakia had signed a defensive pact against a possible Hungarian attack. Later, on April 23, 1921, Czechoslovakia and Rumania concluded an agreement and on June 7 Yugoslavia and Rumania signed a similar treaty.

Thus were forged the three links of the Little Entente, whose purpose was to safeguard the borders of Czechoslovakia, Yugoslavia, and Rumania as defined in the peace treaties. But the treaties were those of St.-Germain,

Trianon, and Neuilly. Thus the Little Entente shortsightedly guaranteed its members only against attack from Hungary, Austria, or Bulgaria— three small states with insignificant armies and representing no real danger. It did not insure Czechoslovakia against a German attack, Yugoslavia against an Italian attack or Rumania against a Russian attack. Despite its publicity as the bulwark of security in central Europe, its practical importance seemed to me negligible, and I so advised my government.

My immediate difficulties in Yugoslavia, however, arose not from general differences in foreign policy but from direct clashes of interest between the two states. There was the problem of Bulgarian prisoners. Although France and Britain had released Bulgarian prisoners of war, Yugoslavia was still holding twenty thousand. Another and thornier problem was a list, prepared in Paris, of more than six hundred Bulgarians accused of crimes in occupied Serbian territory. It was based on reports of the Serbian authorities, but along with real culprits it included many innocent people, often through confusion of names. Under the Treaty of Neuilly, the Bulgarian government had to bring these people to trial, but it naturally acted slowly and unwillingly. Indeed, only one man was ever tried—Major Kulchin, charged with the murder of seventeen civilians in Nish, was convicted and hanged. A general about to be arrested on similar charges had shot himself. What was worse, the ringleaders—the Macedonian chiefs Todor Alexandrov, General Alexander Protoguerov, and Lefterov—had escaped from prison in Sofia by bribing the authorities.

Belgrade accused the Bulgarian government of insincerity, and my attempts to talk of the future met with cold silence. Although able to obtain the release of the Bulgarian prisoners, I got no sympathy for my plea that the Yugoslav government forego the occupation of Tsaribrod and Bosiljgrad in the interest of a future alliance between the two countries. In December, less than three months after my arrival in Belgrade, Serbian troops marched into these territories.

But the greatest difficulty, and one foreshadowing serious trouble for the Stamboliski government, was the formation of a new IMRO under the fugitives Alexandrov and Protoguerov. Into this organization flocked all the unemployed professional Macedonian revolutionists. From their secret strongholds in the region of Petrich, in that small part of Macedonia which remained Bulgarian, Alexandrov and Protoguerov began sending armed *chetas* to raid Serbian Macedonia, thus further embittering relations between the two countries. Worst of all, those higher Bulgarian army officers inimical to the government sympathized with the Macedonians, and the Bulgarian frontier guards permitted the guerrilla bands to cross unchallenged into Yugoslav territory.

[141]

In the latter part of October, 1920, Stamboliski left for the leading capitals—Rome, Paris, London—"to break the ice hemming in Bulgaria" through talks with the government leaders. Late in December he reached Prague, where he summoned a conference of the Bulgarian Ministers to Vienna, Budapest, Belgrade, and Berlin. During his journey our envoys in Berlin and Budapest had publicly expressed anti-Allied sentiments and advocated revision of the peace treaties. Stamboliski at once dismissed them.

While we were in Prague, President Thomas Masaryk gave a dinner in Stamboliski's honor in the Hrcani Castle, and I had the opportunity to meet the great democratic leader who had devoted his whole life to the struggle for freedom of the Czechs and Slovaks. He spoke with reserve and advised us to reach an understanding with Yugoslavia, promising that his government would use its influence with Belgrade to promote it. Foreign Minister Eduard Benes echoed Masaryk's advice, arranged a ball in Stamboliski's honor, and took us to a performance of Smetana's *Bartered Bride*.

Prague had a special beauty, with its medieval castles, Gothic cathedrals, and small Romanesque and baroque churches. On the Charles IV Bridge, above the frozen Moldau, stood statues of the saints, kings, priests, and knights who were the heroes of Czech history. After three hundred years of bondage, Prague was free. The two-year-old Czechoslovak Republic was an excellently administered state, scrupulously respecting the civil rights of the people, including the German minority which had its representatives in parliament, schools, and theaters, and its own university. Lying in the very center of Europe, the little country was important in international politics. And its isolation among hostile neighbors—Germany, Austria, Hungary—inexorably dictated its political course: with France and her Balkan allies against any revision of the peace treaties.

While in Prague, on December 29, I received word from Belgrade that Nadejda had given birth to a son. To celebrate the joyous occasion, I gave a banquet that evening at the Hotel Passage to which I invited Stamboliski and the Russian revolutionary refugees, among whom were Alexander Kerensky, my Foreign Legion comrade Vladimir Lebedev, and Vladimir Zenzinov, a leader of the Social Revolutionary Party and formerly a key member of its Terrorist Brigade. These representatives of the Russian Revolution appealed strongly to Stamboliski because of their sympathy with the peasants, as distinguished from the Bolsheviks with their "proletarian" ideology.

"I was in London not long ago," he told them, "and Lloyd George— who, by the way, presented me with a prize pig for my farm in Bulgaria —advised me to visit Manchester to inspect the factories. I went through dozens of great plants where I saw old workers who had been going through the same mechanical motions for twenty years. I sympathize with the workers, but can people accustomed to nothing but mechanical work be expected to reason wisely and direct the affairs of a nation?

"The mystic cult of the 'proletariat' is the most dangerous illusion in the world. I want freedom for the workers, but I don't believe in their ability to govern. In the name of the 'proletariat,' clever politicians will always run the show while the workers themselves continue for another twenty or thirty years to turn screws. With peasants it's different. Each peasant is an encyclopedia in himself. He understands the life of animals and plants, knows a little astronomy, tills the land, breeds animals, builds and repairs his own wagon, and predicts the weather better than any meteorological station. In the peasant are the seeds of the fully developed human personality. He needs only organization and more knowledge."

Stamboliski's trip put an end to Bulgaria's isolation. Although no immediate practical results could be expected, it gave to our policy the definite line of friendship with the western democracies. In Paris and London Stamboliski had proposed Bulgaria's admission to the League of Nations at the approaching autumn session, for he had great hopes of the League as an instrument of peace.

Working with our Balkan neighbors for a lasting peace, or even a temporary one, was uphill work. "Count Sforza, the Italian Minister of Foreign Affairs," Stamboliski told me, "understands the necessity for collaboration between Yugoslavia and Bulgaria, although the Consulta and nationalist circles keep intriguing against Yugoslavia and trying through flirtation with Bulgaria to wring concessions on the Adriatic from the Yugoslav government. France also favors Yugoslav-Bulgarian collaboration, but Lloyd George, despite his friendly reception, gave me to understand that our policy savors of Pan-Slavism, which the British always oppose."

When I explained my difficulties in Belgrade, he counseled patience. "I didn't expect immediate success. We'll break down Belgrade's hostility by demonstrating our good faith. The course of events will show the Yugoslavs that my policy is not only useful to them, but necessary."

When Nikola Pashich returned from Paris, I called on him at his home. The old statesman who had directed Serbia's policy during so many crises and had finally succeeded in realizing all its national ambitions appeared reasonable and well-disposed toward me; yet I detected an undertone of stubbornness.

The Serbian people worshiped Pashich as the father of their freedom. In his youth he had known Bakunin, the great Russian anarchist, in Switzerland and had later introduced elements of Russian revolutionary idealism into Serbian politics. Under the Obrenovich dynasty he fought wholeheartedly for civil liberty and became virtually a republican. Sentenced to death in 1883 for his part in a peasant insurrection, he fled to Bulgaria where, as a Pan-Slavist who advocated close friendship between Serbia and Bulgaria, he was well received and later employed in the Ministry of Public Works. During the Serbo-Bulgarian War of 1885, Pashich opposed King Milan of Serbia. The King's abdication in 1889 ended his exile and he returned to Belgrade.

Two years later the former refugee from execution became Prime Minister under King Alexander Obrenovich; but his attitude toward the dynasty never changed. Once he even served a brief prison term for *lèse-majesté*. After King Alexander and his wife, Draga, were assassinated and Peter Karadjordjevich became King in 1903, Pashich, as leader of the Radical Party, became the outstanding political figure in Serbia. He established a parliamentary regime, pursued a strong pro-Russian policy, and prepared the ground for a Balkan alliance. He headed the Serbian delegation at the peace conference in 1919 and was Prime Minister of Yugoslavia for most of the time from December, 1920, until his death in 1926.

A keenly practical man of few words, he often feigned naïveté. When I reminded him of his pro-Bulgarian policy in the past, his bright blue eyes twinkled. "All my enemies attack me for it," he said. "I haven't changed much in that respect, but it's still too soon for closer relations. We must be patient."

When Prince Regent Alexander granted me an audience shortly before the death of his aged father, King Peter, I again raised the question of Yugoslav-Bulgarian collaboration. The Prince Regent, who wore the Bulgarian Order of St. Alexander for the occasion, appeared much more receptive than any of the politicians. He was then a man of thirty-three, with extraordinarily expressive black eyes which could change swiftly from severity to velvety softness. His features were sharp, his figure slim and vibrant, and his unusually white teeth made his smile dazzling.

"What does Pashich thing?" he asked.

I reported my two rather unsatisfactory conversations with the Prime Minister. Alexander sighed. "Pashich has done a great deal for the country, but he's an old man now."

I detected a note of irritation in his voice. When we parted he said, "You may count on my help in your mission. And I'm not saying this out of mere diplomatic politeness."

Our legation in Belgrade occupied a spacious sixteen-room house, and I kept it open to all friends and acquaintances, to diplomats, and to Bulgarian subjects traveling through Yugoslavia. Seldom did fewer than ten persons sit down at my table. Twice a month I held diplomatic receptions, for which I ordered the best wines from France and engaged musicians and singers of the Belgrade opera. All the legations entertained well, and in the somewhat provincial atmosphere of Belgrade these parties were the main social attraction. The members of the diplomatic corps mingled on very friendly terms.

The diplomats I met were distinguished neither by great intelligence nor by any great capacity for work. Men of the world, they were accustomed to rise late in the morning and to spend most of their time in purely social engagements, making not the slightest effort to understand the country to which they were accredited. To me such understanding seemed an essential part of a diplomat's duty, and I demanded that the members of my staff become acquainted with Yugoslavia. To insure it, I assigned them special studies in Yugoslav politics and economy and required written reports. In a few months I had at my disposal material covering every aspect of Yugoslav life.

The French Minister, Clément Simon, who became my good friend, was exceptional among his colleagues in knowing the country very well. But when he left for a long vacation just before a general election, the first secretary of the legation, M. de Lens, who had been made chargé d'affaires, came to me.

"Mr. Minister," he said, "my chief, M. Simon, has often told me that you're his best friend in Belgrade and also a good friend of France. He has gone to Paris, and the elections are coming. This is my second year in this country, but I confess I haven't followed its politics. Now the Quai d'Orsay wants a report predicting the probable outcome of the election. What can I say? I don't even know the names of the parties. I asked my British colleague, but he doesn't know any more than I do. For God's sake, help me."

And so the envoy of defeated Bulgaria had to explain Yugoslav politics to a representative of Yugoslavia's ally.

There were three main political currents in Yugoslavia: the Serbian, represented by Belgrade politicians of the old school; the federalist, backed by the majority of the Croats and some Slovenes and the Yugoslav, which aimed at centralism. The Socialist Party was small; the Communist movement fairly strong.

The struggle between Serbs and Croats strained the political structure of the new state. The line dividing the two peoples is elusive: both are Slavic, speaking one language, Serbo-Croatian. The father of Serbian literature, Vuk Stefavonivch Karajich, looked upon the Croats as Serbian Catholics; and Ante Starchevich, patron saint of Croat nationalism, spoke of the Serbs as Croats of the Greek Orthodox faith. Culturally, history has separated the two peoples. The Croats lost their independence to Hungary 800 years ago and later became part of the Austro-Hungarian Empire, within which they were permitted to keep their own language and a parliament in Zagreb which decided local financial questions. As part of a European empire, they naturally adopted European culture. The Serbs, like all Balkan peoples, came under Byzantine influence during the Middle Ages, after which they endured Turkish oppression for four centuries until they won their independence in the revolt which began in 1804 under the leadership of Black George Petrovich, founder of the Karadjordjevich dynasty. Since then they have gone through an endless series of wars and internal upheavals, but have always kept their independence and their limited but indigenous culture. Whereas the Serbs remained a peasant people without profound class differences, the Croats had their social hierarchy—an aristocracy mainly of bureaucratic origin, a middle class which held titles in high regard, and a peasantry which differed little from that of Serbia.

Dr. Voja Marinkovich, the able Serbian statesman who later became Premier, explained this cultural cleavage with the following parable:

"Imagine two brothers born in the same village. One goes to the city, where he becomes a butler in a rich home. The other remains to till the ancestral land. Many years later there is a revolution. The aristocratic home is destroyed, and the butler returns to his native village to live with his brother. He brings with him different customs, habits, and attitudes. His peasant brother seems to him ignorant and boorish. The peasant, on the other hand, looks with distrust on this city creature whose elegant manners seem to him ridiculous."

"How will the misunderstanding end?"

"Necessity will force them to get along. Neither has anywhere else to go. The peasant will adopt some of the ways of his city brother, and the latter will finally understand that it's better to be master in one's own home than a lackey in another's palace."

This brotherly harmony seemed a long way off. The Serbs tactlessly emphasized their rights as victors in the war, while the Croats harped continually on their cultural superiority. One Yugoslav cartoonist, the son of a Serbian father and a Croatian mother, commented pithily on this stupidity in a cartoon depicting a man seized by a gendarme in the act of throwing himself from a bridge. "Let me die!" he cries. "I'm sick of the Serbian civilians who boast of their military prowess and the illiterate Croats who brag about their culture."

The Croats were even divided among themselves. The traditionally Austrophile aristocrats and upper bourgeoisie formed a small but compact opposition to Belgrade. The centralists under Svetozar Pribichevich were supported by that section of the intelligentsia which called itself Yugoslav and recognized no differences between Croats and Serbs.

The vast mass of Croats, however, followed Stepan Radich, leader of the Peasant Party, an able man who understood the peasants and was greatly loved by them. Radich's ideal was a peasant republic, although he did not in principle repudiate Croatian-Serbian co-operation within a democratic order allowing autonomy to Croatia.

The Slovenes were the most highly organized segment of the South Slavs. This small people had a high standard of living, excellent roads and schools, considerable industries, and popular mountain resorts. The entire peasantry was organized on a strongly co-operative basis under the leadership of Catholic priests. With their practical sense, the Slovenes never boycotted Belgrade as Radich did until 1925; therefore, they fared much better than the Croats in obtaining both government positions and large government loans for the development of their province. But it should also be added that their situation on the borders of Austria and Italy made them sensitive to foreign danger and therefore more amenable than the Croats to the idea of centralized government.

In short, the Croats are romantic; the Serbs are politicians; and the Slovenes are practical businessmen.

At Pashich's insistence the new Yugoslav constitution, adopted on June 28, 1921, provided for a strongly centralized government, despite the Croat demand for a federal system and local autonomy. The Croatian Peasant Party refused to recognize the constitution, and its deputies boycotted the Skupshtina (parliament).

On the very day the constitution was adopted by the Constituent Assembly—the seventh anniversary of Sarajevo—a bomb was hurled at the car of Prince Regent Alexander in Milosh the Great Street, not far from the temporary parliament building, which I had just left. Alexander escaped. The act, although laid to the Communist Party, was so inept that rumor called it a police job organized to furnish a pretext for liquidating the Communists. This "red" scare flourished not only in the Balkans, but also throughout Europe and the United States. In any case the Minister of the Interior, Drashkovich, introduced a bill to outlaw the Communist Party, then with fifty-eight deputies in the Skupshtina, because its influence among the disaffected minorities endangered the security of the state.

Drashkovich named his bill "For the Defense of the State." But before presenting it to the parliament, he showed it to the astute Pashich. When the veteran politician had read it, he remarked, "The bill is good, but not the title."

"Why?" asked Drashkovich.

"The people don't love the state," said Pashich, "they love freedom. Let the bill stand as it is, but let's call it 'For the Defense of Freedom.' "

Finally named "For the Defense of Order and Labor," the bill was passed and the Communist Party was outlawed. Drashkovich may have achieved the security of the state, but not his own; in July a young Communist student from Bosnia murdered him at a Croatian mountain resort.

E VERY REFORM IN government provokes the shrill
cry of either "Revolution!" or "Reaction!" A halfway measure cannot
even be a halfway measure, for no such thing exists—in the eyes of the
opposition. Our efforts at collaboration with Yugoslavia were labeled
"treasonable" by all opposition parties; our domestic policy was branded
"Bolshevist" by all but the Communists, who carried on their own
violent campaign against us as "lackeys of the *bourgeoisie*."

My duties were not limited to my diplomatic mission in Belgrade, for
Stamboliski often called me to Sofia—a ten-hour train trip—to help
explain his important reforms to the people. To counteract the hostility
of the press, we started a daily newspaper called *Pobeda (Victory)*, of
which I became chief editorial writer.

The first significant measure introduced by Stamboliski, provoking
the wrath of the opposition, established compulsory labor service—the
first of its kind in modern Europe. Young men were required to serve
one year; older men and women to serve ten days annually. With the
resultant labor corps the government built highways, railways, bridges,
and schools, introduced sewerage systems in provincial cities, and turned
swamps into fertile farm land. Both the left and the right accused
Stamboliski of introducing slave labor and of reverting to the old
Turkish practice of forcing the population to maintain strategic roads
for the benefit of the rulers. Actually, the labor service gave the people
a sense of working for the common welfare.

The second great reform was agrarian credit. The Agrarian Bank,
founded with peasant savings at the beginning of Bulgarian independence, was authorized under a new law to grant all types of credit—
personal credit, credit for improvements, and warrant credit (advances
on unsold crops) —without collateral and at a moderate rate of interest.
These credits had been available formerly only to rich peasants; the
middle and poor peasants had been obliged to borrow from commercial
bankers and speculators, who charged enormous interest. To the great
mass of peasants, therefore, the new Agrarian Bank Law came as a
blessing.

Even more important was a law to limit private holdings of land. The
stream of refugees pouring in from Thrace and the Dobruja, added to
the natural increase in population, had created a land shortage. The
new land law fixed a maximum holding of thirty hectares (about sixty-

five acres)—which a peasant and his family could cultivate without hired labor. Stamboliski hoped thereby to build a stable and self-respecting peasantry. The state expropriated the surplus lands of private owners, but with compensation; and these, plus the government and monastic holdings, constituted a land fund out of which landless peasants and refugees were supplied with farms under conditions similar to those fixed in the United States homestead laws.

A law to safeguard the independence of the peasants made minimum holdings of ten hectares inalienable, regardless of debts or mortgages. Other statutes giving co-operatives certain advantages over private enterprises stimulated the founding of co-operatives for the sale of farm products, thus eliminating many middlemen and enabling the peasants themselves to get the best possible prices for their produce.

Nor did the Peasant government ignore the workers. Raiko Daskalov, as Minister of Trade and Industry, pushed through the eight-hour day and compulsory insurance, whose cost was shared by the government, the workers, and the employers. Wages of railway workers and postal and telegraph employees were almost tripled, while the government economized by denying proportionate increases to its employees in the higher brackets.

The Bulgarian middle class, which owed its very existence to speculation in farm products, fought these measures tooth and nail. Actually the increase in the purchasing power of the peasants benefited honest trade and industry, while it removed the cause of dissatisfaction in the villages. The Socialists and Communists, on the other hand, considered the program reactionary because it lessened the effectiveness of their propaganda. In the elections of April, 1921, the Communists lost nineteen of their forty-nine seats; and they continued to lose ground with every new election until the end of the Peasant regime. In 1923, before Stamboliski's fall, they had only fourteen deputies.

Neither the left nor the right could get anywhere with direct attacks on Stamboliski's sound reforms, and they were astute enough to realize it. The left complained that the agrarian reforms had abnormally raised the prices of food for the workers. The right criticized the all too prevalent official graft, but its main line of attack was "patriotic." It accused Stamboliski of sacrificing the national interest in his efforts for an alliance with Yugoslavia, and even charged that he was ready to sacrifice the political independence of the Bulgarian people in his desire for ultimate union of the two countries. On this ground it found allies in King Boris and among the army officers, both those still in service and those discharged under the Treaty of Neuilly. Gradually a bloc coalesced for the forcible overthrow of the Peasant government. The peasants—nearly 90 per cent of the population—solidly backed Stamboliski. His enemies saw no other way to save the nation—for themselves—than by a coup d'état.

What boded ill for the government, the country, and Balkan peace was the hand in all this of the Italian Foreign Office. From the day Stamboliski turned down Baron Aliotti's offer of a secret military alliance against Yugoslavia, the Italians set out to destroy him. They had three major weapons—bribery, terror, and Bulgarian reparations. Among the Bulgarian opposition, whose hostility to Stamboliski they shared for very different reasons, they found bribable leaders, either sheer opportunists or men willing to take money to promote a cause in which they believed anyhow. And they subsidized the Macedonian leaders who had been in Germany's employ during the war. The Italian press constantly accused Stamboliski of accepting bribes from the Serbs and praised the Macedonians as the real Bulgarian patriots.

By the middle of 1921, the IMRO was in possession of large funds with which it supported numerous terrorist *chetas* and armed them with excellent weapons. From the reports of our agents in the Banco Commerciale d'Italia, which had opened that year in Sofia, we learned that the bank was paying out large sums to opposition lawyers "for legal services." The police arrested one of these lawyers, who confessed after considerable grilling that he handed over the money he received from the Italian bank to an unknown person representing Todor Alexandrov, the IMRO chief. The records of the Banco Commerciale d'Italia showed payments of nearly eight million leva within a few months "for legal services."

The continual forays of these Italian-armed terrorists into Serbian Macedonia served admirably the Italian purpose of maintaining tension between the two countries. They defeated every effort to accomplish my real mission to Yugoslavia. To all my assurances of Bulgarian good faith the answer was, "Then why do you permit Macedonian outrages on our territory?"

Of course we did not permit them. Stamboliski had given orders to the military authorities to keep a close watch on the border, but the officers of the frontier guard considered it their patriotic duty to allow the Macedonians to raid Serbia. In July, 1921, he finally decided to appoint Alexander Dimitrov, unquestionably the most energetic and clearheaded of his followers, Minister of War. Before taking up his new post, Dimitrov came to Belgrade to see Pashich and learn from him directly what he considered the main obstacle to a Bulgar-Yugoslav understanding.

Pashich received us with his usual cordiality, but spoke with marked reticence. To Dimitrov's direct question he answered, "It's difficult to talk of an understanding when every day our borders are violated and our soldiers killed."

"Very well," said Dimitrov. "I return tomorrow to Sofia to take up my duties as Minister of War. I give you my word that I'll put a stop to the Macedonian terror. May I assume that if I do, there will be no further obstacle to an understanding between us?"

Dimitrov at once took drastic measures. First he installed his trusted aid Koslovsky as police prefect of the Petrich region. Then he shook up the command of the garrison and frontier posts and ordered the entire area swept clean of Macedonian *chetniks*. He also ordered the arrest of Protoguerov and Alexandrov, the IMRO leaders. Protoguerov fled to Vienna and Alexandrov vanished. For a while it looked as if the new Minister of War had mastered the situation.

But these efforts to stamp out terror met with terror. In October, Koslovsky was assassinated by the IMRO. Thereupon the military authorities rounded up scores of armed terrorists near the frontiers of Serbian Macedonia and sent them under police guard to eastern Bulgaria. One *cheta,* however, resisted the troops and six *chetniks* were killed. The IMRO retaliated by sending Dimitrov a letter announcing that he was under sentence of death for his "unpatriotic" activities.

In allotting Bulgarian reparations the French and British, with that blindness which characterized their whole postwar policy, gave Italy a strategic position which it used to supplement bribery and terror in its attempts to drive a wedge between Bulgaria and Yugoslavia. For Italy was allotted 40 per cent, as against 40 per cent to Britain and France together and 20 per cent to the other Balkan states. The Italian member of the Reparations Commission in Sofia was therefore the most important of all. He was also the most eccentric. Collins, the British delegate, was sympathetic; the French delegate, Count de Cherizé, was correct; but the Italian delegate, Prince Livio Borghese, had peculiar ways with him, such as leaving a piece of buttered bread on his lawn until it was covered with ants and then eating it, ants and all. He billed the Bulgarian government for even the aspirin he bought in Sofia drugstores. And what was more outrageous than eccentric, he openly condemned Dimitrov's measures against the Macedonian terrorists—whom, of course, his government was subsidizing.

We paid all the commission's expenses, but tried to postpone reparations payments. These had been fixed at about 105 million gold francs ($21,000,000) a year, whereas our entire 1921 budget was only 150 million. We had to convince the Reparations Commission that payment was impossible, and Stamboliski placed the burden on my shoulders.

After many meetings with the commission, I succeeded in getting a one-year moratorium, until March, 1922, when the question was to be reconsidered. But our relief was short-lived. In August, 1921, the commission suddenly reversed its decision on the ground that our budget was balanced and our general economic situation favorable, and demanded immediate payment.

Upon investigation Stamboliski found that the instigator of this action was Prince Borghese, who had been conspiring with the opposition. Several opposition leaders had played their part in the intrigue by delivering to the commission a memorandum purporting to show that Bulgaria could pay. Knowing that the government could not meet the payments, they expected in that way to force Stamboliski's resignation and save themselves the risk of a coup d'état.

Stamboliski decided to send me to Paris to protest against the commission's interference in our internal affairs, while he would leave for Geneva. The sessions of the League of Nations were to begin in September, and it had already been agreed in London and Paris that Bulgaria would be admitted to the League.

On my arrival in Paris I was met by our envoy, General Mikhail Savov, who had been head of the Sofia Military Academy when I was a cadet. During the Balkan wars he had been commander in chief of the Bulgarian army. Knowing the General's weakness, I snapped sharply to attention before him and said, "General Savov, you have been advised of my mission. I have not come here to interfere with your functions, and I shan't take a step without your advice."

The General, who had been somewhat stiff at first, unbent at once. He was a man of sixty, of imposing appearance and bearing, whose voice always sounded like a command. Everyone in Bulgaria respected him, and he was very popular in French political circles.

We got right down to business. The chairman of the Reparations Commission in Paris, M. Dupuis, favored a moratorium, but had told Savov it would be necessary to appeal directly to President Millerand, who made full use of his prerogatives. An official audience was not desirable, however, M. Dupuis had said, and a secret meeting would have to be arranged.

"Tonight," General Savov concluded, "we dine with Millerand's secretary, M. Michel. Tomorrow we'll call on Berthelot."

At dinner, in a private room at the Grand Vautel, I explained the situation to M. Michel, blaming the Italians for what had happened. He promised that as soon as possible he would take us to the President "through the back door."

The next day, at the Quai d'Orsay, I explained to Berthelot the internal and international intrigues connected with Bulgarian reparations. I couldn't tell him of my coming talk with Millerand, because that was confidential. Berthelot took notes while I spoke. When I had finished he agreed to have *Le Temps* print a leading editorial advocating postponement of Bulgarian reparations on the ground that the Stamboliski government had proved its good faith and its will to peace.

A week later M. Michel led General Savov and myself into the Élysée Palace through a small door on the rue St.-Honoré. It was ten o'clock at night. We walked through endless corridors until we reached an enormous waiting room filled with paintings and furniture of the Louis Quinze period. M. Michel disappeared. Five minutes later we entered President Alexandre Millerand's office.

Millerand was tall, his handsome head framed in silver-gray hair, with black eyes under heavy brows, and a thick gray, smartly clipped mustache. He was noted as a great friend of the Serbs, and in explaining our situation I took care to stress once more Italy's use of the reparations question to prevent an understanding between Bulgaria and Yugoslavia. When he asked how the negotiations between Sofia and Belgrade were progressing, I didn't conceal our difficulties, but expressed my conviction that precisely because of the Italian intrigues an agreement between the two states was likely in the near future. He nodded approvingly.

"We're afraid to make Bulgaria a concession on reparations," he said, "because of the precedent it would establish for Germany."

I pointed out that Austrian reparations had already been canceled. He smiled.

"Yes, but Austria really can't pay. Bulgaria, on the other hand, according to the report I have received, is in excellent financial and economic condition."

"That's all relative. If we were to begin paying reparations the situation would become catastrophic at once. I don't believe France wants to pauperize the Bulgarian people. Bulgaria would then not only be unable to pay reparations but even her prewar debts to France."

"But you aren't paying prewar debts anyhow," said Millerand.

Anticipating this argument, I had asked Stamboliski for authority to negotiate terms for the payment of these old debts, which had been contracted for railway construction.

"My government has authorized me to arrange for regular payments on our prewar debts," I answered. "We don't want the small French bondholders, who relied on the word of the Bulgarian government, to lose their money."

Millerand was obviously pleased.

"We're ready," I went on, "to pay our honest debts, but we can't pay debts and reparations at the same time. And since no sanctions can be invoked against us for nonpayment of debts I shall be forced, if we don't get a moratorium on reparations, to express to the French bondholders the regret of the Bulgarian government."

Millerand wagged his head admiringly.

"I confess your government has found a very skillful formula." He rose, and we with him.

"Don't worry, young man, I'll give the necessary orders. Convey my regards to His Majesty King Boris and tell him Bulgaria has a worthy representative in General Savov. He has done much to improve our relations. My regards, too, to M. Stamboliski. When I met him in Paris last year, he impressed me greatly with his forthright character and common sense."

General Savov presssed my hand happily as we drove off. I suggested that he get in touch with the French owners of Bulgarian bonds and propose installment payments in French paper francs.

After learning from Berthelot that Bulgarian reparations had been postponed until June, 1922, I left Paris on September 20 and arrived in Sofia three days later. Stamboliski, who had returned from Geneva, was in high spirits because of Bulgaria's admission to the League of Nations and the temporary solution of the reparations question. He told me that King Boris expected me to report that evening.

The King welcomed me heartily, expressed his great satisfaction with the success of my mission, and kept me with him for dinner. The next morning, while I was shaving, there was a knock on my door and Colonel Kalfov, the King's adjutant, entered. I was in my pajamas and my face was covered with lather. Solemnly he stood before me and said,

"I have the pleasure of delivering to you the Order of St. Alexander, conferred by His Majesty Czar Boris for your services to the Fatherland."

And he handed me a red box. Astonished, I stood holding my shaving brush in one hand and the decoration in the other.

One evening in November, I dined with Alexander Dimitrov at his home.

"I'll soon be killed," he told me. "Kosta Tomov [then Minister of the Interior] has entered into relations with the Macedonians. When they threatened to kill him he agreed to work with them. He has come to me twice, asking me to give them a free hand. When I refused, he said, 'Do as you like. I value my own skin more than yours.' "

"Why doesn't Stamboliski throw him out?"

Dimitrov laughed sadly. "You know Stamboliski. He's busy with big projects. He's a prophet. He leads us to Canaan but we have to clear the way ourselves. I told him everything, but he answered, 'Tomov's a good lad.' I didn't press the matter because I didn't want to give the impression that I was worrying about my own hide."

As he filled our glasses with brandy he added earnestly, "God grant that my death may open Stamboliski's eyes to the danger he himself faces."

A few weeks later, on November 21, a telegram was handed me in the Belgrade Legation:

> WAR MINISTER DIMITROV ASSASSINATED IN AUTOMO-
> BILE ON ROAD TO KOZNITZA. CHAUFFEUR, SECRETARY,
> AND POLICE OFFICER ALSO KILLED. ATTACK STAGED
> BY TWELVE ARMED MEN LED BY VOIVODAS PANCHO
> MIKHAILOV,* IOVAN BRLO. COME TO SOFIA IMMEDI-
> ATELY.
>
> > STAMBOLISKI

I reached Sofia in time for my friend's funeral. Around his bier in the great Sviataya Nedelia Cathedral stood the ministers. The dead man's sallow face was fixed in a stern frown.

When Kosta Tomov kissed him I could not restrain myself. I grasped his arm. "Get out of here, Judas."

Tomov turned pale. "You'll pay for this," he whispered angrily.

The assassins were not caught because Tomov's police did not look for them.

*Pancho Mikhailov was killed in 1927. He is not to be confused with Vancho Mikhailov, later head of the IMRO.

I N 1922 THE grisly specter of economic crisis loomed over Europe. Inflation raged in Germany, Austria and Hungary and dislocated international trade and exchange. Hoping to work out a general European economic agreement, Lloyd George summoned an international conference at Genoa in April, to which virtually all the nations of Europe were invited. Here Soviet Russia, timid but determined, was to make its first appearance on the European diplomatic stage.

Genoa lay stretched out in her beauty under the warm April sun. The Via Garibaldi and the Via Balbi preserved all the magnificent splendor of the epoch when Genoa was queen of the seas and rich Genoese traders built their palaces and adorned them with splendid works of art. The conference sat in one of the most beautiful historic buildings in Italy, the Palazzo San Giorgio, once the meeting place of the aristocracy which ruled the medieval republic.

Our delegation, headed by Stamboliski and Finance Minister Tourlakov, with myself as chief of propaganda, was assigned to the Hotel Savoia in Nervi, a small town on the Italian Riviera. All the delegations except the British and French, which stayed at the Miramar in Genoa, were distributed among small resort towns near the city. The German delegates, headed by Chancellor Wirth and the brilliant Foreign Minister, Walther Rathenau, also were staying in Nervi. The Yugoslavs were in Rapallo. The Soviet delegation, headed by Chicherin, Rakovsky, and Krassin, was in Santa Margherita.

In the trains that took us to Genoa we met the Soviet delegates. Leonid Krassin, a tall, well-dressed man with a reddish beard, showed a thorough understanding of economic problems. In fact, it was said of him that under Bolshevism he continued to make as much money as he had before the war, when he represented the Siemens concern in St. Petersburg. For the Soviet Government, finding his knowledge and experience invaluable, paid him a fabulous salary.

Christian Rakovsky, then President of the Ukraine, had a clean-shaven, somewhat flabby face, like that of an aging actor. The son of a prosperous Bulgarian landowner of northern (Rumanian) Dobruja, he had studied medicine at the University of Grenoble. With his large allowance from home he had put his youthful socialism into practice by supporting a whole group of students. In France and Switzerland he had become acquainted with Russian revolutionists and begun writing for Russian radical periodicals. Later he became the leader of the Rumanian Socialist Party, opposed the war, and was imprisoned, to be liberated by Russian soldiers on the Moldavian front in 1917. Thus he found himself in the thick of the Russian Revolution. After the Bolshevik uprising he became President of the Soviet of People's Commissars of the Ukraine. His good breeding and his knowledge of languages made him a useful Soviet diplomat.

To Stamboliski he said disarmingly in his native tongue, "Let's talk together frankly, like fellow Bulgarians."

He insisted that Bulgaria could improve its international position only with the aid of Russia which, he said, was now growing strong and defending the countries wronged by the peace treaties. Then he asked, "When does Bulgaria intend to recognize the Soviet government?"

"When the great powers have done so," replied Stamboliski.

Georgi Chicherin, Soviet Foreign Commissar and head of the delegation, was about fifty, of medium height and slightly stooped, with a small beard which did not conceal his vague, ironical smile. This Bolshevik diplomat came from one of the oldest Russian families, listed in the supremely exclusive Sixth Book of the Russian Nobility. He was highly cultivated, and spoke French, English, Italian and German fluently. In his youth he had been a Czarist diplomat in Berlin and London, but had suffered a long nervous breakdown which left him incurably attached to liquor. Although a man of innate refinement, at the conference he spoke sharply, always emphasizing the Soviet Government's revolutionary approach to European problems.

Russia was an enigma, and hundreds of journalists crowded around the Soviet delegates to get sensational declarations. The women of high Genoese society waited for the Russians outside the gates of the palace, clamoring for autographs. The bolder ones asked for pictures, but Foreign Commissar Chicherin and his colleagues had none to give. The younger secretaries of the delegation took advantage of the occasion to carry on flirtations with the elegant Genoese ladies.

Rakovsky was especially popular with the journalists. Each evening at six they gathered around him in a private salon at the Miramar Hotel, where he aired the Soviet views on international affairs. A French journalist, Julien of the *Petit Parisien,* once asked him, "What's the difference between you and the diplomats of other countries?"

"We know how to use the same diplomatic phrases and wear the same evening clothes," answered Rakovsky, "but at any moment we can change to a red shirt and a worker's cap and deliver a revolutionary speech to the masses. That's something other diplomats can't do."

Lloyd George had chosen a good city. Nothing more congenial than Genoa in the spring could be imagined. Yet the negotiations did not progress, for the simple reason that every delegation had come to seek not a general solution of Europe's economic problems but a particular solution of its own. The defeated powers, including Bulgaria, came primarily to bring up the question of reparations. The states which had remained neutral in the war had no interest whatever in this question. Those which were concerned, especially France, had a single purpose—to prevent it from being raised.

Stamboliski and I called on Lloyd George, Louis Barthou, head of the French delegation, and the chief Italian delegates, Premier Facta and Foreign Minister Schanzer. In two months our moratorium would expire, and we were eager to set the stage for another postponement. Lloyd George advised us to see Sir Basil Blackett, the financial expert of the British delegation.

"By the way," he added, "I don't believe reparations will ever be collected, but unfortunately the French will prevent the conference from considering the question. Still"—his blue eyes twinkled—"that's what backstage is for. There anything can be discussed."

Lloyd George was right. All the real business at the conference was transacted behind the scenes. On the stage itself, in the hall of the Palazzo San Giorgio, the speeches on the need for international economic solidarity aroused interest only when delivered by political stars such as Lloyd George, Barthou, Rathenau, or the Russians. Most of the delegates soon stopped attending the general sessions; it wasted valuable time. In the hotels on the Mediterranean shore, secret talks were going on between the Russians and Germans and between the Italians and Yugoslavs. The French meanwhile were trying to organize a common front with the Poles and the members of the Little Entente, to resist all demands for revision of treaties or reduction of reparations.

Taking Lloyd George's advice, I called on Sir Basil Blackett with our financial expert. After examining our figures he agreed in principle to the reduction of Bulgarian reparations from two and a quarter to one billion gold francs. He also agreed that another moratorium was needed, but warned us that this depended as much upon the French and Italians as upon himself.

Barthou graciously but unequivocally told us, "I am not authorized by M. Poincaré to discuss the reparations question."

Schanzer, the Italian Foreign Minister, promised to send Count Tosti di Valminuta, Second Assistant Secretary of Foreign Affairs, to discuss the question with us. His first assistant, Signor Contarini, was then negotiating in Rapallo with the Yugoslav delegation for a settlement of that great obstacle to Italian-Yugoslav friendship, the Adriatic problem.

Stamboliski assigned me to deal with Count Tosti di Valminuta. The Count, a stout elderly man, looked at me with an expression of the utmost candor in his big black eyes and said, "I'm a simple man, a sailor who accidentally landed in politics as an Undersecretary of Foregn Affairs. I'm favorably disposed toward Bulgaria, and you know yourself that all Italians love your country."

Thanking him, I remarked, "That makes it easy to discuss the question which interests us."

"Reparations? You know that in this question Italy plays the main role. In the corporation known as 'The Allied Powers' we own 40 per cent of Bulgarian reparations; with the British, 60 per cent—a majority of the shares."

"With the British?" I asked cautiously.

Count Tosti smiled. "Our relations with England permit me to say that."

It was clear to everyone in Genoa that Great Britain and Italy were indeed very close. Lloyd George was constantly conferring with Schanzer, and Great Britain and Italy acted together on almost every issue which arose at the conference.

"Does this mean, Count Tosti, that you speak in the name of England also?"

"Precisely," he said, winking. "Under the circumstances the fate of Bulgarian reparations depends entirely on Italy, and we're ready to help you."

"On what terms?" I asked, anticipating new political demands.

"The terms are purely economic. We're interested in the Balkans as a means of expanding our trade and obtaining concessions—forest concessions, for example."

"What about our relations with Yugoslavia?" I asked point-blank. He waved his hand.

"You're free to conduct any policy you choose. As a matter of fact, now that we're settling all our differences with Yugoslavia, Bulgaria won't interest her."

Then he stated his demands. In the Rila Mountain area of Bulgaria are vast but poorly exploited forests. During the war, a certain Balabanov had obtained a concession from the Bulgarian government to work these forests. The Stamboliski government had repudiated this concession because it had been got through bribery, whereupon Balabanov had gone to Rome and sold it to an Italian bank. The Italian envoy in Sofia had demanded that the Bulgarian government recognize the concession, but Stamboliski had refused. Now Count Tosti was suggesting a deal—the Rila forests in lieu of reparations. I asked him to give me a few days to discuss the matter with Stamboliski and Tourlakov before giving him a definite reply.

"Tell them," said the Count, "that the fate of Bulgarian reparations lies in the Rila forests."

Later I learned that the Banco Commerciale d' Italia, which had bought the concession, had organized a corporation to exploit the forests and had distributed half the shares among influential Italian deputies and other politicians. Among the shareholders were Contarini, the real boss of the Foreign Office, and Count Tosti himself.

Stamboliski turned the Italian proposal down flat.

"The Rila forests are one of the richest natural resources belonging to the Bulgarian people. I can't give them to anyone. I've already refused a number of times to discuss this question with the Italian Minister in Sofia."

I suggested that Stamboliski sign an agreement recognizing the concession in exchange for Italian renunciation of reparations; the agreement to take effect when ratified by the Ministerial Council in Sofia.

"And then?" asked Stamboliski.

"Then we won't ratify the agreement. We'll say the council has turned it down."

"What in the world do we gain by that?"

"A document proving that the Italians are using reparations for blackmail. We'll take the wind out of their sails by the mere threat of publication. Indeed, I count on something even better. Count Tosti, who plays the naïve sailor but thinks himself pretty shrewd, has been speaking not only for himself but for Great Britain. I'll try to induce the Italians to sign a document committing Great Britain as well as Italy. Since the British know nothing of this, the threat of scandal will be twofold. After that we may be confident that the Italians will never dare to raise the reparations question."

Stamboliski and I were strolling slowly on the bench amid the red stones and the flowers. He stopped short, looked at me in astonishment, and said, "Where did you learn such devilish tricks? It's an excellent idea, but I can't believe the Italians would ever sign such an agreement."

They did, though. In Stamboliski's study at the Hotel Savoia, Schanzer and Count Tosti signed for Italy, Stamboliski and I for Bulgaria. In this remarkable document the authorized representatives of the Kingdom of Italy committed not only themselves but Great Britain. Their calculations were simple. The atmosphere in Genoa was such that no one believed reparations would ever be paid. In exchange for the highly doubtful claims of the Italian government, Italian speculators would get concrete resources worth several hundred million gold francs.

The document, which the Italians thought went directly to Sofia for ratification, remained in my possession. A week later, Count Tosti asked me over the telephone, "Well, has it been ratified?" Two days later, I telephoned him. "Unfortunately the Bulgarian cabinet has refused to ratify the agreement."

"I'll be right over to see you," he replied. When he arrived, he was no longer the jovial "simple man."

"We'll demand reparations payments at once!" he stormed.

"And we," I said coldly, "will immediately publish the rejected agreement in all the newspapers of Europe."

Instantly he became affable. "Very well," he said, "it didn't work out. Please return the document."

"The document is in Sofia for safekeeping," I replied.

Count Tosti left in anger and never spoke to me again.

We now had good security against further Italian blackmail, but still no moratorium. Italy would no longer press for payment but Poincaré might. The rumors of an impending Russo-German agreement were disturbing; such an agreement might provoke France to retaliate against Germany by taking a much stiffer attitude on reparations, and that would almost inevitably affect Bulgaria too.

When I asked Chicherin whether there was anything in the report of a pending agreement he made no direct reply, but he did say definitely, "Our policy aims at revision of the peace treaties. On that basis we consider the interests of Soviet Russia and Germany identical. Moreover, we know that Germany can help us increase our industrial production. We intend to take advantage of every opportunity to become economically independent of the capitalist world."

I left him, convinced that an agreement was inevitable. At the conference itself not a single important question was settled. Everything was turned over to commissions of experts. Then two agreements were announced to the world. One met with approbation, the other with agitation. Both were signed at Rapallo.

The first, concerning the Adriatic problem, was signed for Italy by Schanzer and for Yugoslavia by Momchilo Ninchich, recently Foreign Minister of the Yugoslav government in exile in London until January, 1943. The second was the agreement of friendship and economic collaboration between Germany and Russia. In addition to the published Russo-German agreement, it was rumored that there were many secret clauses concerning military collaboration. This was later confirmed by the intimate relations which developed between the Reichswehr and the Red Army and by the transfer of German war industries to Soviet territory to evade the restrictions of Versailles.

Both Rapallo agreements threatened difficulties for us. The Yugoslav-Italian agreement would deprive us of one of our principal arguments for a Bulgar-Yugoslav alliance. The Russo-German agreement infuriated Poincaré. Hoping to forestall the trouble in which sanctions against Germany might involve Bulgaria, Stamboliski wrote a personal letter which I was to deliver to Poincaré in Paris, proposing that Bulgaria pay ten million gold francs a year for three years, payments thereafter to be based on a new survey of its economic situation.

I was replaced at the conference by Petko Petkov, first secretary of our Paris legation, who was to play an important role in subsequent Bulgarian events until his murder two years later. He was the son of a former Premier, and a hero of the three recent wars. We had been friends since military school.

On the morning of May 7, I was back in our Paris legation with General Savov. He was somewhat skeptical when I explained my mission.

"Poincaré," said the General, "looks upon the peace treaties as indivisible. In his eyes there is no difference between Versailles and Neuilly. However, let's stroll a bit and lunch at Fouquet's. Perhaps after luncheon our prospects will seem brighter."

"What shall I do with Stamboliski's letter?"

"Let's send it to the Ministerial Council and ask for an audience. I prefer that you see Poincaré alone. In the meantime I shall work through my own channels."

We decided that I would make use of my old friendships in Paris while the General would sound out his connections in political circles. Once more I visited Mme. Ménard-Dorian, who arranged a political dinner at which I asked Justin Godard, Paul Painlevé, and Albert Thomas to intercede with Poincaré in Bulgaria's behalf. With General Savov I called on Count Peretti de la Rocca, Berthelot's temporary successor in the Foreign Office. He knew much less about Bulgarian affairs than Berthelot, who had been removed because he could not work with Poincaré. De la Rocca promised to arrange an audience for me with his chief but added ominously, "He's very severe."

Poincaré received me on May 11, in an enormous sunny office at the Quai d'Orsay. When I entered he sat at his desk, which was littered with papers. He sprang up quickly, shook my hand, pointed to a chair, and disappeared behind his papers.

I had seen him twice during the war—once when he had presented a banner to the Foreign Legion and again when our regiment had marched before him and King George V on the Somme front. He had aged considerably. His bald forehead, framed on the sides by graying hair, formed a square under which were furrowed brows, severe eyes, a round nose, a drooping mustache, and a small white beard. His voice was shrill and unpleasant.

"I have read M. Stamboliski's letter," he said, "but unfortunately I can't accept his proposal. Reparations are an integral part of the peace treaty. Failure to make the required payments constitutes a disturbance of the juridical order established in Europe."

I repeated to Poincaré all the arguments which had previously impressed Millerand. The Premier listened to me somewhat impatiently, tapping his pencil on the paper before him. I even revealed that Sir Basil Blackett, the British expert, had agreed not only to a moratorium, but also to reduction of the principal. All my arguments were lost upon him save one, and that one purely juridical; that our request was based on the treaty itself, which provided for the reduction, postponement, or even cancellation of reparations should Bulgaria be unable to pay. Poincaré even as Premier was always the jurist.

He pulled out a ponderous text of the Neuilly Treaty, opened it to the section cited, read it aloud to me, and rasped, "The very fact that you propose to pay ten million francs proves that Bulgaria is able to pay."

"Yes, Bulgaria can pay ten million, but not one hundred million," I replied.

"I shall ask the Sofia Reparations Commission for an exact accounting of Bulgaria's finances. On that basis alone the French government will decide." With these words Poincaré bent his head over his papers, and I understood that the audience was over. He rose quickly, shook my hand again, and was back at his desk before I was out of the room.

My old friend Jean José Frappa suggested that we see Briand together and volunteered to arrange an appointment. Briand received us in his small apartment on the Avenue Kléber. A few months earlier he had resigned as Premier after the nationalist press had accused him of being too lenient with the Germans at the Cannes Reparations Conference. Briand's study was almost stark in its simplicity: neither books nor papers on his desk; walls bare save for an enormous signed photograph of Lloyd George.

"You're too late," he told me. "I would help if I were still Premier, but I'm only a deputy now. Poincaré, whom of course I greatly esteem, believes in stern enforcement of the peace terms. I think we can get more by concessions and generosity than by constant threats. I'm accused of being 'tender' with Germany, yet I've managed to get a billion gold francs out of her. What are we to do if Germany doesn't pay? We'll have to invoke sanctions; that means to occupy German territory and set the whole world against us. France, which is rightly proud of its sense of justice, will appear to Great Britain and the United States as an aggressor. The British are already almost hostile and are trying to come to an understanding with the Italians behind our backs."

He paused for a moment, then continued,

"Furthermore, if we send our soldiers into Germany, where the Communist movement is strong, we're menaced by the spread of the revolutionary contagion from Germany to France. I'm as much disturbed by this as by France's possible moral isolation."

Briand promised that if he became Premier again, he would consider our proposals on reparations and other matters in a friendly spirit.

I returned to my post in Belgrade, and several days later Stamboliski stopped there on his way home from Genoa. I reported Poincaré's inflexible attitude and suggested that he make every effort to obtain a favorable report from the Reparations Commission in Sofia.

"But how?" asked Stamboliski.

"Don't spare money," I replied.

T HIS TIME THE Yugoslav capital gave me anything but a warm reception. The Yugoslav cup of patience, I was told in less metaphorical language, had been filled to the brim. Shortly before my arrival Iovan Brlo's *cheta,* which had killed Alexander Dimitrov, had ambushed and killed a Serbian captain and twelve soldiers. This wanton act would have strained our relations at any time. But now the Italian-Yugoslav agreement, although not yet ratified by the two parliaments, gave the Yugoslavs a new sense of security. In view of the intolerable situation on its southeastern border, Yugoslavia was ready to act against Bulgaria. I sent Stamboliski a long ciphered telegram warning that only the firmest measures against the IMRO could prevent a serious clash.

When Stamboliski wired back authorizing me to make whatever proposals I thought necessary, I delivered to Foreign Minister Ninchich a note suggesting a plan for a joint defense of the frontier. Bulgarian and Yugoslav frontier guards were to establish continuous contact with each other by direct telephone and would warn each other of any suspicious person or group seen near the border. Should a *cheta* cross into Yugoslavia, the Bulgarian commandant of that post would be held responsible if he had not warned the Yugoslav patrol. This procedure would gradually eliminate officers of the frontier guard acting in collusion with the IMRO.

In a supplementary note the next day I suggested a conference of both frontier commands, to discuss any additional measures that might be needed. I received no definite reply to either note.

Yugoslavia was preparing to celebrate the wedding of King Alexander and Princess Marie of Rumania. King Boris summoned me to Sofia, gave me a letter to King Alexander, and appointed me his personal representative at the wedding.

On the morning of June 8 a great parade was held in Belgrade, followed by a reception at the palace, where the delegations presented themselves to King Alexander and conveyed the greetings of their governments.

The French delegation was headed by Marshal d'Esperey, victor on the Salonika front. Great Britain was represented by the Duke of York, now King George VI. Crown Prince Umberto was the ranking Italian guest. From Rumania came King Ferdinand, Queen Marie, Crown

Prince Carol, and Prince Nicholas, accompanied by many Rumanian ministers and deputies. The Greek delegates, headed by Gounaris, wore evzone costumes. Less than six months later, Gounaris was to fall before a firing squad for his part in the Greek rout in Asia Minor.

The King received us in the throne room. I had last seen him at a ball in the military club, where we had had a long and friendly conversation. When my turn came, I approached the throne, handed King Boris' letter to Alexander, and conveyed the usual felicitations.

"Tell King Boris I won't tolerate acts of banditry against my frontier any longer," he replied angrily.

Taken aback by his tone, I said, "I shall convey Your Majesty's words to my sovereign, but I have the honor to advise you that I have already transmitted a note to your Foreign Minister suggesting a plan to correct the situation."

The King didn't seem to hear me. His eyes, usually so soft, flashed with indignation.

"My patience is exhausted," he said, and nodded to indicate that I was to pass on. Fortunately no one in the large crowd seemed to notice that our brief interview was really a quarrel.

That evening at a wedding ball in the palace we were introduced to the new Queen—less striking than her mother, Queen Marie, but gracious and unaffected. During dinner there were many toasts to the royal couple. Old King Ferdinand of Rumania, who had drunk these toasts in full measure, rose to speak.

"I drink to my august son-in-law, the King of the Serbs and the Slovaks," he said, ending with a hiccup. Amid embarrassed smiles, Queen Marie whispered something in his ear. Ferdinand smiled, nodded his head, and added, "Yes, yes—and King of the Croats."

After dinner, the Rumanian palace chamberlain introduced me to King Ferdinand. He looked at me with glassy eyes, smiled expansively, and when I conveyed greetings in the name of King Boris, said, "But King Boris has fled from Sofia."

I could only maintain a startled silence. He continued to smile broadly and added, "I read in the papers that there was a revolution in Bulgaria and Boris had fled to Varna."

"There must be some mistake, Your Majesty. I saw the King yesterday and he asked me to convey his regards to you."

"You're wrong, Mr. Minister," he giggled. "Hee-hee-hee, you're wrong. The King has fled."

His long gray beard danced as he laughed, and his whole face became a pitiful, tragicomic mask. I felt certain that the man was half mad. His chamberlain blushed with shame and looked at me imploringly, as if asking my pardon. To his sovereign he said, "There has been no revolution in Sofia; King Boris has not left the city."

Ferdinand winked knowingly. "Very well, have it your own way."

In official Rumanian publications this man was called "Ferdinand the Great."

The chamberlain introduced me to Ferdinand's son, Crown Prince Carol, who wore a splendid uniform bedizened with medals. Only when Carol laughed did he somewhat resemble his father. His mother, Queen Marie, despite her years, was still a beautiful woman who found a gracious word for everyone. In her whole bearing it was clear that she was the real monarch of Rumania.

Nadejda did not attend the ball for a simple reason: that very night she gave birth to a daughter whom we named Tatiana. My personal joy was marred by the feeling that Bulgar-Yugoslav relations were hopelessly tangled; that instead of being near an alliance with Yugoslavia, we were on the verge of war.

Several days later, Sofia informed me that the Bulgarian Minister in Bucharest had been handed a collective ultimatum by Rumanian Foreign Minister Ion Duca, in the name of our three Balkan neighbors, Rumania, Yugoslavia, and Greece. The note demanded that Bulgaria destroy all organizations directed against the security of its neighbors, and said that unless Bulgaria gave a satisfactory reply the three states would take upon themselves the task of restoring order in the Balkans— a clear threat of occupation. Somewhat frantically, Sofia asked for my advice.

I realized that during the wedding celebration in Belgrade the bonds between our neighbors had been strengthened and the old alliance of the Second Balkan War was being renewed against us. As a member of the League of Nations, Bulgaria could appeal under Article II of the Covenant for a special session of the League Council to deal with the dispute. I suggested that course. I also advised a protest against the collective character of the note, which indicated the existence of a secret treaty in contravention of the spirit and letter of the League Covenant.

Acting on my suggestion, the government demanded an immediate convocation of the Council. The League Secretariat thereupon advised all the powers concerned that the Council would meet in London in the middle of July and that in the interim action by any of the Balkan countries would be deemed a violation of the Covenant.

With this breathing spell I returned to Sofia at the end of June to find Stamboliski greatly disturbed by our delicate international position and by a rift in his cabinet which even danger of invasion did not heal. The death of Alexander Dimitrov had irreparably hurt the Peasant regime. Dimitrov had been completely fearless and incorruptible;

there was no one to replace him. Five ministers, through fear of the Macedonians, now opposed Stamboliski's foreign policy. Tomov himself, now Minister of War, continued to help the IMRO while pretending to suppress it. Yet Stamboliski could not make up his mind to break with these disloyal ministers, although they were also implicated in financial swindles. He was afraid of splitting the Peasant Party.

The only good news was that the Reparations Commission had recommended to Poincaré the postponement of our payment until the spring of 1923.

"How much did it cost us?" I asked.

Stamboliski sighed. "Twenty-five million leva."

That was only a tenth of what Stamboliski had offered in his letter to Poincaré.

The opposition to Stamboliski was growing steadily, with the press playing up all his vices, real and fancied. Although he drank very little, according to the newspapers he was always drunk. They also accused him of keeping dozens of mistresses. Women were, in fact, his weakness; he had led an ascetic life in his youth and was easily deceived. His mistresses used him and took advantage of his good name.

The present one, a plump, pretty young adventuress, took all his money and forced him to give jobs to various incompetents. Her brother had opened an employment agency where, under the camouflage of a legitimate business, he sold government jobs. Learning of this from my old Brussels friend, Mikhailov, to whom he had offered a job as consul general for 100,000 leva, I informed the chief of the secret police and we set a trap. Mikhailov went to the "employment agency" with marked thousand-leva notes. That same evening the police arrested the scoundrel. We discovered that he had a dead telephone line over which he "spoke directly" to Stamboliski about government jobs in the presence of his clients. I went to Stamboliski at once and told him bluntly that I had brought about the arrest of his mistress's brother. He was angry because I had done so without warning him, but promised to break off with the woman; a promise he couldn't bring himself to keep.

Appointed chief of the Bulgarian delegation to the meeting of the League Council in London, I accepted with the understanding that whatever the results I would resign as envoy to Belgrade, since our appeal to the Council meant that my mission to Yugoslavia had failed.

London struck me by its air of stability and sobriety. Even the trees in Hyde and Regent Parks seemed stable and sober, as if they would say, "We are not ordinary trees; we are British." The bronze lions at the base of the Nelson column in Trafalgar Square were fat, contented, and pacific; their bellies were full and they didn't want to molest anyone. They seemed symbolic of the British Empire. Instinctively I compared them with the Bulgarian lion on our coat of arms, its great jaws gaping in hunger.

The sessions of the Council, with Lord Balfour presiding, were held at the St. James Palace. In addressing the Council I did not deny that *komitajis* who had killed our own Minister of War had raided Yugoslavia. I admitted the justice of Yugoslav demands that the border raids be stopped, but pointed out that I had made a proposal for dealing with this condition, to which the Yugoslav government had not replied. Moreover, I denied the right of Rumania and Greece to interfere since they could cite no instance of violation of their borders.

Nicolai Titulescu, then Rumania's envoy to London and later its Foreign Minister, answered me. He was considered one of the leading orators of the League. Sensing the tenor of sentiment in the Council, he adopted a conciliatory tone. The Council decided that the dispute could be settled by direct negotiation and, in effect, advised us to reach an agreement along the lines of the note I had submitted to Belgrade. Our success was greater than we had anticipated.

Lord Balfour invited me to luncheon at his house. I was impressed by the physical and spiritual beauty of this tall, slender, sensitive man. Balfour approached European problems from a philosophical point of view.

"Old Europe," he said, "has had many wars and revolutions, but it has done nothing to achieve a moral revolution. We must make the League of Nations an instrument to promote genuine and permanent understanding among the nations, to disarm the spirit and explain the futility of war, to bring about the solidarity of poor humanity, which still can't cure the common cold yet fights for the illusion of power."

Contact with a man like Lord Balfour made all the intricate political questions we were fighting about seem trivial and the resort to intrigue and threats contemptible. In his presence I felt that it would be easy indeed to settle everything if the human conscience were only permitted to speak.

No sooner had I reached Paris than Stamboliski wired me to go to Prague, to ask Benes' aid in reaching an understanding with Yugoslavia. I left Paris by plane at six in the morning and reached Prague at noon. When I spoke to Benes that afternoon, he promised to help Stamboliski at the regular session of the League of Nations, in September. I stopped in Belgrade only long enough to see my family and went on to Sofia, where Stamboliski told me that I was to head the Bulgarian delegation to the League sessions.

[170]

A few days before I left for Geneva, Count Aldovrandi, the Italian envoy, served notice that since we refused to recognize the Rila forest concession, Italy would be forced to raise once more the question of reparations. I answered that I was taking with me to Geneva the agreement signed at Genoa, and would turn it over to the press.

At the Hôtel de Russie, where I stayed in Geneva, appeared a beautiful woman who made friends with the members of the Bulgarian delegation. She spoke excellent French and was introduced to me as a countess. Her speech suggested the South and her large black eyes and musical voice suggested Italy; but she assured me she was French, spoke of her château near Cannes, and after a brief two days acquaintance startled me by declaring she loved me and proposing that we spend the evening together on the French shore of Lake Leman, at Evian-les-Bains.

My suspicion was aroused, for I had never considered myself an Adonis. Moreover, I had noticed the colorful figure of my old friend, that "simple sailor" Count Tosti di Valminuta, in the Italian delegation. Still, I agreed to dine with the countess in Evian-les-Bains. We returned by automobile at two in the morning, and during the drive she succeeded in making me forget my suspicions and scruples. She went with me to my room.

Half asleep, I felt her slip out of bed. A few minutes later I heard papers rustling. I waited several seconds and then suddenly switched on the light. The Countess was holding a sheaf of papers she had taken from my portfolio. She trembled. I realized that she was looking for the document which plagued the Italian government.

"Put down the papers, Madam," I said. "You won't find anything of interest to you."

Helplessly she sat down, and the papers fell at her feet.

"I'm sorry to see such a splendid woman engage in espionage."

I took two hundred Swiss francs from my coat pocket. She flushed and turned away. "You're insulting," she said, and left the room before I could say another word.

The next day the "countess" was no longer in the hotel and Count Tosti had disappeared from the Italian delegation.

September was not chosen by chance for the sessions of the League. It was the best time of year in Geneva. The air was warm, the lake as clear as the sky. Foreigners swarmed into the city; not only delegates and correspondents, but tourists come to spend the autumn season on Lake Leman. Night clubs did a flourishing business, with international spies and girls from Montmartre rubbing elbows with the delegates of the nations of Europe, Asia, and Latin America.

In the midst of all this beauty and bustle, the League occupied itself with trivia. I sat in the Fifth Commission, which discussed such piddling questions as the struggle against obscene literature and the use of Esperanto in international relations.

I asked a Scandinavian spinster who spoke on the necessity of adopting measures against obscene literature whether she would outlaw de Maupassant.

"Of course," she cried.

I countered by suggesting that we ban the Old Testament because of its many lewd passages. This caused a minor scandal. On the question of Esperanto I reminded my colleagues of what Anatole France had said—that he preferred the ugliest living woman to the most beautiful mechanical doll. This caused a second flurry. The one useful thing our commission did was to create, at Fridtjof Nansen's suggestion, a League of Nations passport to protect stateless political refugees. When the sessions ended we left feeling frustrated. Virtually all business had been handled by the Secretariat, headed by Sir Eric Drummond, who was "clever" enough to exclude every troublesome question from the agenda.

Stamboliski came to Switzerland during the sessions, and on the day of his arrival, September 17, the newspapers carried disturbing reports. At an opposition meeting in Trnovo, the ancient Bulgarian capital, peasants had attacked and beaten the leaders. The next day, Acting Premier Daskalov had ordered the arrest of all opposition leaders, charging them with responsibility for Bulgaria's defeat in the war— because they had been ministers at some time between 1912 and 1918. This highhanded action hurt the prestige of our government both abroad and at home. Several of the arrested men had been in Stamboliski's first cabinet. If they had been arrested in 1920 with Radoslavov's lieutenants at the beginning of the war-guilt trials, the action could have been justified, but coming at this time the purpose of their arrest was only too apparent.

Stamboliski disclaimed responsibility for Daskalov's measures and wired to Sofia ordering the release of former Premier Malinov and a number of others. Instead of complying, Daskalov announced that a popular referendum would be held to decide whether to try the prisoners or release them. When fuller reports reached us, we discovered that the principal instigator of these actions was that tool of the Italian-paid Macedonians, Kosta Tomov, who was deliberately fanning unrest by announcing that he had nipped an incipient uprising at Trnovo.

From the League sessions I returned to my post in Belgrade, which I retained by special request of Ninchich, the Yugoslav Minister of Foreign Affairs. I had told him in Geneva that I didn't expect to return.

"When Stamboliski comes to Geneva," he had replied, "I'll ask him to keep you in Belgrade. It's not only my personal wish, but that of His Majesty King Alexander."

The atmosphere in Belgrade had thawed considerably. Benes had kept his promise to speak to Ninchich in our behalf. And at once I began to prepare the ground for a visit by Stamboliski to King Alexander and Pashich, to speed an understanding with Yugoslavia. Early in November Stamboliski came to Belgrade.

I went with him to call on Pashich and Ninchich, but no one was present during his audience with the King. When he left Alexander he was enthusiastic, especially because the King had understood his Bulgarian and he had had no difficulty with the King's Serbian. The close kinship of the two Slavonic languages seemed to him a favorable omen.

When Alexander had twitted him with having been a republican most of his life, his answer was, "If monarchy doesn't destroy freedom, I've no objection to it. It may even be useful if the King remembers that he is only an arbiter."

Alexander was equally enthusiastic.

"I believe," he said, "that an alliance between us is now possible."

During a dinner given by Ninchich, Stamboliski was asked what he thought of Yugoslavia. He replied, "I like it a great deal, but you remind me of people who have suddenly acquired great wealth. You aren't yet accustomed to it and you're always afraid someone will want to take it away from you. For that reason you're suspicious of everyone— even of me."

IN THE MIDST of the League sessions came news of the crushing Greek defeat in Asia Minor. The Turks under Mustafa Kemal and Ismet Pasha routed the Greek army and occupied Smyrna early in September, 1922. Once more King Constantine was forced into exile. He was succeeded by his son, George II, and a provisional military dictatorship was established.

The Turkish victory changed the political balance in the Balkans. The ambitious project of a Greater Greece, to include Constantinople, western Thrace, and most of Asia Minor, had collapsed. The Treaty of Sèvres, concluded in 1920 between Turkey and the Allies, no longer existed, and Greece and the great powers were forced to negotiate with Mustafa Kemal Pasha.

To arrange the terms of Turko-Greek peace and to settle the question of the Straits, a new conference was summoned to meet in Lausanne in November. As a Black Sea nation, Bulgaria had a vital interest in the Straits. We also hoped, at this conference, to obtain the outlet to the Aegean provided for in the Treaty of Neuilly but not yet ceded to us. The treaty provided for a *trade* outlet, and the Allies wanted us to accept the use of the harbor of Dedeagach (Alexandropolis). But we insisted on a *territorial* outlet—the cession to Bulgaria of a corridor along the railway and full control over the port.

Our delegation of thirty members was headed by Stamboliski, with myself as second ranking delegate. The evening we arrived in Lausanne we held a meeting which Stanciov, our delegate to London, and General Savov also attended. Stanciov had been persuaded in London that Bulgaria should accept a trade outlet, and had succeeded in convincing Stamboliski that taking London's advice would ease our whole future political course. When Stamboliski announced this at the meeting I flared up.

"In that event," I shouted, "I renounce my obligations as second delegate. This decision is against the basic interests of the Bulgarian nation."

Stamboliski was furious, but Morfov, our chief expert on railways and harbors, rose and said, "I wish to explain why I agree completely with Todorov."

Dedeagach, Morfov reminded us, really had no harbor. Building one would cost a minimum of ten million dollars. Yet unless we controlled the port, in case of the slightest conflict with Greece, we could expect to lose our right to its use.

Stamboliski turned to me. "Why didn't you explain it that way? Your way shows that at heart you're still a terrorist."

During the conference our delegation repeatedly raised this question of an outlet to the Aegean; but Venizelos, who headed the Greek delegation, protested strongly against our efforts to get a corridor through territory which the great powers had so lately ceded to Greece. Once he spoke so bitterly that Stamboliski remarked,

"If the honorable Greek delegate speaks in that way, you can imagine what would be the conduct of the Greek gendarmes under whose supervision Bulgarian trade in Dedeagach would be conducted."

The delegates laughed. Several days later, Venizelos offered to grant us a free zone in Salonika.

"As a peasant people," I answered, "we prefer a cottage of our own to the best apartment in the mansion of a stranger."

Venizelos had to face a storm in Lausanne because of events in Athens. Eight of former King Constantine's ministers and advisers were tried before an extraordinary court-martial, and six were sentenced to death. They were shot the same day, before Venizelos could intervene. They were unquestionably responsible for the Greek catastrophe in Asia Minor, but their execution shocked the diplomats, and the British considered breaking off diplomatic relations with Greece.

The big three of the Lausanne Conference were Curzon, Poincaré and Mussolini, now making his first appearance on the diplomatic stage, a month after the march on Rome. The general attitude toward Mussolini in Lausanne was one of benevolent optimism; conditions in Italy, it was felt, would soon return to normal, and Mussolini's policy would differ little from that of the preceding regime. The French were even pleased, remembering in him a friend whom they had paid to advocate Italian participation in the war against Germany.

Stamboliski and I called on Poincaré, Curzon, and finally Mussolini the day after our arrival. Mussolini was staying at the Hôtel Beau Rivage in Ouchy, a suburb of Lausanne, on Lake Leman. His appearance was unquestionably impressive, and he spoke with moderation and tact. He assured us that Italy would pursue a policy of friendship toward Bulgaria, and that he understood our financial problem, although in principle he favored the stern enforcement of treaties.

"I entirely approve of M. Poincaré's policy and the measures he proposes to take against Germany for refusing to pay."

Poincaré had declared that if Germany defaulted on its reparations installment, France would invoke sanctions and occupy German terri-

[175]

tory. French troops were already poised to move into the Ruhr.

We were about to raise the question of our own reparations when Mussolini's secretary entered and whispered something to him. He nodded. A moment later, two cameramen entered. Mussolini helped them move the desk into a better light and sat down. The photographers opened the door leading to the balcony and focused their cameras. We stepped aside. Then something very strange happened. Mussolini changed completely. He adopted a stern Roman air and made such ludicrous grimaces and gestures that I had to cover my mouth, vainly trying to stifle my laugh. The Italian Premier had become a ham actor playing Caesar.

The performance over and the photographers gone, Mussolini turned to me. "You thought it funny?"

I tried to apologize, but he laughed. "So do I, but it impresses my people."

We left feeling that the man looked upon politics as a lurid melodrama in which he was playing the star part.

The British delegation, under Lord Curzon, was a group of tedious experts; except for Harold Nicholson, it was almost impossible to talk to any of them. Yet each knew his own narrow field very well. One specialized in extraterritorial rights, another in maritime law, a third in the question of the Straits. Collectively they formed an excellent staff, able to furnish their chief on short notice with any information he needed. The French delegation, on the other hand, was full of brilliant men who knew everything but the problem before the conference—with the exception of Poincaré, General Secretary Massigli, and the military expert, General Maxime Weygand.

This French military hero refused to posture and grimace, like Mussolini, in the spotlight of history. At an official dinner I found myself seated beside him. To make conversation I complimented him on his victory in Poland in 1920, about which so much had been written.

He smiled. "What victory? I had nothing to do with it."

Hearing a general disclaim a victory was a unique experience, and I expressed my surprise. We had dined well and drunk good wine, and General Weygand felt talkative.

"I'll tell you what happened. When I took charge of the operations of the Polish army, I ordered the Poles to stop the Russian offensive on the Niemen River. But they kept retreating. Then I ordered them to stop it on the Bug, but they didn't. The third time I ordered them to stop it on the Vistula, and they did—not because of my order, but because fresh troops arrived who decided to fight."

"Very well," I said. "But the battle of Warsaw?"

"Confidentially, there was no battle. Of course there were a few shots from both sides. But what really happened was that the Russians, who had chased the Poles in the hope of surrendering, finally caught up and surrendered. That was all."

The Soviet delegation, headed by Chicherin and Rakovsky, stopped at the Hotel Savoie, where our delegation and the Yugoslavs were also staying. Thus the Savoie became the headquarters of the Slavs.

From the beginning of the conference Chicherin worked in close collaboration with the Turkish delegation and engaged in a number of bouts with the British. A French journalist told me that upon his arrival in Lausanne he had called on Lord Curzon. The head of the British delegation, who had been Viceroy of India and was known as the enemy of everything Russian, Czarist or Bolshevik, had kept the Commissar waiting fifteen minutes in his anteroom. When Chicherin was at last admitted to his study, Curzon pretended to be writing and raised his head only long enough to point to a chair. Chicherin didn't sit down.

"I only came," he said, "to remind you that the Chicherin family has been illustrious since the thirteenth century, while the Curzons have been aristocrats only three generations." Then he turned and left.

Si non è vero, è molto ben trovato. In any event, Lord Curzon, for all his intelligence, was haughty and cold, and little liked by the other delegations. Probably his bad behavior was partly due to ill health. When he spoke to the Russians he was irritable and tactless. In reply to one of his biting remarks, Chicherin smiled ironically and said in clear English,

"The honorable chairman seems to forget that Russian Cossacks are already on the Pamir Plateau."

Lord Curzon had once predicted that the appearance of Russian Cossacks on the Pamir Plateau would mark the beginning of the end of British rule in India. Curiously enough, despite Russia's territorial losses in the first World War, the Pamir Plateau fell into Russian hands.

At the Lausanne Conference our relations with the Soviet delegation were friendly because both Russia and Bulgaria preferred to have Turkey rather than Greece or any great power control the Straits. I became better acquainted with Chicherin and found that he was erudite enough to know Bulgarian history. I was also on excellent terms with Ismet Pasha, now President Ismet Inonu, who headed the Turkish delegation.

Ismet, who earned his surname by defeating the Greeks at Inonu, was Mustafa Kemal's right-hand man. He was short, with a large head and protruding brow, small black eyes, a hooked nose, and clipped mustache. He spoke a little French, but his hearing was so defective that he used a horn in conversation. At the conference he behaved with icy calm, never yielding a single point. The delegates of the other powers would deliver long speeches. Ismet would listen, smile, and reply curtly,

"The answer of the Turkish delegation is No!"

When he failed to grasp a purely juridical question, he would say, "The Turkish delegation will reply tomorrow." No amount of coaxing could induce him to change his mind. His strength lay in his knowledge that not one European power was prepared to continue the war in Asia Minor, while the Turks had 100,000 men before Constantinople, ready to attack at any moment. In Lausanne the Allies demonstrated that they had no policy at all, except an all-consuming desire to get from Turkey as many trade concessions as possible.

The Soviet delegates stood fast on all questions concerning Russia, but they still played the diplomatic game like amateurs. The first version of the agreement on the Straits, prepared by Lord Curzon and nearly accepted by Turkey, was really directed against Russia, but the Russian delegation didn't realize it. Our expert, Morfov, a rabid anti-Bolshevik but Russophile, appealed to me, "For God's sake let's go to Chicherin and explain the situation."

"What?" I laughed. "Do you want to help the Bolsheviks?"

"Never mind the Bolsheviks. This question concerns Russia."

We went to warn Chicherin. Morfov explained that the plan the Turks were ready to accept really bottled up Russia in the Black Sea. Not a single Russian warship would be allowed to pass through the Straits, whereas each of the western powers could send 50,000 tons of warships into the Black Sea. Chicherin thanked us. The next day Ismet Pasha rejected Curzon's plan. Under the final text, no power could send more than 30,000 tons of war vessels into the Black Sea, and Russia was granted the right to send out an equal tonnage through the Straits.

After Poincaré and Mussolini left, the French and Italian delegations remained in strange hands. The French spokesmen were two old diplomats, Bompard and Berrère, promptly dubbed "the Siamese twins," who read their written declarations in trembling voices. The chief of the Italian delegation, seventy-year-old Marquis Garroni, former Ambassador to Turkey, was bald and fat, with an enormous nose, sagging cheeks, and a triple chin. He usually dozed off during the sessions. When it came his turn to speak he would shake off his sleep, smile pleasantly, and intone, "Italy joins in the proposal of our illustrious chairman. . . . Italy is always for the freedom of the seas and all that."

Then he would lapse into beatific slumber while his secretary translated his insignificant remarks into impossible French.

Rakich, Yugoslav Minister to Sofia and a noted poet, whispered to me, "Thank God, Todorov, you and I can never be ambassadors."

Stamboliski also was obliged to leave before the conference was over. In Bulgaria, the Macedonians were carrying on guerrilla war against the government. Early in December one of Pancho Mikhailov's *chetas,* with the local police and the military authorities conniving, occupied the city of Kustendil. This was a feint to test the government's power to resist a coup d'état. Instead of ordering Mikhailov's band dispersed at once, War Minister Tomov went to Kustendil, met the Macedonian *voivoda,* posed with him for a picture, and left without disturbing the rebels. Stamboliski asked me what measure I thought necessary to restore the authority of the Peasant government.

"Overhaul your cabinet," I advised. "Proclaim martial law, mobilize and arm the peasants, and arrest all unreliable officers."

"Very well," he agreed. "We'll return to Sofia. I'll proclaim martial law and appoint new ministers."

But the next day he had a change of heart. "No," he said humbly, "I'm afraid it would mean spilling too much blood. I can't do it."

"I'm afraid that eventually blood will be spilled," I replied sadly, "but it will be ours."

Stamboliski bowed his massive head and remained silent for several minutes. "Very well," he said at last, "let it be my blood."

He left for Sofia the next day and I remained in Lausanne as head of the delegation.

Because of our unsatisfactory relations with Greece, we needed to drag out the conference as long as possible. To that end I often conferred with the Turkish delegation—so often that Taponier of *L'Information* wrote, "Every time Todorov, the Bulgarian delegate, comes from Ismet Pasha, we know the conference will be prolonged another week."

Chicherin invited me to dine, and brought up the question of restoring diplomatic relations between Russia and Bulgaria. Stamboliski and I both favored recognition of the Soviet government; it was abnormal to have no representatives in the vast Slavic country which was our Black Sea neighbor. But the reactionary press all over the world was accusing us of Bolshevism because of our reform program; therefore we could not safely recognize the Soviet government before the great powers did so.

In urging recognition, Chicherin assured me that the Soviet government had nothing in common with the Communist International and didn't intend to conduct Communist propaganda in Bulgaria.

"That's too bad," I answered. "If I'm correctly informed, the Bulgarian Communist Party now gets about twenty million leva a year from Moscow. That's only $200,000. I'd be overjoyed if Russia gave them 100 million leva, in American dollars. For a poor country like

Bulgaria, that would represent a sizable increase in the national income and diminish the chance of an uprising."

Chicherin was puzzled. "How would it diminish the chance?"

"Because big money would corrupt the party. The countless functionaries would buy homes and land and become respectable citizens, though they might go on talking revolution. Give a Bulgarian a few acres of land and he's satisfied."

Chicherin laughed. "If all the bourgeois representatives talked your language, we'd be ruined. No one would be afraid of us. Is your government so sure of itself that it fears nothing?"

"Certainly not. We're afraid of patriotic romanticism taking the form of a military conspiracy, but we don't fear the people. Stamboliski's reforms have met their needs. Our only danger is from the right."

To my surprise, Venizelos also invited me to dine with him and his wife. After dinner we retired into a corner of the salon to talk politics. I reminded him of the offer Stamboliski had made to Greece, Yugoslavia, and Rumania when the Treaty of Neuilly was signed.

"If you, the Serbs, and the Rumanians had accepted, you wouldn't have suffered defeat in Asia Minor, and the entire situation in the Balkans would now be different."

"I was always in favor of a Balkan alliance," said Venizelos. "I'm not responsible for the fact that Bulgaria destroyed it in 1913. But that's history. Let's speak of the future. What do you really want?"

"Only what we've already suggested at the conference, a territorial outlet to the Aegean. If you feel that a Balkan alliance is necessary, you should be willing to make that small sacrifice."

The Greeks now feared a Bulgar-Yugoslav agreement for a joint move southward; the Yugoslavs to Salonika and the Bulgarians to Kavalla and Dedeagach. This gave me a strong bargaining position. I told Venizelos that our relations with Yugoslavia were steadily becoming closer and that we were about to sign a friendly agreement.

"After this agreement," I said, "Greece can play only one of two roles—the maritime guardian of the united Balkans, or the vanguard of an outside European power. In the first case, Greece is protected against any surprise; in the second, an eventual struggle between us is inevitable."

"Very well," said Venizelos, "if Greece gives you Dedeagach and a corridor, will that be your last demand?"

I couldn't answer without consulting Stamboliski, but promised to act in that spirit with my government's consent. Since he was not yet Premier, Venizelos asked me to wait until he returned to Athens before beginning negotiations.

Two days later Sir Edward Boyle, chairman of the Balkan Committee in London, came to see me. He told me he had spoken with Venizelos.

Then he took out a map showing possible Greek concessions.

"I've marked it myself," he said, "under Venizelos's supervision."

The map indicated that in exchange for a strip to Dedeagach, we were to cede an equal amount of land along our Thracian border with Greece. This document is still in my archives in Sofia.

The territory was never ceded, for Venizelos was to discover after the fall of Stamboliski that a Yugoslav-Bulgar alliance need not be feared.

A<small>T</small> L<small>AUSANNE,</small> Mussolini had promised Stamboliski Italian friendship. Actually he continued the policy of that clique in the Italian Foreign Office which had first betrayed its enmity to the new Yugoslav state when Italian officers of the army of occupation cultivated friendships in Sofia drawing rooms; the clique which had inspired Aliotti's offer of an anti-Yugoslav military alliance and when refused had begun to subsidize the enemies of the Peasant government. The keystone of Italy's policy in the Balkans continued to be Yugoslavia's isolation, and no Bulgarian government could look for Italian friendship on any other basis than that of connivance in Mussolini's schemes for penetration of the Balkan Peninsula through the eastern shore of the Adriatic.

When I returned to Belgrade in January, 1923, after the Lausanne Conference had been recessed until April, I found King Alexander and Pashich ready to discuss broader problems than that of securing the border. The Italo-Yugoslav agreement had not been ratified in either Rome or Belgrade. Mussolini's press was now clamoring for Dalmatia, and once more the two countries were at odds. At the same time Mussolini notified our minister to Rome that he would demand payment of Bulgarian reparations, and that the stupid document signed by the representatives of the late Facta government did not interest him.

The threat was, of course, another attempt at blackmail, designed to frighten the Bulgarian government into renouncing its policy of alliance with Yugoslavia. The imperative need of such an alliance, for the mutual protection of the two Balkan states and the eventual solidarity of the whole peninsula against Fascist aggression, was clearer than ever. The Yugoslav government, alarmed by the Fascist hue and cry for Dalmatia, was at last ready to negotiate.

Before leaving Belgrade for Sofia I arranged with Ninchich for a conference in Nish between Yugoslav and Bulgarian military and police authorities, to work out a practical plan for safeguarding our frontiers against the depredations of the Macedonian terrorists as the necessary first step toward complete agreement. The Fascist dictatorship was continuing to finance the Macedonian *chetas* and to supply them with contraband arms and explosives.

Mussolini was as good as his word. It was not long before the Reparations Commission, at Prince Borghese's insistence, delivered an ultimatum threatening to invoke sanctions unless Bulgaria paid, and citing as a precedent the recent occupation of the Ruhr by French troops.

Stamboliski was alarmed. "The Italians," he said, "are irritated by our policy. The coming conference in Nish frightens them."

Chicherin had promised me at Lausanne that in case of any attempt at forcible collection of Bulgarian reparations, Soviet troops would mass on the Rumanian frontier and the Soviet press would begin a campaign for the return of Bessarabia. That would eliminate Rumania. I wasn't worried about Greece, still punch-drunk from its recent defeat. And I was sure that with Mussolini threatening Dalmatia I could persuade Belgrade to take no part in sanctions against Bulgaria.

Returning to Belgrade, I offered Pashich and Ninchich a practical argument: Yugoslavia's interest in Bulgarian reparations was 5 per cent as against Italy's 40 per cent; yet Mussolini wanted Yugoslavia to take on the burden of collecting, by seizing the Bulgarian customs and occupying the Pernik coal mines—after which he would probably use his 40 per cent of the money thus extorted to arm Italy against Yugoslavia. Besides, the occupation would force Stamboliski to resign and would irreparably harm Bulgar-Yugoslav relations. Pashich and Ninchich heartily agreed with me and promised that Serbian troops would not collect for Mussolini. King Alexander promised to ask the Rumanian government for similar assurances.

Armed with these pledges, I returned to Sofia. Stamboliski, greatly relieved, assigned me the unpleasant task of negotiating with the Reparations Commission.

The French delegate argued that since France had occupied the Ruhr he could not in good conscience recommend leniency for Bulgaria. The British representative said he had made every effort to ease Bulgaria's position and could do no more. But Prince Borghese declared bluntly, "Either you pay at once or we invoke sanctions."

"Who, in your opinion, will enforce them?"

"Your neighbors."

"Allow me to assure your Excellency that our neighbors will do nothing of the kind. I have the honor to advise you that I have come to an understanding with M. Pashich."

Prince Borghese spluttered.

"Then—then—Italy will send warships and troops to Varna."

"If you send one Italian division," I answered, "two thousand Bulgarian soldiers are enough to handle it. If you send two divisions, four thousand Bulgarians will dispose of them."

I left quickly, before he could explode.

An hour later, Stamboliski telephoned. "You've insulted Prince Borghese again. He's threatening to leave Bulgaria."

"Very well," I said, "appoint someone with better manners than mine."

I was replaced by Petko Petkov, who was now Chief Secretary of the Foreign Office.

When, in March, the Reparations Commission in Paris authorized our neighbors to seize the Bulgarian customs and the Pernik mines, the Yugoslav government refused, saying that it did not wish to jeopardize its friendly relations with us. Bucharest followed Belgrade's example and Greece made no move. Mussolini did not attack Varna—his object was not to strengthen Stamboliski but to destroy him.

There was plenty of explosive material within the country. In January, Stamboliski had at last overhauled his cabinet and dismissed the doubtful ministers, thus necessarily creating new enemies. And he had lost none of his old ones. The new ministers were loyal, but many were young and inexperienced. To add to his difficulties, the Russians were making trouble.

A few days before the League sessions closed two strangers had called on me in Geneva—a Frenchman who introduced himself as Count du Chayla and a Russian calling himself Korotkov. They asked permission for the Soviet Red Cross to establish an office in Bulgaria, to send back to Russia those refugees who wanted to return and were eligible for amnesty. They stressed that the Russian Red Cross was an exclusively humanitarian organization.

There were more than forty thousand Russian refugees in Bulgaria. In Gallipoli, thousands of others, the remnants of General Piotr Wrangel's army, clamored for Bulgarian visas. I told Korotkov that his proposal might be acceptable if the Soviet government would guarantee the safety of every Russian exile who returned voluntarily to his own country. Later I introduced the two men to Stamboliski, who agreed to admit a delegation of the Soviet Red Cross into Bulgaria. The delegation of twenty men had arrived at the beginning of the year and occupied the Grand Hotel Bulgaria, the best in Sofia. Their titular head was Korotkov, but it was clear that this modest man had no authority. A tall, blond man who boasted that he had defeated the British in Turkestan, seemed to be the real boss.

In this Soviet delegation I encountered men who had all the earmarks of hardened Chekists. They spoke with coarse self-assurance, drank a great deal, and bragged about their exploits during the Civil War. Not one of them was traveling under his real name. I was often in their company, but when I asked any one his name, he would answer, "Well, let's say Maxim."

The delegation sent about four thousand Russian refugees from Bulgaria to Constantinople, where they sailed for their homeland. Between the Russians who wanted to go home and those loyal to the White General Wrangel there was bad blood; and the Wrangel men hated the Bulgarian government for facilitating the repatriation of the homesick refugees. Many of them attended secret meetings of the opposition, promising the help of their regiments in the event of a coup d'état against Stamboliski.

The most troublesome of these people, General Kutiepov, called himself Commander in Chief of the Russian Forces in Bulgaria. In Trnovo with his staff, he behaved as if entirely independent of the Sofia government. In the early spring of 1923, he even went as far as to court-martial and hang four Russian officers for disobeying his orders. This exhausted Stamboliski's patience, and he ordered the expulsion of Kutiepov and General Shatilov, his Chief of Staff. The Sofia police thereupon raided the Russian legation, where Wrangel's representatives lived, and seized stores of ammunition as well as detailed plans for Stamboliski's overthrow. Several hundred Russian officers and their families were instantly deported to Yugoslavia.

A year later I learned that this "Russian plot" had been framed up by Stancho Trifonov, assistant chief of the Sofia police, who told me the truth about it in his Belgrade exile. The Soviet Red Cross delegation had bribed him to organize the "plot." On an ordinary map of Sofia, Trifonov and a White Russian *agent provocateur* had marked points near the ministry which were to be "seized" and listed the Russian officers who were supposedly to take part in the coup. This forged document served as the basis for the accusation against the Russian exiles. The guns found in the cellars of the Russian legation, Trifonov told me, had been planted there by his men.

"How much did you get for it?"

"Very little," he replied bitterly. "They promised plenty, but all I got was 20,000 leva and this gold cigar case."

He showed me the case—solid gold set with several precious stones. Not his conscience but his indignation made Trifonov confess.

"I went to Prague, where I found that blond young man who boasted of his victories over the British in Turkestan. He was in the Soviet trade delegation. I asked him for my pay. After all, I not only broke up the White Russian organization in Bulgaria, but I also got General Pokrovsky."

"Pokrovsky?"

"General Pokrovsky disappeared after the arrests in Sofia, but the Bolsheviks told me where he was hiding. I sent my police with orders to bring him back dead or alive, preferably dead. He was hiding in a small house outside Kustendil. When he saw my men he tried to get away, but they killed him."

"Well, what did your young man in Prague say?"

"He treated me to vodka and didn't give me a kopeck."

A very real plot was taking shape against Stamboliski; Mussolini was working feverishly to forestall the impending Yugoslav-Bulgarian alliance. Heading the map division of our War Office was Colonel Ivan Volkov, who had become an Italian agent and handled the money sent from Rome to the IMRO after the device of the Banco Commerciale d'Italia was exposed. This traitor, with Professor Alexander Tsankov, who had taken no part in politics but during the War had been Germanophile, had organized a secret "Military League" into which flocked all sorts of disgruntled people—opposition leaders, army officers both employed and unemployed, and of course the IMRO chiefs. The purpose of this organization was the forcible overthrow of the Peasant government.

In March, a Macedonian *cheta* fired on Daskalov's automobile, but missed him. A bomb landed in Stamboliski's box one night at the National Theater. Luckily it failed to explode, but the lights went out and the assassin escaped.

Early in April Colonel Lichev, chief of the Sofia garrison, came to see me.

"The general opinion is that you're a man of good sense," he began, "and that's why I'm here."

I asked what was wrong.

"A military coup d'état is being plotted. If I'm given the authority, I'll deal with it at once. I've already warned the government several times, but no one takes me seriously. I want to know once and for all whether the government intends to defend itself. If not, there's no reason why I should lose my head. I'll join the conspirators."

I went with Colonel Lichev directly to the War Office and saw Muraviev, the new Minister of War, who was Stamboliski's nephew and could be trusted.

The Colonel explained the situation and gave the names of several leading conspirators, including Volkov. The Minister of War, a man of limited ability, sat smoking a thick cigar in an effort to look important.

"I'll look into the matter," he promised.

When the Colonel had left, Muraviev said to me, "All this is nonsense. The officers he mentioned are loyal men. Pay no attention to that ass."

He spoke with such assurance that I confess I believed him.

[186]

The Nish conference, which blackmail and terrorism had failed to prevent, took place early in August. The representatives of the two countries speedily agreed on a plan for joint control of the Macedonian frontier against the IMRO raids. The way was at last clear for a comprehensive Bulgar-Yugoslav agreement. The IMRO and the political opposition at once began to circulate the slanderous charge that Stamboliski had forever renounced Bulgaria's claims in Macedonia and had sold out to the Serbs. Yet the Nish agreement was signed by the leading Bulgarian officers, including the commander of the frontier guard, Colonel Davidov, who later took part in the coup d'état against the government.

A few days after the signing, Stamboliski received a letter signed by Todor Alexandrov, informing him that the IMRO had sentenced him to death. I received a similar letter. Leaflets scattered by the Macedonian Organization called us "traitors" and "Serbian spies."

The Council of the League was about to consider, at Geneva, the treatment by the Greeks of the Bulgarian minority in eastern Thrace. Stamboliski sent me to represent Bulgaria there and at the Lausanne Conference, reconvening in mid-April.

On my way to Geneva, I stopped in Belgrade to arrange with Ninchich for a military alliance. The talks would have to be conducted in complete secrecy to prevent a violent reaction from Italy and uneasiness on the part of our Balkan neighbors. The chiefs of staff of the two armies—Colonel Noikov, who had accompanied me to London and Geneva, and General Peshich—were to work out the details. We arranged that Colonel Noikov would go to some Yugoslav resort as a civilian on vacation, and General Peshich, who also would mask his identity, would meet him there. As soon as the alliance was concluded, the Yugoslav government was to ask France to permit the sending of military equipment into Bulgaria from Yugoslavia. When I left for Geneva, I felt that Bulgaria's situation was more favorable than at any time since the war.

At the sessions of the League Council nothing important was done; the resolution adopted merely advised the Greeks to be more considerate of the Bulgarian minority in Thrace. Before the League Secretariat I raised the question of allowing the Bulgarian army to reintroduce conscription for military service. To my amazement, Sir Eric Drummond advised me to get the subject discussed in the German press.

"Why?" I asked. "How does Germany enter into the picture?"

"Because our London newspapers are very sensitive to what is written in Germany. A question raised in the German press will at once find a response in British public opinion."

I decided to drop the matter and left for the Lausanne Conference. This time most of the stars were absent. Sir Horace Rumbold succeeded Lord Curzon. Vorovsky, newly appointed Ambassador to Rome, headed the Soviet delegation. In place of the senile Marquis Garroni came Montagna, younger and more alert. The French delegates were the same old men, with the addition of Bargeton, a high Foreign Office official, no fool but an incorrigible pessimist. The contending Turks and Greeks were still represented by their aces, Ismet Pasha and Venizelos.

Turkey had already won a complete victory, and the sole concern of the Allies now as before was to get as many economic and financial concessions as possible from the new Turkish regime. The French were primarily interested in the Banque Ottoman and the tobacco monopoly, which had been founded with French capital. The British were trying to organize an oil monopoly. The Italians suddenly began to court the Turks in an effort to get favorable terms for the export of Italian manufactures to Turkey.

Ismet Pasha listened, smiled, and repeated his stock rejoinders: "The answer of the Turkish delegation is No!"; "The Turkish delegation will reply tomorrow."

But he told me privately, "Turkey no longer intends to be a colony of the European powers."

Anticipating a long conference, I sent for Nadejda and the children, of whom I had seen very little in recent months. The placid life on the shores of Lake Leman made the latent conspiracy in Bulgaria seem unreal and distant. Weeks had passed since Colonel Lichev's warning of a military plot, yet no disturbing news came from home. An April election to test public confidence in Stamboliski after the break with his Ministers had given the Peasant Party an overwhelming majority in the Sobranje—somewhat too large, indeed, for a completely fair election, yet indicating that his hold on the people was as firm as ever.

Two decorations which I received at this time added to my feeling of confidence. King Alexander conferred upon me the Order of St. Sava of the first class, and I became a Knight of the French Legion of Honor because of the Paris treaty on Bulgarian prewar debts, for which General Savov gave me the credit. For risking my life in 1916 I had received no recognition. Now, for having arranged a routine business deal, I became a member of the Legion of Honor.

Just when I felt most secure, a clap of thunder shattered my calm and changed the whole course of my life.

PART IV

EXILE

1923-1943

Only the mind cannot be exiled.

OVID

O<small>N</small> J<small>UNE</small> 9 <small>THE</small> Lausanne delegates made an excursion on the lake aboard a chartered steamer. The weather was perfect. A band played on deck. The mountains were reflected in the calm water, and the clean white cities of Lake Leman gleamed in the sun. When the boat stopped in Montreux, I bought a newspaper. The headline stood out large and clear: COUP D'ÉTAT IN BULGARIA.

During the night of June 8, the Sofia garrison had overthrown the Stamboliski government, and a new cabinet had been formed under Professor Tsankov. Later in the day, the newspapers reported that most of Stamboliski's ministers had been arrested and troops were being sent to seize him in his native village.

I hardly needed to verify the reports; the available details convinced me only too well that the Peasant regime had been overthrown. That evening, I sent a telegram to Sofia expressing my loyalty to the fallen government and resigning as delegate to the League of Nations and the Lausanne Conference. Our technical expert, Morfov, replaced me. I turned over to him the delegation's cash and sent my family back to Bulgaria, while I left for Paris to learn through the Quai d'Orsay exactly what was happening. The newspapers emphasized that the coup had been accomplished with little violence. I little suspected the bloody turn events were about to take.

Reports of revolt in the provinces and contradictory accounts of Stamboliski's death began to come through. The official version put out by the Tsankov government claimed that Stamboliski had been killed in southern Bulgaria during a struggle between the Sofia troops and armed peasants who had attacked the army automobile in which he was being driven to Sofia under arrest. At the Quai d'Orsay, Peretti de la Rocca showed me the report of the French Minister in Sofia, telling what had really happened. Piecing this together with other information I gathered later, I was finally able to reconstruct the whole gruesome story.

During the coup d'état in Sofia, Stamboliski was in his native village of Slavovitza, guarded by a platoon of loyal soldiers and peasants. When a detachment of troops arrived to arrest him, his men drove it off. Stamboliski then ordered that rockets be sent up—a prearranged signal for armed peasants to join him. Several thousand men arrived, but most of them were unarmed, although a few months earlier they had been furnished with all available rifles in anticipation of a possible army coup d'état. Officers in the conspiracy had convinced the gullible Minister of War, Muraviev, that the guns should be sent to an arsenal for cleaning and repair; and on his order most of the peasants had turned over their rifles to the army. No more than eight hundred of those who joined Stamboliski in Slavovitza carried guns and ammunition.

With these limited forces, Stamboliski moved on Tatar-Pazarjik, hoping to rally the peasants to his support. Regular troops moved out of the town against him, were defeated, and withdrew. Then Stamboliski repeated Daskalov's mistake in the uprising of September, 1918; he halted his peasants outside the town until morning. During the night, artillery arrived from the near-by city of Plovdiv, and the next day the peasants fled after resisting briefly. Stamboliski, left alone with his brother Vasili, managed to reach the village of Goliak, but was seized there and brought back to Tatar-Pazarjik, which was under the command of Colonel Vasiliev, his former schoolmate.

Some hours later several automobiles arrived from the capital, filled with Todor Alexandrov's Macedonians commanded by a Captain Harlakov and a professional assassin named Velichko. Harlakov produced an order from the Italian agent, Ivan Volkov, as Minister of War, and Vasiliev handed Stamboliski over to the Macedonians. They drove him back to his villa in Slavovitza, where they tortured him sadistically while he pleaded in vain for a quick death.

Velichko cut off his right arm and cried, "Here is the hand which signed the Nish Agreement with the Serbs!"

When at last Stamboliski was dead, Captain Harlakov and his men pillaged the villa and stole all the belongings of the murdered leader. They dismembered the corpse and buried the parts in several spots along the banks of the Maritsa River.

The men who overthrew the Peasant government represented widely divergent elements. Some of them, like Volkov, were paid agents of Italy. Others proclaimed themselves Fascists immediately after their victory. Some were Macedonian terrorists who served any cause for money. Many were honest men, mainly army officers, who had been convinced that Stamboliski intended to sacrifice Bulgarian independence for an eventual union with Yugoslavia. In short, the conspiracy was of the type later to be known as "fifth column"—Fascist agents and fellow-travelers, paid thugs, and innocents. Some of the innocents later broke with Tsankov and Volkov and stanchly supported the Peasant Party.

The King played a somewhat ambiguous role in the uprising. Rumors were widespread that he had ordered Stamboliski's murder, and his subsequent protection of Volkov proved that at the very least the crime had pleased him. On the night of the coup he returned late to his summer palace at Vrana, near Sofia, to find the conspirators waiting for him. He kept them in suspense until morning before signing the decree appointing Professor Tsankov head of the new government; he wanted to be sure that there could be no counterblow.

Stamboliski was killed just as his basic foreign policy was about to succeed—the policy of alliance between Bulgaria and Yugoslavia, constituting a bloc of twenty million Slavs around which all the Balkan peoples could group for their common defense against outside aggressors. His death blocked that alliance and served the immediate interests of Italy more clearly than those of any faction in Bulgaria. And it was Mussolini's paid agent, Volkov, who delivered Stamboliski to Mussolini's paid Macedonian assassins. Mussolini murdered Stamboliski, and thereby perpetuated Balkan disunity for the ultimate benefit of his future overlord, Hitler.

At news of the coup d'état the peasants rose against the slayers of their leader. In the north Stamboliski's Minister of Agriculture, Obov, massed 17,000 poorly armed men and attacked Plevna. The Tsankov-Volkov forces defeated the desperate peasant army and Obov fled to Rumania with thousands of his followers.

The Central Committee of the Bulgarian Communist Party, in its official newspaper, justified the Fascist coup. A month later, in July, the Executive Committee of the Communist International in Moscow condemned the attitude of the Bulgarian Communist Party during the coup as a grave tactical mistake, and *Pravda* published the Comintern's appeal to the Bulgarian workers and peasants to overthrow the new regime. This put the Bulgarian Communists in an embarrassing position, but they attempted to save face and justify their behavior on the ground that "the Peasants, by their policy, had destroyed the faith of the masses."

The new regime rounded up every Peasant leader on whom it could lay hands. Prisons became so overcrowded that hundreds of schools were turned into temporary jails. More than two hundred Peasant deputies were arrested, and all of Stamboliski's ministers except Obov, who was safe in Rumania, and Raiko Daskalov, whom Stamboliski had sent to Prague.

In the first days after the coup, twenty Peasant deputies were removed from prisons at night, driven on trucks into the mountains, killed, and their bodies hurled into ravines. On a fast-moving train between Tatar-Pazarjik and Sofia, the Peasant Minister of Justice was shot and his body thrown from the compartment window. When the corpse was found, the government announced that he had leaped from the train to escape arrest. This was the first phase of the Tsankov terror. A few months later it would seem almost mild in retrospect.

Daskalov, who had been elected Vice-President at a congress in 1921, now became the leader of the Peasant Party. I remembered my promise to Stamboliski to join the party when it was no longer in power, and with Obov joined Daskalov in Prague to plan our future work. With Bulgarian refugees pouring into Yugoslavia, Daskalov suggested that I go to Belgrade to make arrangements with the Yugoslav government to feed and shelter them.

In Belgrade I found even greater sympathy than I had anticipated. Now that Stamboliski was dead, all Yugoslavia paid tribute to him, and everyone recalled that he had been the first "Yugoslav" when in August, 1914, in defiance of the anti-Serbian sentiment in the Sobranje, he had made an impassioned speech praying for a Serbian victory over Austria.

One deputy had cried: "You're no Bulgarian! You're a Serb!"

"You're right," Stamboliski had answered. "I'm no Bulgarian. Neither am I a Serb. I'm a Slav of the South—a Yugoslav!"

King Alexander, when I called upon him for a farewell audience, expressed his sorrow that all Stamboliski had worked for had been destroyed on the very eve of success.

"But it has only been postponed," he said, "because sooner or later the Peasant Party will return to power."

Old Pashich heartened me. "You don't know the peasants as I do. When a storm comes, they bow their heads. But later they raise them once more. The most important thing is that they forget neither good nor evil. And they know how to wait. We city people are always in a hurry. We demand immediate payment for our work. But the peasant plants the seed in the autumn and gathers the harvest only the following summer."

Pashich stroked his white beard and almost chanted, "The peasants are accustomed to wait for the harvest—and there shall be a harvest."

While I was busy organizing camps for our refugees, news of more government murders came from Bulgaria. Realizing that return to Sofia was impossible, I decided to go to Geneva as soon as the League of Nations convened, to work against the Tsankov-Volkov regime. Meanwhile, I went to Paris to urge French intervention in behalf of a number of the arrested Bulgarians who faced death.

Peretti de la Rocca promised me that the French government would do everything possible. From that moment until the Communist uprising in September there were no killings, with one notable exception—Nikola Ghenadiev, my Sofia prison comrade through whom I had made most of my Paris connections. Ghenadiev, one of the best lawyers in Bulgaria, never had been a member of Stamboliski's government. But when the Tsankov regime began a series of trials against all who had resisted the coup d'état, he took upon himself the thankless task of defending the accused peasants. He succeeded in getting a number of acquittals, but they cost him his life. One of Volkov's aides murdered him.

In Paris I arranged to work as a caricaturist for several newspapers. I had not done caricatures since my brief stay in Sofia before the war, when my lampoons of King Ferdinand had forced me to leave the country. My technique was rusty and I spent a great deal of time in cafés, sketching every interesting face I could find. By the time I reached Geneva for the League of Nations session I had regained a certain dexterity.

My standing as a former League delegate enabled me to move freely in otherwise inaccessible circles. I explained the situation in Bulgaria to all the delegates I could corner, from Lord Robert Cecil to the South American representatives, while doing caricatures of them. Thus I combined my political mission with my new profession. My caricatures were more successful than I had anticipated. An issue of *L'Europe Nouvelle,* dedicated to the League of Nations, contained many of my drawings. Others appeared in the *Petit Parisien,* the *London Daily Mail,* the local Swiss newspapers and the Belgrade *Politika.* For a time I found myself earning more as a cartoonist than I had as a diplomat.

The Bulgarian delegation to the League was now headed by Foreign Minister Kalfov, former adjutant to the King, who had presented the Order of St. Alexander to me two years before. During one of the sessions he approached me.

"His Majesty King Boris asked me to give you his best regards."

Somewhat surprised, I answered that I was pleased.

"I want to talk to you," said Kalfov. A number of delegates saw us conversing and promptly spread word that I was rejoining the Bulgarian delegation.

When Kalfov and I met the next morning he spoke plainly. "The government believes that you and Petko Petkov were the ablest diplomats of the fallen regime. I'm authorized to offer you the following terms: you'll be reappointed a plenipotentiary minister, but without a fixed post. Your headquarters will be Paris and your job will be to conduct Bulgarian propaganda in France and Yugoslavia. Because of the special nature of your work you'll receive an appropriate salary and all necessary expenses."

"What interests me," I said, "is not a soft berth for myself, but the foreign policy you intend to follow. What you call my diplomatic skill was only the sound Balkan policy of Stamboliski. What's yours to be?

[195]

If I find it acceptable I'll undertake the work you suggest without an official position or a salary."

Kalfov began by explaining that in his opinion Bulgaria had to pursue a careful course, without commitments to anyone. "The recent policy of close collaboration with Yugoslavia, for example, prejudiced our relations with Italy. For that reason we can't accept it."

"In that case there's little more to be said," I answered. "The future safety of the Balkan peoples depends upon their solidarity. To accept your offer would make it necessary for me to deceive both the Yugoslavs and the French. What's more, your internal policy is based on force and violence."

Kalfov tried to assure me that things had calmed down and civil liberty would soon be restored. I rejected his proposal.

A few days later, I received an agitated letter from Nadejda. Realizing that I could not return to Sofia I had asked her to join me in Switzerland. Now I learned that she and the children had been removed from the train as they were about to leave the country. What was even more alarming, the police were threatening to exile them to Petrich, in Bulgarian Macedonia, where they would be at the mercy of Todor Alexandrov's *chetas*.

I telephoned Kalfov, asking for an immediate interview. His voice sounded almost affectionate over the telephone, and he invited me to come to his hotel at once. I drove down in a cab, controlling my rage with difficulty.

"Well, so you've decided to work with us?" Kalfov beamed.

Instead of answering, I handed him Nadejda's letter. He shrugged his shoulders.

"That's in the hands of the police; there's nothing I can do. However, if you accept the government's offer I'm sure arrangements can be made for your family."

"Colonel Kalfov, you've probably heard that I wasn't always a diplomat; that I've had occasion to use a revolver and even to throw a bomb."

He looked mildly amused.

"I give you my word of honor." I said, "that if in twenty-four hours I don't receive a telegram from my wife informing me that she is on her way to Geneva, I'll shoot you down like a dog."

"What, you dare to threaten me!" he shouted.

"It's a promise, not a threat. I repeat: I give you my word of honor I'll kill you unless I hear from my wife tomorrow."

That same evening Nadejda wired that she was leaving with the children on the first Orient Express.

On September 19 came news of a Communist uprising in Bulgaria, and I hastened at once to Belgrade. From the new refugees streaming into Yugoslavia, I learned what had happened. The Communists had expected that in return for their benevolent attitude during the June coup d'état, the new government would give them a free hand in their political activity. Instead, the Tsankov-Volkov government late in August outlawed the Communist Party and confiscated its property, including the great headquarters in Sofia which it converted into police headquarters.

The Sofia workers didn't respond to the Communist call for an uprising. Of the cities, only Stara Zagora revolted, but an attack on the barracks there was repulsed. In northern Bulgaria, near the Yugoslav frontier, several thousand peasants rose under Georgi Dimitrov and Vasili Kolarov, the Communist leaders. They organized a "provisional government" in the mountains, with a Peasant Party schoolteacher as Minister of Education and all the other cabinet posts in Communist hands. The peasants defeated several battalions of soldiers, but were finally crushed with the aid of Macedonian terrorists and White Russians of General Wrangel's former army.

A week later, Dimitrov and Kolarov crossed the Yugoslav border with 2,000 peasants who were disarmed by the frontier patrol. The Communist leaders asked to see me; they wanted me to get them passports to Vienna and money for the trip. They justified their behavior during the June coup on the ground that Stamboliski had persecuted them. Now, they said, we must organize a united front which would overthrow Tsankov and set up a "workers' and peasants'" government in Bulgaria.

I telephoned the Ministry of the Interior in Belgrade, and several hours later passports arrived at the border for Dimitrov and Kolarov, on the understanding they would be surrendered to the Yugoslav legation in Vienna. I gave them money to cover their immediate expenses. I couldn't resist the temptation to remind Dimitrov that his "proletariat" had failed to respond and that the recent uprising had been staged entirely by the "petit bourgeois" peasants. This time he took my taunts good-humoredly. I agreed to meet him later in Vienna to discuss plans for joint Peasant-Communist action against the Tsankov-Volkov regime.

The usurpers soon set out to rid the Peasant Party of all its leaders, in Bulgaria or abroad. Raiko Daskalov was murdered in Prague by an assassin who admitted to the Czech police that he had been sent by the IMRO. Daskalov's death coincided with the beginning of an unprecedented reign of terror in Bulgaria. In every city, village, and hamlet the Tsankov-Volkov government conducted pogroms against its opponents; in some villages not a single male was spared. An investigation subsequently conducted by Émile Vandervelde, the Belgian Socialist leader, revealed that some seventeen thousand persons perished in the terror of 1923-24.

It was now morally impossible for me to remain aloof from the armed struggle against the usurpers. As soon as I had arranged with the Yugoslav government for the care of our new refugees, I left for Prague. There Obov and I founded a Revolutionary Committee to work for the overthrow of the dictatorship in Bulgaria.

First of all, we needed money. At the very outset the Czech Agrarian Party gave us half a million crowns. Then I went to Paris and in Mme. Ménard-Dorian's salon explained the connection between the Bulgarian terror and Mussolini's Balkan policy.

Returning to Yugoslavia, I began to organize the Bulgarian exiles into a fighting force—about 4,000 men, mostly followers of the Peasant Party, but also a good many Communists. I dispersed them at various places near the Bulgarian border and organized them in military units under commanders who were to be responsible to me.

Within two months, the framework of our organization was complete. The 4,000 men were divided into four battalions, and each battalion into ten companies of 100 men each. The refugees who had work paid 10 per cent of their wages to the Revolutionary Committee. The best men became our secret couriers, slipping into Bulgaria to deliver communications to local Peasant leaders in the name of the committee. Soon in the villages on the other side of the border we had our secret revolutionary network organized in the tradition of the *chetas* which had fought the Turks. Conspiracy was almost instinctive with the peasants of the frontier. Some of my couriers penetrated deep into Bulgaria to paste on telegraph poles leaflets reading:

THE COURIERS OF THE REVOLUTIONARY COMMITTEE HAVE PASSED THROUGH HERE.

These notes meant more than the longest proclamation, for they gave the people hope and alarmed the authorities.

Obov and I continued our efforts to win the support of the democratic governments against Bulgarian dictatorship. They were adamant. As far as they were concerned, the Tsankov-Volkov regime, although it had destroyed the people's government, was legal because it had the King's approval. At the Quai d'Orsay, Bargeton, the new director of the political section, invariably gave me the same answer, "We can't meddle in Bulgaria's internal affairs." During our Peasant regime, almost every time a speculator was arrested, M. Piquot, the French Minister, would protest that the man represented French interests. Now the usurpers' bloody pogroms were classed as a "purely internal" affair in which the democracies could not meddle. In vain did I argue that this "internal affair" was closely bound up with the Balkan ambitions of Fascist Italy and that the Tsankov-Volkov government itself was the monstrous creature of Italian intervention in our affairs.

Success in Bulgaria made Mussolini bolder. His next Balkan move was open aggression, made possible by Allied stupidity and sanctioned by Allied pusillanimity. In 1921, the Conference of Ambassadors of Great Britain, France, Italy, and Japan had recognized Italy's special interest in Albania, thereby opening the way for Italian interference in Albanian affairs under the guise of protection. Since the Albanian frontier had not been entirely defined by the Conference of Ambassadors, Italy sent to southern Albania a military mission headed by General Telini, to fix the border with Greece.

In August, 1923, Telini and four officers of his staff were killed on Greek territory near the border by unknown assassins, in all probability Albanian bandits. Mussolini chose to blame the Greeks, delivered an outrageous ultimatum, then bombarded and occupied the island of Corfu. Greece appealed to the League of Nations, which instead of adopting sanctions against Italy, permitted it to collect half a million pounds in damages. But world opinion forced Mussolini to evacuate Corfu. Even so the incident was valuable to him; it proved that he need not fear the League of Nations. The man chiefly responsible for the League's capitulation was Sir Eric Drummond, later Lord Perth, then chief of the League Secretariat and afterward British Ambassador to Rome. The precedent led not only to the disintegration of the League; it led to the disintegration of Europe.

W HILE THOUSANDS OF our supporters lay in prison, the Tsankov-Volkov government held an election to test its "popularity." Terror gave it a decisive victory; even so the Peasant Party elected twenty-six deputies, most of them newcomers to the party. My friends Petko Petkov and Lieutenant Nicolas Petrini, outraged by the crimes of the usurpers, had joined the Peasant Party and were both elected to the Sobranje. These two fearless men led the Peasant deputies in parliament while secretly joining our Revolutionary Committee. Through my couriers I received word from them urging me to enter into negotiations with Georgi Dimitrov for united action against the dictatorship.

In January, 1924, Dimitrov and I met in the Park Hotel at Schönbrunn, near Vienna. A few months of life abroad had had a remarkable effect on Dimitrov. He was perfumed and elegant. During our conversation, only Gavril Genov was present. Genov, in charge of the activities of Bulgarian Communists in Yugoslavia, was a man of exceptional cunning and organizing ability who knew how to appear modest and naïve. He asked me for money for his men in Yugoslavia, and for a long time concealed the fact that the Comintern was sending him $3,000 a month for the Bulgarian Communist exiles. I learned this when the Yugoslav authorities showed me letters they had intercepted; but by that time I had already given Genov 50,000 dinars, which he used to organize his own courier service. In fairness to the man, it must be said that he never used party funds for himself.

Dimitrov's proposals were interesting. He wanted us to acknowledge that the goal of our struggle against Tsankov was the establishment of a "workers' and peasants'" government, with the Communist Party dominating. The government would consist of ten members: six Peasants and four Communists. We would hold the premiership, but the key ministries of war, interior, and communications would be in Communist hands. The fourth post for his party was immaterial, Dimitrov said, provided the army, the police, and communications were under Communist control. In return he promised full Russian support—the creation of a Bulgarian revolutionary base in Odessa and the shipment of arms into Bulgaria by way of the Black Sea. All the material resources necessary for an insurrection would be placed at the disposal of our Revolutionary Committee, which would be reorganized to include Communists.

The government Dimitrov proposed was impossible not only from our own point of view, but from that of international relations. In all but name it would have been a Communist dictatorship against which our neighbors certainly would have acted. To accept would have been to risk a repetition of the Hungarian experience of 1919, when the Béla Kun government was overthrown by Rumanian intervention. Dimitrov's unyielding insistence on all three government posts which controlled the life of the country proved clearly that he planned a Communist dictatorship rather than a coalition government. When I flatly rejected his terms he adopted a conciliatory tone and suggested that I go to Moscow, where all our differences could be ironed out. "I'm sure we shall find a basis for agreement," he concluded.

I promised to answer in a few days. From Prague Obov and I consulted the members of the Revolutionary Committee in Bulgaria, who urged me to accept Dimitrov's invitation.

As a further precaution I saw Benes and told him that if I didn't return from Moscow within a reasonable time, it would mean that the Soviet authorities were holding me as a hostage. He advised me to call on the head of the Czech trade mission in Moscow, who if necessary would communicate with Prague about me.

"The Bolsheviks are trying to establish diplomatic relations with all the countries of Europe and aren't likely to make a scandal by holding you," he said.

When I returned to Vienna to arrange the details of my trip, Dimitrov had already left for Moscow. In his stead I saw Charsky, chief representative of the Comintern in Vienna and director of Communist propaganda for the Balkans. We met in the Hotel Imperial. While we ate, all sorts of people stopped at our table to greet him. Most of them were extremely well dressed and did not look like Communists.

"Who are they?" I asked.

"*Schieber*" (profiteers), he laughed. "They deal with us in the Soviet trade mission. We find them very useful."

I explained to Charsky that going to Moscow with my Bulgarian diplomatic passport would cause me trouble upon my return. If I traveled on a Soviet passport no questions would be asked because I could easily pass as a Russian. He promised to arrange the matter, and several days later informed me that a passport awaited me in Berlin.

I arrived in Berlin late in January. Somewhat to my surprise I was received at the Soviet Embassy by Ambassador Krestinsky himself. Nikolai Krestinsky looked like a typical Russian intellectual—beard, spectacles, and all. His manner, however, was businesslike. He questioned me briefly about the situation in Bulgaria, listened attentively, and commented, "I trust that now the Bulgarian Communists will correct their mistakes. They made a capital error during the Tsankov uprising."

Krestinsky impressed me favorably, although I was slightly annoyed by his use of certain hackneyed expressions which betrayed an ideological fanaticism. He handed me the Soviet passport and wished me the best of luck. I never saw him again. In 1938 he was executed in Moscow with Bukharin, Rykov, and Yagoda.

On the train to Moscow I met S. A. Lozovsky, now Vice-Commissar of Foreign Affairs, to whom it has fallen to be the press spokesman of the Commissariat during these heroic days of Russian history. He was then head of the Red Trade Union International, and was returning with his wife and young secretary from a mission to Paris. All three were elegantly dressed; but as we neared the Soviet frontier remarkable changes took place in their appearance. Lozovsky and his secretary now wore shabby old suits, and the rings had disappeared from their fingers. Mme. Lozovsky, who had been wearing a bracelet and earrings, appeared in a plain wool dress and no jewelry. I asked Lozovsky why this change.

"Returning to our Soviet fatherland," he said scornfully, "we cast aside the bourgeois appearances which are necessary in western Europe."

At the Latvian-Soviet frontier the baggage of my three friends was not inspected, but as a simple "Soviet citizen" I was undressed, my clothing was carefully searched, and when nothing else was found my foreign newspapers and a few French books were confiscated. In vain I protested that the books were harmless novels.

"Novels, perhaps," said the Soviet customs officials, "but bourgeois novels."

I arrived in Moscow on January 28, 1924, the day after Lenin's funeral. It was fearfully cold, and I froze in the sleigh that took me to the address Charsky had given me. The driver was a Tver peasant who worked in Moscow during the winter months.

"Well, it's better now that the peasants have land," I ventured.

"What land?" he asked. "I had my four acres before the Revolution and I still have four acres. And my land is good for nothing—all sand." With a sigh he added, "It's a hard life, *barin*."

The word *barin* (master), a relic of Czarist days, surprised me. "What makes you think I'm a *barin*?"

"I can tell by your clothes."

"But there are no masters in Russia."

"How so? There are new ones," he answered with a shrug.

In the lobby of the Hotel Lux on the Tverskaya I was stopped by a determined individual in a leather jacket, armed with a revolver. For half an hour I tried in vain to convince him that I had an appointment with Vasili Kolarov, Secretary of the Communist International. His only answer was, "Are you a Communist or aren't you? If you aren't, you've no business here." The Lux, I afterward learned, was reserved for foreign Communists and was always closely guarded.

I was about to leave when by chance Georgi Dimitrov walked in. He professed to be delighted to see me and told the human barrier, evidently a Cheka agent, that I was his comrade. I was taken to a large room on the second floor where I found Kolarov, his wife, and one of his sons sitting around a table having tea with bread and cheese. Kolarov told me I could not stay at the Lux, but sent me to the Hotel Europa near the Alexander III Museum, where a room had been reserved for me. It was richly furnished in pre-Revolutionary style, but it had no washing facilities, nor was there one usable bathroom in the entire hotel. I had to wash at a faucet in the hall and use a shirt for a towel.

That evening I wandered about the city, still decorated with the placards and banners of Lenin's funeral, with their enormous inscriptions of which the most common was, "Lenin is Dead, but Leninism Lives." In the Red Square, close to the Kremlin wall, Lenin's body lay in a temporary frame mausoleum, a squat, incongruous structure over which towered the belfries and cupolas of the Greek Orthodox churches and palaces.

In the food stores everything from white bread to the most expensive smoked fish and caviar was available for those who could pay, and there were no queues, for this was the era of the New Economic Policy. The people on the streets were plainly but warmly dressed—excepting the enormous number of half-frozen, homeless children who roamed the city, selling matches, snatching purses, or huddling together in restaurant doorways hoping someone would give them bread.

The first proposal of Dimitrov and Kolarov was identical with the one I had already rejected in Vienna. I answered quietly that those terms were still unacceptable.

"Suppose you make a counterproposal," Kolarov suggested, whereupon I offered the following agreement: The Peasant Party and the Bulgarian Communist Party would fight jointly against the Tsankov-Volkov regime. For this purpose a United Revolutionary Committee of the two parties would be formed, consisting of an equal number of representatives of the two parties in Bulgaria and abroad. Our immediate common objective would be to organize an insurrection. That achieved, a provisional Peasant government would be formed which would restore civil liberty, legalize the Communist Party, and hold democratic elections to determine what the future government would be.

"According to you, then, we're not even to be represented in the government?" Dimitrov exploded.

"Of course not. That would result in foreign occupation. I prefer any Bulgarian government to foreign occupation, which might end with the partition of Bulgaria."

"In other words, you want us to fight to bring you to power?" sneered Dimitrov.

"True. But it's in your interest to do so, because we'll give you full freedom."

"We know all about your freedom," said Kolarov. "Dimitrov and I spent several months eluding your police."

The whole conversation was in a semijesting tone, but I understood that there was no common ground on which we could stand. Our debate went on for several days without result. At last Dimitrov made a new proposal. He agreed to give us either the Ministry of War or that of the Interior; but in exchange for this "big concession" the Peasant Party was to enter the newly created Peasant International.

"What sort of international is this?" I asked.

"Polish and Baltic peasants are already joining it, together with the Russians," said Dimitrov. "All the progressive peasant organizations of Europe, including the Croatian Peasant Party, will be invited to join. The secretary of the organization is Dombal, a Polish deputy. I'll introduce you to him."

"And the purpose of this international?"

"A united front of workers and peasants throughout the world," was his grandiloquent reply.

"Listen, Dimitrov," I said, "I'm not here to settle world problems. My authority is strictly limited—to negotiate with the Bulgarian Communist Party for a united struggle against Tsankov. Nothing else interests me."

Dimitrov then played his trump card. "If you sign this agreement," he said, "twenty million French francs will be placed at your disposal in the Lenderbank in Vienna. You'll have a free hand in spending it for arms and whatever else you need, provided you turn over half the weapons you buy to the Communists in Bulgaria. Gavril Genov will be your assistant. You may take as much as you find necessary for your personal use."

"Money is of secondary importance," I answered. "When there are brave men willing to fight, money can always be raised."

"Then this is a rejection?" he asked angrily.

"Yes. My original proposal represents the only possible basis for an understanding."

"Then it's clear that you never intended to come to any agreement with us," said Kolarov triumphantly.

"Would you really prefer that I deceive you by accepting your terms and later disregarding them?"

"We'll find others who'll agree to them," said Dimitrov.

"Perhaps, but in the event of a successful uprising, they won't keep a single promise."

On that we parted. I intended to leave Moscow and told them so.

"Let's have a few days' recess," Kolarov said. "We'll continue our talks later. I must discuss the matter with Zinoviev and Bukharin."

I agreed to wait until February 15, thinking to see Chicherin meanwhile. Perhaps I could convince him that my proposal should be accepted as the basis for an agreement. At the Commissariat of Foreign Affairs I was received by Herman Sandomirsky, chief of the Balkan Division, whom I had known many years before in the Odessa prison. He had been an anarchist then. He explained that he was still an anarchist but had decided to work for the Soviet regime "to save the people from reaction." He promised to speak with Chicherin and let me know the outcome the next day.

The Balkan Section of the Foreign Commissariat was a sorry sight. On the wall hung an imposing map of the Balkan Peninsula, but not a single newspaper from any Balkan country was visible. Sandomirsky himself knew nothing about Balkan problems.

"Where do you get your information on the Balkans?" I asked.

"From the Comintern in the form of weekly reports," replied Sandomirsky. "By the way, there's a Bulgarian here who knows you. He works under me."

"Who is he?"

He mentioned a name I didn't know. Sandomirsky sent for the Bulgarian. A self-assured young man appeared, with a cigarette between his teeth.

"Vasiliev, your compatriot," Sandomirsky introduced me.

"I hear that you know Kosta Todorov," I said. "Unfortunately I've never met him. What's he like?"

My compatriot proceeded to describe me in great detail. "I was with him almost every day in Sofia," he assured us.

Sandomirsky looked on amused. "This is Kosta Todorov," he said at last.

The young man lost his composure for a moment, then muttered, "Well, it must have been another Kosta Todorov."

In the Commissariat of Foreign Affairs I found another old Odessa prison comrade, Jacob Schmidman, who had been sentenced to twelve years for armed resistance to the police. He was a weaver from Kishinev who could neither read nor write when I met him in prison. He was one of my least promising pupils. I taught him to write, but that was about all. History and literature were too much for him. Strangely enough, he now belonged to a Moscow literary circle. Proudly he gave me a brochure he had written on Bessarabia, which began with Pushkin's words,

> O, Godforsaken Kishinev,
> My tongue grows tired cursing you.

I recalled that those were the only lines of poetry he had ever been able to memorize, because they dealt with his native city. Pushkin was not yet an official Soviet idol, and Schmidman's pamphlet continued,

> That is how the contemptible aristocrat, Pushkin, described our splendid city.

My prison comrade occupied an important post as the chief of railway transportation between Moscow and Orel. He told me that another of our Odessa prison mates, the noted anarchist writer, Novomirsky, was editing a publication in Moscow. I called on Novomirsky forthwith. When he saw me he wept. He had lately been released from the prison to which he had been confined after the Kronstadt revolt.

"How did you get your job?" I asked.

"For a simple reason. They haven't enough intellectuals. They give us jobs, but force us to write as they dictate. I'm no longer young and I have my wife to think of."

I asked him about his economic situation.

"It's not bad. I get twice as much pay as a commissar, but the moral yoke is intolerable. I'd rather dig ditches in France than hold a high post here." He said this almost in a whisper; he had become a frightened and broken man. Under the Czar he had spent twelve years in prison but had never made the slightest compromise.

"You understand," he continued hoarsely, "these people deform the soul and cripple the mind. Under the Czar we believed that the Revolution would bring universal freedom. The Revolution came. What are we to cling to now that the princess of our dreams has turned into an ogress?"

The next night I was told that Chicherin expected me. The Foreign Commissar, who habitually slept most of the day and worked in a frenzy at night, seldom received callers before two in the morning. He wore a strange, slightly intoxicated expression and no longer talked as freely as in Lausanne. I asked him whether, in the event of an uprising in Bulgaria and the intervention of our neighbors, he could guarantee to help us. Could he help us against Rumania, for example?

"There is an alliance between Rumania and Poland," he answered.

"Then I take it the answer is No."

He nodded. I told him what the Bulgarians of the Comintern were demanding. He smiled wryly, shrugged his shoulders, and said, "You know I can't interfere in the affairs of the Comintern."

I realized for the first time that this man who seemed so important was mere window dressing.

Learning from the French papers that Henri Rollin, my friend of *Le Temps,* was in Moscow, I looked him up and told him of my feeling that the Soviet authorities might not let me leave the country if I didn't sign an agreement with Dimitrov and Kolarov.

"In that case, come to me," he said. "They're very anxious at the moment to have no unpleasant reports reach the foreign press. I'm sure you won't be detained. The Soviet government knows I've been working for French recognition, and my good will is valued here."

At tea in the Hotel Europa next day I saw Count Manzoni, the new Italian Ambassador. We had been colleagues in the Belgrade diplomatic corps, but this meeting was embarrassing for us both, and we spoke for only a moment. Later a beautiful, well dressed young woman who had seen me talking with the Italian Ambassador sat down at a table next to mine.

"I'm happy to find someone who speaks French," she began. "May I join you?"

"You're Russian, of course?" I asked.

"Yes, but I've spoken French since childhood. I had a French governess. You see," she added quietly, "I'm a former aristocrat."

"Are you living at this hotel?"

"Yes. I'm looking for another place, but so far I haven't found any."

The Hotel Europa was expensive. It occurred to me that this beautiful creature was working for the Cheka, and when she asked me to introduce her to Count Manzoni I was convinced of it. By becoming better acquainted with her, I thought I might discover what the police had in mind for me. When she suggested a drive, I agreed at once.

In a fast sleigh we drove off through the snow-packed streets. My lady spoke openly against the regime and praised the good old Czarist days, although the driver could hear her. She suggested that we drive to a club where we could dine well and spend a gay evening. The place was not far from the Kuznetsky Most. Singers and dancers performed, but couldn't always be heard above the din of the crowd. There was also gambling.

"Is the club open to the public?" I asked.

"Of course not. It's entirely private."

"How do the police tolerate it?"

"You know," she smiled, "it's always possible to come to an understanding with the police."

The dinner was excellent, but the prices were fantastic; when my lovely companion asked for wine, the bill amounted to about thirty dollars. With my limited budget this was quite an expense. When she asked me to come with her into the gambling salon I hesitated, but curiosity won out. In spite of her urging, however, I refused to play.

"Let me play," she begged. Not wanting to appear stingy, I gave her a *chervonetz* (value about $8), which she quickly lost at roulette. When I refused to give her more she became incensed, called me a miser, and left. Although I was sure the woman was a Cheka agent, her game mystified me, but when I told Rollin the story he laughed knowingly.

"This sort of thing happens regularly to foreigners whom the government wants to use. Pretty women induce them to gamble away every kopeck. When they're cleaned out, the Cheka agents who run the place generously lend them money. They've caught many a fish in that net. People who take their money once continue to take it and do whatever is asked of them. If you hadn't stopped in time, I'm afraid that sooner or later you'd have signed any agreement handed to you."

"If that's your opinion of these people, why are you in favor of an understanding with the Soviets?"

"Because I'm a Frenchman and I fear Germany. Whatever its government, we need Russia as an ally."

With Rollin and his wife I visited the Tretyakov Galleries, home of the masterpieces of Russian painting. In the room containing the works of Repin was a class of students from thirteen to sixteen years old, conducted by a drawing instructor and a political mentor. The first soberly explained the artistic qualities of a picture which showed Ivan the Terrible killing his eldest son. Then the political tutor spoke.

"Citizens, from our Communist standpoint the painting has another significance. It shows how in the sixteenth century, nearly 350 years ago, the ruling class treated the proletariat. Ivan the Terrible represents the bourgeoisie. His son Ivan wanted to become the champion of the proletariat. That's why the Czar killed him. Thus you see the class struggle of that epoch."

As a former Czarist prisoner I was invited to a banquet given by a society of former political prisoners who had served terms at hard labor in Siberia. At that time the society included veterans of all the revolutionary parties. Only a few were Bolsheviks. The dinner took place in what had once been the home of a rich merchant, not far from the Kitaigorod section of Moscow.

I was seated between two Communists. Of the guests I knew only Sandomirsky, Novomirsky, and Schmidman. But I recognized a man who sat almost directly opposite me. He was fair, with astonishingly clear eyes and a pale, ascetic face. He had once known anguish in a Siberian prison; now it was his turn to inflict it on others. Looking at him it was hard to realize that his name inspired dread; for this pale, sensitive man was Felix Dzerzhinsky, founder and chief of the Cheka, now called the G.P.U. Yet he was known to be incorrigibly honest; it was whispered that he had recently shot one of his closest friends for embezzling public funds.

Despite Dzerzhinsky's presence, the party became gay after we had drunk a good deal of wine from the Crimean cellars of the late Czar. We sang our old prison songs, and men spoke almost with nostalgia of Siberia. Dzerzhinsky drank little and seemed sad and tired. The tipsy Communist at my right began to pump me with questions about how I liked what was going on in Soviet Russia. I had had a lot to drink and his persistence finally annoyed me. I replied with four lines of verse which for several days had been forming in my head:

> *Tsarstvo bezumnikh ekstazov*
> *Tolko geroi ne novi*
> *Lenin-Ivan Karamazov*
> *Bratya yevo—Smerdyakovi*

(Kingdom of insane raptures, your heroes are ever the same! Lenin is Ivan Karamazov. His comrades in arms are Smerdyakovs.)

Dzerzhinsky heard me distinctly. A fleeting smile lit up his face; then he turned his head away as if he had not heard.

"What does it mean?" asked my neighbor.

"Ivan Karamazov said that everything was permissible, so Smerdyakov stole and murdered."

Fortunately my neighbor still didn't understand. Later, when I remembered what I had said, I trembled to think what Dzerzhinsky might have done had he taken me seriously.

When I finally spoke to Kolarov and Dimitrov again, I realized it was hopeless. Their new proposal differed from the first only in wording. I insisted on leaving at once, explaining that I had a great deal to do and already had stayed too long in Moscow.

"That's no concern of ours," said Dimitrov. "Leave, if you can get permission from the authorities."

"Is that a threat?"

"No. We simply aren't interested in arranging for your departure, and you may find it difficult to leave Russia on a Soviet passport."

It was almost midnight when I left my compatriots and went to a restaurant. Two youngsters standing at the door threw themselves upon me with the cry, "Citizen, buy matches!" I gave them all the change I had in my pocket and entered amid savage shouts as they fought over their spoils.

Inside, at a table loaded with elaborate foods, fruits out of season, and choice wines, sat a man in Caucasian costume, with a sword. With him were four heavily painted women. I ordered only one dish and a bottle of *kvas*—all I could afford. Suddenly the Caucasian staggered toward me, a cigarette in his mouth.

"Bourgeois!" he said insolently, "get up and light my cigarette."

I ignored him.

"Light my cigarette, or I'll beat the hell out of you!" he shouted.

I stood up, my hand in my right pocket. When he swung at me, I pulled my revolver and hit him across the face with the butt. He reeled back with a bloody nose, but the waiters came to his assistance. Then I took out the red card which Kolarov had given me when I arrived in Moscow, issued only to foreigners enjoying the protection of the Comintern. The waiters at once apologized and the drunken Caucasian came up to me with arms outstretched.

"I didn't know you were a comrade," he cried.

I pushed him aside and said, "I'll see that Dzerzhinsky hears how you spend Soviet money."

The Caucasian quickly paid his bill and left without his ladies. I finished my meal in peace.

The next day I went to the Commissariat of Foreign Affairs for my visa. Sandomirsky took my passport and promised to arrange it. I waited two days, then telephoned.

"There's some complication," he told me. "I don't know what it is myself."

I went at once to Henri Rollin. He picked up the telephone, called the Foreign Commissariat, and said that if I didn't have a visa the next day, he would be forced to communicate with Paris. The next morning my passport was returned with the necessary visas. Ten minutes later Kolarov's voice came over the telephone. "Drop in before you leave." This time both Kolarov and Dimitrov were agreeable enough, but I understood that they now considered me their enemy.

When I crossed the Soviet frontier and saw behind me the inscription, "Greetings to the Proletariat of the West," I felt greatly relieved.

Back in Belgrade, I found that the Communists had begun a whispering campaign against me—even accusing me of being Tsankov's agent. Gavril Genov seemed as friendly as ever and stoutly denied responsibility for the slander, but my own people told me another story. The Communists were doing everything in their power to disrupt our organization, spending money freely to bribe some of my lieutenants. Making a hasty inspection of our camps, I removed ten doubtful commanders and replaced them with more reliable men.

Our supporters in Bulgaria were clamoring for guns and money, but we had only fifty revolvers. I decided to visit Paris and Prague to raise money for our needs. With the help of Mme. Ménard-Dorian, I collected nearly 250,000 francs in Paris. At her suggestion I went to see Émile Vandervelde in Brussels. Acting for the Socialist International, Vandervelde had gone to Bulgaria and seen with his own eyes the effects of the Tsankov-Volkov terror. He was more than eager to co-operate with us, and aided by him I added 200,000 francs to our fund.

In Czechoslovakia the Socialist Party enabled us to publish our newspaper, *The Peasant Banner,* in Bulgarian and in French. We distributed the French edition among European statesmen and journalists. The Bulgarian edition, printed on thin cigarette paper, our couriers smuggled into Bulgaria and distributed among the peasants. Antonin Svehla, the Czech Agrarian leader, and Beheny, the Socialist minister, gave us 350,000 crowns.

From Prague I went to Vienna. Everything was sold in Vienna in 1924, but the biggest trade was in government secrets and guns. Through Austria passed the arms Mussolini was secretly sending to the Hungarian Irredentists. The Austrian railway workers stole a good part of this contraband, so I was able to buy at a very low price twenty Schwarzlose machine guns and five hundred Parabellum automatic revolvers, with the necessary ammunition.

With the help of a firm selling agricultural implements, we packed the guns in boxes with a few farm tools on top and sent them down the Danube to Belgrade, to a friend connected with a farm co-operative, who had no trouble with the customs officials. The total cost was about 150,000 francs. By the middle of April the crates reached the Bulgarian frontier, and within ten days most of the guns had been smuggled through well-organized channels to our comrades within the country. We kept only a few machine guns and about a hundred automatic revolvers for ourselves in Yugoslavia. Although the quantity of arms was small, the moral effect was great. The knowledge that the Revolutionary Committee could get weapons filled our men with confidence. Accumulating enough weapons for an insurrection was only a matter of patience.

The Bolsheviks were spending enormous sums in the Balkans and paying in American dollars. The main center of their activity was now Vienna, where they published the *Fédération balkanique,* which attacked me scurrilously. Much of the money which passed through their hands stuck in their coatsleeves. Balkan Communists who for one reason or another had left the Comintern told me that they had been forced to sign receipts for twice the amounts they received, on the pretext that there were other people who had to be paid but couldn't sign.

The most remarkable achievement of the Communist Balkan center in Vienna came in the spring of 1924, when they formed an alliance with the IMRO. Two trends had continued in the IMRO, even after its degeneration into mercenary terrorism. One wing wanted to incorporate Macedonia into Bulgaria; the other, the so-called "federalists," wanted an autonomous Macedonia within a general Balkan federation. The Communists had decided to play upon the idea of Macedonian autonomy within a federation, to serve the purposes of the Comintern's *Fédération balkanique.*

At this time a triumvirate—Todor Alexandrov, Alexander Protoguerov, and Peter Chaulev—controlled the IMRO. An independent Macedonian federalist group was led by the legendary *voivoda* Todor Panitza, reputed slayer of more than a hundred men. Panitza arrived in Yugoslavia early in 1924 to place his organization at our disposal, but was soon won over by that wily political confidence man, Gavril Genov, who sent him to the Communist center in Vienna. Upon his return, Panitza told me that those who sabotaged a Peasant-Communist alliance were enemies of the people. When I ordered him to leave he reached for his revolver, but my men quickly disarmed him and threw him out.

The Vienna center succeeded in establishing contact with the IMRO triumvirate and induced them to enter into an agreement whereby the Macedonian Organization would work for the Comintern in return for a large subsidy and the support of the underground Yugoslav Communist Party.

When Todor Alexandrov returned to Sofia, he consulted Tsankov and Volkov about this agreement, saying that by maintaining the appearance of working with the Comintern the IMRO would get valuable

Communist support of its activities in Yugoslavia. They flatly refused to have any dealings with Moscow and warned Alexandrov that they would tolerate the IMRO only as long as it obeyed their orders. Alexandrov thereupon published in the Sofia press a letter repudiating the Vienna agreement. Protoguerov followed his example, but Chaulev announced that he would keep his word—and was soon murdered in Milan, where he had been living, by a Bulgarian student.

By repudiating the agreement with the Comintern, Todor Alexandrov placated Volkov and Mussolini, but he still had to reckon with the Communists. In August he was shot dead by their agents at a meeting in Petrich. The next day the slain *voivoda's* lieutenant, Vancho Mikhailov, aided by General Volkov with regular Bulgarian troops, fell upon the *komitajis* suspected of Comintern sympathies and killed several hundred. Mikhailov, donning the mantle of his dead commander, then proceeded to carry out a wholesale purge of the federalists, even killing a number of veteran *voivodas* who had long since withdrawn from the Macedonian movement. Thus the IMRO remained under the control of the Bulgarian government and, through General Volkov, under that of Mussolini. The Comintern's agreement with the IMRO leaders had boomeranged and wrecked the grandiose *Fédération balkanique* scheme. Its failure brought Georgi Dimitrov back to Vienna in the spring of 1925 as the new Comintern chief for Balkan affairs.

Through its agents among the exiles the Bulgarian government had enough information about our activities to offer two million leva for my capture dead or alive. Assassins twice tried to reach me in Yugoslavia. My men caught the first one at night on a train in Nish, disarmed him, and brought him to Belgrade. When he was searched at the police station my photograph was found in his pocket, and he admitted he had come to kill me. The second gunman slipped across the frontier into Serbian Macedonia and went to Belgrade, where the police seized and disarmed him and found he carried a false passport, a bomb, and two revolvers.

In August Petrini sent word from Sofia urging the need to discuss certain problems of the underground organization. Rather than have him risk his position in the Sobranje by an illegal trip across the border, I arranged to meet him in the village of Gramada, about ten miles inside Bulgaria. Accompanied by twelve men armed with rifles and one light machine gun, I crossed the frontier on the night of August 14. We had to be on guard against both the Yugoslav and the Bulgarian patrols, but our experienced scouts guided us safely through the hills into northern Bulgaria.

At the outskirts of Gramada we were met by three men waiting to take us to a friend's house. I refused to go. "Show me where your mayor lives," I said. The mayor was a stanch supporter of Tsankov, which was precisely the reason I decided to meet Petrini in his house. If I went to a member of our organization and the police were later informed, mass arrests and killings would follow. The mayor's home was the safest place; he wouldn't dare to report us after we had gone, for fear of being suspected of disloyalty to the government.

We surrounded his house, and I rapped loudly on the door. From within came an irate voice, "Who's knocking at this hour?"

"The police," I answered.

That word always alarms any peasant, no matter what his office. When the mayor opened the door I pointed my revolver at his head, exclaiming, "In the name of the Bulgarian Revolutionary Committee!"

He offered no resistance and I entered, followed by my men. Several of our supporters remained outside to watch for Petrini.

I ordered the mayor to sit down, put my revolver back into its holster, and asked, "Where are your wife and children?"

With a look of distress he indicated the closed door of the adjoining room.

"At the slightest move to call the police," I said, "your family will suffer. We intend to stay here until tomorrow night. Tomorrow you will prepare food for us, for which you will be paid."

I stationed sentries outside the house and lay down to rest. Petrini arrived at five o'clock in the morning, disguised as a peasant. The mayor didn't allow the members of his family to leave their room. Outside two of our supporters stood guard—natives of the village who could loiter near the mayor's house without arousing suspicion.

Petrini told me that our men inside Bulgaria were forced to work with the Communists because they were getting guns from the arsenals by paying enormous bribes to local military authorities. They had also succeeded in organizing cells in the Sofia artillery regiment. A number of officers who sympathized with us were organizing, and in Breznik, not far from the Yugoslav border, a cavalry regiment stood ready to join our forces when the uprising began.

"We've already armed several thousand peasants," said Petrini, "mainly in the north and near Sofia. The peasant masses are with us solidly, but we need money."

Our host the mayor fed us well, served wine, and even joined us at table. When night came, Petrini left on foot for the interior, while we headed toward the border after warning the mayor that if he talked our men would return and kill him.

Despite the risk, Petrini insisted upon visiting me secretly in Belgrade a few weeks later. He told me that we could hardly expect to be strong enough for an uprising until the next spring. I parted with him reluctantly, and he returned to continue his double role as a Peasant deputy in the Sobranje and leader of the underground Revolutionary Committee in Bulgaria. In June, Petrini had to shoulder most of the burden of leadership. For Petko Petkov, after a strong speech in the Sobranje condemning the Tsankov-Volkov terror, was murdered in the streets of Sofia.

Late that summer, two former Peasant ministers, Athanasov and Stoyanov, escaped from prison and arrived safely in Yugoslavia. We received them joyfully, and as members of Stamboliski's cabinet they entered at once into the Revolutionary Committee. Obov and I were soon surprised to discover that both men insisted on full collaboration with the Communists. We explained our unsuccessful efforts to find a basis for understanding with them. But Athanasov and Stoyanov stubbornly insisted that I try again to come to terms with Dimitrov.

Once more Dimitrov and I met in Schönbrunn. He had shaved his beard and was more perfumed and elegant than ever. He expressed dissatisfaction because of Genov's reports that all the arms I received went exclusively to our organization.

"If you send guns," I said, "I'll see that half of them reach your Communists."

"Half? Why not all?"

"Because we'll take half as our commission for smuggling them into Bulgaria."

I told Dimitrov he could see Athanasov and Stoyanov in Prague, and returned to Belgrade. I could still see no basis for a Peasant-Communist agreement.

Earlier in that summer of 1924 southern Albania had revolted. Premier Ahmed Zogu fled to Yugoslavia with a number of his followers, and a new government was formed, headed by Fan Noli, a Greek Orthodox bishop. Everyone suspected Mussolini's hand in this, although Fan Noli was also accused of being under Soviet influence.

Several days after this upheaval a bearded man in the uniform of an Albanian officer appeared at my apartment, which also served as the Belgrade headquarters of the Bulgarian Peasant Party. Snapping to attention before me, he announced,

"I have the honor to present myself in the name of His Excellency, Ahmed Zogu Bey."

He announced that his chief wished to call on me. The next day Zogu appeared, accompanied by six officers who remained in an adjoining room while I spoke with him through an interpreter.

The Albanian leader impressed me most favorably. He had a well-built, erect figure and a proud, aristocratic face, blue eyes, and blond hair. He was an hereditary *bayraktar* (standard-bearer, or chief) of the Mata tribe of central Albania, distinguished for its courage, had studied in Constantinople, and from the age of twenty had been a leader in his country. He was now only about thirty. He told me that he hoped to return to power soon through an armed uprising and that his policy was that of Balkan solidarity.

"How can I help you?" I asked.

"I have enough men who can handle rifles," he answered, "but I shall need experts for machine guns and artillery."

He said he had many relatives and friends among the Albanians in Yugoslavia, the most important being his sister's husband, Tsena Bey of the noted Beloglavich family, who would furnish him with several thousand fighters.

In Serbian villages near the Albanian frontier many Austrian cannon and machine guns had remained hidden since the World War, and Zogu asked me to provide him with volunteers to handle them. I agreed to help him as much as possible in exchange for his promise to furnish us with weapons should he return to power. Although we had bought a thousand machine guns in Vienna, they were far from enough.

I saw Zogu often. One day his handsome young brother-in-law, Tsena Bey, called for me and drove me to Zogu's suburban villa. We dined on the veranda overlooking Belgrade and the bridges of the Sava. Despite the hot July day, it was cool here.

After dinner, Zogu declared that our alliance must be sanctified according to Albanian custom. Each of us added a few drops of his blood to a glass of water, which we then drank. This, the sacred Albanian *besa* of brotherhood and loyalty unto the grave, made us blood brothers. To a primitive Albanian, the *besa* is the holiest of oaths. In the future, Zogu could not refuse anything I might ask of him. For the moment, however, he wanted my help. When he took power, he swore, Albania would be at my service.

Eighty of my men, including two officers of the Hungarian army, had already volunteered to take part in the coming revolt. Tsena Bey said that preparations were proceeding very rapidly, and the blow could be expected in the autumn. He assured me that Bishop Fan Noli was an Italian agent, and I believed him. When later events forced me to have serious doubts, the damage had already been done.

In December, Zogu told me he was ready for insurrection and asked me to move my men to the Albanian frontier. His forces were concentrating in the Yugoslav border village of Djakovo, and I sent my men under the command of Captain Petrov and Lieutenant Tsvetkin to join Tsena Bey there. Maintaining that he was short of funds, Zogu asked me to cover their expenses. I advanced 60,000 dinars which he promised to return as soon as he occupied Tirana.

On Christmas Day, 1924, Zogu's forces moved into Albania, with my men in charge of a battery of Austrian mountain artillery and ten machine guns. Bishop Fan Noli had no real army with which to oppose him. Moreover, he made the fatal mistake of proclaiming that Zogu was a Yugoslav agent backed by Serbian infantry and artillery. His men became panicky. They might have fought Zogu, but a struggle against the Yugoslav army seemed hopeless, and many of them deserted. The attempt of the remaining troops to make a stand on the road to Tirana was shattered with the aid of Lieutenant Tsvetkin's battery of mountain guns. This easy victory opened the road to Tirana, and within ten days Zogu was back in power. In January he proclaimed himself President of the Albanian Republic.

Ahmed Zogu never remembered his sacred oath of blood brotherhood. He sent my men back to Yugoslavia with a few gold coins apiece. When my messenger brought him my gift, a silver sword, and asked when his Excellency could see me, his answer was, "Not now. In a few months, when I've restored order."

Later, when Tsena Bey became Albanian Minister to Belgrade, I asked him to return the 60,000 dinars I had advanced Zogu. He replied that he and Zogu were on bad terms and that he had really been exiled to Yugoslavia after serving a few months as Minister of the Interior.

In November, 1926, Zogu came to terms with Mussolini and signed the Treaty of Tirana, making Albania a virtual Italian dependency. Tsena Bey, who opposed his brother-in-law's foreign policy, was sent to Prague, where Zogu's agents murdered him in the street. Two years later, in September, 1928, the *bayraktar* who had become an Italian puppet proclaimed himself Zog I, King of Albania. If I had wanted revenge, it came eleven years later.

WHEN ATHANASOV AND Stoyanov returned to Belgrade after meeting with Dimitrov, they were more insistent than ever that we join with the Communists. They had agreed to accept the rejected formula of a "workers' and peasants' government." "We've succeeded in getting big concessions from the Communists," they told me proudly. "The posts of War and Interior will go to our party!"

The formula included a new trick clause. The titular government would be in our hands, but above it would be a Central Committee consisting of three Communists and only two members of the Peasant Party. Obov and I at once repudiated this absurd agreement. Still, the two former ministers seemed sincere, and I agreed to turn over to Stoyanov the organizational work on the frontier and to Athanasov the care of the exiles. This left me free to concentrate on our general plans and to handle foreign contacts. For about a month everything moved smoothly.

I received word from Vienna that an important personage from Bulgaria wanted to meet me there. To my extreme surprise he turned out to be one of our leading bankers, whose name must remain secret because he is still in Sofia. He told me that the situation at home was critical, and that he considered the return of the Peasant Party to power imperative. He offered to place a large sum of money at our disposal if we would promise not to touch his concern. We needed money badly, and this banker represented large French interests that we had no intention of molesting in any case. I gave him the necessary assurances and received a check for 500,000 francs, then about $25,000, on the Banque de Paris et des Pays-Bas.

"If my colleagues hear of this, they'll take me for a madman," were his parting words.

As I was paying my hotel bill a Bulgarian spy saw me and reported me to the Austrian police. I was taken to police headquarters and searched. They found my revolver and a passport under an assumed name. I thought I was in for it, until they discovered something else in my pocket—a letter from the French Premier Édouard Herriot. When Herriot, whom I had known in Geneva, had come to power after the elections of May, 1924, I had sent him a letter of congratulation to which he had cordially replied. The effect of the French Premier's brief note was instantaneous. The police apologized, returned my passport but they confiscated my revolver, and told me that I was free to leave.

Outside my friends were waiting for me, and five minutes later I had another revolver in my pocket. In Vienna this was essential because the city was filled with Macedonian terrorists who boasted in the coffee-houses that they would kill me on sight.

Knowing that no action could be expected for the next few weeks, I went from Vienna to Paris for a brief Christmas vacation. I had been working incessantly for a year and a half, had slept little, and was exhausted. Nadejda and the children were living in a small but comfortable house in the suburbs. In contrast to the way I had been living in Belgrade, in an apartment where our revolutionary couriers came at all hours of the night and I often had to surrender my bed, that suburban villa seemed the last word in luxury.

While in Paris, I wanted to make the best use of my Sofia banker's money. I looked up my old friends among the French aviators who had been in Salonika, for I intended to use planes over Sofia during our insurrection. My friend Bertchet found three Spad planes which could be bought very cheap by any former French army pilot for his private use. Bertchet and two of his comrades bought the three Spads for 75,000 francs. They were somewhat obsolete biplanes but in good condition and capable of doing 135 miles an hour. Bertchet promised to get them to Yugoslavia for me.

He went to the Yugoslav legation in Paris and explained that he wished to go to Belgrade with a few friends to stage acrobatic demonstration flights before members of the Yugoslav air force. The legation gave him all the necessary papers and free passage for the planes, but it turned out that he had to call for them in person in Belgrade. Bertchet agreed not only to do so, but also to lead the three planes in flight over Sofia with five of his comrades for a fee of 10,000 francs each.

I also bought five trucks for 200,000 francs from the firm of Renault and paid the shipping costs in advance. In Yugoslavia they would be converted into armored cars.

When I returned to Belgrade early in February, I found our organization in an alarming state. During my absence, Stoyanov had ordered several unnecessary and foolhardy raids into Bulgarian territory, in one of which a number of Bulgarian soldiers had been killed and we had lost Lieutenant Tsvetkin, who had commanded the battery for Zogu in Albania. Nor was that all. The Macedonian federalist, Todor Panitza, freed from my supervision, had made several attacks on the IMRO and had hanged several local *voivodas*. Panitza had not lost a single man, for he was a master at that type of raid. These actions served no real purpose and jeopardized our cause by depriving us of the advantage of surprise. Stoyanov's excuse was that the raids were needed to train the men. Their immediate effect was to annoy the Yugoslav government. Ninchich warned me that if they continued he would be forced to disperse our men in small groups in the interior.

Our preparations were reaching the point where we could plan our operations, and I anxiously wished to avoid conflict. We had about sixty former Bulgarian officers among us. I chose two of the most intelligent and assigned them to work out the details. We could count on about 8,000 men, most of them veterans, in the Bulgarian frontier villages. They had about 3,000 rifles and 50 machine guns and were awaiting the signal to attack. The noted one-armed Serbian war hero, Ilya Birchanin, promised to help us with 3,000 Serbian volunteers, all veterans, whom he had secretly signed up. He also gave me 5,000 hand grenades which belonged to his Yugoslav National Organization and were kept hidden in an enormous wine cellar in Nish.

My men and Birchanin's volunteers were to form an army of six to seven thousand for a sudden attack on Sofia, while our units in Bulgaria would start an uprising and seize strategic Kustendil and the city of Vrattsa in northern Bulgaria. We planned to cross the frontier at night and move on Sofia by train after taking over the railway station at Tsaribrod, about seventy kilometers from the capital. Simultaneously a picked unit was to occupy the barracks of the Twenty-fifth Bulgarian Regiment in Slivnitza, forty kilometers from Sofia, to assure the movement of our trains. We expected to have from ten to fifteen armored trucks, equipped with machine guns, moving parallel with the railway line to protect our trains from a possible flank attack. When we reached Sofia, we counted on the support of part of the garrison in overthrowing the Tsankov-Volkov government.

Early in March Petrini warned me from Bulgaria that the Communists were working behind his back, but that he couldn't get to the bottom of their plans. Soon an agitated letter from Deputy Kosovsky, Petrini's chief aide, informed me that the Communists, led by Lieutenant Colonel Yankov, were preparing for a big move and had lately received enormous sums for the purchase of arms. I sent for Obov, Athanasov and Stoyanov and read them Kosovsky's letter. All three seemed to agree that we had to forestall the Communists by acting first, and we accordingly revised our timetable. But Athanasov and Stoyanov at once went to Georgi Dimitrov's lieutenant, Gavril Genov, and gave him a full report on our conference. Unknown to us they had been meeting regularly with Genov to report all my movements and plans.

On March 27, Genov, Athanasov, and Stoyanov went to our main camp in Nish, summoned all the men, and proclaimed that Obov and

I had been expelled from the Revolutionary Committee as Premier Tsankov's agents, and that they were taking over complete authority. The response was divided. Most of the men protested that the charge was a lie and refused to take orders from the self-appointed leaders. One of them rushed to a telephone and put through a long-distance call to warn me in Belgrade.

I realized that this was an eleventh-hour Communist attempt to destroy everything we had been building up since the fall of 1923. Obviously it was connected with the warning of Petrini and Kosovsky about Communist preparations for action. I left for Nish the following morning.

To my great relief, I found that only about thirty-five men had definitely lined up with Athanasov and Stoyanov. They had already heard of my arrival and were waiting outside the Hotel Europa, not quite certain what to do next. I went there at once, accompanied by a crowd of my supporters, to the great bewilderment of the local Serbs. In the square before the hotel I halted my men and advanced alone toward the hostile, jeering group. I tried to appear calm, but inside I was boiling at the thought that treachery at this last hour might ruin everything. As I drew nearer, my hand grasping the revolver in my right pocket, the taunts gradually subsided. When I was close upon them, I shouted, "So, you've turned traitors!"

From the crowd a voice replied, "You're the traitor yourself."

They moved forward. Without thinking, I brought out my revolver and began hitting everyone near me with the butt. For an instant they were too startled to act. Before they could pile on me, my men pitched into the fray. Ironically enough, two of the men I knocked down that day, Kakhariev and Dimov, later became cabinet ministers. The first is now vice-president of the Sobranje and supports the pro-Axis policy of King Boris.

When the local police finally arrived, I went with them to the prefect to explain what had happened. Athanasov and Stoyanov took cover in a private home and appealed through their emissaries for police protection. Upon returning to the camp where my men were massed, I expelled the Communists and the Peasants who had sided with them. Then I left for Belgrade to try to counteract the mischief that had already been done.

Reports of the Nish battle were already appearing in the Yugoslav newspapers. To protect themselves, my enemies brazenly declared to the press that I was a paid agent of the Communists! This was too much even for Georgi Dimitrov, who sent a letter from Vienna to the Belgrade *Politika,* saying, "Todorov is our political opponent and has never received money from us."

After the Nish affair we realized that insurrection in Bulgaria had become a race between the Communists and ourselves. We were beginning to move our forces and Birchanin's Serbian volunteers from Nish to Pirot, twelve miles from Tsaribrod, when on April 14, 1925, all our calculations were spoiled by two events—an attempt on the life of King Boris, and the assassination of General Gheorgiev, Chief of Military Justice of Bulgaria.

The King was attacked in the mountain pass of Araba-Konak while returning by automobile from a trip to northern Bulgaria. The first volley killed one of his bodyguards, wounded the chauffeur, and caused the car to crash. The King leaped into a ditch and stopped a passing omnibus which he himself drove to Sofia. The next day, Premier Tsankov announced in the Sobranje that documents found at the scene of the ambush indicated that the Peasant Party had organized the attempt on the King's life. Almost simultaneously the official version issued by the Bulgarian legation in Vienna claimed that the attempt was the work of bandits and had no political significance. Neither account was true.

The band which ambushed King Boris in the Araba-Konak defile escaped to Yugoslavia, and I met their leader, Tumangelov, who told me what had really happened. Tumangelov, one of those intrepid men who did not stop fighting the Fascist usurpers after the suppression of the September uprising, took refuge with his band in the Sredna Gora mountains of southern Bulgaria, where for a year and a half he defied the police and the army. In the spring of 1925, feeling that Volkov's military police were closing in on him, he decided to leave Bulgaria. He crossed the Balkan mountains with his men and reached the Araba-Konak Pass. While they were camping there, eating their bread and cheese, Tumangelov peered through his field glasses and saw in the distance an automobile filled with uniformed men. The opportunity to take a farewell shot at Volkov's officers was too good to miss, and as the car came within range Tumangelov ordered his men to open fire. He had no idea that the King was in the car.

When Tumangelov and his *cheta* left Araba-Konak, they carelessly left behind copies of our newspaper, *The Peasant Banner*. These were the "documents" to which Tsankov alluded in his speech in the Sobranje. Tumangelov told me, laughing, that his men had used our newspaper to wrap up their cheese.

General Gheorgiev's murder caused general surprise because he was not politically active and had taken no part in the government terror. His death, in itself of little significance, had a terrible aftermath.

On the morning of April 16 Premier Tsankov and War Minister Volkov, with the entire cabinet and the generals of the Sofia garrison, gathered in the Sviataya Nedelia Cathedral to attend the funeral of General Gheorgiev. The great crowd was awaiting the arrival of King Boris when a deafening explosion shattered the silence. Many were killed outright and more than a hundred injured, but not a single member of the government was killed.

Volkov proclaimed martial law and sent out his military police to round up all opponents of the regime. Once more the terror gripped Sofia. Thousands were seized and many killed that night. Some were taken outside the city in trucks to be shot; others were killed in the cellars of police headquarters, once the Communist stronghold. Lieutenant Colonel Yankov, the Communist leader, resisted arrest and was shot down in his home. Two of Stamboliski's former ministers as well as Petrini's aide, Kosovsky, were murdered in the cellars of police headquarters. But the most frightful end was reserved for my friend Petrini. The police themselves later described it.

He was taken below in police headquarters and led before the great furnace. Its door stood wide open. Police Inspector Bichev faced him, his face aflame in the glow of the furnace, and threatened, "If you don't give me the names and addresses of all members of the Revolutionary Committee, we'll throw you in."

Proudly Lieutenant Petrini replied, "You fool, don't you know you're talking to a Bulgarian officer?"

And pushing Inspector Bichev to one side, he leaped headlong into the flames.

In the course of several days, two thousand persons were murdered in Sofia alone. How many victims met death is unknown, but probably not under five thousand.

My parents spent nearly two months in prison; my brother-in-law, director of the Technical Institute and a professor of mathematics at the Sofia University, also was arrested, though he had never taken part in politics.

In the provinces, especially near the Yugoslav border, peasants were searched for arms, tortured, and murdered, but not one of them betrayed his comrades. Among the Communists, however, there were numerous informers who helped the police round up their own leaders as well as our men. Consequently every important Communist in Bulgaria was seized. We lost about fifty of our best men; our revolutionary organization was hopelessly shattered.

And the bombing that caused all this?

Early in March, Gavril Genov bought several hundred kilograms of ecrasite, a powerful explosive that could be had only in Yugoslavia, and sent it to Lieutenant Colonel Yankov in Sofia. The Communists then bribed the sexton of the Sviataya Nedelia Cathedral to plant in the cupola a time bomb they had made of about fifty kilograms of the ecrasite. The Communist plan called for a general uprising immediately after the explosion in the cathedral. But when the bomb failed to kill the King or his ministers, the Communist leaders went into a panic and the workers made no move to revolt. Had the explosion decapitated the regime, the Communists probably would have been able to seize power during the ensuing chaos.

Gavril Genov left Yugoslavia for Vienna immediately after the débâcle and continued on to Moscow. He later died in Moscow of tuberculosis, taking with him to the grave the secret of the instigation of the terrorist act which led only to the death of thousands of innocent people.

Our ties with Bulgaria were cut off, and part of our hidden store of arms was discovered by the Bulgarian police. To complete the disaster, the Yugoslav authorities broke up our camps and confiscated our arms and our three airplanes. Everything was lost. In May, I announced that the Revolutionary Committee was dissolved and that henceforth we would retain only the foreign delegation of the Bulgarian Peasant Party, with headquarters in Prague, and the Émigrés Committee in Belgrade.

The Communist attempt to forestall the Peasant insurrection had destroyed not the Bulgarian Fascist government but the Bulgarian revolutionary movement.

A LTHOUGH BULGARIAN DEMOCRACY had suffered a blow from which it never recovered, fascism was not yet firmly enough entrenched to slaughter with impunity. Premier Tsankov's triumph was short-lived. The April terror aroused a wave of resentment which split the Military League that had destroyed the Peasant government in 1923. The honest officers, the "innocents" of the conspiracy, accused Volkov of embezzling money earmarked for military expenses, of working secretly with Vancho Mikhailov of the IMRO, and of conducting a perpetual reign of terror through his military police, which everyone in Bulgaria called the military Cheka. King Boris soon realized that unless there was a change in the ministry, the throne would be imperiled. On December 31, 1925, he gave a dinner at the palace for the Premier and his cabinet. After the ministers had been properly wined and dined, the King rose.

"I thank you for your service to the country," he said, "but a change in the government has become necessary to pacify the people. I must ask Premier Tsankov to submit the cabinet's resignation at once."

As Tsankov was about to protest the doors at both ends of the banquet hall opened and armed officers appeared. Tsankov paled and with a trembling hand wrote his resignation. The next day a new cabinet was formed, headed by André Liapchev, who had been Minister of Finance under King Ferdinand. But Volkov, secretly supported by the King, entered the new ministry. Tsankov, the symbol, was removed but Mussolini's paid agent, the man who had conducted the terror, remained in office with Boris' connivance. Sensing the temper of the people, he stopped the pogroms of his military police, but he still permitted Vancho Mikhailov and his men to murder federalists in Bulgaria and Serbian officials in Macedonia. The Italian Fascist press defended these murders and called Vancho Mikhailov "the hero of the Macedonian revolutionary movement."

This "hero" was used by his Italian master to purge that movement of leaders who would not take Mussolini's orders. The first victim was the Macedonian federalist *voivoda*, Todor Panitza, who had joined our insurrectionary movement in Yugoslavia. After the Sofia bombing Panitza told me that his *chetas*, which had jeopardized our plans by their ill-timed raids on the IMRO, would have to lie low for a time, and that he wished to go to Austria. I gave him the money, and he moved with his family to Vienna. There a young Macedonian girl, Mencha Karnicheva, made the acquaintance of Panitza's wife and gradually became a friend of the family. Panitza was an extremely cautious man, yet he not only accepted her invitation to a performance at the Burgtheater, but allowed her to sit behind him in the loge when she complained of the glare of the footlights. After the play had begun Karnicheva took a small revolver from her handbag and fired three shots into the *voivoda's* back, killing him instantly.

Brought to trial, Karnicheva had the help of excellent lawyers engaged by the IMRO and the Bulgarian legation. Besides, she was beautiful. The Austrian court acquitted her on the ground that she had acted "from idealistic convictions." This "idealist" then returned to Sofia, collected 500,000 leva for her work, and promptly married Vancho Mikhailov.

Another victim of the purge was the old Macedonian chief, Alexander Protoguerov. In 1927, after Mussolini had bought from Ahmed Zogu the right to "protect" Albania in return for a loan of fifty million gold francs, Protoguerov visited Rome. Mussolini offered him the following agreement: Italy would support a Macedonian insurrection, even to the point of unofficial military intervention through Albania. When Macedonia had been liberated from the Serbs and Greeks, it would become an "independent" state controlled by Italy, like Albania. To Protoguerov, Mussolini offered the "crown of Macedonia," with the same powers as Ahmed Zogu.

Protoguerov had made many mistakes and committed many crimes, but he was a passionate Bulgarian patriot whose single purpose was to unite Macedonia with Bulgaria. Mussolini's offer opened his eyes. He decided to abandon his guerrilla war against the Serbs and work henceforth for an understanding between Bulgaria and Yugoslavia. He conferred secretly with Ninchich, then Yugoslav Minister to Bulgaria, who later told me the story. He also went to Macedonia and told Vancho Mikhailov all that had happened in Rome, believing Mikhailov to be a sincere patriot like himself. Mikhailov at once went to Sofia and betrayed Protoguerov's plans to Volkov, who called that same day on the Italian Minister. When Protoguerov went to Sofia in July, 1928, he was shot dead on the street, and of course the police did not find the assassin.

Protoguerov's murder split the IMRO wide open. His followers, many of them officers, formed their own organization, and the conflicting Macedonians started killing one another, often on Sofia streets in broad daylight. On Volkov's order the members of the anti-Italian Protoguerov faction were arrested on sight and disarmed, while Mikhailov's followers were allowed a free hand.

All this was part of an intensified effort to promote the policy of

Italian penetration in the Balkans by isolating Yugoslavia. At the same time Mussolini was supporting Hungarian irredentist claims, seeking Rumanian and Greek friendship, and trying to repeat in Yugoslavia the fifth-column tactics that had succeeded against Stamboliski.

The Treaty of Tirana had forced the resignation of Ninchich as Yugoslav Foreign Minister; his foreign policy based on friendship with Italy was bankrupt. In November, 1927, his successor, Dr. Voja Marinkovich, concluded with Briand an alliance providing that an Italian attack on either France or Yugoslavia would automatically bring the other into the war. Mussolini's agents and their stooges in both countries fought this alliance tooth and nail. Meanwhile he attempted to win over the Croat Peasant Party, which had finally settled its quarrel with the government and whose leader, Stepan Radich, had entered the cabinet in 1925 with three of his supporters.

Having vainly tried to bribe Radich, Mussolini began to deal with Ante Pavelich, who represented extreme Croat nationalism. Pavelich's popular following was small but resolute and did not shrink from violence. He would pay any price to become the ruler of an independent Croatia. And he joined forces with both Mussolini and the IMRO— an alliance which was to have tragic consequences in 1934 and again in 1941.

While this witch's brew was being stirred up in the Balkans the only political activity open to me was to try, through my personal connections, to explain its sinister meaning to European statesmen, and, if possible, to make them see that it threatened the peace of Europe. For this purpose I had moved to Paris, after doing what I could to find work for our refugees. To support my family, I arranged to send dispatches from abroad to Yugoslav newspapers, and also became the Paris representative of several Yugoslav co-operatives exporting pork products. What property I had in Bulgaria had been confiscated in 1926, when I was condemned to death *in absentia* for my revolutionary activity, along with Dimitrov, Kolarov, Athanasov, Stoyanov, and Obov.

My political and business interests obliged me to shuttle back and forth between Paris and Belgrade. Fortunately Berthelot was again General Secretary of the French Foreign Office, under Briand, and, on the basis of my military service, he gave me a French passport. My travels were not confined to Europe. In the winter of 1927-28 I visited the United States, where I lectured on Yugoslav-Bulgarian union to audiences of South Slavs in New York, Boston, Philadelphia, Akron, Pittsburgh, Cleveland, Detroit, Chicago, Indianapolis, and many other cities and towns. Everywhere I found some enemies, but on the whole my audiences were friendly. One Serb from Herzegovina, who ran a Chicago speakeasy, became so enthusiastic that he left his business in his son's care and traveled with me wherever I went. He was enormous and extraordinarily powerful, and when at meetings he rose with clenched fists and glared at hecklers they usually lost interest in expressing their dissent.

In Chicago a Serbian journalist introduced me to Joe Morgan, a rival of Al Capone, who ran a four-story place called Illusion House, with a speakeasy, gambling rooms, a dance hall and girls. Joe took a liking to me—for one thing, my nine-chamber Parabellum revolver fascinated him. He invited me to have some real old Canadian whisky in his private apartment on the third floor. Through the corridors sauntered silent men whose doubles I later saw in gangster films. The walls of the room Joe called his study were covered, and not for decorative purposes, with Colt revolvers and submachine guns. In his living room I was startled to find paintings of the seventeenth- and eighteenth-century French and Flemish schools.

"Are these all originals?" I asked.

"They'd better be," said Joe. "I warned the guy who sold them to me that if they were fake he'd get twenty-five slugs in his hide. They're real, all right."

I returned to France in May, 1928. That autumn a letter from my mother told me that my father had died. I had not seen him for more than five years, and it would be nearly four years more before I could visit his grave.

All over the continent of Europe democracy was breaking down, and communism and fascism were contending for the succession. It was becoming all too clear that the Allied reorganization of Europe was unworkable. Yet the League of Nations, which should have brought about the revision of the peace treaties and led the continent toward a workable federation, was paralyzed. Its capitulation to Mussolini in his aggression against Greece had proved its impotence to bring major powers to time. Mussolini was sabotaging it at every turn, and the Polish delegates, now that the Pilsudski dictatorship had been established, were acting truculently. Yet the original purpose of the League could not have been frustrated if the conservative press of Great Britain and France had not worked against all the broader proposals made in Geneva and derided the ideas of European federation and of collective security enforced by sanctions.

In September of each year I went to Geneva for the League sessions. Aristide Briand dominated the proceedings. He would approach the rostrum slowly, stooping as if he literally carried the burden of Europe on his shoulders. When he spoke, it was without oratorical art but with something much greater. His voice had a quality profoundly moving, and his words always stirred the hearts of his listeners and touched the best in everyone. While he spoke, an atmosphere of spiritual rapport pervaded the League sessions.

When this man, nine times Premier of France, uttered such simple words as, "I recall my long life, full of mistakes," the pompous diplomats and stuffed shirts understood for a fleeting instant at least that they, too, were mere mortals. I saw cold, monocled Sir Austen Chamberlain, usually as stiff as if he had swallowed a pole, jump from his seat, applaud wildly, and shout, "Bravo!" Once he even jumped up on his chair to applaud Briand.

Briand sincerely wanted to insure peace through a European federation, but contrary to popular conception, he was never willing to jeopardize the safety of France by pacifism. Never did he lose sight of the fact that his policy of concessions might not prevent Germany from seeking revenge.

For Mussolini he had supreme contempt. In September, 1929, Mussolini delivered a speech in Turin, trying to alarm France with the words, "I'll show the whole world how high the temperature of the Italian people can rise!" A crowd of correspondents surrounded Briand in Geneva directly after Il Duce's speech, clamoring to know what he thought of it. Digging into his pocket for a crumpled cigarette, Briand lighted it, inhaled several times, and said with an indifferent shrug, "I think it must be extremely embarrassing to travel through Italy with a thermometer in one's backside."

The Italian correspondents stormed away, badly ruffled.

That same evening I went to see Briand at his hotel. We discussed the situation in the Balkans, and he expressed his pleasure at the excellent relations between Paris and Belgrade, adding that Foreign Minister Marinkovich of Yugoslavia was one of the most intelligent men he had met in Geneva.

I asked him how he reconciled his policy of peace with his recent request in the Chamber of Deputies for new military credits.

"To have a lasting peace with the Germans," he replied, "it is essential first of all to be strong. Our arms safeguard both the Germans and the French against a new conflict, because France will never abuse its strength."

"And if extreme nationalism should triumph in Germany?"

"Then I shall consider my effort for peace a failure. I shall resign and suggest the formation of a government capable of pursuing another policy."

Briand's pacifism differed significantly from that of the French Socialist

Party, which maintained that the first prerequisite to a lasting peace was French disarmament. Its party congresses always adopted this kind of resolution:

> The Socialist Party of France favors national defense, but demands disarmament as the best assurance of national defense.

While the Left wanted France disarmed before its enemies, the Right was making good friends with them. Virtually the whole rightist press was pro-Mussolini. Commert, press director of the Quai d'Orsay, later told me that Mussolini spent forty million francs a year for his propaganda in France. Consequently, even the Radical Socialist *La République* remained friendly toward Mussolini while he ranted against France.

This was only an aspect of the corruption which menaced the Republic. Senators and deputies engaged in shady transactions and held financial stakes in irresponsible promotion schemes. They accepted blocks of stock in Italian enterprises from Mussolini's agents. Henri Bérenger, chairman of the Senate Committee on Foreign Affairs, had a substantial interest in Italian industry, and when Senator Justin Godard gave me a letter to him he warned me, "In God's name, when you discuss the Bulgarian problem, not a word about Italy!"

The postwar parvenus who dominated French society were destroying French prestige throughout the world. They regarded the country's Central European allies as colonies, insolently demanded economic concessions, and corrupted the politicians of those states no less than their own. Thus, because of a vile clique, the French lost their true face as a great and honest people and appeared before the world in the mask of international swindlers.

In the Balkans, too, the worst elements were rising to the top. The peasants, living under primitive conditions and toiling on the land from daybreak to nightfall, are an honest, upright people. But Balkan peasants who are uprooted and become city dwellers quickly abandon the simple code of their village and find nothing to replace it. Almost the entire Balkan bourgeoisie, with the exception of a handful of old families, springs from peasants who left the soil a relatively short time ago. These people, burdened by no traditions or scruples, seek political power primarily because it offers them opportunities for enrichment. Dictatorship appeals to this primitive Balkan bourgeoisie because under authoritarian rule bribery and unlimited corruption can flourish with little public notice and no redress.

In February, 1929, I had word that one of the chiefs of the Protoguerov wing of the IMRO wanted me to meet him in Munich. Since he is still in Belgrade, I cannot name him without jeopardizing his safety.

When Protoguerov was alive, this man had marked me for death. Now Vancho Mikhailov's men were hunting him. We met in the lobby of the Wittelsbach Hotel. The Macedonian approached me slowly. Instinctively we extended our left hands, while holding revolvers in our right coat pockets. Then we both burst out laughing.

"Why don't you give me your right hand?" I asked.

"Why not?" he laughed, and we shook hands properly.

The *voivoda* told me that his organization was prepared to work with us for a Bulgar-Yugoslav alliance. His only condition was that we supply guns to his men; the police, by continuing to disarm them, were giving Mikhailov's killers easy prey. We still had revolvers in Sofia that we no longer needed, and I told him where to go for them.

There was a complete split in the Military League, he said. Colonel Damian Velchev, leader of the anti-Volkov faction, finally had been forced out of his position by Volkov in the summer of 1928. Velchev then openly charged the Minister of War with being an Italian agent and having embezzled large sums of money in buying Swedish machine guns for the army. Volkov had sued for libel but the action boomeranged, for the court acquitted Velchev.

His most astonishing news was that Volkov and Vancho Mikhailov had convinced King Boris that they were protecting him against a plot of the Yugoslav government to have him assassinated.

"Last summer," said the *voivoda*, "Mikhailov's gang killed one of our men and threw his corpse into the garden of the King's summer palace at Vrana, with a note stating that the murdered man had come to the palace to kill Boris. At about the same time, Deputy Stoicho Mushanov, who was in the delegation to the League of Nations, returned from Geneva with a 'document' on the stationery of the Yugoslav Ministerial Council, purporting to show that the Yugoslav Cabinet had decided to kill King Boris. The thing was forged, of course, in the office of *La Macédoine*, in Geneva."

"Does Boris really believe such rubbish?"

"Of course he does. Since they shot at him in 1925 he's been convinced that the refugees are plotting with the Serbs to kill him."

I was in Munich on my French passport, and when I gave it to the hotelkeeper, he said in correct French, "I'm very happy to have a Frenchman stay at my hotel. I worked in France for several years, in restaurants and hotels, and I love your country."

That evening he came to me. "Tomorrow we have a big affair. Adolf Hitler himself will speak. If you like, I'll take you. He's a great man."

I knew little about Hitler, except that he ranted against the Versailles Treaty and bitterly hated France.

"This morning you told me you loved France," I said, "yet now you're enthusiastic about a man who wants to destroy it."

My host smiled. "Don't believe Hitler wants to make war. No one in Germany wants war again. But Hitler will destroy a great evil." And he explained why he had become a Nazi sympathizer: "I still owe 200,000 marks on this hotel, and I owe it to Jewish banks. If Hitler comes to power, he'll liquidate all debts to Jews. Do you understand?"

I understood. I also understood for the first time that Hitler's propaganda, by playing on the primitive instinct of plunder, had a greater chance of success than communism. It dealt in a few simple and brutal formulas instead of the complicated abstractions of Marxism.

But the Communist skirmishers who locked with Hitler's yeggs in the physical clashes between the two ideologies dealt in no abstractions. One day a rather shabbily dressed man accosted me on the street in Belgrade, told me he was a Serbian Communist worker wanted by the police, and asked for 200 dinars to get him to the Austrian border. After hesitating a moment I gave him the money. Several months later, in Vienna, I was dining at a restaurant near the Opera when a flashy young man, dressed in expensive bad taste, came to my table and said in Serbian, with a broad grin, "I'm delighted to see you, Mr. Todorov. Naturally you don't know me. I borrowed 200 dinars from you in Belgrade last year."

I remembered him then. "Well, thank God you saved yourself."

"Yes, and now I live splendidly." He reeked of cheap perfume and wine. "Do me the honor of joining me at my table. I have a young lady with me," he coaxed. The girl was a typical Viennese blond, to whom he spoke in an incredible Serbo-German jargon.

"How in the world do you make yourself understood?" I asked. "She doesn't seem to understand a word you're saying."

"What sort of talk do you need with a woman?" he laughed. Then he added pompously, "You're my guest now, and I shall return the money I borrowed." He handed me twenty-five shillings and poured out drinks. "This is the life. Nothing like it in Belgrade—beautiful women, swanky night clubs, and fast motorcars."

As he drank he grew more and more expansive, forgot his dull-eyed blond, and began to boast of his importance. "I'm working here in the Balkan Section of the Comintern. You're accustomed to conspiracy and will understand what I mean when I say I'm used for *special jobs*. Often I cross the frontier secretly. I've been in Yugoslavia three times. You know, when it comes to rubbing out someone, we Balkans are experts. All those 'Swabians' are good for nothing. As far as I'm concerned—just show me the man!"

"Whom have you been ordered to kill?" I asked.

"Oh, you know, all sorts of Fascist bastards and traitors."

In the hope of learning more, I agreed to go to his apartment, where he said he had a few bottles of choice old wine. He threw the girl twenty shillings, hailed a cab, and we drove to a handsome house on the Eckergasse. His room was lavishly furnished in the same execrable taste as his clothes. While looking for the wine, he opened a large closet, revealing an array of suits of many colors and an unbelievable collection of shoes.

"How many pairs of shoes have you?" I asked.

"Sixty!" he answered. And he added sardonically, "The time has come for the proletariat to live well."

Shortly after King Alexander proclaimed a royal dictatorship in Yugoslavia, I went to Belgrade to live at the home of Dr. Milan Gavrilovich, vice-chairman and later head of the Serbian Peasant Party. He had been forced to quit his position as editor of *Politika,* the largest paper in the country, and now lived in temporary retirement.

After Stepan Radich's murder in parliament, in June, 1928, the Croats, headed by Pribichevich and Vladimir Machek, had once more begun to fight the government. The King sent for the two leaders and tried to induce them to co-operate. But they demanded full autonomy for Croatia, Bosnia, Dalmatia, and Voivodina, joined to Serbia only through the crown. Then the King dismissed parliament and in January, 1929, proclaimed the necessity of dictatorship to preserve national unity. He placed the press under strict censorship, denied the right of assembly and dissolved political parties.

Not long after I arrived in Belgrade Alexander sent word that he wished to see me. I had not seen him since 1923, and the idea of meeting him again under the existing conditions disturbed me. Within twenty minutes, however, a car came and whisked me off to the new palace, on a hill not far from the city. Alexander received me in his study, which was filled with flowers although winter was barely over; flowers were almost a passion with him. He had begun to gray and looked thinner and tired.

"How much has happened since we last met," he said, "in your country and in mine! While you were engaged in revolutionary work—of which I knew, of course," he added with a smile—"I couldn't see you out of loyalty to King Boris. Now that you've returned to peaceful political activity, I want to have a talk with you about international affairs."

We spoke of the general European situation and of Bulgaria. He was astounded to hear that King Boris believed the Yugoslav government was plotting to kill him.

"I'm a soldier and at the same time a King. I would never permit anything so shameful."

[233]

I suggested that he act through his Minister in Sofia to make King Boris realize the absurdity of his suspicions. In my opinion, I told him bluntly, Italy was behind most of the Balkan intrigues, trying to divide the Balkan peoples and open the way to fulfillment of Mussolini's imperialist ambitions east of the Adriatic.

"My information is very much the same," said Alexander. "We must do everything to thwart Mussolini's plans."

Suddenly, when I thought our talk was nearly over, the King asked point-blank, "How do you like my new government?"

I was embarrassed. It seemed to me wholly improper to discuss the internal affairs of a country which had sheltered our refugees and whose government had been so kind to me personally. I told Alexander this. His eyes grew sad.

"I so seldom hear the truth," he said. "Everyone tries to deceive me with flattery. Not long ago, one of my former ministers stopped as he entered my room and said, 'Your Majesty, I see a halo around your head.'" Alexander laughed. "You can imagine what sort of halo! But it's my job to preserve Yugoslavia. Will you really refuse to speak the truth?"

"What if the truth should be unpleasant?"

"So much the better. For a long time I've heard nothing but uncritical praise."

I expressed my opinion somewhat indirectly.

"I know several of your ministers, Your Majesty, and I'm sure most of them are decent men with the best intentions. But without a parliament and a free press they're like actors performing before a mirror. Each, locked in his own room, recites a loud monologue heard only by himself. All actors have high opinions of themselves and like their own performance, but you know that they need an audience to discipline their talents."

The King looked at me with his velvet eyes which were so expressive when he was in a good mood.

"How, in your opinion, can I show my actors to the public?"

"Only by restoring a free press and liberty in general."

"Do you think I broke so easily with the tradition of my family?" he asked excitedly. "The Karadjordjeviches came from the people and understand and treasure freedom. But you don't know what went on here —how liberty was abused."

He walked up and down the room with quick, agitated steps, then stopped at his desk and took out a sheaf of papers.

"Look!" he said. "Here's a list of 110 deputies to the last parliament. They got their salaries, but that wasn't enough. They also took salaries from the police. They became police agents of their own free will. Tell me, under such conditions can one respect parliamentary government?"

[234]

I glanced at the list long enough to note several well-known names, and answered, "Since you want me to speak frankly, this is not the result of freedom, but of its precise opposite."

"Why?"

"Because all the elections I witnessed in Yugoslavia were accompanied by police intimidation. Naturally, under such conditions the most unworthy were often elected, and of course they served the police who elected them."

The King hardly heard me.

"Freedom! At a moment when the country is faced with complete internal collapse! That I cannot do! When everything calms down, I shall gradually restore parliament and freedom of the press—but only gradually."

Before we parted, he said, "You're staying with Gavrilovich. He's an honest man, but he doesn't understand me. Some day he will. . . . And don't forget that I'm your friend. Talk to me always as you did today, frankly."

While dictatorship threatened democracy all over Europe, Spain, which had endured dictatorship for years, suddenly reversed the trend. In Paris early in 1931 I met Ramón Franco, who had led the abortive aviators' uprising against the dictatorship of General Berenguer at the Quatro Vientos airport near Madrid the preceding December. Franco assured me he would soon return to Spain. That had a familiar ring; all refugees believe revolution to be imminent in their countries. We had believed it ourselves for a long time; former Premier Nitti of Italy continued to demonstrate with statistics, in Mme. Ménard-Dorian's salon, that Mussolini could not survive the next three months; even the Russians in Paris always saw Bolshevism on its last legs. But on the evening of April 14, I heard the radio reports of revolution in Madrid, the proclamation of a republic under Niceto Alcalá Zamora, and the flight of King Alfonso XIII. Several days later Ramón Franco sent me a telegram inviting me to come to Madrid as "the guest of the Spanish Republic." He had just been appointed chief of the air force.

Within a week I was in Madrid. Everywhere I saw inscriptions demanding General Berenguer's head. On the Via Alcalá, one of the main thoroughfares, workers and students were still demonstrating; radios blared the *Marseillaise;* and the tricolor of the new republic mingled with the red banners of the anarcho-syndicalist labor organizations.

Franco introduced me to many of his friends—journalists and young professors full of enthusiasm and optimism. The naïveté of these young republicans amazed me: they seemed to regard the magic word "republic" as the answer to all evils.

[235]

I knew enough about Spain to realize that its most urgent problem was the enormous class of landless peasants laboring in virtual serfdom on the great estates. Yet none of my new friends discussed the land question. To my argument that by introducing agrarian reforms which would satisfy the peasant mass they could establish a solid social foundation for their democratic regime, they answered, "Ours is a coalition cabinet. Most of the ministers, and President Alcalá Zamora himself, are opposed to any basic land reform." Nor could they deal seriously with the centrifugal force inherent in the Catalan and Basque claims to autonomy.

Ramón Franco thought it necessary to set up a revolutionary dictatorship and liquidate all enemies of the republic, but he seemed to have no constructive economic program. Another Franco (not related to Ramón), a handsome young professor at the Salamanca University who had just been appointed director of a bank for foreign trade, explained, "Our chief enemy is the Catholic Church. Under long-established tradition an aristocratic family sends its first son into the priesthood and one of the others into the army. The Church, which itself owns great estates, is thus closely bound to the aristocracy and will always be our enemy."

"What about the army?"

"In the army the situation was abnormal. We had 28,000 officers for 100,000 soldiers. Most of them did nothing but meddle in politics. Of course, some of them are good men, like Captains Hernández and Galán who were executed by General Berenguer after the uprising last December. But the majority are reactionaries. The government has taken steps to dismiss half of them."

I couldn't help thinking of the time when we had been forced to dismiss many of our own officers, only to have them form the nucleus of the conspiracy which overthrew our government.

The next day Ramón Franco introduced me to the Minister of War, Manuel Azaña, a fat, jovial man who later became Premier and subsequently President of the Spanish Republic. Azaña made a pleasant impression but no more than that. I asked him whether he expected any trouble from the retired officers.

"I've ordered that they receive half-pay so they won't go hungry," he answered.

Franco interrupted, "I told you yesterday, I tell you today, and I'll continue to tell you: if you want to preserve the republic, order the immediate arrest of my brother!"

From the conversation, I gathered that Ramón's brother, General Francisco Franco, head of the Military Academy at Saragossa, had a large following among the officers. It struck me as strange when Ramón insisted, "If you don't arrest him, he'll try to organize a coup d'état. I know my brother."

"You exaggerate," said Azaña. "General Franco is a splendid officer. We'll make a good republican of him."

Under Primo de Rivera and his successor, General Berenguer, the relations between Spain and Italy had been very close. The proclamation of the republic not only dealt a moral blow to fascism; it threatened to thwart all Il Duce's Mediterranean ambitions. In the cafés and restaurants I met many Italian exiles who had come from Paris, expecting the Spanish Republic to help them against Mussolini. To one of these refugees Ramón Franco boasted that as soon as the Spanish air force was properly organized, he would send a plane to bomb Mussolini's palace. Six years later Ramón Franco's plane, which may well have been Italian, was bombing the homes of Barcelona instead of the Palazzo Venezia.

Several times I flew with Ramón Franco on his inspection tours of airports and aviation centers—Bilbao, Barcelona, and Seville. The diversity of Spanish types fascinated me. The type traditionally known as the Spaniard is an inhabitant of Old Castile or Aragon, parched provinces of rock and sand where the rivers flow through deep ravines, making irrigation difficult. Centuries of living in this austere land have developed that strength and pride which marked the conquistadors. In Andalusia, with its pastures, olive trees, and orange groves, life is easier and gayer, and people need less cause to laugh and sing. In Castile, men walk slowly with a melancholy air, as if still carrying a hidden sorrow for the sunken armadas of the past. In this ancient land of knights and conquerors, pride is the dominant note. Even the beggars of Madrid are proud. When one of them extends his hand for alms he seems to say, "I happen to need a little money now, but don't think I'm less a gentleman than you."

Sitting on the terrace of a café in Madrid, Professor Franco explained to me the psychology of these beggars, whose haughty independence astonished me.

"He has too much self-respect ever to betray your confidence. He'll pick your pocket in a crowd, but if you give him a hundred pesetas to buy something for you, he'll bring back the exact change."

Seeing my skepticism, he called the first passing beggar, told me to give him a hundred pesetas, and said, "Please buy some cigarettes for this foreigner."

I considered my money as good as gone. But the man soon returned with the cigarettes and my change and refused a tip. I looked at Franco.

"We can invite him to join us at coffee," he said.

I asked this hidalgo in rags to sit down with us and he did so, completely at ease. When he had finished his coffee, he nodded his head in thanks and left.

With Professor Franco I motored to Toledo, city of beautiful churches, of fountains and flowers, of El Greco and Cervantes. As we visited the ancient inn where Cervantes had lived, Professor Franco suddenly turned to me and said,

"Do you know what the Spanish revolution is? It's Don Quixote's revenge for Sancho Panza's wisdom."

We visited the great Cathedral of Toledo where, a guide told us as bitterly as if it had happened yesterday, Napoleon's soldiers had stabled their horses. And we stood before El Greco's immortal *Burial of Count Orgaz,* with its splendid Toledan knights whose Semitic features remind the spectator that virtually the entire Toledo aristocracy, with their resounding names and pride of valor, came from Jewish origins.

When I mentioned this later to Ramón Franco, he remarked, "I wouldn't be surprised if my own ancestors were Jews."

On the way back to Madrid through the rich countryside of New Castile, Professor Franco said, "I'll take you to the home of the oldest republican in this region.

We stopped before a small house. "Álvarez!" Franco called out.

A dark, grave face appeared in the doorway. Álvarez the peasant received us with the measured grace of a Spanish grandee. In a room poor but clean he brought us oranges and an earthen pitcher of wine. Professor Franco asked him to explain how he had become a republican and translated his answer:

"Ten years ago, Don Alfonso came to Toledo. He stopped his automobile here on the road and went for a walk. I was working in the fields. Seeing the King, I took off my hat and welcomed him. He looked at me and didn't respond to my greeting. Then I understood that he was not a worthy man and I became a republican."

As we continued on our way to the capital, Professor Franco said, "Our task seems simple; yet it's really difficult. Simple because the struggle against the power of the king long ago developed a deep-rooted republican tradition. Difficult because every Spaniard is a kind of independent republic in himself. This makes the establishment of an organized democratic government quite a task. When Aragon united with Castile at the end of the fifteenth century the oath of the Aragonese to the king was something like this: 'We who are as worthy as you, and perhaps worthier, recognize you as king on condition that your conduct, just as ours, be subject to control by the High Judge of Saragossa.' About three-quarters of a century later, King Philip II hanged the High Judge of Saragossa. Since then the Aragonese have not recognized the monarchy, and every year on the anniversary of his execution the people gather around his monument to keep alive the memory of the ancient liberties they lost four hundred years ago. Nor have the Catalans forgotten the rights they enjoyed until the eighteenth century; nor the Basques, who kept their rights until a century ago. When we proclaimed the republic, the thirst for freedom was so great that it took an almost anarchic form.

"Our first republic of 1873 was of that type. Spain was divided into 20,000 independent districts, each with its own laws and refusing to pay taxes to the state. In less than two years, the republic was gone and the monarchy restored."

I couldn't help thinking that Spain sorely needed some of Sancho Panza's healthy common sense.

I N 1931 A GENERAL election took place in Bulgaria which led to my return from exile. The entire opposition united against the Liapchev government, which for almost six years had been wallowing in an orgy of public plunder. This opposition bloc—Malinov's Democrats, the remnants of the Liberal Party, the so-called Radicals, and the Peasants—had no common program beyond Liapchev's overthrow. From Sofia emissaries of our party leaders, Gichev and Muraviev, came to ask my advice and seek financial help. The amount they asked was substantial, and to raise it I was forced, among other measures, to mortgage a six-acre property I had bought near Orléans.

Although the usual police terror accompanied the election, the opposition scored a smashing victory and the government was forced to resign. Malinov headed a new cabinet which included three Peasants, and the people believed a new era had begun. We exiles naturally expected the new parliament to vote an immediate amnesty. But the government was in no hurry to act. Curiously enough, our own party comrades, fearing we might demand the cream of the political posts, were not at all eager to see us in Sofia.

The new regime did not keep faith with us, but what was far more important, it did not keep faith with the people. The impoverished peasants remained as miserable as under Tsankov and Liapchev. Corruption still flourished, and so did the pro-Italian foreign policy. Vancho Mikhailov continued his terrorist activities and his old boss, the discredited General Volkov, who had been made Minister to Rome, remained at his post because King Boris wished it.

The new Peasant ministers seemed chiefly concerned with keeping in the King's good graces and hanging on to their jobs. As popular discontent increased, the Communists rapidly gained strength, and for a time it looked as if they would become the leading opposition party. But when the attitude of the Peasant spokesmen in the government became clear, Obov, myself, and other leaders organized an independent party which we called the Alexander Stamboliski Peasant Union to emphasize our continued faith in Stamboliski's principles—political and economic peasant democracy, and an alliance with Yugoslavia as the keystone of a united Balkans. We soon diverted the current of popular unrest from the Communist channel to a mass political party reflecting the aspirations of the peasants.

[240]

In July, 1932, at an international conference on reparations in Lausanne the Bulgarian delegation was headed by the new Premier, Nikola Mushanov, who had succeeded Malinov when the latter became ill. At Evian-les-Bains, where I was staying with my family, I ran into my old friend, Batolov, the Bulgarian Minister to France. "Mushanov wants to see you," he said. "We've been looking for you for three days."

The next day Premier Mushanov invited me to dinner. This was ironic. I was not only a refugee but was still under sentence of death, and Mushanov was the head of a government which had refused to grant an amnesty. But Balkan customs permit anything.

"Your friends attack me very violently," Mushanov complained. "Tell them to stop."

"We aren't fighting you personally, but your government."

"What do you want? We have democracy."

"What sort of democracy is it with five killings a day in the streets of Sofia?"

He shrugged his shoulders. "The Macedonians killing off one another. What business is that of ours?"

Mushanov was handsome and gay and had a great weakness for women. He seemed too indolent and frivolous to tackle any problem seriously.

"Tell me," he asked, "do you want an amnesty?"

"Not at all," I answered indifferently. "While we're abroad our prestige continues to rise while yours falls. If you grant an amnesty, we'll have to return to Sofia and take a direct part in politics. We'll probably make the usual mistakes and perhaps some compromises. While we're in exile our names are connected in the minds of the people only with the ideals of our party."

"Which is precisely the reason you shall be pardoned," said the Premier. And that fall he introduced an amnesty bill which became law on January 6, 1933. We were free to return to Bulgaria. Having a great deal of business to clean up in Paris, Prague, and Belgrade, I could not leave for Sofia until March. Nadejda remained in Paris with the children, for we had no great faith in this amnesty.

Before I left Belgrade for Sofia, King Alexander sent for me. I had met him a number of times since 1929, and we had become good friends. The King often made mistakes in his domestic policy. He was impressionable, frequently acted on impulse, and tired easily of his ministers. His constitution of 1931 satisfied neither the Serbian opposition, the Croats, nor the Slovenes. Censorship of the press continued and parliament consisted almost entirely of government deputies elected without opposition. Among these deputies artificial opposition groups arose which in no way reflected the real divisions in political opinion. In his foreign policy, however, Alexander was clearheaded. He was strongly pro-French and pro-British, favored the extension of the Little Entente, and more than ever wanted an alliance with Bulgaria.

The King was uneasy about my return to Sofia. He showed me reports of his legation there as well as police reports, predicting that I would be murdered at once. I told him that assassins had been on my trail for years. One of them had even come to Paris in the summer of 1930. My friends in Sofia had warned me and sent me his picture. He was a Macedonian terrorist who had attempted to kill two federalists in Vienna. I knew the usual haunts of the Bulgarians and Macedonians in Paris, and with a revolver in my pocket I went to look for him. In a small Bulgarian restaurant in St-Michel I showed his photograph to the proprietor.

"Does this man come here?" I asked.

"Yes. He left half an hour ago."

"Very well. Tell him Kosta Todorov is looking for him and will kill him on sight." I repeated the threat in other cafés, thus following the old law of the Balkan haiduks, "If you don't want to be the prey, become the hunter."

Alexander was not reassured by my story. "It's much more serious now in Sofia. Men are being killed daily and the police do nothing about it. As your friend I ask you to stay here."

"I can't. If I don't return I'll be morally destroyed in the eyes of the Bulgarian people. They have no use for leaders who are cowards."

"But why must you risk your life now, when big things are happening in Europe? Think of the future."

"What would you do in my place?"

The King paused for a moment, then said, "I'd go. . . . If anything happens to you," he added, "I'll look after your family."

On the evening of March 5, Obov and I with twenty other exiles, all armed, left for Sofia. None of us slept that night; we were too much excited over returning to our homeland after almost ten years in exile. At the first stop in Bulgaria, we were met by several thousand peasants, including delegations from every part of the country. Opposition newspapers were saying, "To the disgrace of the Bulgarian people, the traitor Kosta Todorov is returning to Sofia." I went out on the platform and shouted to the crowd, "Behold the traitor, Kosta Todorov!" There were cries, tears, shouts of "Bravo!" and the train moved on. But at the next station the police were waiting to take us to Sofia by automobile, explaining that a hostile crowd had gathered at the Sofia station and might cause trouble. They forgot to add that they themselves had organized the hostile crowd, which numbered no more than two hundred men, and that thirty thousand peasants and citizens of Sofia were waiting to welcome us and the government was determined to prevent this ovation.

In Sofia, I stopped at the apartment of my old companion of Brussels days, Mischa Mikhailov. My friends organized a bodyguard of three men, each armed with two revolvers, who protected me constantly. Unknown persons were searched before being admitted to see me. I lived as if in a beleaguered fortress and moved about the city only in an automobile, with my bodyguards.

I found my mother greatly aged, and when I spoke with her I realized how much she had suffered. Together we visited my father's grave.

Plunging at once into political activity, I became the editor of two papers and also traveled about the country organizing the peasant struggle against the government. In the village I found appalling distress. All Stamboliski's reforms had been wiped out. The peasants had no money for clothing or kerosene, or even the few leva to send their children to school. Several families would share a box of matches, for which they paid with a half-dozen eggs. Our Peasant Union had about 17,000 members, led by Dr. Georgi Dimitrov (no relation of the Communist leader), an honest man and a splendid orator. As our activity increased thousands more flocked to our standard, although many peasants, disillusioned by the behavior of their leaders in the Mushanov government, told me frankly, "We'll support you, but if you deceive us too we'll all go drown in the Red Sea of Bolshevism."

The feud between the Macedonian factions continued, with daily murders in Sofia and the provinces. Vancho Mikhailov's terrorists, arrogant in their immunity from arrest and punishment, inspired such fear that few Bulgarian politicians dared to speak a word against them. I decided to bring the issue into the open. At our mass meetings I said, "All of you have known battles and wars. Aren't you ashamed to be terrorized by an organized band of hoodlums in the pay of the brigand Mussolini?"

Men who until then hadn't dared utter a word suddenly began to applaud and shout, "You're right! It's time we cleaned out that gang!"

I called for alliance with Yugoslavia in a common Balkan front, a policy no one had dared to discuss for ten years. Mussolini's Macedonians were furious, and the newspaper *Macedonia* called me "a Trojan Horse sent by King Alexander to seize Bulgaria from within." The Minister of the Interior warned me that they had decided to finish me off at any cost. Several times my bodyguards stopped suspicious-looking men on the street corner near my house and turned them over to the police, who disarmed and released them.

Finally the IMRO resorted to a different stratagem. One day a young woman came with a note from Obov, told me she had heard me speak at several meetings, and declared she was madly in love with me. I pretended to be taken in, and when she gave me her telephone number and asked me to visit her, I promised to do so. Upon investigation we found that her name was Nencheva and she was the mistress of Kurtev, one of Vancho Mikhailov's lieutenants. With my three bodyguards I went to her house, at a lonely spot near the Military Academy. We held our revolvers in readiness as I rang her doorbell. A maid opened the door and asked cautiously, "Who are you?"

"Please tell Mme. Nencheva we're from the Macedonian Organization."

In a moment we were admitted into the spacious dining room. Seeing me, Nencheva blushed but immediately regained control of herself.

"How happy I am to see you!" she exclaimed.

I kissed her hand, motioned to my men to wait outside, and said, "I've kept my promise."

"Why didn't you telephone me you were coming?"

"So that you could tell Kurtev?"

Her eyes betrayed both anger and fear.

"What Kurtev?" she asked, playing for time.

"Your lover, the so-called *voivoda* Kurtev, aide of Vancho Mikhailov, the notorious Macedonian assassin."

She wasn't in the least embarrassed. "Oh, that! A little adventure which ended long ago. Excuse me for a moment, I'll telephone for some pastry. You and I will have tea together, won't we?"

"Certainly, but don't trouble yourself about the pastry."

When I left, I told my men to shadow her. Several days later a truck came to her house and loaded her furniture. That was the last I heard of Mme. Nencheva.

The Protoguerov men were now our allies. This wing of the Macedonians had grown stronger in recent months. Aided by a sympathetic customs official I had managed to smuggle 150 revolvers to them from Prague. The killings continued but most of those slain now were Vancho Mikhailov's followers. Mikhailov didn't dare leave his stronghold in Macedonia. He was as cowardly as he was arrogant.

When Mikhailov received foreign correspondents, he would arrange mock raids for their benefit. His men took them to a false border guarded by Macedonians wearing Serbian uniforms. On this theatrical frontier they fought synthetic battles. The correspondents were then led on horseback through mountain passes to a village which they were told was in Yugoslavia. At night, in a secret place in the forest, they were brought before Vancho and his wife Karnicheva, Todor Panitza's murderer, who was dressed as an Amazon. Around them stood a guard of thirty or forty *komitajis* armed to the teeth. All this took place safely in Bulgarian territory under the eyes of the authorities, yet throughout

Europe passed stories of the mysterious *voivoda*, the uncrowned King of Macedonia, and his great power in the Balkans.

This "King" had an annual income of about 100 million leva from Italian subsidies and from pillage, which he used for his terrorists in Bulgaria and Yugoslavia. He took no risks himself. Protoguerov's men now had him so scared that he dared not remain in one spot more than two days, but kept moving from one mountain village to another. A year later, when another coup d'état in Bulgaria brought to power men determined to end the Macedonian terror, Mikhailov fled to Turkey with his wife and sixty million leva. Later he would turn up in Nazi Germany.

In August, 1933, a French Parliamentary delegation headed by Édouard Herriot came to Bulgaria. When I called on Herriot he told me he had been invited to visit King Boris at the Euxinograd Palace near Varna on the Black Sea.

"What do you think of the King?" he asked.

Avoiding a direct answer, I replied, "He'll receive you very graciously, tell you pleasant things, and will no doubt quote from your books."

Herriot smiled. "We'll see," he said. When I saw him after his return I asked,

"Well, how was it?"

"Just as you said."

I laughed. "He quoted *Madame Récamier, La Forêt Normande,* and *Beethoven?*"

Herriot grinned. "Of course."

That was the King's way. Whenever he expected a distinguished foreign guest, he studied his tastes and his hobbies and boned up in the *Encyclopaedia Britannica,* to appear well informed. With writers he went further, even skimming through their works. Consequently most people left this shallow man charmed by his grace, his culture, and the wide range of his interests.

In September, the Reichstag fire trial began in Leipzig, and Bulgarians forgot political differences in their concern for the fate of Georgi Dimitrov, who was certainly innocent of this crime. Dimitrov's emergence as the hero in the courtroom gratified the national ego. His conduct contrasted sharply with the supine behavior of Ernst Torgler, the leading German Communist defendant. "In all of Germany there's only one courageous man, and he's a Bulgarian," was the quip which went the rounds in the Sofia cafés.

The Central Committee of our party sent a telegram to the court in Leipzig, stating our conviction that Dimitrov was not guilty. When the text was published in the Sofia press, an old woman of about seventy came to see me. She introduced herself as Dimitrov's mother and asked me to lend her money to go to Leipzig to see her son, "perhaps for the last time."

After giving her what she needed, I asked, "Don't the Communists have money to help you get to Germany?"

"They have it, my son, they have it; but that money is for the unfortunates, for those who are in prison, for the families of those who've been killed. I don't want to take anything out of such money."

She looked at me with serene and luminous eyes. I don't know whether Dimitrov was really a hero; on the world stage, before an audience of millions, he played the part well. But his mother, this simple old woman, was a heroine without the slightest pose. I was happy to help her and pleased when she thanked me simply, with one word. Then she added, "I can't return this money to you. If my son lives, he'll repay you."

"Yes, of course," I said, knowing that Dimitrov, alive or dead, would never pay a debt.

The time was approaching for a congress which would test the strength of our party, and I redoubled my political activity. On the morning of November 1, 1933, with three deputies and two bodyguards, I arrived in Lom Palanka on the Danube to address a mass meeting. Local supporters told us that Dimov, the Minister of Public Works, had suddenly appeared in the city. Dimov was one of the men I had injured in the brawl in Nish in 1925. My men told me he had been seen conferring with the Macedonians and former Premier Tsankov's Fascists. They suspected a plot to assassinate me. I knew that Dimov, who owed his post to his friendship with Vancho Mikhailov, was capable of anything.

The meeting started at eleven in the morning in a theater seating more than a thousand. Outside in the square, about four thousand peasants from the neighboring districts heard the speech through loudspeakers. When I spoke of the pressing need of a Bulgar-Yugoslav alliance in the face of mounting international danger, a group of Macedonians who had managed to slip inside tried to silence me with their jeers but were quickly thrown out. They gathered in the square outside, where they were joined by about two hundred local Fascists. When we left the theater and walked toward the hotel, accompanied by the crowd, the Fascists and Macedonians shouted, "Down with Todorov!" and threw stones at us, but my followers routed them.

There was no train to Sofia before eleven P.M., so we went to the hotel to wait and the peasants left for their villages. By nightfall the six of us were alone. We dined and went upstairs to rest until train time. Soon we heard shouts and noises from below; armed Macedonians and Fascists were crowding the lobby. Suddenly a squad of Fascists rushed up the stairs and into our room, but retreated when we fired in the air. The chief of police arrived, but instead of protecting us he left after speaking quietly to the ringleaders. Several minutes later men were on the stairs again, brandishing revolvers and knives, shouting, "We'll fix Kosta Todorov, the traitor!"

We barricaded ourselves in the room with chairs and tables. They began ramming at the door, and we knew we couldn't hold them off. The window of our room looking out into the court offered the only chance of escape. We leaped before they could break down the door. Two of the deputies fractured their ankles. They groaned as we helped them to hobble along, consuming precious time. The assassins, having broken into the room and found us gone, dashed out after us, and a group of about fifty men, accompanied by four police officers with rifles slung across their shoulders, blocked our way to the street. The situation looked hopeless. The Fascists approached us slowly and cautiously.

"In the name of God, don't shoot, they'll kill us," my comrades urged. But there was no choice. More out of desperate fury than courage, my bodyguards and I rushed into the crowd and began swinging the butts of our revolvers at everyone in sight. Suddenly I felt a sharp pain in my left side. In the light of the street lamp I saw a man with knife upraised. I fired at him and at another who rushed toward me, and ran for all I was worth. Several shots followed me, but on I ran as fast as my legs could carry me. Suddenly police headquarters loomed before me. I dashed in, revolver in hand. To my good fortune, the local prosecutor had arrived. The chief of police at once disarmed me and I slumped into a chair. Then for the first time I felt blood oozing slowly from my left side.

The prosecutor called a doctor, ordered the Fascists dispersed, and turned angrily to the chief of police.

"This is all your work; you've disgraced the city."

The other answered insolently. "This is no business of yours. It's a police matter. And we'll arrest this one. Two men are dead back there."

When the doctor arrived, he found that my wound was not deep. The knife had passed through a thick leather wallet before penetrating. Meanwhile the prosecutor had been in an adjoining room, telephoning Sofia. After a long conversation he called the chief of police. "The Minister of the Interior wants to talk to you."

The chief returned scowling. "My orders are to see that you reach Sofia safely."

My injured companions were taken to the hospital and my bodyguards and I were escorted to the station in a carriage by a young lieutenant of cavalry, who told us, "The army is fed up with these Macedonian scoundrels. You may be sure we'll soon attend to them. I'd like to see them attack the station. If they try it, I'll order my soldiers to kill them all on the spot."

He surrounded the train with his men, commandeered a car, and placed at the doors two soldiers whom he ordered to remain on board until the first stop. I reached Sofia to find the morning papers full of the most fantastic versions of what had happened in Lom. The headlines had me seriously wounded.

In Paris, Nadejda heard an exaggerated report over the radio and wired frantically to Sofia. My mother, who unfortunately had seen the papers, came running to see me without stopping to put on her coat. Her teeth were chattering with cold. I gave her tea, ordered a car, and sent her home. She became sick at once and died nine days later of pneumonia. I was with her at the end and closed her eyes.

During the day after the attack, visitors came from every part of Bulgaria. From Belgrade came Milan Stoyadinovich, former Minister to Sofia, to bring me the good wishes of my friends in Yugoslavia. Stoyadinovich, then my good friend, was later to become the pro-Axis Premier of Yugoslavia.

On November 21, in Sofia, we held our party congress. In seven months our ranks had swelled from 17,000 to 128,000. The sessions lasted three days, climaxed by the election of a seven-man Central Committee and a governing Party Council of thirty-two members. I received the largest number of votes; of the sixteen administrative areas, twelve demanded that I represent them in the Central Committee.

The election for half the local councils of Bulgaria, which were coming up in January, would be the first big test for our party. In the midst of the campaign Nadejda wired that our daughter Tatiana was seriously ill. I left for Paris at once and had to remain there during the elections. The result showed us running second to the government coalition and well ahead of Tsankov's Fascists and the Communist Party.

I was still in Paris on February 6 when the Stavisky affair shook the foundations of the Third Republic. It is worth recalling that Stavisky had previously come to the attention of the police several times for minor crimes and had been in prison. Yet he found easy access to important men in the government and the *Sûreté Nationale*. In organizing the Hungarian reparations bond swindle he had important political help, mainly from the Minister of Finance, Georges Bonnet. The reactionary press, of course, exploited the scandal and blamed the Third Republic. In reality, politicians of every camp were involved.

The big men were disappearing from the French political scene. Clemenceau, Poincaré, Briand, and Painlevé were dead. Édouard Herriot, by far the wisest and ablest man in the Radical Socialist Party, was being pushed aside by new men headed by Édouard Daladier who, although personally honest, was weak and surrounded himself with such dubious figures as Bonnet and Chautemps. Pierre Laval, who had begun life as a poor butcher's son and had become a millionaire owning fifteen provincial newspapers and ten Paris apartment houses, was much more concerned with his private fortunes than those of France. Pierre Étienne Flandin, spokesman of the Right and friend of Germany, was engaged in many shady enterprises such as the bankrupt France Aéronautique which had swallowed 100 million francs in government subsidies. Somewhat earlier, there had been the scandal of Mme. Hanau's *Gazette du Franc,* involving many politicians.

The public was tired of it all. On February 6, when the Royalists staged a demonstration against the Daladier government, the enormous crowd which massed in the Place de la Concorde included outraged Parisians of every political shade, united only by their desire to put an end to the canker of corruption destroying France. I was in the crowd on the rue Royale near the Madeleine Church when firing came from across the Seine and bullets whistled over our heads. The rioting crowds were dispersed, but not without many casualties. The next day Premier Daladier resigned in panic.

I could gauge the feeling of the French people from that of my friend Professor Louis Brun, whom I had known on the Western Front as an excellent officer and a passionate patriot. Now he said, "I'm personally ready to shoot any minister who declares war. I won't fight again. For whom would I be fighting? For these scoundrels!"

All his savings had been wiped out in a bank crash, and he had nothing left but his miserable academic pay. There were millions like him in France. The average hard-working, thrifty Frenchman who saw his savings vanish overnight could feel nothing but rancor or cynical indifference toward his government.

While Frenchmen lost heart, on their eastern frontier Nazi Germany was forging its weapons.

H ITLER'S SEIZURE OF power changed the polit-
ical outlook for the Balkan countries as for the rest of Europe. Italian
fascism had meddled in Balkan affairs for ten years, bribing, corrupting,
murdering in a determined effort to prevent any real defensive alliance
against Mussolini's predatory designs. Now the peninsula lay weakened
by its divisions before a fascism as predatory as that of Italy and poten-
tially far more powerful. The immediate reaction was a tendency to
strengthen existing defensive ties and to seek new ones. Once more the
idea of an alliance of all the South Slavs as the nucleus of a United Balkans came to the fore. And this time its chief protagonist was the man
who, thirteen years before, had assured me of his sympathy with Stamboliski's foreign policy—Alexander of Yugoslavia.

The chief obstacle to this alliance remained the pro-Italian policy of
the Bulgarian government. Mussolini had poured money into Bulgaria;
he had controlled one government after another; he owned the IMRO.
And he had somehow managed to win King Boris' support at the very
outset of his successful attempts to control Bulgarian policy; the King
had never ceased to protect his agent, Volkov, who had plotted Stamboliski's murder. Moreover, Mussolini had succeeded in convincing Boris,
through Volkov and Mikhailov, that the Yugoslav government was planning to kill him. In 1930 the Bulgarian king had formed closer ties with
Italy through his marriage with Princess Giovanna of Savoy.

All of which is simply another way of saying that Bulgarian resistance
to an alliance with Yugoslavia was chiefly Mussolini's resistance. If
Alexander should succeed where Stamboliski had almost succeeded, all
Mussolini's criminal activity, all his enormous outlay of Italian money,
would have been in vain. In the next act of the tragedy of the Balkans
between world wars, the chief protagonists would be the Yugoslav King
and the Italian Dictator.

My first experience of the renewed trend toward Balkan solidarity
came in April, 1933, when the Rumanian Government, through its Minister to Sofia, invited me to come to Bucharest. In the Rumanian Ministry of Foreign Affairs, Undersecretary Savel Radulescu received me
because Foreign Minister Titulescu was then abroad. Radulescu told me
that his government believed Hitler's rise to power necessitated closer
ties among the Balkan peoples, and was ready to begin negotiating with
its Balkan neighbors for a general alliance.

"Splendid!" I answered, "but why not address the Bulgarian government?"

"We'll do so at the proper time. For the moment we want to sound out the leaders of the Bulgarian political parties."

He arranged an audience for me with Premier Vaida-Voevod, an experienced old politician who had once represented the Rumanian minority of Transylvania in the Hungarian parliament. With unusual candor the Premier said, "I'm in power for only a short time. Duca, the Liberal leader, will no doubt follow me. You must see him."

I knew Duca from Lausanne. He was wise, exceptionally honest, and a sincere democrat.

"If I come to power," he said, "I intend to make every effort for a Balkan alliance."

Duca did come to power, but was murdered that December by the Fascist Iron Guard.

Shortly after this interview I was invited to speak on the subject of an alliance at the University of Belgrade. The evening I arrived King Alexander sent for me. He shook hands warmly and asked, "Well, when will your party take power?"

I told him I wasn't optimistic, for both King Boris and the army were against us and it was a long time until the next election.

"That's unfortunate," he said. "Events may take us by surprise and once more we shall be unprepared. I've already begun talks with Rumania, Turkey, and Greece; but a Balkan alliance without Bulgaria is worthless. Both strategically and for the quality of her soldiers, Bulgaria is essential for a powerful Balkan alliance."

"Why don't you try to meet King Boris?"

"He doesn't trust me. He thinks I'm his enemy."

At that time I believed that winning King Boris' collaboration was simply a matter of overcoming the fears aroused in him by the lies of Volkov and Mikhailov. I told King Alexander I was sure he could convince Boris in one conversation that these fears were baseless.

That was in May, 1933. On October 3, King Alexander arrived in Varna on his destroyer *Dubrovnik,* and was welcomed at the port by King Boris. The two kings had already met briefly at the Belgrade railway station in September, as Boris and his queen returned to Sofia from a tour of Europe. Now they spent the day together at the Euxinograd Palace. That moment, it seemed to me, was the turning-point in the postwar history of the Balkans. Confident that it meant a Bulgar-Yugoslav alliance at long last, I summoned a mass meeting of my followers in Preslav, the ancient Bulgarian capital, and said to them,

"As late as yesterday so-called patriots, for whom patriotism is a profitable profession, declared that any collaboration with Yugoslavia was treason. Today the King of Bulgaria meets the King of Yugoslavia in Euxinograd, kisses him, and calls him cousin. If their kings are cousins, the Bulgarians and Yugoslavs are brothers."

From Varna, the *Dubrovnik* proceeded to Istanbul, where Alexander conferred with President Kemal on the impending Balkan pact. The new Turkey, which made no territorial claims against its neighbors, was following a policy of collaboration with all Balkan peoples, and the Foreign Minister, Rudji Aras, had visited Athens, Belgrade, Sofia, and Bucharest to advocate a Balkan alliance.

As soon as Alexander returned to Belgrade I hastened to see him, to learn what had been accomplished at Euxinograd and Istanbul. He didn't consider his trip to Bulgaria a success. To his offer of alliance, Boris had replied, "Unfortunately, the Macedonians are very strong in my country. They'll kill anyone who makes an alliance with Yugoslavia." And with a sigh he had added, "You know the fate of Stamboliski."

"I warned him," continued Alexander, "that Rumania and Turkey were insisting on the immediate conclusion of a Balkan pact, but that I didn't want to sign until I had done everything possible to bring in Bulgaria. 'That's nothing,' he told me. 'If it's necessary, sign the pact!' A few minutes later he reconsidered. 'Yes, you'd better wait,' he said.

"But the most interesting thing," laughed Alexander, "was when he asked me about you. 'Do you know Kosta Todorov?'

" 'Of course,' I answered. 'He was your minister to my country.'

" 'Yes, yes, of course,' said Boris, and he praised you highly, adding that you had a great future in Bulgaria, but that the time wasn't quite ripe for you."

It was my turn to laugh. "Boris told you that because he was sure you'd repeat it to me. It's one of his methods of flattery. But what about the results of your talk?"

"So far none." And he added sadly, "I'm afraid we shall have to conclude the pact without Bulgaria."

Shortly thereafter Alexander sent for me from the spa near Nish. The King was agitated.

"France," he said, "demands a Balkan pact at once. Titulescu also insists. The Turks and the Greeks are in a hurry. I'm holding it up, but that breeds distrust, especially among the Greeks and Rumanians who were already disturbed by my meeting with Boris. They're afraid I'll make an alliance with Bulgaria which might be directed against the Greeks. I can't wait any longer."

Knowing only too well that a Balkan pact without Bulgaria could easily be directed against Bulgaria, I remarked, "It would be a pity if the conclusion of a pact now were to cut short the progress toward a Bulgar-Yugoslav understanding."

"I myself would prefer an alliance with Bulgaria to any kind of Balkan pact," said Alexander, "but I can't hold them off any longer."

"I think you can," I said. "The Greeks recently tried to come to an understanding with Italy. The talk of an alliance between our countries made them suspect a secret agreement to enable us both to reach the Aegean, and they sought Italian aid against that possibility. I believe you might suggest, as one of the conditions of a Balkan pact, that all the signatories recognize the solidarity of the Balkan states against any great power which might attack any of them. Since this condition would be directed primarily against Italy, Greece will be reluctant to agree. Yet without that clause, the Balkan pact would be worth very little."

"You're quite right," said Alexander. "That clause will lead to long debates and I shall gain time."

"Why don't you use the usual diplomatic channels?" I asked.

"Because I want no documents on this. My proposal is oral. In the event of an alliance, I'm prepared to return Tsaribrod and Bosiljgrad to Bulgaria."

"May I tell that to the Bulgarian envoy?"

After a pause, Alexander said, "Yes—unofficially."

The minute I reached Belgrade I went to the Bulgarian legation. I had known the Minister, Kiosseivanov, for many years and had always considered him honest if not too bright. During the Peasant regime he had been dismissed from a diplomatic secretarial post on the ground of incompetence, but Stamboliski had reinstated him in the service at my request. Now, a decade later, he occupied my old post in Belgrade. In 1935, after King Boris became absolute dictator, Kiosseivanov suddenly became Prime Minister, and held that position when the present war began.

I told him of my talk with Alexander and asked him to advise Sofia in strict confidence of the Yugoslav proposal. He promised to do so, declaring that he believed deeply in a Bulgar-Yugoslav alliance.

Returning to Sofia, I immediately reported Alexander's offer to my old friend of *komitaji* days, Petko Penchev, who was a political friend of Premier Mushanov. After transmitting it to the Premier, Petko told me, "It's no use. The man refuses to take anything seriously."

In November the Balkan pact was signed without Bulgaria but with a proviso, upon Alexander's insistence, that Bulgaria might become a full partner at any time. Alexander had not given up hope of winning King Boris. Early in December Boris paid a state visit to Belgrade, but Alexander told me that while the meeting was cordial no agreement had been reached.

Still, this state visit, following so closely on the conclusion of the Balkan Pact, evidently aroused in Mussolini fears that Boris would either be won over to the pact by Alexander or be driven over to it by the growing Bulgarian sentiment in its favor. He moved immediately to forestall a complete alliance.

On December 17, 1933, King Alexander and Queen Marie visited Zagreb to celebrate the King's forty-fifth birthday. In the great crowd which cheered as they drove to the Cathedral of St. Stephen, were three assassins armed with bombs to kill the royal pair. But when their leader saw the enthusiasm of the people and the smiling faces of the King and Queen he lost his nerve, and his failure to act caused his confederates to lose theirs. Seized by the police after killing a gendarme, the leader, Peter Oreb, frankly confessed that they had been sent from Italy on false Hungarian passports by Ante Pavelich, and that Mussolini's prefect at Brescia had supplied them with money and weapons.

Pavelich, leader of the extremist Croat *Ustasha,* whom Mussolini had bought shortly after the conclusion of the French-Yugoslav alliance, had been in Italy since 1929, organizing terrorist units on the model of the IMRO. He and his activities were financed by Mussolini on a most extravagant scale. In the summer of 1932, operating from the isolated port of Zara on the Dalmatian coast, Pavelich attempted with his terrorists to provoke an uprising in the Lika area between Bosnia and Croatia. On Pavelich's assurance that the moment of Croatian liberation was at hand, Mussolini held his fleet ready to intervene. But the revolution fizzled out for the simple reason that no one joined the Italian-armed terrorists. Now the assassination of King Alexander in the Croatian capital had been expected to serve as a new signal for revolution in Croatia and the creation of an independent state headed by Pavelich.

King Alexander saw through the Zagreb attempt. "It's clear that Mussolini wants to kill me and will stop at nothing," he told me. "Could you imagine that the head of a government with which we maintain normal relations would send assassins to kill me? I intended to place the issue squarely before the League of Nations, but the French and the British advise me to avoid open conflict with Italy. They still hope Mussolini will side with them, but I'm convinced he's secretly negotiating with Hitler."

The King realized that the Reich under Hitler's leadership was heading Europe toward a general conflict, but he also firmly believed that France would take the necessary steps to prevent Hitler from growing too strong.

"The Germans are courting us now," he continued. "They're trying to make us break away from France and Czechoslovakia, and to frighten us with the specter of Bolshevism. I told the German envoy we would handle the Bolsheviks ourselves and that we intended to remain loyal to our allies."

Six months after this attempt on Alexander's life a coup d'état in Bulgaria resulted in an anti-Italian, pro-Yugoslav government—and my own exile. Premier Mushanov's frivolity had disgusted the people. The economic situation was calamitous, the cabinet was forever squabbling, the Macedonians were killing with impunity and the government even allowed them to frame up and murder an army colonel who had condemned their activities.

Not realizing that his government was on its last legs, Mushanov had begun secret negotiations with our party for our entry into the cabinet in place of the right-wing Peasant deputies. We demanded a new economic policy in favor of the peasants, Volkov's dismissal from his position as Minister to Rome, collaboration with Yugoslavia, and the suppression of Tsankov's Fascists who had begun to accept German subsidies. Mushanov agreed to all conditions except the Yugoslav alliance. That, he said, was not within his power; the King must decide.

So matters stood when, on May 18, 1934, the coup d'état brought to power a group of men who had taken part in the Tsankov coup of 1923, and who in 1929 had formed a political organization to demand a new foreign and internal policy beginning with the abolition of the IMRO. This group, led by Kimon Gheorgiev and Volkov's old enemy, Colonel Damian Velchev, called itself the *Zveno* (link). Most of its members were honest men who regretted their part in Stamboliski's overthrow.

The *Zveno* detested Tsankov, was strongly anti-Italian, and wanted an alliance with Yugoslavia; and it considered King Boris largely responsible for the unwise foreign policy and the intolerable internal situation. But under Gheorgiev as Premier it set up an authoritarian regime, suspended the constitution, outlawed all political parties, and banned all party papers. It also outlawed the IMRO, and the military and police authorities swooped down to make the ban effective. Mikhailov fled to Turkey. Many of his men were arrested and large quantities of arms were seized. To the amazement and relief of everyone in Bulgaria, the dreaded IMRO collapsed overnight. Mussolini had lost one of his most effective—and expensive—means of terrorizing Bulgarian politicians and harassing the Yugoslav government.

The masses of the Peasant Party were ready to support Gheorgiev, but the new regime alienated them by declaring that it would push through its domestic and foreign policy without the people's help. The suppression of civil liberty was intolerable to me, and I attacked it at once. A few days after the coup, the chief of police informed me that the government had decreed my expulsion from Bulgaria, and within an hour I left for Belgrade, again an exile.

King Alexander sent for me immediately. "Can the new government be trusted with regard to an alliance?"

"Completely. They're honest men. However, they can't last very long."

"Why?'"

"Because they have the support of neither King nor people. Only part of the army is with them. It's possible to be with the King against the people or with the people against the King, but not against both while the King remains in power."

Alexander frowned. "What about the King's position? I shouldn't like anything to happen to him, especially since the Gheorgiev government has announced its desire for an understanding with us. King Boris might think me a party to any move against him."

Such rumors were already spreading in Sofia. Our conversation turned to the question of dictatorship.

"It's not easy," Alexander sighed. "When something succeeds, my ministers take the credit; when it fails, they say it's my fault. Recently I saw my brother-in-law, King Carol. We met on a yacht on the Danube and spent two days together, during which he must have worn at least a hundred medals. He asked me whether I didn't think it might be better if he introduced dictatorship in Rumania. Do you know what I told him?"

"To follow your example?"

"No, no," said Alexander morosely, "I told him that dictatorship outwardly resembles a splendid palace, but once you're in you can't find a way out. You get lost in labyrinths and dark corridors, and there's no door open for escape."

From Belgrade I went once more to Paris, where I called at the Ministry of Foreign Affairs to discuss with Bargeton, director of the political section, the alarming spread of German influence in the Balkans and the German drive to capture Balkan markets.

"Well, what of it?" he asked. "We're not interested in Balkan trade. Let Germany exploit that market; it will pacify Hitler."

"But you know," I warned him, "that the German soldier inevitably follows the German salesman."

Bargeton smiled complacently. "You exaggerate."

He viewed with equal indifference my reports of Italian intrigue. With Berthelot gone, I realized, the Quai d'Orsay existed in name only.

When I returned to Belgrade early in September, the first hints of a possible Italian attack on Ethiopia could be detected. I mentioned this to King Alexander.

"What are you driving at?" he asked.

"I think Mussolini will attack Ethiopia because it's the only country which can't defend itself against him and because Italy has long dreamed of grabbing it."

"Perhaps . . . perhaps."

"Then let me advise you to send Haile Selassie as large a quantity of guns and ammunition as possible, to force Italy to become involved in a long war and to leave the Balkans in peace."

Alexander brightened. "An excellent idea! When I have more definite information we'll discuss it."

A week later he sent for me again. "Our envoys in London and Rome confirm your suspicions. We have a large supply of old Austrian machine guns and ammunition that I could send to Ethiopia, but who can take charge of them? Would you agree to go?"

I answered with a laugh, "No, Your Majesty. As it is, I'm always being accused of seeking out adventure. Besides I'm too much occupied with matters nearer home to undertake such a distant mission."

I suggested that he send to Ethiopia several priests and experienced reserve officers under the guise of a Greek Orthodox delegation, as the Russian Czar used to do. The Ethiopians belonged to the kindred Coptic Church. By this device he could not only arm the Ethiopians, but also send them Yugoslav military instructors. Alexander said he would try to find the right men.

Then he turned to his recent meeting with Hermann Goering in Belgrade.

"Goering told me, 'I come to you as one soldier to another. We want to maintain good relations with Yugoslavia. We respect the Serbian people and have no aggressive intentions in the Balkans. But the union of Germany and Austria is just as essential to us as your union with the Croats, which formed Yugoslavia.'

"I replied that on that question Yugoslavia could only act together with her allies, France, Rumania, and Czechoslovakia. I've been dissatisfied with French policy lately, but Barthou seems to have an excellent grasp of our problems and wants to strengthen our ties with France. I look forward to much good from my trip to Paris, in the way of stabilizing the European situation."

I never saw King Alexander again. A few days after our last talk I went to Paris and the King left for Sofia, accompanied by Foreign Minister Yevtich. He arrived on September 17 and received an enthusiastic welcome. Old animosities seemed at last to have disappeared; the IMRO no longer existed, and Gheorgiev was eager for an alliance with Yugoslavia. Alexander returned to Belgrade in high spirits.

Early in October General Atsa Dimitrievich, his marshal of the palace, came to Paris to make arrangements for the King's visit. Alexander sailed for Marseille on October 6 aboard the *Dubrovnik*. He was to reach Marseille on the ninth and Paris the next day. General Dimitrievich telephoned me that the King wished to see me at the Ritz on the evening of his arrival.

On the evening of October 9 I came home to find Nadejda waiting for me, pale and shaken.

"I've just heard on the radio that King Alexander has been killed in Marseille."

I called up the Yugoslav legation.

"Yes," came the reply, "the King is dead. The assassin is a Petrus Keleman, carrying a Czech passport."

It very soon became known that the assassin was no Czech but a Bulgarian. When his body was stripped the initials IMRO and the Bulgarian words for "Liberty or Death" were found tattooed on his arm. From that clue it was easy to establish that he was Vlado Gheorgiev Chernozemsky, better known as Vlado the Chauffeur, one of the most notorious IMRO assassins.

No attempt had been made to guard Alexander upon his arrival. No soldiers lined the streets through which he was to pass. Only a small troop of cavalry was detailed to act as escort, and it streaked away so far ahead of the royal car that it was useless for protection. The newsreel men were allowed to delay the procession and create confusion. Two mounted officers flanked the car, but the one who at last felled the assassin was a colonel of infantry who handled his horse so clumsily that by the time he could strike the King was dead, and Foreign Minister Barthou, General Georges, a police agent and two bystanders wounded.

Moreover, Barthou was allowed to bleed to death from a wound which with proper medical attention need not have proved fatal. The whole spectacle of ineptitude and confusion was a disgrace to France. Yet the *Sûreté Nationale* must surely have been informed that a Serb agent had seen three assassins on the Orient Express, going from Hungary to Paris at the same time that Alexander was leaving Yugoslavia. It must surely have known that the *Ustasha's* death-sentence against Alexander had been published in its official paper. By making it easy for King Alexander to be assassinated the minute he reached French soil, it provided good ground for suspicion that agents of some interested foreign power had a hand in its disregard of elementary precautions.

As if to make up in belated zeal for its lack of the merest interest before the crime, the police began to work on the case with considerable energy. Three of the killer's accomplices were caught before they could get out of France—Mio Kralj whose appointed task had been to facilitate Vlado's getaway by throwing a bomb into the crowd, but who had lost his nerve; Popishil and Raich, who were to have killed Alexander at Versailles if the Marseille attempt failed. Within two weeks the French

[258]

police had most of the important clues in its hands. Those clues led directly to Ante Pavelich and his confederates, and beyond them to Mussolini, Horthy, and even farther.

Almost at once a mysterious influence began to make itself felt. The affair was suppressed. During the King's funeral the representatives of the Little Entente unanimously declared that the assassination was no mere blow against Yugoslav unity but had been aimed at the existing order in Europe. But the French government, under Barthou's successor, Pierre Laval, intrigued busily to keep its Italian origin from being mentioned. The British government wanted both Italian and Hungarian complicity ignored, lest Alexander's murder, like that at Sarajevo twenty years before, lead to a European war. No doubt the danger seemed even greater than then, with governments the real assassins.

Prince Paul, the Yugoslav regent, was amenable. When Yugoslavia appealed for redress to the League of Nations, its memorandum was moderate in tone and mentioned only Hungary, against which it had lodged an earlier complaint for harboring Pavelich's terrorists on its territory. The Hungarians, while denying their own complicity, loyally refrained from mentioning the Italian inspiration of the crime. Mussolini made sure that the trial in France should not take place before the League session, by arresting Pavelich and his lieutenant Eugene Kvaternik, holding them incommunicado, and refusing the French request for their extradition. And Laval was too obliging to push the request with any embarrassing vigor; he was negotiating with the Duce for a French-Italian agreement. At the opening League session, on December 5, he intervened to prevent any mention of Italy's part in the crime. And when Anthony Eden, by a speech extremely painful to Yugoslav national feeling, had driven the Yugoslav delegation to the point of withdrawing from the sessions, Laval, with a series of shrewd backstage moves worthy of the confidence man he is, managed at once to keep the Yugoslavs in the League and bamboozle them into accepting a "Tut, tut" to Hungary, along with a condemnation of the murder which cost no one anything and a demand for justice which M. Laval would be able to take care of when the time came.

Once more the League had sacrificed the just claims of a small nation to its craven desire to appease the Italian dictator. Laval was pleased; he had served Mussolini slickly and successfully, and others, too, whose identities remained obscure. The British statesmen, who during this period raised obtuseness to the dignity of a profession, were also pleased. The King he had killed had seen that Mussolini would cast in his lot with Hitler; the British politicians saw nothing. They believed that the travesty of justice staged at Geneva had averted a European war. In fact it had enormously increased the danger.

For the Little Entente was right. King Alexander's assassination was aimed at the existing order in Europe. It was the first concerted assault on that order by the Axis and its satellites. The success of the Geneva conspiracy which prevented Yugoslavia from getting justice before the League of Nations proved to these criminals that the League would not dare oppose their aggressions—in other words, that the League as an instrument of European peace was useless.

The fact that Pavelich was back of the Marseille assassination proved that Mussolini was its instigator. Already he had tried, through Pavelich, to assassinate Alexander at Zagreb. In this case the precaution taken by Pavelich of sending his agent, Eugene Kvaternik, to Zurich for French francs before any of the conspirators left Italy, did not really shield Mussolini; the world knew that he had supplied the wherewithal to finance the crime.

Hungary's part in the conspiracy was less important. One of Pavelich's agents, Eugene Perchets, had maintained at Yanka Pusta, in Hungary, an *Ustasha* terrorist training center under the protection of the Hungarian government, and three of the assassin's confederates went from that camp to France on Hungarian passports. Perchets was an intelligence officer in the Hungarian army, and Horthy protected his terrorists because he hoped their outrages in northern Yugoslavia would weaken the Belgrade government and enable him to make good his claims to Yugoslav territory. A series of sensational articles in the Zagreb *Novosti* by Perchets' former Croat mistress, Yelka Pogorelets, had exposed the Italian and Hungarian connections of the *Ustasha* leaders, and had obliged Perchets to disappear; but Horthy continued his hospitality to the *Ustasha* and was extremely generous with Hungarian passports for its terrorists. Not only those of Alexander's assassins who went to France from Hungary but those who went from Italy were supplied with an ample assortment, in various names. The Hungarian government's direct knowledge of the reason for their trip was proved by the fact that one of its secret agents who had followed the three reserve assassins to Zurich, warned Kvaternik that a Serb agent had overheard them talking in the train.

The Yugoslav investigation was carried much further than the French and established certain facts which linked the German and Bulgarian governments with the crime. From the chief of the Yugoslav political police I learned that Kvaternik had gone to Munich to buy the German weapons to be used against the King—the Mauser automatic with which he was killed and those kept in reserve in case the Marseille attempt failed. And what was more significant, Kvaternik had carried this arsenal into France under the protection of a German diplomatic passport.

Nor was this Hitler's only contribution to the crime. The weekly paper of the *Ustasha* appeared first at Berlin and subsequently at Danzig, which had already come under Nazi control. This paper, the *Nezavisna Hrvatska,* was financed by Joseph Goebbels on the sole condition that it be published at **Danzig** instead of Berlin, so the German government might, in case of necessity, be able to disclaim responsibility for it. A few weeks before the assassination this sheet published the death sentence pronounced against Alexander by the *Ustasha,* and accompanied it with violent threats against Barthou. Hitler's complicity in the plot against the King thereby became an open secret—a secret which must surely have been known to the *Sûreté Nationale* even before Alexander left Yugoslavia for Marseille.

Mussolini, Horthy, Hitler—and the fantastic biography of the Bulgarian gunman whose hand had pulled the trigger for them pointed to the complicity of yet another ruler—Boris of Bulgaria.

It would have been impossible to ascertain the facts about Vlado the Chauffeur if Alexander's murder had not taken place while the *Zveno* government was in power. The *Zveno* was anti-Boris and anti-Italian. It had wiped out the Macedonian Organization. It was under compulsion from no quarter to conceal the truth.

Vlado Chernozemsky in the course of his criminal career had used a number of aliases, two of which were recognized as legal by the Bulgarian police, who had provided them. Twice he had been condemned to death—in 1924 for the murder of a Sofia Deputy, Dimo Hadji Dimov, and in 1931 for the murder of Naum Tomalevsky, a journalist who had been an important member of the IMRO and had acted as Vancho Mikhailov's deputy in conferences with Pavelich to arrange for co-operation between the two terrorist organizations. Tomalevsky had broken with Mikhailov, and knew too much to be allowed to live.

But the IMRO's crack assassin was not to be spared for anything so trivial as satisfaction of justice. Each time Vlado was sentenced to death a fake execution took place, registering the "death" of his name. After which the killer was released under a new name, to await orders for a new assassination. Obviously Vlado the Chauffeur enjoyed protection from some very powerful Bulgarian official quarter. It was indeed powerful; one of the best-informed men in Bulgaria, who held a high office in the police force under the *Zveno* government, told me frankly that after both sentences Vlado had been released on the personal order of King Boris. Moreover, after his second release he became the King's personal chauffeur.

In February, 1934, this expert gunman was sent by Kurtev, Vancho Mikhailov's lieutenant (whose mistress had tried to trap me for him some months earlier), to the Yanka Pusta camp to be subject to Ante Pavelich's orders. This move resulted from an exchange of letters between Pavelich and Kurtev which were found in Kurtev's possession—the original of Pavelich's letter and the copy of Kurtev's reply. In substance they were as follows:

Pavelich to Kurtev: "Send me a tried terrorist. Mine aren't worth much."

Kurtev to Pavelich: "I'm sending you a first rate assassin. Use him only against a victim of the utmost importance."

Pavelich's appeal was inspired, of course, by Oreb's failure to assassinate Alexander in Zagreb. He used his new killer for a time at Yanka Pusta, to instruct the assassins reserved for the possible Versailles attempt. Then he sent him to Italy. Pavelich convinced Vlado that in France no one ever went to the guillotine for a political murder, and that even if he were caught he would only be sent to prison, from which money and influence would soon release him. Vlado was unafraid. In Bulgaria he had committed a dozen murders for which he had never been arrested, and even when condemned to death he had been saved by powerful influence. His immunity had mightily increased his courage.

Thus King Boris's personal chauffeur, whom he had twice saved from the extreme penalty for murder, left Bulgaria on the order of the IMRO, necessarily with Boris' consent, to be used by Pavelich against two victims of the utmost importance, the Yugoslav King and the French Minister of Foreign Affairs. That the King was willing twice to misuse his power to save the IMRO's crack killer is proof enough that he was himself as much Mussolini's agent as the IMRO leaders for whom he acted. And that he permitted Vlado to be sent to Pavelich proved that he was well aware against whom the killer would be used. Pavelich's designs, and Mussolini's, could be no secret to anyone after the Zagreb attempt. Possibly Boris still harbored the made-in-Italy suspicion that Alexander had designs upon his life, and therefore welcomed the opportunity to forestall them by helping to kill Alexander. But it is rather more likely that he was moved to connive at the murder by greed for territory.

For there is no question that the conspirators expected the King's death to be followed by the speedy dissolution of Yugoslavia. Mussolini expected this to facilitate his penetration of the Balkans; Horthy expected it to enable him to make territorial gains in the northern provinces of Yugoslavia; Boris entertained the same hopes in regard to the southern provinces. And Hitler believed, rightly, that Alexander's death would be a crippling blow to the Franco-Yugoslav alliance and to the Little Entente with its fifty million people and its powerful armies which could be equipped by Czech industry.

These hopes were not immediately realized. Yugoslavia remained united before the tomb of its King. But they were realized ultimately.

With Alexander died the last hope of united Balkan defense against the aggressive designs of the fascist dictators. Prince Paul, who as regent succeeded to Alexander's power, did his best to bring about the destruction of his country, lending himself to the designs of Mussolini and later of Hitler, and thus paving the way for Yugoslavia's destruction. When that destruction had been completed in 1941 by German armies invading from Bulgaria, which Boris had turned over to Hitler without firing a shot, the conspirators who had murdered Alexander helped themselves to the fruits of their crime. Here is the picture at the moment of writing:

In Croatia, Pavelich, installed as "chief" of state by the Germans and Italians, maintains a hideous reign of terror and assassinates all who oppose him, whether Serbs or Croats.

King Boris has occupied a large part of Yugoslav territory.

Horthy has invaded the northern provinces and massacred the Serbs.

Mussolini has annexed Dalmatia and part of Slovenia, peopled by pure South Slavs.

Hitler, as chief of this gang, rules over all of them, and has taken some slices of Yugoslav territory.

And to complete the picture, another accomplice, Pierre Laval, who suppressed the affair of Marseille, cheated Yugoslavia at the League sessions, and turned the trial of the accomplices into a nauseating mockery of justice, became Hitler's Quisling at Vichy, where he continues, after complete German occupation of France, to do his master's bidding.

Once before, an understanding between the two South Slav peoples had threatened to thwart Mussolini's Adriatic and Balkan plans. Then, too, an Alexander had died by his order. Both Volkov, who planned the murder of Alexander Stamboliski the peasant, and Pavelich, who directed the assassination of Alexander Karadjordjevich the King, served Mussolini. But Pavelich, in serving Mussolini, also served Boris of Bulgaria, whose ministers were about to ally his country with Yugoslavia against his will; he served Horthy of Hungary; he served Hitler; and above all he served the designs of the Axis conspirators upon European civilization.

THE PRIME MOVER in the plot to murder Alexander had been Mussolini. Its prime beneficiary was Hitler. With the strongest advocate of defensive Balkan union out of the way, the *Führer* lost no time in helping himself to the results of Mussolini's work. From the end of 1934—that is, from the date of Alexander's death—Italian influence in the Balkans began to decline before that of Germany, as Hitler's propaganda elbowed out and supplanted Mussolini's. In short, to Hitler's role of Antichrist, Mussolini had quite unintentionally played that of John the Baptist.

What made the German propaganda so much more successful than the Italian was its pretense of disinterestedness. "Germany has no unfriendly or imperialistic designs in the Balkans," said Goebbels' agents. "On the contrary, it wants peace and understanding among the Balkan peoples. Its sole aim is to destroy Bolshevism and thus save European civilization from its menace. Germany is also against capitalism which is represented by the Jews. By destroying Bolshevism and the Jews it will insure the independence of the nations and the well-being of the workers."

Meanwhile the Nazis were pushing their commercial offensive and planting "tourist agencies" everywhere, which carried on German propaganda and soon became centers of corruption and espionage.

I had ample opportunity to observe this process at work in Yugoslavia during the summer of 1935, after a sojourn of one day in my native land. My recall from exile followed interesting political changes in Bulgaria. On January 22, 1935, King Boris forced the resignation of Kimon Gheorgiev, head of the *Zveno*, who was succeeded by his Minister of War, General Zlatev. This amounted to a royal coup d'état. Gheorgiev had attempted to give his authoritarian regime a legal stamp through a new constitution modeled upon the Portuguese, which would have deprived the King of many of his prerogatives but transferred them to the Ministerial Council rather than the Sobranje. The attempt displeased the people as well as the King. In ridding himself of Gheorgiev, Boris showed great skill and cunning, splitting the ranks of the *Zveno* by encouraging the ambitions of General Zlatev and a small group of his followers. Gheorgiev's eight months in power remained notable for two things—the liquidation of the IMRO and the recognition of Soviet Russia.

With Gheorgiev out of the way and the threat to his growing personal power removed, Boris soon got rid of General Zlatev. He had not forgotten that Zlatev's wing of the *Zveno* had also conspired to reduce him to a puppet. In April, he installed a cabinet headed by Andre Toshev, former Minister to Vienna and close adviser of former King Ferdinand —that is to say, pro-German—with Kiosseivanov as Minister of Foreign Affairs. Kiosseivanov, whose skin I had once saved because I thought him honest, had climbed to this position through duplicity. Gheorgiev had appointed him Minister to the Palace to keep an eye on the King's moves. Instead he had acted against Gheorgiev as a secret intermediary between General Zlatev and Boris, and his new post was the King's reward for his services. The cabinet was now responsible to one man—the King. It no longer even reflected the will of the army, as had the *Zveno* regime.

Word reached me from Sofia in June, 1935, that I could return to Bulgaria and that the Bulgarian Minister to Belgrade was expecting me in that city. I was living in Marseille at the time, where in late October, 1934, I had converted a garage in the working-class section into a small bakery to produce strudel. There were only two of us, Nadejda's brother and myself, to prepare the product and distribute it among the cafés and restaurants of the city. Our strudels were both good and cheap, and by the end of the year we were selling a thousand a day. In promoting our product I was obliged to resort to a stratagem to conceal its German origin. Our strudel became *bûche normande*.

The summons home from exile meant that I was obliged to sell this prospering business and to leave Marseille for Belgrade and Sofia.

The envoy to Belgrade told me little more than that Kiosseivanov wished to see me on an important matter. At the Dragoman station on the Bulgarian frontier, friends met me with an automobile and told me Sofia was buzzing with rumors that I was being summoned to take a cabinet post. Naturally I had no intention of entering a cabinet which had officially proclaimed that it ruled only in the name of the King. Since Gheorgiev's coup d'état, however, a strange practice had arisen of "requisitioning" men for ministerial positions without asking whether they were willing to serve.

About halfway to the capital we suddenly found our way blocked by a large police car. This looked like arrest; perhaps the invitation to come to Sofia was a trap. A pompous police official emerged, stepped up to our car, saluted, and said, "By order of the Prime Minister, I have come to welcome you and escort you to Sofia."

This was worse than arrest. "You've been requisitioned," my companions remarked sadly.

When our car stopped before the home of my friend Mischa Mikhailov, a half-squadron of gendarmes stood at attention outside. Again it looked like arrest. But the officer in command shouted, "Attention!" and I was greeted by a salute of raised sabers.

"It's plain to see you've been appointed a minister," sighed my friends.

We had barely sat down to dinner when Kiosseivanov telephoned. "I'm sending a car for you; I want to see you at the Ministry."

He received me cordially, reminded me of the favor I had once done him, and said that the government counted on my help in the grave tasks before it.

"How can I help you?" I answered. "My party is banned, and you rule without the Sobranje."

"But we know," said Kiosseivanov, "that your party continues to exist secretly and that you have great influence with the people."

"If you're looking for popular support, restore liberty and hold an election. We believe in taking power only with a mandate from the people. Your government is illegal."

"What do you mean, illegal?" shouted Kiosseivanov. "We derive our authority from the King!"

"According to our constitution which, though not enforced, still exists, the King is merely the arbiter. In that capacity he is over the government. But a government can rest only on what is below it, as we are leaning on this table. Because he is above your regime, you cannot lean on the King. You can only hang from him."

Kiosseivanov assumed a pose of weariness, expressed regret that we couldn't come to an understanding, and let me go. The next day, the police invited me to leave the country. I had left my profitable strudel business in Marseille only to become once more an exile in Belgrade.

Prince Regent Paul now ruled Yugoslavia, and his Prime Minister was Dr. Milan Stoyadinovich, who had visited me in Sofia after the attempt on my life at Lom Palanka. Curiously enough, this man, who later tried to establish a totalitarian regime with himself as *Führer*, became Premier on his promise to restore parliamentary government and freedom of press and speech. And there seemed no reason at the time to doubt his word. Under King Alexander's dictatorship he had been a stanch oppositionist and had even advocated a republic.

The Regent, too, was thought to be a liberal. Prince Paul was the son of Arseni Karadjordjevich, the brother of King Peter I, who married a Russian princess of the illustrious Demidov family and served as a general in the Russian army. Paul was educated at St. Petersburg and Oxford, developed the habits of an English gentleman, and often expressed his keen admiration for British political institutions. Therefore, when he became Prince Regent and soon made Stoyadinovich Prime

Minister, it was generally expected that the dictatorship established in 1929 would shortly be liquidated. The opposite happened.

Paul was too elegant for his peasant subjects. They had forgiven Alexander many things because he was a soldier-king who had won victories on the battlefield. The Prince Regent was cold, aloof, arrogant, a patron of the arts whose chief passion was collecting paintings by the great French masters, which demanded large expenditures.

The pro-Italian line which he adopted almost at once, culminating in the Italo-Yugoslav friendship pact of March, 1937, had an interesting origin. Paul's aunt, Princess Demidova-San Donato, died in Italy, leaving him a legacy of 350 million lire. Under Italian law bequests to foreigners were heavily taxed, so that Paul was legally entitled to no more than a tenth of the estate But by courting Mussolini and seeking the Concordat with the Vatican against which the Greek Orthodox Church of Serbia rebelled, he obtained the whole of the legacy, free of inheritance tax.

Hitler found a similar way to the Prince Regent's heart. King Alexander had felt an emotional aversion to the Bolsheviks as regicides; he never forgot that Czar Nicholas, whom they killed, had entered the war on behalf of Serbia. But Paul hated them for a much more personal reason. Until the Bolshevik Revolution the Demidov family had been one of the richest in the world, owning fabulous mines in the Urals, great estates throughout Russia, and more than twenty palaces. The Bolsheviks had confiscated all this wealth, estimated at more than a billion and a half gold rubles. When Prince Paul began to visit Hitler, there is no doubt that Hitler promised to restore this fortune to him if he joined with Germany in the crusade against Bolshevism.

This "crusade" was one of the Nazi propaganda devices from the first. The "Organization for Struggle against the Third International," with headquarters in Geneva, had a Belgrade section whose secretary, Senator Popovich, went to Berlin every month, lived in great luxury, and preached a Yugoslav-Nazi alliance for the coming war against Bolshevism. Another device was the stock Nazi appeal to race prejudice. An anti-Semitic paper edited by one Tsitsvarich began to appear in Belgrade. Meanwhile Hitler continued to grab markets—and to buy apologists. A former Communist writer whom I had known for years now spoke of him as a genius and insisted that only by selling its farm products to Germany could Yugoslavia prosper. Trade between the two countries had doubled during the year, and the market was glutted with German products, from stockings to radios and automobiles, at remarkably low prices. People arriving in Belgrade from Bucharest, Athens, and Sofia described the same developments there.

The Yugoslav people remained pro-French, but they blamed France, with good cause, for its complete indifference to its ally's economic interests, notably its failure to buy Yugoslav farm products. Among the politicians it was said that Laval's pro-Italian policy, marked by the recent Stresa agreement, meant that Yugoslavia would be left to its fate. Count Dampierre, the new French Minister to Belgrade, had been counselor to the embassy in Rome for many years. An admirer of Mussolini, at his very first meeting with Stoyadinovich he advised the Premier to come to an understanding with Italy. A year later, when Stoyadinovich went to Rome and the rapprochement between Italy and Yugoslavia began, Dampierre protested in the name of the French government. Stoyadinovich could reply with justified cynicism, "I acted on your advice."

At the Egmont Palace in Brussels, in November, 1935, I attended the Interparliamentary Conference of the left parties of Europe as a representative of the Bulgarian Peasant Party. From France came Pierre Cot and Grumbach; from Belgium, Senators de Broughère and Rollin; from England, Lord Lister and several Labor members of Parliament. Spain was represented by Álvarez del Vayo, who demanded the support of the conference for the liberation of Francisco Largo Caballero, then under arrest in connection with the terror of October, 1934, conducted by José Marie Gil Robles, the Catholic reactionary, in the Asturias.

The British delegates protested vehemently against Laval's tacit support of Mussolini's Ethiopian adventure. There was not a single Communist delegate to this conference, but I later learned in Paris that it had been arranged by Willi Muenzenberg, who was then organizing "united fronts" for the Comintern in western Europe.

Upon my return to Paris from Brussels, I was caught between the Communist and Nazi propaganda mills. Willi Muenzenberg met me at the Café La Coupole and asked me to contribute to his German publication, appearing in Paris. With him was a short, dark German worker whom he introduced as a former Reichstag deputy and "Dimitrov's best friend." The two tried to persuade me to go to Moscow to consult Dimitrov, now Secretary of the Comintern, about my future work in the Balkans, and Muenzenberg offered to advance my expenses. I refused.

A few days later, a Bulgarian named Mincho Stoyilov called at my hotel. He told me he had tried unsuccessfully to reach me in Brussels and had finally got my address from the German Embassy in Paris.

"How did the German Embassy know it?" I asked in surprise.

Stoyilov smiled. "They know everything. They follow the activities of everyone who interests them."

He suggested a drive in his excellent Mercedes. I knew the man slightly and had a vague knowledge of his activities. He lived in Berlin, apparently engaged in the tobacco trade, and was always traveling through Europe in his car, supposedly to find customers for Bulgarian tobacco. Once before he had visited me in Belgrade and offered to take me to Colonel Parvan Draganov, the Bulgarian envoy in Vienna, known to be King Boris' closest friend and rumored to be King Ferdinand's illegitimate son. I had seen Draganov in Vienna in 1934, when he hinted that King Boris was not averse to coming to an understanding with me provided I gave proof I was not working against the dynasty.

Stoyilov was on a new mission now. He asked me to accompany him in his Mercedes to Berlin.

"You have a brilliant future before you," he said, "and from the way you seem to be living in Paris, your business must be pretty bad. I'm stopping at the Hotel Majestic on the Avenue Kléber," he boasted.

"What would I do in Berlin?" I asked him.

"Goebbels himself wants to see you."

I laughed. "Doesn't Goebbels know what I think of Hitlerism? I certainly haven't kept it a secret."

"That's only a misunderstanding. You and your friends don't understand the meaning of National Socialism. Hitler wants a new Europe based on justice. He's on the side of the people against capitalism. And Bulgaria can expect great advantages—economic, political, and territorial—from an alliance with Germany. You're for the people and for Bulgaria, aren't you?"

I was interested in knowing what Joseph Goebbels could offer and listened attentively to Stoyilov's proposals.

"Germany needs energetic new men in the Balkans. Tsankov was in Berlin recently, but Hitler wasn't impressed with him. He considers him too old and too badly compromised to be of much use. On my advice, Goebbels decided to approach you."

"Then I take it you're very close to Goebbels?"

Stoyilov gave me a broad, slow smile. "Yes, we're friends. . . . Well, what about it? Suppose we leave for Berlin today?"

"I'm afraid that's impossible."

He flushed with agitation. "What do you mean? This is the opportunity of a lifetime! They'll give you 100,000 marks a month!" He fairly gasped, "Nearly a million francs! Perhaps you don't believe me? Come with me right now to the German Embassy. I'll phone Goebbels himself and you'll get an invitation direct from him."

I got up and left, Stoyilov tugging after me almost hysterically. "I took the responsibility of bringing you to Berlin," he wailed.

Every morning Stoyilov appeared at my hotel, entreating me, "In

God's name, come with me to Berlin! When you get there you can turn down their offer."

And alternating with Stoyilov's frantic pleas came the cool voice of Willi Muenzenberg over the telephone: "When may I notify Moscow that you're coming?"

I went neither to Berlin nor to Moscow.

Over the Christmas holidays, my family and several supporters from Sofia joined me in Belgrade, bringing with them the latest news from Bulgaria. Kiosseivanov had become Prime Minister in November and the Sofia Communists were now proposing the creation of a united front for the struggle against fascism and the dictatorship. I was hardly surprised. Since George Dimitrov's "Trojan Horse" speech before the Seventh Congress of the Communist International in July, the Communists everywhere had been agitating for a united front with other political parties. In Bulgaria, they were prepared to join forces with all parties, excepting Tsankov's Fascists but including the reactionary elements we had been fighting ever since the war. I advised my followers to delay their decision until we saw how the united front worked in France.

I was in Belgrade when the most important event of postwar history took place. On that day, March 7, 1936, despite the treaties of Versailles and Locarno, Germany sent troops into the Rhineland. And France did nothing. Several months later, when I saw Mme. Geneviéve Tabouis in Paris, she told me, "I have unimpeachable information that if French troops had crossed the Rhine on March 7, the Germans would have retired without a fight, and Hitler would have shot himself. The German forces occupied the Rhineland without ammunition, to avoid any conflict with the French. Everything depended at the moment on a single decisive gesture by Flandin."

"Why wasn't that gesture made?"

"Partly because of England and partly because the government couldn't bring itself to order general mobilization, which would have involved great expense. General Gamelin refused to agree to partial mobilization because he considered it ineffectual."

Mme. Tabouis explained that Hitler knew from his French agents that he was running little risk in sending his unprepared army into the Rhineland. Fernand de Brinon, who traveled frequently between Paris and Berlin and was very close to Laval, Flandin, Bonnet, and Chautemps, had assured Hitler that apart from perfunctory protests, France would not act.

The effects of Hitler's success were immediate. France's inaction shook the faith of her allies, especially Poland and Yugoslavia. In Belgrade I could see this plainly even in military circles traditionally close to France. General Arachich of the General Staff told me that if France couldn't defend herself he didn't see how she was going to protect Yugoslavia.

The remilitarization of the Rhineland had an even greater influence on the Belgrade government than on the army. When Stoyadinovich later tried to explain to me his policy of rapprochement with Italy and Germany, he argued that after March 7, 1936, the entire strategic balance in Europe had changed.

Our conversation took place in the Ministry of Foreign Affairs about a year after Hitler had moved into the Rhineland.

"I hear," said the Premier with a smile, "that you speak against my policy."

"Yes. It seems to me very shortsighted."

"If you were anyone else, I'd kick you out and never give you another visa, but we're old friends," he said without rancor. Then he rose, went over to the large map of Europe on the wall, and, running his finger along the Franco-German border, said, "Facing one another here are the Maginot Line and the fortifications the Germans are building. In the event of war, France and Germany will sit behind impregnable positions, while the main German forces will be free to strike in another direction. This means that if we get into a war because of France, no one will help us. I'm as pro-French as you are, but my first duty is to save Yugoslavia."

But Stoyadinovich by that time was really pro-German and indeed a Nazi agent. And the reasons were chiefly personal. This man, powerful in physique and cynical in spirit, cared for just two things in life—gambling and women. Both required money. The Germans saw their opportunity and supplied it without stint. By a secret arrangement—but secrets quickly become known in the Balkans—he received a percentage on all import-export trade between Yugoslavia and Germany. In return he undertook to work for the destruction of the Little Entente, and did so methodically. On the other hand, at Germany's instigation, he began a rapprochement with King Boris, who was already allied with the Axis.

In Rumania the Iron Guard was also at Hitler's disposal, and its leader, Cornelieu Codreanu, was receiving enormous German subsidies. Thus, at the moment when German policy was becoming more and more active, it had at its disposal important forces in the Balkans with numerous agents in all political parties of every Balkan country.

The victory of the Popular Front in the French May elections brought hope that the new government would follow a more vigorous policy, root out Hitler's agents, and restore the badly damaged prestige of the Republic.

I knew Léon Blum, the new Premier, from Mme. Ménard-Dorian's salon and had also met him at several congresses of the French Socialist Party. He is a man of refined intellect and great moral qualities, but his sensitiveness proved a serious fault in the critical moment drawing near. The Popular Front in France came as the result of social and political necessity, after years of frightful corruption and a series of cabinets which had offered no program at all.

Although the reforms of the Blum government came too late to produce decisive results, they improved the morale of the people. The great mistake of the Popular Front was its failure to clean out the corrupt diplomats, the old and incompetent generals, and the bureaucrats in administrative positions. In the supreme military council sat the same old reactionary generals who didn't even suspect the nature of the new warfare. True, France did not arm fast enough, yet it did more to prepare for war than the conservative government in Great Britain, and Blum introduced the largest military budget in French peacetime history. Military production was sabotaged to a much greater extent by manufacturers inimical to the Blum reforms than by the workers, although here the Communists played a double game, inciting a number of strikes which greatly impaired the government's prestige. Moreover, the right Radical Socialists, led by Chautemps and Bonnet, opposed Blum at every turn. When the Spanish Civil War broke out in July, 1936, Vice-Premier Chautemps threatened to resign if help were sent to Republican Spain.

Shortly before the beginning of the war, I arrived in Paris from Belgrade. A number of my friends were in the new cabinet, and I spoke several times with the Minister of Trade, Paul Bastide, and with Marius Moutet, the Minister of Colonies. To Bastide I explained the danger of Germany's growing economic domination of the Balkans. He told me he was buying a large quantity of grain in Yugoslavia to prevent the Germans from cornering the market. He also promised to influence the French tobacco monopoly to buy Bulgarian tobacco. In a few months Bastide ordered 15,000 carloads of wheat and corn from Yugoslavia for which France, unlike the Nazis, paid in cash. But this French help, to use a phrase since famous, was "too little and too late."

With Moutet I discussed the personnel of the French diplomatic corps abroad—mainly incompetents and enemies of the Blum government— citing Dampierre in Belgrade as an example. At a banquet he had given at the legation his wife had declared loudly within easy hearing of the Nazi diplomats, "Blum is a Communist, a Mason, and a dirty Jew. I hope a patriotic Frenchman will soon be found to kill him."

Moutet sighed. "Yes, but any change will depend on Foreign Minister Delbos. He's extremely intelligent, but he has one shortcoming. He was graduated first in his class at the École Normale Supérieure, and he thinks himself too wise to take advice from anyone."

A good part of that summer I spent with my family in the village of Igl in the Tyrolean Alps. Suddenly Stoyilov, about whom I had completely forgotten, arrived in his Mercedes, accompanied by his wife, and again urged me to go to Germany.

"You have only to go as far as Munich," he coaxed. "I'll arrange for you to meet a right-hand man of Goebbels, and if you want to meet Goebbels, Berlin isn't so far."

"I've already given you my answer."

"Yes, but there's a new situation now."

"What's new about it?"

"Are you still in favor of an alliance between Bulgaria and Yugoslavia?"

"As always."

"Well," he declared triumphantly, "so is Germany! Goebbels himself told me so. You can continue to work for the alliance and direct propaganda in both countries—Bulgaria and Yugoslavia. Furthermore, you may return to Bulgaria tomorrow if you wish."

"I was expelled from Bulgaria," I reminded him.

"If you like, I'll drive you to see Colonel Draganov in Vienna, and you'll see for yourself. You're free to return to Sofia at any time with the King's personal approval."

I didn't want to break off with Stoyilov completely because his wagging tongue told me more than he realized. Evidently, Nazi Germany already had reason to consider itself so firmly in control of both the Bulgarian and Yugoslav governments that their alliance now would be merely a consolidation of German interests. I allowed Stoyilov to suggest all the combinations he had to offer. They seemed to have originated in a brain far more fertile than his own. When he finally realized he was getting nowhere he told me what a fool I was; that this profitable job would simply go to someone else.

I was aware that there were plenty of profitable jobs for those Balkan politicians who would work for Hitler. Earlier that summer, with the co-operation of my friend Dr. Milan Gavrilovich, I had addressed 4,000 persons at the University of Belgrade in a lecture, "Hitler and the Slavs," which I repeated thereafter wherever I could find an audience until Stoyadinovich forbade me any further political activity in Yugoslavia. There were notorious German agents present at each gathering. Addressing them I said:

"A Slav can be Germanophile only for one of two reasons: either he is stupid and understands nothing; or he is a paid agent. There is no other choice." At that a few pro-Nazis walked out; so did the staff of the German legation, snapping their fingers while the audience sped them with a roar of laughter.

[273]

This lecture was published in Paris, in the *Monde Slav* for November, 1937. It predicted that Hitler would occupy Austria, then attack Czechoslovakia, then Poland, and then undertake the conquest of the Balkans or Russia—not bad prophecy, except that the "or" should have been "and."

In December, 1936, I received official permission once more to return to Bulgaria. I discovered that despite the government ban our organization had continued to grow and that the recurrent arrests and mistreatment of our spokesmen had had the opposite effect of that intended. Not long after I arrived, Kyril Stanev, a Communist formerly in the Sobranje, came to me with an official proposal for a Popular Front, and this time, because of the growing strength of naziism, I accepted.

A few days later Raskolnikov, the Soviet Minister, invited Nadejda and me to dinner. His strange fixed, pale eyes had a somewhat hypnotic effect on me. A Bolshevik of the Old Guard, he had taken an active part in the seizure of Petrograd in November, 1917.

After an excellent Russian dinner with fine wines, Raskolnikov and I retired to his study, where he smilingly offered me cigarettes bearing the Bulgarian crown.

"A gift from your King," he said.

"How did you like him?"

"A very charming person. He told me he considers Stalin the greatest statesman of our time."

"I was sure he would tell you that. What do you think of Premier Kiosseivanov?"

"A soft pillow on which King Boris finds it convenient to sleep," Raskolnikov answered. A few minutes later he suddenly asked, "Why don't you go to Russia?"

"I was in Soviet Russia once and published my impressions. The Communists didn't seem to like them at all."

"That was a long time ago. Much has changed since then. If you go, you'll see for yourself."

I promised to think it over. We spoke of Bulgarian literature, which I found he knew very well. He was a writer himself and told me he was working on a new book. Under Raskolnikov the Soviet legation became one of the leading literary and cultural centers of Sofia. Strangely enough, it was most popular among the conservative old Russophiles who forgot about the Czar they had once admired and insisted that Russia, whatever its regime, was Bulgaria's truest friend.

One year later Raskolnikov broke with the Soviet regime, addressed an open letter to Stalin protesting against the purges, and died soon after, a completely broken man.

[274]

For the first time in years I could now move freely through the streets of Sofia. Mikhailov's assassins had gone out of business. I ran into many of them in the cafés on Marie-Louise Street, gloomily drinking coffee instead of wine and complaining of hard times. Until Gheorgiev suppressed the IMRO, the Marie-Louise cafés had been the curb exchange for their hired labor as far back as I could remember. In their heyday they could command wine on credit, paying up after each job. Now they sat around grumbling, without their revolvers, unemployed. Several of them smiled when they saw me.

"You scoundrels!" I shouted. "Here's twenty leva for wine, but clear out of here!"

They took the money gladly and left, to drink in another café a liter which would remind them faintly of their former glory.

One day I met Stoyilov loitering aimlessly outside the Café Bulgaria. He greeted me bitterly.

"What's wrong?" I asked. "How's business?"

"Business? I'm ruined—flat broke."

"What about your tobacco commissions?"

"What tobacco? I've been kicked out of Germany. And all because of you!"

"Because of me? What have I got to do with it?"

I took him inside for a drink, but he began at once to reproach me.

"The Germans turned out to be bastards," he said. "They threw me out because I couldn't bring you to Goebbels. I had to sell my car and furniture and come home. And you're responsible."

I understood that if I were generous, I might learn something. "Since I'm to blame for your troubles, I'll help you out a bit," I said, giving him a thousand leva.

His spirits rose at once and he began to talk. "The Germans are the most ungrateful race in the world. For three years I served them loyally, and they fired me without even giving me a chance to make good on some other job. One failure, and I could no longer see Goebbels or even General von Massow, who's in charge of Bulgarian affairs—you remember, the Major von Massow who was here in Sofia during the war. General Ganchev took advantage of my failure to advise them to expel me from Germany."

I knew Ganchev. He had been the Bulgarian military attaché with the German army during the war, had fled to Germany with King Ferdinand, and had been supported ever since by the German government. For the past few years he had been working to create pro-German sentiment in Bulgaria, often inviting Sofia politicians to Berlin as his guests.

"What's Ganchev's position in Germany now?" I asked.

"He's back in the government's good graces. Last year he was nearly liquidated because he took money from Goebbels for various Bulgarian politicians and pocketed half of it. The Gestapo found him out soon enough, but old Ferdinand himself intervened to save him. Now he's in favor with Goebbels and Fritsch. Do you know that Fritsch, the Bavarian Minister of Education, is chief of German propaganda for the Balkan peninsula? When I wanted to take you to Munich it was to meet Fritsch."

"Are the Germans spending a lot of money in Bulgaria?"

"Enormous sums. Nearly all the large newspapers are in their hands. *Zora, Utro,* and *Dnevnik* get their newsprint free from Germany, and several million leva a year go to the managers of those papers for their personal expenses. German agents are in every Bulgarian political organization, paid according to their importance. Tsankov's still on the pay roll, but they're looking for a man to replace him. They're now organizing Professor Kantargiev's Brown Shirt Warriors for Bulgarian Progress!"

"Where does all the money come from?"

"That's easy. All German firms which export to Bulgaria must leave 10 per cent in local currency here to be used for German propaganda."

"Ten per cent of their profits?"

"No, 10 per cent of the gross receipts."

"That's more than 100 million leva."

"Much more—from 150 to 200 million."

"Does it all go for propaganda?"

"No. There are other expenses, chiefly for the Gestapo, which works independently and about whose activities I can tell you very little. I only know that practically all the trade representatives of the German firms work for the Gestapo. There are more than a thousand of them in Bulgaria, all doing political and military espionage."

A few drinks later, Stoyilov hit upon a bright idea.

"Couldn't you find a spot for me in the British or French intelligence? You see I could be very useful."

I answered that unfortunately I had no connections with any intelligence service. Obviously he didn't believe me.

Several days later a smartly dressed man, a Todorov but no relative, came to see me at my home. Years before, as a courier of the Foreign Ministry, he had delivered the diplomatic mail to me in Belgrade. He began to express regret that such a "remarkable" journalist as I had no paper.

"What's to be done?" I asked. "You know the government won't allow it."

"Well," he said importantly, "that's easily arranged. That's why I'm here. I represent a financial group which is prepared to organize at once the biggest paper in Bulgaria—possibly in the Balkans—with the most modern printing plant, provided you agree to be the manager and editor."

The offer looked good, and I was more than pleased at the prospect of having a paper again in which to express my views.

"Who are these people, and how can they get permission for the paper to appear?" I asked eagerly.

"You'll learn soon enough if you agree to a few minor conditions."

These "minor conditions" turned out to be an editorial policy which would hammer away at the idea that Bulgaria's national interests were inseparable from Germany's and would attack the Comintern, French imperialism, and the Little Entente as the enemies of the Bulgarian national ideal.

"In other words, this paper would be a German enterprise?" I inquired, suppressing my anger.

After stalling for a moment he said, "No—it's only that the people who will help are associated with German firms."

"How much money do they intend to invest?"

"As much as necessary—ten, fifteen, twenty million leva. You can pick the location for the plant. You'll receive your equipment from Germany and newsprint without cost, plus whatever cash you need for your initial expenses."

"Yes," I laughed, "all coming out of the 10 per cent tax on German trade receipts in Bulgaria."

"Who told you that?" he demanded.

"The British Intelligence Service," I replied ironically.

"Listen, Mr. Todorov," he said with a great show of sincerity, "an opportunity like this comes to a man only once. Most of the Sofia papers are trash. I know that you're capable of producing the best newspaper in the Balkans. You'll be in full charge. You can even advocate an alliance with Yugoslavia. You'll be able to take care of all your friends. The government will remain completely benevolent, and you'll become the leader of public opinion in Bulgaria. Is it possible that you really don't understand where your own interests lie?"

Apparently I was stupid enough not to understand. I never saw my namesake again

WHEN THE SPANISH Civil War broke out in July, 1936, followed by the quasi-official intervention of Mussolini and Hitler on the side of Franco, the peoples of the world understood that this bloody game was no internal Spanish affair, but menaced the liberty and progress of all Europe. A year earlier it had been Fascist aggression against Ethiopia, and popular sympathy everywhere was with the Ethiopians. Popular instinct is rarely deceived. This time it was violently manifested in the Balkans against the aggressors and the medieval Franco reactionaries in Spain. I remember a conversation with a Bulgarian peasant who had made a long trip to see me on behalf of his fellow-villagers and ask for news of Spain.

"But you read the newspapers," I said.

"Nobody believes them. We know they lie, and that you'll tell us the truth."

"But why are you so much interested in Spain? It's so far away."

"The people know," replied my visitor a bit acidly, "that it's a question of our skins too. If the Germans and Italians are allowed to attack Spain, we, too, may be attacked tomorrow if we want to get rid of the King and his lackeys who have made slaves of us by robbing us of all our liberties. Do you understand?"

Of course I understood, and I felt as the people felt. What astonished and exasperated me was that the statesmen of the Western democracies understood nothing—or through cowardice preferred to understand nothing. Their cynical "non-intervention agreement," under which Germany and Italy helped Franco while France and Britain comfortably pretended that all Europe was keeping hands off, forced the Loyalists to accept Soviet aid, with all the Communist interference it implied. When I visited Spain both Indelacio Prieto and his assistant, Deputy Balanos, complained, "We're accused of being Communists, yet it's hard to find one real Communist among a hundred Spaniards. If France and England would help us, we could refuse all aid from Moscow and rid ourselves of its interference."

In June, 1937, I went to Paris with my family to attend the Exposition. The rightist press was openly clamoring for a Fascist victory and the leftist newspapers in the main were supporting the suicidal policy of non-intervention. Only a handful of journalists were reiterating that the

Germans and Italians were testing their weapons in Spain for a future attack on France.

One July evening at a café on the Boulevard Montparnasse I met my old Serbian friend, B.P., one of the most interesting men I have ever known. He was a member of the Sarajevo group which assassinated Archduke Francis Ferdinand in 1914, escaped to Serbia, and fought as a volunteer in the Serbian army. After the Bolshevik Revolution he became a Communist. He never returned to Yugoslavia but lived abroad, mainly in Paris, sometimes vanishing for long periods. He was one of those typical Russophile Balkan Slavs who joined the Communist movement because to them it represented Russia. I found him elated that summer evening.

"Even the blind must see now that Russia is right. Stalin's policy is directed against Germany, the eternal enemy of our people."

Since Russia's current foreign policy met with my approval, I didn't dispute the point.

"Have you been in Paris long?" I asked.

"Only two days. I've just come from Spain. I was secretly in Franco territory—for the second time. I'll tell you everything as a friend, but in strictest confidence. I'm sure that sooner or later you'll all join us, because the final struggle for the future of mankind will be between Russia and Germany."

He had twice reached Burgos through Portugal on a false German passport, taking advantage of his fluent German—he had been graduated from a German gymnasium and could easily pass for a native.

"What did you do in Spain?"

"I was on a special sabotage mission. I wanted to organize the assassination of General Franco, but that's impossible without a widespread network. Two assistants were sent to me, but they were seized at the frontier. It's a good thing they didn't talk."

"Do you expect to go back?"

"No, it can't be done. Besides, I have other work here."

"What kind of work?"

"Liquidating traitors and German spies."

"How do you know who is a traitor and German spy? You might be misled."

"That, of course, is possible," and some of the confidence left his voice. "Acting on instructions, I recently shot a man on the rue Denfert-Rochereau. Thank God I only wounded him, because it all turned out to be a mistake. Yes, mistakes occur, but there are so many traitors, so many German agents, like those now being shot in Russia, that I don't hesitate to carry out any order I get."

He told me how urgently Republican Spain needed volunteers. I knew that there were many Bulgarians and Yugoslavs who wanted to go to Spain to fight, but lacked the money. Besides their governments took legal measures against them if their desire became known, whereas those few dozen who wanted to fight for Franco—all Croats of Pavelich's group —had been provided with every facility. Not long before, a Bulgarian village teacher had visited me and told me he was going to Spain; that he had enough money to reach Vienna and from there would go on foot. When I asked him whether there were many more like him, he had answered that all the young men in his village were ready to go because "they realize that Spain's fight is our fight."

Remembering this conversation, I now asked my Serbian friend, "Instead of shooting people who may be innocent, why don't you arrange to get volunteers from Yugoslavia and Bulgaria to Spain?"

"We're trying. You know yourself that a shipload of volunteers recently sailed from Split but were betrayed to the Yugoslav authorities and stopped at sea." Slamming his fist on the table, he growled, "Well, what would you have us do with traitors except shoot them!"

One morning soon after this meeting B.P. turned up at my home. "I'll introduce you to the most important Soviet representative now in Paris," he said with an air of mystery. "He's on a special mission—a high officer of the Red army who enjoys the full trust of Stalin himself. I've spoken to him about sending Balkan volunteers to Spain, and he wants to see you about it."

I arranged to meet the Soviet representative at the Pavillion Bleu in Saint-Cloud. When I arrived, I found sitting with B.P. a fair-haired man of about fifty in civilian clothes. When he rose to shake hands with me, I noticed that he limped.

"From our own Civil War, you know." He smiled, indicating his left leg.

He spoke a simple Russian and was evidently of peasant or working-class origin.

"How shall I address you?" I asked.

"Call me Alexei."

I outlined to Alexei a plan I had devised for sending Bulgarian volunteers to Spain. "First of all, I suggest the creation in Marseille of an employment agency for agricultural workers. France is importing agricultural labor, and the Bulgarian government is issuing passports and visas to peasants who want to work here. I'll find men to organize a bureau in Sofia who will make connections with the Marseille office. In that way several thousand men can get to Marseille. From there it's your job to get them to Spain."

Alexei was enthusiastic. "That's a splendid idea!"

"But money will be needed for the passports and railway tickets," I added. "I'll cover the expenses of the Sofia agency, but that's all I can manage to do."

"Money is the easiest part of it," he answered. "I'm going to Moscow to discuss the plan and I'll be back as soon as possible. We've no time to lose. I'll place $1,000 a month at your disposal for your expenses."

He was astonished when I answered, "I don't want it. With $1,000 you can send at least fifty volunteers."

Alexei left for Russia by plane, expecting to be back in two weeks. I remained in Paris until September, but he didn't return. B.P. became uneasy. "He was probably detained by important business," he said.

About a year later, he confided to me, "I think Alexei was liquidated in Moscow."

By that time, B.P. himself had been expelled from the Communist Party, was completely destitute, and had lost faith in the cause he had served so long.

Although my plan thus came to nothing, those Bulgarians and Yugoslavs who succeeded in getting to Loyalist Spain numbered some three thousand. Invited to go to Spain to visit these valiant men, I gladly accepted. At the Spanish embassy in Paris I received a permit to enter Spain, and in November, 1937, I left for Barcelona.

After the gray, rainy autumn of Paris, I found myself under a pure, warm sky in a city incomparably picturesque and charming. In spite of the Italian bombing and the food shortage, life seemed gay and carefree. The cafés which served atrocious sugarless coffee were crowded at night with people who danced even when the sirens warned of approaching enemy air-raiders. At the luxurious and well-kept Hotel Ritz I found many old acquaintances, journalists who were habitués of international conferences, all of whom regardless of political differences had become friends of the Spanish Republic.

To Swayer, the Reuter correspondent whom I had known at Sofia, I posed some questions which had troubled me in spite of my sympathy for the Republican cause. He answered, "It's true that here in Catalonia the anarchists killed some priests before the government was able to get the situation in hand. Since then there have been no killings. A number of churches are open and services are held without the slightest incident. Violence is sternly dealt with, and there is perfect order. In spite of the blackout, crimes at night are rare."

We were talking in the basement bar of the hotel. Suddenly an explosion very near by shook the walls. Others followed, accompanied by cries and the wail of the siren.

"There it goes again," he exclaimed. "I've got to go; it's news."

I went with him to the scene of the bombing two blocks away but the police were there already and forced us to turn back. Not until the next morning did we learn that twenty civilians had been killed. Farther away more houses had been hit.

"Several days ago forty children sheltered in the basement of a church were killed during a bombing in broad daylight. . . . If you could have seen those poor little mangled bodies and the frantic mothers bending over them, trying to identify them! And in London sits a non-intervention committee!"

I visited Premier Juan Negrin, Prieto, and Balanos, whom I had met during my first visit to Spain. Now he was Undersecretary of State for War and aide to Prieto, whom everyone recognized as the organizing genius of the Republican defense. One and all they made the same complaint: "We are without arms and munitions in the face of German-Italian intervention which is becoming more and more insolent and more and more formidably armed. Has democracy lost all its vigor and its sense of reality? This is the dress rehearsal for tomorrow's war on France and England. Every bomb that falls on Barcelona, Valencia, or Madrid is aimed at Paris. Tell them that when you go back."

I traveled through the country: Catalonia, gay as a garden in bloom; bare and rocky Aragon with its stones as red as if they had been washed in blood—the blood of a chivalrous, proud and passionate people. And what a people! One couldn't help loving them, for dignity did not prevent them from being good, polite, and generous.

Soldiers were besieging Huesca and Saragossa, armed chiefly with rifles. Cannon were few and of various models, grouped in heterogeneous batteries. The whitewashed, red-roofed houses of Huesca seemed very near. The Republicans occupied the heights which dominated the city, but the defenders were powerfully armed. At night their searchlights and rockets searched the horizon, preventing any surprise. Besides, the besiegers were Catalonians, brave but recognizing no discipline. They left the ranks whenever they pleased and went home to rest. Most of them were anarchists.

"May one man command others?" To this question they answered, "In principle, no."

But how, then, can a war be conducted? After long discussions they admitted that one may obey in a zone of thirty kilometers from the front; but even in this zone they obeyed reluctantly. Durutti, their heroic leader who tried to get himself obeyed, was killed by a bullet from the rear.

The foreign volunteers were superb. Their idealism, their morale, their discipline were beyond praise. And our Balkan volunteers were among the best. Of 580 Bulgarians, 350 became officers. Several became brigade commanders. The Chief of Staff of the International Brigade,

Colonel Belov, was a Bulgarian. In December, 1941, he was heard from in Russia as commander of the cavalry which took Stalinogorsk on the Moscow front. Serbs and Croats outdid one another in bravery. The Serbs invented a way to fight tanks by throwing under their treads bottles filled with gasoline provided with a lighted fuse. The tanks caught fire and burned like torches.

But everyone agreed that the best of all, the bravest of the brave, were the Poles.

General José Miaja received me at his headquarters in the basement of a large Madrid house. Small, sallow, tired, with a big nose and glasses, he had the look of an old savant. But the protruding eyes behind his spectacles were steely.

"We need tanks, guns, planes. Of men we have enough—more than 450,000. And we have succeeded in organizing them well. Soon we shall have a half-million. If we can get arms we are sure to win. So far only the Russians have helped us; that's why they're so popular."

And indeed, when the foreign volunteers passed by, the children cried enthusiastically, "Russians! Russians!"

The Communists directed the International Brigade, because they were the most numerous and because it was Russia which furnished arms and munitions to the Republic. If the democrats had done the same thing, they would have had the upper hand in Spanish affairs. They did almost nothing—and yet they seemed to resent the Russian influence.

There was plenty of it. Quite unexpectedly a handsome young Bulgarian lieutenant arrived from Valencia and announced that he had been appointed my personal aide. At first I was flattered by this attention on the part of the Spanish government, but I very soon realized that my "aide" was a watch-dog sent by the Communists to spy on me. On the pretext that he was responsible for my safety, he never left me alone with anyone for a moment. Like the other Bulgarians and Serbs whom I met in Spain, he used a fictitious name and a Spanish one at that— Francesco. At every possible opportunity he urged upon me the necessity of a united front in Bulgaria, in the identical words used by the Communists in Sofia. I was always amazed by the ability of Communists to learn phrases by rote and to repeat them simultaneously in all the languages of the world.

The man who actually controlled the 45,000 foreign volunteers, the French Communist Deputy, André Marty, was brutal, repulsive, arrogant, with the manners of an under officer playing Napoleon. The soldiers, Communists included, frankly detested him. He did not conceal his fanatical hatred of all those who were not members of the party, and he was said to be responsible for the disappearance of several foreign democrats who had come to offer their services to the Republic. Marty thus provided the pretext for those who wanted to justify their policy of abandoning Spain to its fate. Nervous and haughty, he paraded his little bird's head, perched on its reptilian neck, through the army camps, giving contradictory orders, yelling, screaming, and leaving behind him trouble and disgust.

The Russian pilots, on the other hand, were liked by everybody for their bravery, intelligence, and amiability. With their little pursuit planes they sowed panic among the Fiats and Savoias which outnumbered them five to one and operated from well-organized bases plentifully stocked with gasoline.

I spent several weeks with the army, weeks which made me relive my memories of that other war; days and nights passed on the straw of the trenches or in villages, with their houses of cut stone and no sign of vegetation, behind the front in the depths of the dry Aragon mountains. And I saw pass before me ardent idealists, come to sacrifice their lives; professional revolutionists doing their job dutifully but without exaltation; disillusioned men who sought forgetfulness in adventure; young men dreaming of heroic deeds—a repetition of what I had seen in the Foreign Legion more than twenty years before. Often during the clear, cold nights I talked with the son of a Yugoslav minister who, having run through his father's fortune, had left his unfaithful wife to purify himself, as he said, in the fight for liberty. I met the typical professional Legionnaire in Captain Alvarez, who had come to spend on the Spanish front the three years of paid rest due him after twenty-five years of service in the Foreign Legion without leave or absence from his regiment. "I was bored in Paris," he said. "I had nothing to do. Here I breathe an atmosphere I like. Only," he frowned, "these people don't even know how to wear a uniform properly."

Finally, there was that young Bulgarian teacher who had crossed Europe on foot to find out how to make a revolution; for, said he, "We need to know how, for Bulgaria's sake, when the moment comes." He talked constantly of his native village. But he never saw it again—he died in the battle of Ebro.

Back in Paris, I felt suffocated, as if I had descended from a mountain peak into a cellar full of smoke, foul odors, tarts and pimps. In vain I appealed to the political masters of the hour. I met with cowardice, hesitation, and indifference. The democracies did not want to take advantage of the opportunity offered by the Spanish War to check the destructive force of fascism. Once more they supported it.

Nevertheless, in Yugoslavia I succeeded in finding arms. A friend of

Stoyadinovich, with his help (he would have sold his mother for money), succeeded in selling rifles and ammunition to Republican Spain. However, he also sold munitions to Franco.

At the end of January, 1938, the Spanish government invited me to represent Bulgarian democracy at the solemn session of the Cortes which was to take place early in February. I traveled to Spain with the Swedish Senator Branting, Émile Vandervelde, a group of French Communist and Socialist deputies and British laborites. We arrived in Barcelona on February 2, and the next day were taken in automobiles to the monastery of Montserrat, perched on a mountain height dominating a fantastic landscape of forests, cliffs, deep ravines and cascading waters. Montserrat is the legendary home of the Holy Grail and the setting for Wagner's *Parsifal*. From its serrated towers in clear weather one can see Barcelona and the Mediterranean.

Military music and a company of the Spanish Republican Guard did us honor on our arrival. Then, in a hall hung with Gobelin tapestries, the Cortes held its session in the presence of a hundred foreign delegates who mingled with the deputies. All parties acclaimed the Negrin government, and their spokesmen one after another mounted the tribune to voice their approval of its policy.

The noted Communist, La Passionaria, with her fading traces of former beauty, spoke with considerable eloquence. Negrin, on the other hand, was crisp, businesslike and reserved. During the banquet which followed, the question was raised, who was to speak in the name of the foreign delegation. Most of us wanted Vandervelde, but the Communist Ramette proposed André Marty. The suggestion provoked a tumult of protest and invective—"We won't listen to that scoundrel," cried someone, and Marty, turning over his chair with a hysterical gesture, left the room.

Vandervelde spoke. But he was no longer the man of 1914 and the sessions of the League of Nations. His voice shook, and his phrases, still well turned, fell dead upon the silence. We applauded out of respect for a veteran who had served humanity all his life and who was visibly nearing his end.

I was able to speak to him afterward. He heard badly with the aid of an apparatus.

"What's the attitude in Belgium toward the Spanish war? How much influence have the Rexists?"

"It's not a question of the Rexists," he answered, suddenly alert, his voice clear and angry. "It's the King who is playing a detestable role. He has nothing of his father in him. All his preferences are for fascism. He has found support even in our party, men who are at this very moment agents of Hitler, such as De Man. He's playing a tragic game. He has cut our ties with France and England and looks for support to Germany, believing it will respect Belgian neutrality. Everything we've built up since the war is menaced with ruin. We're without alliances and without protection. And European democracy is on the way to commit the most stupid of suicides."

He was seated with his wife on a stone bench on the terrace of the monastery. After this effort his voice failed and his eyes became dark and troubled. His wife soothed him. "Come, Émile, don't get excited. You know the doctor has forbidden it."

"Yes, dear," he answered with a discouraged gesture. "It's time to go."

And for the last time I shook the hand of my old professor. He died soon after his return to Brussels.

The next day I visited the Balkan volunteers, who were with the Forty-fifth Division at Calenda, near Lerida. Many were already missing. They had been at Teruel. The division passed in parade step before me and I saluted it with raised fist.

Before leaving Barcelona we saw Negrin and Prieto, who demanded only one thing, "Tell your countries the truth about Spain." There was nothing we could say. But in France I tried once more. I went to see the chief secretary of Delbos, Minister of Foreign Affairs, who introduced me to Deputy Laugier, director of the Minister's political cabinet. Dr. Laugier understood. He sympathized with Republican Spain, was ready to help in any way possible, and promised to do his best to get Delbos to act. But two days later Delbos resigned.

In Bulgaria, the opposition had formed a united bloc to fight the rise of fascism. Only Tsankov and his Fascists were excluded—the Communists, on my insistence, having been admitted. We had small chance of success because of a unique electoral law, but we wanted to manifest our unity against the dictatorship. The police had excluded most of our candidates from the lists. Those who had been accepted because of personal connections with the judges or because they were little known, having been hitherto inactive politically—those candidates we had recommended to the voters in secret letters.

When I returned to Sofia in March the electoral campaign was in full swing. The chief of police asked me to call on him.

"Where have you been?"

"In Paris."

"Oh, no! You were in Spain, in spite of the government's formal prohibition. Your passport!"

My passport was innocent of any trace of my Spanish journey. He frowned. "No matter. You were there." And he showed me a photograph of the Calenda parade in which my silhouette was visible in the background, saluting the soldiers. But my head was turned, and the profile was not clear.

"Who is it?" I asked innocently.

"You!" he shouted, thumping the table. And I realized that some foreign police had its agents even on the Spanish Republican front.

The next day I was interned in the little town of Yamboli, where I lived in the house of a physician, a member of our party. It was almost a pleasure; I so much needed rest. Besides, I had begun a political history of modern Bulgaria which I could nowhere have finished as tranquilly as in this little place where there were no amusements, no political conferences, and no boring visitors. In the two weeks before the elections I made progress. The elections were a great success for us. Of the twenty candidates who had got past the preventive police censorship, eighteen were elected. And more than 300,000 ballots declared void bore the slogan, "Long live the flag of Stamboliski."

A little incident ended my internment and opened a new chapter in my homeless wandering. One Sunday I was working in my room when shouts in which I thought I heard my name came from the market place before the house. I went to the window. Every Sunday as many as 500 to 600 peasants came to sell their grain, chickens, eggs, butter and cheese to the villagers. But on this day the market place swarmed with several thousand people crying, "Long live Kosta Todorov!"

I had withdrawn to the back of the room when the district police chief, pale and breathless, appeared in the doorway.

"Mr. Todorov, I beg you! Something terrible may happen. The guards are in danger of being killed if you don't calm the peasants."

"What can I do?"

"Go out on the balcony and ask them to leave."

"You want me to talk to them? But you know the kind of speech I'm likely to make."

"Say what you will, but help me to avert a tragedy."

"Very well." I went to the balcony. "There he is," shouted the crowd. "Long live Kosta Todorov!"

When everything was quiet I said, "Brothers! I ask you to return peacefully to your homes, to avoid an incident. There's no reason to shed blood in vain—either yours or that of the police, who are just as much a part of the people as yourselves. Save your strength for the day when I summon you to come. Then you'll come with guns and settle accounts once and for all with those who rule by force and rob the people. Goodby."

The peasants shouted for a few minutes and slowly began to leave the square. But the chief of police was frantic.

"What have I done? What have I done?" he cried, clutching his head.

"You've made a revolutionary speech with my consent. I'm as good as finished."

"I gave you fair warning," I reminded him.

He called Sofia, told the Minister of the Interior that my presence in Yamboli was provoking demonstrations against the government, and asked that I be removed from his district. He was told to send me to Sofia, and I left for the capital that evening.

During my internment something far more important had happened. On March 12, German legions had occupied Austria. Without firing a shot, Hitler had taken the first step in the program of conquest outlined in *Mein Kampf*. Presumably he had made his preparations in utmost secrecy, so that few people outside the Reich knew the timetable of annexation. Yet I discovered that King Boris had known what was coming. In February he had visited Berlin, as he had done several times before, on the pretext of visiting his aged father. Each time he met Hitler quietly, without pomp or official notice. Ten days before the German occupation of Austria, he transferred his favorite minister and alleged half-brother, Colonel Draganov, from Vienna to Berlin and sent to the Vienna legation Peter Neikov, a diplomat whom he was known to dislike heartily. To anyone who knew the King's character this was evidence enough that Boris had been forewarned of Austria's impending annexation.

German prestige was mounting steadily in the Balkans, with all the governments on the peninsula now dictatorships. In Greece, under the restored monarchy, General Metaxas had become dictator. In Rumania, King Carol had established a personal dictatorship and abolished all civil liberties. In Yugoslavia, the Stoyadinovich dictatorship continued to become more Fascist and to draw closer to Italy and Germany, although on paper the Little Entente and the Balkan Pact still existed. The ties between western Europe and the Balkans were weakening, with France's dominant place in trade and politics going by default to the Nazis.

In Bulgaria this trend was now all too clear. The army was restored to full strength and when in May, 1938, a motorized division appeared in Sofia, all the armament was of German manufacture. German instructors came to teach military aviation. Even the new uniforms of the Bulgarian officers were patterned after those of the Reichswehr. Trade with Germany so flourished that German "salesmen" filled all the leading hotels in Sofia and the provinces. The government no longer allowed anything which might even indirectly offend Germany to appear in the press. An anthology, *On the Racial Question*, in which most Bulgarian political leaders and writers, including myself, expressed their antipathy to anti-Semitism, was confiscated and destroyed by the authorities.

Anti-Semitism was implanted artificially in Bulgaria, for it was utterly alien to the traditions of the Bulgarian people and their deep-rooted racial tolerance. In Bulgaria in all there were about 60,000 Sephardic Jews, whose influence was very slight and who had lived on the most friendly terms with the rest of the populace. Most of them were poor artisans—shoemakers and tailors—who played no role either in politics or in the press, yet they had helped fight Bulgaria's wars, and their percentage of casualties was even higher than that of their Slav compatriots.

German propaganda tried to incite the people against the Jews by blaming them for the economic difficulties of the country. But a typical example of how the seed developed on Bulgarian soil is that of Stancho Trifonov. While assistant chief of the Sofia police during our regime, he had been on the Soviet pay roll. During our party congress in November, 1933, he had proposed that we include an anti-Semitic plank in our platform, charging that the Jews were speculating in agricultural products. His proposal was howled down without a vote. When I investigated Trifonov's sudden dislike for the Jews I soon discovered the cause.

He had gone to Prague to sell tobacco to the Czech government tobacco monopoly, but the monopoly had preferred to give its order to two Bulgarian Jews who offered better quality at a lower price. This was the secret of Stancho Trifonov's sudden anti-Semitism, which he tried to turn against the entire Jewish people.

When the Sobranje convened on May 21, 1938, and the King delivered his speech from the throne, the eighteen deputies of my party shouted, "Long live the Constitution! Down with the Personal Regime!"

Within a few days they were all expelled from the Sobranje. On May 22, I was summoned by the chief of police, who handed me a passport.

"Orders from above," he said. "You must leave Bulgaria forever."

I N BELGRADE, I found the government dishonestly maintaining that the annexation of Austria was useful to Yugoslavia because it ended the danger of a Hapsburg restoration, but the people recognized their own peril. One of my friends, the journalist G., who wrote for a non-political Zagreb newspaper, described to me the incredible nightmares he had witnessed in Vienna during the first days of Nazi occupation—the first phase of the spread of Nazi *Kultur*. Similar nightmares have followed its further spread with unfailing regularity, and their nature is too well known to require description here. Suffice it to say that G., a former Austrian officer, never interested in politics and with no motive whatever to lie or exaggerate, summed up his account with the words, "I have come to the conclusion that the Germans have ceased to be human beings."

Needless to say, he was not permitted to publish in the Yugoslav press one word of what he told me.

With Austria safely engorged, Germany now stirred up the Sudeten caldron. It was obvious that the German demand for Sudeten autonomy was only a pretext to attack Czechoslovakia as the second move in Hitler's blueprint of conquest. In both Yugoslavia and Bulgaria, the people sympathized strongly with Czechoslovakia, and the Czech consulates were besieged by Yugoslavs and Bulgarians trying to enter the Czech army as volunteers. Maksa, the Czech envoy to Sofia, had told me before I left Bulgaria that he had had to hire several clerks to handle his mail because of about 40,000 requests from Bulgarians eager to volunteer. In Belgrade, I learned from my friend Kerbel, the Czech press attaché, that in Yugoslavia about 70,000 volunteers stood ready to join.

With this information, I left for Prague to arrange for a mixed South Slav legion to fight for Czechoslovakia in case of war. I knew that the Hungarian authorities did not permit transit to volunteers and had already turned back several shiploads on the Danube; but I believed that with proper organization a large number of men could be sent through Rumania.

I reached Prague on May 31, 1938, to find the people in a mood of heroic determination. The superbly equipped Czech army was ready— the mobilization of May 20 had been accomplished in five hours! The excellent technical resources of the Republic had enabled the army to take up its positions on the frontier in that incredibly short time.

Even the women were ready to fight. A lady of Prague, a leader of society, told me, "I intend to drive a truck, and I shall turn over all my property to my country as soon as the war begins."

The people were confident that if war came, France, England, and Russia would spring to their aid; and that gave them faith in ultimate victory. Despite the tension, however, not a single German in Prague was molested; the patriotism of the Czechs was combined with an exemplary democratic discipline.

I had not come to Prague to talk politics. For decorum's sake only I called on Foreign Minister Krofta. I met one-eyed General Jan Syrovy, chief of the Czech armed forces, who impressed me as a strong and energetic character (I was wrong!). He introduced me to Colonel Moravac, an officer of the General Staff (now a German agent) with whom I was to deal in organizing the South Slav legion.

There were already more than 2,500 Serbs, Bulgarians, and Croats in the country, registered as volunteers and ready to answer the call to arms. The international situation seemed somewhat improved in June because the Germans had backed down in the face of Czech mobilization. But on the advice of London and Paris the Czech government now began to treat with Konrad Henlein, leader of the Sudeten German party.

At a tea given by Foreign Minister Krofta to foreign correspondents, I met Shcheglov, councilor of the Soviet legation, who insisted that Russia would live up to her obligations in the event of war. I also met the Soviet air attaché, a pug-nosed young man whose hair was plastered down with vaseline. After a few drinks he said, "When war comes 2,000 Soviet airplanes will attack Berlin, and instead of a city there will be an epitaph reading, 'Here stood Berlin.'"

He spoke as a passionate Russian patriot, declaring that the Soviet Union continued in the great fighting tradition of the past. He spoke with contempt of Pokrovsky's orthodox Marxist history of Russia, which described Catherine the Great as a whore. "Perhaps she was," he said, "but she was also an empress who gave Russia great territories."

About June 10, I left Prague for Paris. On the train through Germany I described myself as a Bulgarian merchant traveling to Paris on business. There were few passengers, but the Germans with whom I talked were panic-stricken at the prospect of war. One man of middle age, going from Nuremberg to Munich with his wife and two children, asked me whether I believed there would be war.

"I think so."

"*Mein Gott, mein Gott!*" he moaned, "is it really going to begin all over again?"

I remained in Munich for a day to try to capture the German mood.

Except among the youth, I read anxiety and depression in most faces. The city swarmed with troops; the rumors abroad, however, of a food shortage were greatly exaggerated. There was plenty of bread, meat, and vegetables. Only milk and butter were scarce.

On the morning I reached Paris, I visited a number of my newspaper friends. To my surprise, they were extremely pessimistic. In their opinion, rightist circles in France were exerting strong pressure on the government to abandon the Czechs. An article by Professor Barthélemy, who later became Minister of Justice in Vichy, had just appeared in *Le Temps,* attempting to prove that the mutual-assistance pact with Czechoslovakia did not bind France if the Czechs, by their refusal to make concessions, brought war upon themselves. Léon Bailby's *Le Jour* was conducting a systematic campaign against the Czechs, calling President Benes a Bolshevik agent and insisting that the Germans were right in demanding the Sudetenland.

Professor Dominois of the Slavonic Institute told me, "Paris is seething with German spies whose job it is to turn French opinion against help to Czechoslovakia."

"What about the Quai d'Orsay?"

"It does anything the British demand; and the British Conservatives, with the exception of Churchill and Eden, want to force the Czechs to make big concessions."

With Professor Dominois I went to see the General Secretary of the French Ministerial Council, M. Chataignaux, later Vichy's Minister to Afghanistan, whom I had known for many years. He had held this key post since 1936 and was in a position to know the political currents in high circles better than anyone else.

His wise, sensitive face expressed embarrassment as I questioned him about French policy. I described the situation in Czechoslovakia, the enthusiasm in Prague and the people's faith in France. He didn't answer my questions directly, but asked me to write a report which he would transmit to Daladier, Chautemps, and Bonnet. And he hinted cautiously that Britain was exerting very strong pressure. In the Czech question, as in the Spanish, he said, France could only follow the British lead.

The next day I visited Pierre Commert, chief of the press bureau of the Foreign Office, who told me that he was fighting desperately against hostile influences, but that his hands were tied by Foreign Minister Bonnet, who wouldn't allow him to publish documentary evidence in his possession of the enormous sums received from the German and Italian embassies by *Le Jour, Le Matin,* and the weeklies *Candide* and *Gringoire.*

What I saw and heard in Paris shook me profoundly. I wanted to go to London, but the British Embassy refused to grant me a visa. It turned out that I was blacklisted because of my activities against King Boris. I appealed to Miss Ellen Wilkinson, Labourite member of Parliament, to Lord Lister, and to Voight of the *Manchester Guardian*. But the Home Office considered me a Bolshevik, and despite their intercession would not grant a visa.

Apparently the Germans were well informed through their espionage network of the real situation in England and France. For this reason, although they had adopted a more moderate tone after the Czech mobilization, they were now increasing their pressure. At first they spoke only of Sudeten autonomy, but after the appearance of articles in *Le Temps* in Paris and *The Times* of London which by implication went further than their own demands, they became more intransigent, and Konrad Henlein, in his talks with Premier Milan Hodza, demanded complete independence for the Sudetenland, with the right to join Germany.

During this whole period, from the end of May to the middle of September, I shuttled among Paris, Prague, and Belgrade, trying to the limit of my strength to do whatever I could. Had London and Paris shown resolution then, Hitler would not have ventured war. His boldness was his reaction to the weakness betrayed by the British and the French.

The Nazis were not ready for war in 1938. They had not yet managed to stock up enough reserves of food; they had only five motorized divisions. Moreover, feeling against Germany ran so high in Rumania and Yugoslavia that if Hitler had attacked Czechoslovakia, those countries would probably have entered the war against him at once. Yugoslav officers whom I knew told me that in the event of war they would overthrow Stoyadinovich and help the Czechs. According to reports in Prague, King Carol was even ready to permit the passage of Russian troops, because he understood clearly that the destruction of the Czech Republic would mean disaster for Rumania. Poland, which in September helped Hitler, would never have gone against Czechoslovakia if France and England had decided to defend it.

In July, I witnessed the great celebration in which the Czech and Yugloslav Sokols and Bulgarian Yunaks participated. The Sokols were an athletic society which stressed Slav solidarity. There were 300,000 in Czechoslovakia alone, and the delegations which came from Bulgaria and Yugoslavia numbered several thousand.

At the Ministry of Foreign Affairs I was told that the French and English were already warning the Czechs that if they did not yield on the Sudeten question, France and England would leave them to their fate. The policy of the Western democracies was beginning to undermine the spirit of the Czechs.

Our volunteers now numbered 5,000 men, but Colonel Moravac told me with disgust, "If England and France betray us to the Germans, we ourselves will go over to their side and accept union with Germany."

I still did not think betrayal possible. But when Lord Runciman arrived from London at the beginning of August, Masardjik, secretary to Krofta, the Minister of Foreign Affairs, said frankly, "Our impression is that Runciman is here to persuade us to capitulate and accept the German demands." And Herbert Ripka, a noted Czech journalist, one of Benes' closest friends and now in his London cabinet, said, "I believe catastrophe is inevitable."

When I went from Belgrade to Czechoslovakia for the third time, early in September, I stopped for a day in Bratislava where I found a much more optimistic mood. The city, only a short distance from Vienna, was filled with troops, but that was not the reason for the improved morale of the people. I learned that there were Soviet planes at the airdrome. Access was barred by the police, but from a distance I saw several large bombers bearing the Soviet hammer and sickle.

The tragic climax was approaching. On September 7, an editorial in *The Times* of London suggested that Czechoslovakia might become a more homogeneous state if it gave up the Sudetenland. That same afternoon the Henleinists staged a bloody riot in Moravská-Ostrava (Mährisch-Ostrau). On the twelfth, Hitler delivered the most aggressive of his speeches, demanding *for the first time* the cession of the Sudetenland to Germany—five days after *The Times* had in effect offered it to him. On the fifteenth, Prime Minister Neville Chamberlain of Great Britain conferred with Hitler in Berchtesgaden, and the end was in sight.

When I read of the Munich agreement, I collapsed on the street in Belgrade and awoke to find myself in a hospital. A few days later I learned that in Paris my friend Professor Dominois of the Slavonic Institute had dropped dead from the shock.

I took my cross of the Legion of Honor, wrapped it up, and sent it off to Premier Daladier with the following letter:

"If my comrades, the volunteers who died in the war, could arise from their graves in Champagne and Artois and on the Oise and the Somme, they would spit in the faces of those who betrayed humanity and France by concluding the shameful Munich agreement."

I could not return to my own country and I did not want to live in France. As quickly as possible I completed my political history of Bulgaria. The book appeared on November 15, and I earned enough to leave Europe. I spent the Christmas holidays in Belgrade with my family, who came from Bulgaria to meet me, arranged to send articles to the *Politika* from the United States, and left for Paris.

Again I stopped in Munich, where I found an entirely different spirit. The spectacular victory over Chamberlain and Daladier had convinced the people that Hitler could realize all the aims of the Third Reich without bloodshed.

In Paris, my old friends halfheartedly justified the behavior of their government by placing the blame on Britain. When I visited Paul Bastide, the former Minister of Trade, he kept his eyes on the floor during our entire conversation. Commert had become chief of the American section of the Ministry of Foreign Affairs.

"Bonnet considered me a nuisance as press chief," he said, as he gave me a letter to Raoul de Roussy de Sales, the brilliant French journalist and representative of the Havas News Agency in New York.

It was common knowledge among the initiated that Georges Bonnet had cleaned up 200 million francs on Munich. The September mobilization had caused a sharp decline in stocks. Bonnet, who knew there would be no war then, bought up a great block of securities, which rose as soon as the Munich agreement was signed.

During the mobilization, Chastenet, director of *Le Temps,* who represented the Comité des Forges, had sent a reporter to the Gare de l'Est to observe the conduct of the departing troops. His object was to confirm *Le Temps'* thesis that war in behalf of the Czechs was unpopular. The reporter returned late at night with word that the soldiers seemed to think it necessary to put a stop to Hitler's eternal threats.

Chastenet was terribly upset and irritated.

"Nom de Dieu!" he shouted. "It is clear that these people have nothing to lose."

He was right. The mobilized shopkeepers, artisans, workers, and peasants had nothing to lose but their lives. They had already been swindled out of their savings by such men as Bonnet and Laval. When I left Paris I could almost smell the decay of that great city I had loved so long.

I sailed from Le Havre on the *Isle de France,* about a month before Hitler occupied Prague. On the deck, with my face turned to the vanishing lights of the French shore, I felt that I was saying a last farewell to everything I had loved. All my life I had fought for freedom, yet everywhere tyranny, force, deceit and darkness reigned. I had spent seven years in a Czarist prison for a revolution which had aborted. In the Balkans, proud of their age-old tradition of struggle against oppression, dictatorship and corruption had prevailed; the idea of a democratic union of the South Slavs remained a distant dream. France was wallowing in filth, and the memory of the Foreign Legion seemed an obscene mockery. The Spanish people were putting up their last resistance in an already hopeless struggle. Everywhere lay the graves of my friends. I felt like Don Quixote, hurled from his saddle in final defeat, with neither sword nor helmet.

Among my shipmates were André Maurois, former German Chancellor Wirth, and Paderewski, who was ill and did not leave his cabin. I became acquainted with Maurois, whose *Disraeli* and *Byron* I greatly admired. As a Frenchman he was even more ashamed of Munich than I. I reminded Wirth of our brief acquaintance during the Genoa Conference in 1922, when Weimar Germany had sat side by side with the nations of the West, and we sadly recalled the past.

On the sixth day, New York gleamed in the red glow of sunset, as if nothing had changed.

Hoping to repeat my Marseille success, I opened a pastry shop and tearoom on Seventy-second Street. This time I failed. Often working eighteen hours a day, I envied my two employees: I was boss, but they had steady wages and an eight-hour day. I realized the dilemma of the small proprietor and sold the business.

Six months passed, and war came. France and England were fighting at last, but for the first time I was far from the front. I wrote to Paris, volunteering to return to the French army, but received no answer. For eighteen months I was forced to watch developments from afar: the partition of Poland, the fall of Denmark and Norway, the seizure of the Low Countries, the incredible French disaster, the heroic British resistance, the approach of the conflict to the Balkans.

On the day the German army entered Bulgaria—March 1, 1941—I knew I could remain no longer on the sidelines. I wrote at once to Winston Churchill, repudiating the contemptible action of King Boris and offering my services as a soldier. While awaiting a reply, I followed the heroic drama of Yugoslavia, climaxed by the Revolution of March 27, when the Serbian people rose against Prince Paul and his ministers who had signed the supine Vienna Pact delivering the country to the Nazis. I was happy when young King Peter, son of Alexander, mounted the throne of the fighting Karadjordjeviches. Many people thought the Serbs mad to defy Hitler. But I remembered the story of Kara George himself, who summoned his chieftains in conclave to vote on war or peace with the Turks.

One of his wisest counselors spoke, "We must not fight, Black George. We're only a handful against a mighty Turkish army."

The Serbian leader took out his pistol and shot down his adviser.

"What have you done, Black George? What have you done?" his chieftains cried.

"I have killed logic," George replied, and raised the standard of revolt which brought the Serbs their freedom. That was almost a century and a half ago. By tearing up the pact with Hitler, the Serbs again "killed logic" to fight for liberty.

A few days after the battle of the Balkans had begun, I received a favorable reply from England.

On THE EVENING of April 25, 1941, as I strolled
with several friends through the brightly lighted streets of New York, I
suddenly realized that I loved it. For the first time its harsh noises sounded
like powerful music. More than ever the bluish vista of lighted sky-
scrapers towering above the delicately interlaced trees of Central Park
moved me by its majestic beauty.

On that evening a farewell dinner at the Peter Stuyvesant Hotel had
brought together more than two hundred friends of all nationalities
whom I had known during my stay. I was deeply touched. As I took
leave of them I saw an old man I didn't know, watching me with ironical eyes. Shaking his hand, I remarked,

"I'm especially pleased to see here someone who has done me the
honor to come even though we've never met."

"The reason is simple," he answered smiling. "I just wanted to see
what kind of fool would be leaving America at a time when any sane
European would give his eye-teeth to be here and most of them are
doing their best to get here."

The huge airliner took off for Los Angeles. I expected a city like
Nice, fair and gay under the radiant spring sun. But it was industrial
and commercial. In Hollywood I found several Russian friends, dreaming the classic dream of stardom while they lived in penury. Beverley
Hills was disgusting in its blatant wealth. But when the steamship
Lurline left port on May 2 I found myself in the company of good
American workers on their way to the Hawaiian Islands to work on the
fortifications. What fine, open, friendly faces! It was the American people, strong, good, intelligent, who escorted me as I left their continent.

What would be impossible in Europe, they came freely into the first-
class salons, and the passengers in dinner jackets and evening gowns
saw nothing incongruous in mingling with these brawny men in caps
and shirtsleeves. Were they not all descendants of the pioneers who had
established this sacred Land of Liberty?

As we docked in Honolulu my friends, the workers, and I responded
to the love songs and plangent Hawaiian guitars with the warlike *Marseillaise* which I had taught them en route. And garlanded with the leis
which the Hawaiian girls brought aboard in profusion, we disembarked
in that enchanting city. Even beauty should have its limits. So many

flowers, so many colors, so much sweetness and light all at one time overwhelmed me—perhaps because my spirit rebelled against this almost insolent happiness in the face of universal anguish. I didn't regret leaving Hawaii, with its enervating climate in which human energy seemed to melt like the snows of yesteryear.

Then the ocean. Flight over desert isles where the sand shone immaculate and the great sea birds, clumsy and comic on land, lived at peace with a few soldiers and Pan American Airways employees. Wake, Midway, Guam, then Manila with its gay, carefree natives, its Spanish churches, its broad avenues lined with palms and cacti.

In the plane I brooded on the miracle of our troubled civilization. I reflected that I was born when the gasoline motor didn't exist and when steam and electricity seemed the last word in progress. Since then—the automobile, the airplane, and the radio! Were they perhaps too much for one generation? Too many secular human desires realized all at once, upsetting traditions, beliefs, and dreams? Space robbed of its mystery, distance annihilated, souls surfeited and emptied. And all for what? For murderous torpedoes launched at children. For evil and stupefying propaganda borne on the waves of the air. For the great symphonies to be followed by the raucous hysterics of a mad assassin like Hitler.

Hong Kong. Coolies side by side with powerful machines. Chinese girls like Sèvres porcelain, fragile, elegant, sweet-voiced. Then the tortuous streets of the native quarter where human skeletons beg and die on the pavement, to be collected like so much garbage and tossed into a common trench in the cemetery of the poor. Music, triumphal, rhythmic, insistent; dragon banners and a procession of glad faces. A wedding? No; a rich man's funeral.

At the Hotel Gloucester I met a few Chinese, cultured and hypocritical, ambitious to prove themselves not inferior to Europeans. When I assured them I didn't think Chinese civilization inferior to ours they were almost disappointed; they had so wanted to impress me with their Europeanization.

"Why is there such frightful poverty here?" I asked.

"Three hundred thousand refugees from Canton have crowded into Hong Kong and Kowloon. The population of the city has grown one third; it's already over a million."

"And no one helps them?"

Involuntarily I glanced at the huge diamond sparkling on the finger of one of my companions. We were having tea near a window of the salon, looking out over the bay crowded with brown-sailed junks and black ships.

"Everyone is so poor!" he answered with an affected sigh and a polite smile—and drew out a $100 bill to pay the check.

"The Chinese haven't the slightest social sense," said a British officer. "There are several rich men here, any one of whom could feed all the refugees. But it doesn't even occur to them. Only the European hospitals, English and French, make any attempt at relief. The city is autonomous, you know. The administration, the police, and all institutions are in the hands of the Chinese. Those of the old regime—there are a few left —are corrupt and indifferent. The younger ones do nothing but talk. Do you know how many of them have volunteered for the army of Free China? Eleven, out of a population of one million."

"Are they cowards?"

"No. But traditionally the soldier's calling is regarded as almost shameful. Forced to fight, they show a real if somewhat passive courage."

A former French consul who had resigned to join General Charles de Gaulle's Free French gave me much light on the Far East, from his fifteen years' experience in China and Japan. He speaks both Northern and Southern Chinese; also Japanese. A physician by profession, he knows Chinese life.

"Neither the Chinese nor the Japanese," he said, "is afraid of death, but the Japanese wants to die beautifully, brandishing the ancestral sword and exciting admiration and envy. The Chinese regards death as a thing so commonplace that it would be ridiculous either to fear it or to be proud of it. He doesn't invite it, but he accepts it without fear. For example, I once witnessed the execution of a Chinese. His family and friends came to see him in prison. The executioner was there with his sword, and everybody—the doomed man included—tried the edge of the sword to make sure it was sharp enough. Up to the very moment of the execution they sat in a circle discussing family affairs and eating rice, for all the world as if they were gathered around the domestic hearth. And they were all smiling; indeed, they smile continuously."

We were driving in his car across the wooded hillocks of Kowloon toward the Japanese-held frontier. It was a charming landscape, dotted with beautiful villas; also with filthy villages whose half-naked inhabitants lived on frail junks at the water's edge—a cemetery of stinking little boats tied up there for five years and full of tubercular beggars. At the frontier stood Japanese guards, small, broad-shouldered, and ugly, looking not at all like fierce soldiers. Astonished when the doctor addressed them in their own language, they came up to us. An officer came also and queried us, suspicion in his eyes. Where did we come from, and why? Weren't we British officers in civilian dress?

Afterward my friend told me that the Japanese were a predatory race, false, lying, brutal and stupid; also corrupt. They sold gasoline to the Chinese, even the troops. They sold passes to the Canton refugees for twenty Hong Kong (five U.S.) dollars. Among their officers few Samurai were left, for many of them died in the Chinese war. But their navy was formidable—and intact.

"Are their losses so great?"

"Not in battle. The Chinese are badly equipped and not always well trained, but they kill a good many Japanese in another way. This evening I'll have my cook talk to you after dinner. He has fought the Japanese."

We dined, in the intolerably humid heat, on the terrace of his house in Kowloon. After dinner my host summoned the cook, questioned him, and translated his answers.

He had been three years in Free China and in the zone occupied by the Japanese. The Chiang Kai-shek government paid from ten to twenty Chinese dollars for a Japanese rifle. In China that's real money and so the Chinese would go Japanese-hunting, sneaking through the Japanese lines with bags of hand grenades, which were to be had from the government for the asking.

"And then?"

"Alone or in groups we would attack isolated Japanese and bring back weapons taken from them. Before I came here I made several expeditions, sometimes as far as 300 miles. In all I brought back fourteen guns and a horse, and that enabled me to bring my family here."

"And what if you'd been caught?"

He smiled as if announcing something pleasant. "They cut off your head on the spot."

During my ten days in Hong Kong I often watched military maneuvers. They were ridiculous, adapted to the training of soldiers for the Crimean War. The principal concern was alignment, the military salute, and the rhythm of marching. No motorized equipment; hardly a plane. I have never understood why the Hong Kong garrison, the minute war was declared, wasn't evacuated to a more important front —Singapore or Java.

Not one of the officials believed that a Japanese attack was imminent. On London's order they were building bomb shelters, but regarded the work as a useless pastime. The patent espionage of the Japanese and the Vichyists disturbed no one. The Vichyists, indeed, were the preferred French inhabitants of Hong Kong. The French Consul-General was rather looked down upon because he favored de Gaulle. On the other hand, a former captain in the French Navy, a man of shady business affairs who ran a boat between Indo-China and Hong Kong and who openly admired Vichy politics—this dubious person was in the good graces of the local authorities.

When I expressed astonishment to Colonel C. that the Hong Kong

French language radio was always at the disposal of the Vichyists, he asked,

"And to whom do you think I should entrust it?"

"But there's an important group of Free French here."

"Oh! They're traitors. They're against Marshal Petain."

"I don't think Mr. Churchill agrees with you."

"Possibly," said this astonishing Colonel, "but that's his personal opinion."

My friend the doctor told me sadly, "That's not, unfortunately, the only case. At Shanghai the British Consul-General is on the best of terms with the Vicomte de Margérie, Vichy Consul-General and an avowed pro-German, 'because he's so elegant and comes of such a good family.' This gentleman of good family had several anti-Vichy Frenchmen arrested, and they disappeared without leaving a trace."

At last I left Hong Kong for Chungking on a plane of the Chinese Aerial Navigation Company. I was glad the pilot was American, for the Chinese pilots are reckless. In a general way the Chinese are rebels against modern technique. They love fine handwork but when they touch a motor they ruin it nine times out of ten. The Russians, who furnished them with planes, never allowed a Chinese to approach the hangars where they were kept.

We left during the night to cross Japanese-occupied territory before daybreak, and climbed to a dizzy height—almost 20,000 feet—with no oxygen. At seven A.M. we landed at the Chungking airport. Airport! A few huts of thatched straw, no hangars, no shelters. A stormy wind blew up clouds of dust. The city stood on a height reached by a steep path. As we neared the top a Japanese plane appeared.

"They come almost every day," said an Englishman who often made this trip on business. The exploding bombs shook the cliffs, and loosened stones rolled into the ravine. Strangely enough the three planes on the airport were not bombed; the Japanese fliers concentrated on the city. The rude board houses, which formed the principal part of the pitiable temporary capital of China, burned like match boxes. The crowd scurried for shelters; a few were killed. Starving children searched the ashes for remnants of food. Two young girls near a demolished wall cried shrilly as they beat an unresisting poor devil who smiled under their blows.

"A thief. He'll lose his head," said the Englishman. And indeed, two soldiers quickly nabbed him. Other soldiers solemnly shot at the planes with their Parabellum pistols. That was the only anti-aircraft defense I saw at Chungking.

The houses burned noisily. The Englishman explained, "That's not important. They will be rebuilt tomorrow. They take a hundred boards each, and there's an enormous supply of lumber here. Of course the dead can't be revived, but here in the Orient death is the rule and life is only a more or less happy accident." After a moment he added, "That's the case in Europe too, today, and perhaps all over the world tomorrow—with the difference that it will be much more painful for us because we don't have the Chinese philosophy."

The next day we were at Lashio near the Burma frontier, on the famous Burma Road. The air-line's hotel for travelers was overflowing and all the other hotels were full—above all, of vermin. On the foul sheets enormous lice and bedbugs paraded, awaiting the next victim. I decided to do without sleep, and repaired to a restaurant which was open all night. There were a dozen people at the tables, all merchants attracted to Lashio by the fabulous profits to be realized from the Chinese war. Two were English, three Greek, two American, one Portuguese, and the rest Chinese. They received me well, especially when they learned that I wasn't a competitor. They told me that the China trade had suddenly transformed Lashio from a wretched village to a wretched but sizable city. Houses sprouted like mushrooms on a manure pile. Money flowed in by the millions.

Caravans of trucks loaded with all sorts of merchandise passed through Lashio, where the railway ended and there were enormous supply depots. One trip to Chungking netted three times the price of the truck—two or three thousand dollars profit—and the trucks themselves were sold in China for twice their original cost; there was nothing to be gained by sending them back empty to Lashio. Thus international speculators were making enormous fortunes on the tragedy of the Chinese people, without risk and almost without danger, for thus far all the trucks had reached their destination although the road was bad and the rains often transformed it into a gluey marsh.

One of the Greeks, enchanted when I addressed him in his native tongue, confided to me that in a few months he had made $200,000. "And I gave $2,000 to the Greek national fund," he added proudly. That 1 per cent was salve to his conscience.

That same evening I was in ill-fated Rangoon. I took a ride on an elephant for the sake of learning that it is better to glide along the road in an American car, with shady paths unrolling on either side and the gilded cupolas and open gates of the Buddhist temples beyond. It is better to see them from afar; when you go near to those enormous, whitewashed Buddhas with their stupid masks, the illusion of mystery is destroyed. And the crowd of lepers make you shudder with horror. The natives, even those who take your alms, look at you with eyes in which hate is barely restrained by fear.

The barber at the Grand Hotel was a Japanese, submissive and over-polite. "According to my information," said the manager, "that fellow is an officer of the Tokyo General Staff. But he baffles every attempt to find him out, and the authorities really have nothing on him. He knows he's suspected of being a spy, never protests against grilling, and wouldn't leave the country for anything in the world."

"Why do you rent him your shop?"

"Because it's easier to watch him here than elsewhere. He'd be freer anywhere else."

"And why don't they deport him by force?"

"Impossible! The Japanese Consul would defend him to the limit. There's only one way to get rid of him, but it's not in the English style. It's the classic Balkan method—a bullet from around the corner which accidentally hits him exactly in the head."

Afterward, when the Japanese attack was let loose, I reflected that in certain cases the Balkan method is not to be neglected.

In Thailand, with the complicity of the government which the Japanese had bought en bloc, more than 30,000 camouflaged soldiers were concentrated with their arms at Bangkok from March, 1941. The Free French told me this at Hong Kong, and the former French Minister at Bangkok, my friend M. Garveau, confirmed it when I met him later in London. But in this case as in others certain diplomats continued to believe in the good will and loyalty of the Thai government. It was the same with Prince Paul of Yugoslavia, King Boris of Bulgaria, Horthy of Hungary, the King of Iran, who never was anything but a brigand, and even with Petain. *Stultorum infinitus numerus est.*

Not everyone was blind. Many English officers at Rangoon and elsewhere saw what was coming, especially those in the British military intelligence. But the diplomats treated them like incompetents and refused to take their warnings seriously. Hence the tragic surprises which led to the catastrophe of Singapore and a series of avoidable defeats.

Our hydroplane made two stops on the Ganges. After the first we had as a passenger a white-clad Hindu, a member of the National Congress, who spoke excellent English. He was my neighbor, and when we had soared far enough above the stifling heat to breathe once more, we struck up a conversation.

"You're a Bulgarian? A country that loves liberty. We Hindus love it too and we'll win it sooner or later."

I informed him that I was pro-British but he said, "No matter. We have the right to talk. Besides, we say the same things to the English themselves. We're not afraid."

"Alas!" I answered, "We Europeans envy you at present; we're not only denied the right to talk; under the various dictatorships we're forbidden even to think."

"But the English exploit us and treat us like dogs! They deny us the right of self-determination. We're a nation of 300 million people with the oldest civilization and the deepest philosophy in the world."

And he talked passionately and vehemently against the English, while two British officers calmly listened. I wanted to say, "You who complain of the English, what would you say if for a tenth of your criticisms you'd be sent to the gibbet, as you would be under Hitler?" But I restrained myself because of the British officers who no doubt were listening attentively.

"Without denying to any people the right to manage its own affairs," I said, "it seems to me that at this moment the English are defending the liberty of all nations, including India. What would happen to your people if the English got out right now and left you to your own devices?"

The question astonished him. "But who says they should get out?"

"If I understood . . ." I began.

"You didn't understand, sir. We don't want them to leave right away. We demand our liberty, that's understood. We want to govern ourselves, but the English can stay and help us defend ourselves until the end of the war. For I assure you I know the Japanese and the Germans —I've traveled a lot. They'd make us slaves forever. Oh, yes! I know them!"

The English officers exchanged rapid glances followed by almost imperceptible smiles.

The market of Calcutta was crowded and noisy, a permanent fair. In the booths was "Oriental" junk, mostly from Dresden and Munich—bracelets, rings, necklaces enameled in so-called symbolic designs. Oily-eyed merchants lied in every language and sold them to the Americans and the English as genuine antiques. In the garden a fakir worked miracles which I had already seen in Paris. Like everyone else, I bought "real" cashmere which the hotelkeeper assured me came from Chicago. The Indies too had been stripped of their mystery. All around me was bluff: the priests of Brahma, the fakirs, the antiques. Only the misery was real. And in the Orient only death does not lie.

Poor Orient! Its greatest achievement is aping the Occident. Even the Chinese and Indian dishes that I ate en route are much better prepared in New York. And often, in that unbearable heat, eating dishes too rich or too spicy, I dreamed with nostalgia of the comfort of a simple, air-conditioned American cafeteria where one could drink a fresh fruit juice and enjoy good, savory coffee. It was with fervid enthusiasm that on my first night in Calcutta, after a few drinks, I joined some American travelers in singing *God Bless America*.

But there was something worse than Rangoon and Calcutta—Karachi, the last stop in India en route to the Mediterranean. This city of 400,000 on the edge of the desert has a port from which ships sail for Arabia and a caravan route which leads to Persia. But except for a wealthy section near the sea where one can breathe, it is poor and depressing. Trains of camels cross the city day and night. In the villages the animals were dying of starvation. In the courtyard of a native I saw a cow of Biblical thinness gobble up a piece of underwear hung out to dry.

"Underwear?" laughed a casual friend. "For them underwear is a delicacy. They even eat newspapers. You might say they're full of information."

He was from the Middle West of the United States, and he had been waiting two months in Karachi for a ship to Arabia, where he was to be foreman in a gold mine. His good humor was unfailing, and he invented all sorts of amusement. He took to me because the English seemed to him too cold and silent.

"What do you think! I've just had an accident. An Englishman—a real one—whom I've been meeting every day for two months was suddenly inspired to say, 'Good morning.' This event merits celebration. Waiter! Two whiskies and soda—double!"

Once more I admired the calm, the patience, and the discipline of the English. They never complained; they accepted everything—bad food, heat, and discomfort—with exemplary stoicism. The officers to whom I had to appeal to arrange the rest of my trip did everything possible to relieve the boredom of my enforced stay of seven days in that hole.

The road from Lydda to Jerusalem passes through mountains where new pine forests have been sown at random. But the vines and orange groves attest the determined labor that has reconquered an ungrateful soil devastated by centuries of Moslem neglect. My Arab chauffeur, a Roman Catholic, spoke good French: "The Carmelite Convent; the Church of the Blessed Virgin; a feudal castle." The poverty of the Arab villages contrasted with the flourishing plantations of the Jews; but the shepherds with their flocks were straight out of the illustrations I had seen in Russian editions of the Bible. The young girls and women along the way were majestically beautiful. On their heads they carried jars covered with white kerchiefs, and under their dark tunics one could divine their firm, slender bodies and their strong hips. The landscape was nobly austere; the green on the cliffs seemed darker, the sky deeper and clearer than elsewhere.

Jerusalem was not seductive—until I stood on a balcony of the King David Hotel and saw the old city etched upon the horizon. Then emotion suddenly choked me—whether caused by the direct impression or by historical association I couldn't decide.

A joyful surprise awaited me in Jerusalem. A big, handsome English officer came to tell me that dear friends who had escaped from Bulgaria were waiting for me in the lobby. And to cap that he informed me that the Gavrilovich family, my best friends in Belgrade, were safe and sound and living in the city.

Among my Bulgarian friends I found Dr. Georgi Dimitrov, who had replaced me as head of our party in Sofia. Arrested, he had succeeded in fooling the police and after incredible adventures had reached Turkey and then Yugoslavia, from which he escaped by plane after the disaster. Another, the lawyer Matzankiev, as a deputy to the 1938 parliament had won nation-wide respect by his courageous conduct and had been arrested on King Boris' order. The third, Professor Ivan Kostov, was my comrade in arms during my first exile in Yugoslavia. He, too, had secretly crossed the frontier while the police were looking for him.

Then I hurried to the Gaviloviches, and there was a deliriously happy reunion. But the head of the family was absent in Turkey. As Yugoslav Minister to the Soviet Union he had been forced to leave on the demand of the German Ambassador, and he was now in Ankara awaiting developments.

From my friends I learned the details of what had happened in Bulgaria and Yugoslavia.

Although Boris had long been tied up with Hitler and Mussolini, he was careful not to betray his real sentiments before the collapse of France. He even assured the Allies of his sympathy for their cause. His old trick of compliments and little attentions to the Allied diplomats succeeded marvelously. In extreme cases he played innocent, and although he was the sole master of the country he affected to be the victim of mysterious forces—military conspiracy and all kinds of pressure which, so to say, forced his hand. After the Petain-Laval treason his game became more and more obvious. But before the British Minister he continued to lie. To the American journalists he would remark, sighing, "My army is pro-German, my wife is Italian, my people are pro-Russian. I'm the only pro-Bulgarian in this country." In this cheap rigmarole one thing was true: the people were pro-Russian. The King had expelled from the army all anti-Axis higher officers. His wife, Queen Joanna, had no influence, while he had been devoted to Hitler since 1937 and to Mussolini since 1923.

My friends, seeing the danger, tried to act. Dimitrov offered a united front to the other opposition leaders. They accepted, and the united opposition demanded an audience with the King. But Boris refused to receive them, remembering that other audience of the opposition leaders in 1915, when Stamboliski had threatened King Ferdinand. He avoided a repetition of the scene and prepared his coup in the shadow. On February 15, his representative at Vienna signed the pact with the Axis and on March 1, German troops occupied Bulgaria with his consent.

"Why was the popular reaction so weak?" I asked.

"For several reasons. The people were taken by surprise, and they were unarmed. Besides, the German-kept press—the King prohibited any independent press—declared that Russia had consented to the entry of the German troops and that Yugoslavia too would soon join the Axis and permit German troops to cross its territory in order to attack Greece. Even so there were isolated attacks on German patrols; trains were wrecked and bridges blown up."

"But the German papers said that the people along their line of march across the country made joyous demonstrations."

"In some places the police forced them to demonstrate, but on the whole they were hostile or indifferent. After having escaped arrest by a miracle, I had to remain in hiding for three weeks, and the peasants everywhere concealed me at the risk of being shot."

The Yugoslavs in Jerusalem told me that Prince Paul in his hatred of Russia decided also to join the Axis when Hitler assured him he was about to attack the Soviet Union. And this although he knew how the people, especially the Serbs, detested the Germans and Italians. Tsvetkovich's government was divided. He decided to submit to the Prince's will only after long hesitation. The discussions in the Council of Ministers were more and more heated, with the agrarians and independent democrats protesting vehemently against capitulation. The rest is known—how three Ministers, Chubrilovich, Constantinovich, and Boudisavljich resigned, as did Gavrilovich, Minister to Moscow; how the army and the people of Belgrade arrested the Prince and the government two days after the pact was signed; how young King Peter took supreme power, with General Simovich, head of the military conspiracy, as President of the Council.

"You should have seen the enthusiasm in Belgrade," said Dimitrov. "People hugged one another in the streets and wept for joy. Not one forgot the danger hanging over the country, but everyone said, 'Better death than shame!' It was a cry that came from the depths of the national conscience, nourished by the heroic traditions of the past."

"Then why was the débâcle so rapid?"

The Yugoslavs, whether ministers or army officers, answered that Prince Paul and his general staff had not only failed to prepare for defense, but had deliberately sabotaged all military arrangements. The "fifth column," which included several generals, interfered with the orders of the new government. There were also some naïve optimists who believed war could be averted. And so, instead of thirty-eight divisions, only five had mobilized, not to mention the inferiority of Yugoslav armament in the face of the formidable German war machine.

The Yugoslav government was at Tentoura, an old monastery of the Knights of Malta, and I found old friends there, bowed by misfortune but still believing in ultimate victory. There were also other politicians who had escaped from Yugoslavia, thanks to the self-sacrifice of the English. Those most compromised by their anti-Axis activity had succeeded in escaping from Belgrade to small towns on the Adriatic. There, too, were a number of British subjects, among them the staff of the British legation. Many of these Englishmen had played an important part in the struggle against the Axis and if caught would be in great danger. Yet when British planes arrived to evacuate them they insisted upon yielding their places to the compromised Yugoslavs and to the few women and children. "The captain of a ship is traditionally the last to leave his post, after having insured the safety of his passengers and crew," declared one Englishman, refusing to leave until the Yugoslav civilians had been evacuated. And so twenty-six Englishmen remained to become prisoners of the Italians.

At Jerusalem I also met several Rumanians who had been forced to flee their country when Hitler's agent, Antonescu, took power. They all praised the Peasant Party of Maniu, the old Peasant leader of Transylvania, which continued its resolute opposition. They told me about the last acts of King Carol who, having forfeited his country's respect, fled despised and execrated by the politicians, the army, and the people. A year earlier he had forced his government to make him a present of five sugar refineries at a cost of some twenty or thirty million dollars. When he decided under German pressure to cede Transylvania to the Bulgarians and under Russian pressure to cede Bessarabia to the Soviets, he resold these same refineries to the Rumanian state for an enormous sum, demanding payment in dollars. The refineries were in ceded territory!

The Serbs who had succeeded in escaping through Rumania to embark at Constanza for Istanbul bore witness to the great kindness of the Rumanian people, who fed and sheltered them throughout their flight. Others who had escaped through Bulgaria told the same story of the Bulgarian peasants.

Some of the Balkan countries were conquered by treason; others by treason and force. Had they been united they would have constituted a bloc of fifty million people without even including Turkey, and Germany and Italy would perhaps not have dared attack them. Or had they attacked, the united and co-ordinated Balkan resistance would have cost the aggressors dear and appreciably weakened them. But it was not to be—and now we all lie prostrate under the German heel. Now, after the catastrophe, everyone seems to understand; the old formulas of Balkan solidarity ring with a new sincerity. But man, contrary to legend, is a being more illogical than the animals which are guided by instinct.

If proof were needed, the Syrian campaign would provide it. That campaign had just begun. We naturally expected that the French troops would seize the opportunity to go over to the side of those who were fighting for the liberation of France, where Germans were shooting hostages, stealing food and art objects, and reducing the country to tragic misery. Instead, the French resisted. They had capitulated before Hitler's destructive hordes who brought them death and slavery—and they refused to accept liberty.

The general staff of the Free French, headed by General Catroux, was at the King David Hotel. After several days, General de Gaulle appeared—tall, erect, and calm. My old friend André Glarner, formerly an habituée of the League of Nations, was there, too, representing the Telegraph Exchange of London. He had just returned from the front, and I was eager to hear the news.

"We're advancing, but it's a hard job. They're resisting stubbornly. That same General Dentz who surrendered Paris to the Germans doesn't want to surrender Beirut to the French."

"What do the prisoners say—especially the officers?"

"They cite military discipline, and orders. In reality Vichy has tripled their penalties and threatened reprisals against their families in France in case of desertion. It's very sad."

He was silent, then added in a low voice, "It's funny, but deep down I feel something like spiritual satisfaction. We'll take Syria, but at least the French have shown that they can still fight bravely when they want to. I know it's illogical."

But I understood. We've had too much talk about "French degeneracy" since the French débâcle.

The Holy Land enchanted and moved me more and more. There one realizes that the God of Israel was no fiction. Often one seems to see on a height the severe profile of a prophet, and one wouldn't even be surprised to meet somewhere the mild, inspired face of Jesus Christ. But only away from those places which attract tourists! The landscape looks as if it had been carved with a sword out of the living rock. The air is pure, fresh and invigorating, and all the land seems kissed by the breeze of legend. Naturally we went to the tomb and the birthplace of Christ, and heard the sighs of devout Jews at the foot of the Wailing

Wall. But our great delight was to visit the Jewish colonists whose gigantic efforts were reviving the former prosperity of this arid land. In Palestine more than anywhere else one sees what this ancient people is capable of when inspired by a noble passion.

Forty miles from Haifa is the Bulgarian Jewish colony of Maobaroth. When some hundred colonists settled there seven years ago, the soil was sandy and sterile—as it is today around the colony, which looks like an oasis in the desert. The magnificent work of the Jewish youth has transformed it into a flowering garden. Orange groves, vegetable gardens, pastures, vineyards, and potato fields—this colony strives to achieve a synthetic rural economy which will make it self-sufficient. The results are surprising—four tons of potatoes per hectare, for example, whereas the American record is only two. Fifty cows were in the stable. The cowherd was a former teacher from the Pazardjik district of southern Bulgaria. She was very proud of her soft-eyed charges, and caressed one of them as she informed us precisely of their regimen—food, hygiene, and rest. To their regular food oranges were now added, for the war had spoiled the market. Only Egypt and Syria could consume them, but at the moment Syria was under Vichy and in Egypt King Fouad had planted his own orange groves, which yielded a miserable fruit. Nevertheless he had placed a prohibitive duty on Palestine oranges.

In spite of this crisis the colony was prospering and was planning to buy more land, for its eighty hectares were not enough. All the colonists lived in one big house. The children were admirably cared for, and forty children of recent refugees were being hospitalized there for the summer. They were robust, lively and good-natured, and had nothing in common with the poor rachitic children of the various ghettos I have seen.

The colony had its own mill, its bakery, and its electric plant.

"Do you earn enough money?" I asked the colonist who was conducting our tour of the property—a tour on which we were accompanied by a number of colonists delighted to see compatriots and to speak their native Bulgarian.

Our guide smiled. "We have no money. The treasurer keeps it for collective purchases. What would we do with money? We lack nothing here, and we go to the city only when we're sent."

"Then this is really a sort of *kolkhoz?* A collective farm?"

"Yes, and very successful, as you see."

"I see. And I explain it by the fact that it's a *kolkhoz* of free people whom no one has forced to accept this communal way of life. Am I mistaken?"

"Perhaps you are right."

We ate fresh bread, cheese, and juicy grapes. They urged us to spend a few days with them, but we had to go to visit the camp where, behind barbed wire, were interned 250 Bulgarian Jews who had entered Palestine without permission. Although they were well fed and housed in clean barracks, it was pitiable to see these young people—for most of them were young—in this lamentable situation.

"We ask only one thing," they told us, "to be mobilized and allowed to fight." Most of them had served in the Bulgarian army and some of them had been officers. "Let them take our wives and children into the colonies, where they can work, and give us rifles."

We often heard that cry in Palestine. "Let us fight!" The Jews wanted to raise an army of 50,000 men. But the British were afraid of displeasing the Arabs—as if the majority of the Arabs were not already against the British; as if this attitude had prevented the Iraq revolt and hostile agitation in most of the countries called Arabian. I say "called," for almost fifty mutually hostile peoples are called by the collective name "Arab." They are equally against Christians and Jews, and against strangers generally. And it is ridiculous naïveté to think they can be appeased by restraining the Jews. To refuse the Jewish demand is to deprive the Allies of a dependable and even fanatical army, without gaining Arab friendship. The colonists whose idealism has brought them from their various countries and who have already wrought the miracle of reviving their ancestral language and of returning to their land after 2,000 years, merit consideration as an element of the highest moral value; and every man not blinded by stupid race prejudice should take account of it.

We gave our Bulgarian Jewish brothers what money we had to cheer them a little in their captivity. And we took steps to get them liberated —I don't know with what success, for we left for Cairo a few days later.

Before leaving I twice visited that charming new city on the sands of the Mediterranean coast, Tel-Aviv. It has neither Jerusalem's majestic sobriety nor its reminders of the past; but it symbolizes the future if the Jews are allowed to build it in Palestine. It is something of a miracle. All these gardens of palms and flowers, all these light, cheerful, clean houses have been built by intellectuals turned masons, artisans, and painters. Doctors, lawyers, musicians, professors, and artists with the work of their hands have given this city—raised as if by enchantment on the dunes—its pleasant air of a Riviera town, and it prospers in spite of German and Italian bombings. Those bombings have not prevented the orchestras from playing on the café terraces, facing a sort of "Promenade des Anglais" along the beaches. It was gay—yet I heard a little girl with great shining brown eyes, whose right arm had been torn off by an exploding bomb, say, "Tell me, Mama, my arm will grow again when I'm big, won't it?" And the mother, winking back her tears, answered, "Yes, dear, of course."

[311]

My Bulgarian friends had long since created a National Bulgarian Committee—of free Bulgarians—most of whom, well camouflaged and belonging to other groups and parties, remained in Bulgaria. They invited me to join. But I had left New York two months earlier intending to fight, therefore I reserved my decision until my military situation should be clarified. Going to the military authorities in Jerusalem, I asked to be sent to the general staff of the army in Egypt. Their answer was evasive.

"Why fight at the front when you can serve your country and the Allied cause in the Bulgarian Committee?" In vain I insisted, demanding to be assigned a front-line battalion. "We'll see. Wait."

Meanwhile, each evening, in the villa rented by the Committee, we discussed our future action—restoring contact with the country, organizing propaganda and collaboration with representatives of other Balkan countries.

"You want to join the army," said Dimitrov, "and yet there are so few of us to do what's necessary. Don't you think you have more important things to do than die in the sands of Libya?"

In my heart I knew that Dimitrov and the British were right, and that my reasons for wanting to fight were largely personal—the wish to gratify a passion, and perhaps to finish "beautifully." Perhaps also I had been trying to escape the contradictions of a life which had begun to grow wearisome.

And when at last the British general staff refused me the desired command, I shouldered the heavy burden of my new task as a member of the Bulgarian Committee—but with the reservation that having finished my duties I might still go into actual combat. And my work, as we conceived it, would be to confer with other Balkan representatives; to go to London and make contact with British government officials; then to tour America enlisting the active support of Bulgarian emigrants in the United States and Canada. After that I would follow my own inclination.

Often, after our sessions, we anxiously discussed the possible effects of our activity upon our families in Bulgaria. Dimitrov's wife, never politically active, had already been held responsible for her husband's actions, arrested and accused of conspiracy. She was a person of rare charm, gentle and good, who adored her husband and lived for him and her two children. That child—for she was very young—had behaved like a true heroine, responding to all questions of the examining judge with the one remark, "You are a servant of executioners and I will not talk to you." She really knew nothing, for her husband had been careful not to involve her in his dangerous and necessarily clandestine activities.

We discussed my family—my wife, my son and daughter. Would they on my account suffer the cruelties inflicted on the families of all those branded "traitors" by Hitler's police? But if those who have families they love should refuse to fight, who would rise up against the tyranny and barbarism which menaces the world? And to keep our nerve we banished from our minds the thought of our loved ones.

At the Jerusalem station were several cars filled with Italian prisoners. As I arrived each one was receiving a well-baked roll and a slice of rich cheese. They were radiant. In a haphazard Italian which they nonetheless understood, I asked them, "Well, how goes it?"

"Very well!"

"Are you well treated?"

"Oh, sir, the English are fine folk. We're glad the war is over."

"Over?"

"Certainly—for us."

From behind the spokesman came a grumbling remark in which I distinguished the word "Madonna." Someone was swearing. My soldier turned and answered with a sonorous "Swine!" Then he turned to me, smiling. "He's a Fascist. But me, I'm a peasant, and in the villages we don't like the Blackshirts. All our troubles are their fault."

The next morning we arrived in Cairo. Dimitrov and I went to stay at Mena House outside the city at the foot of the Pyramids. For me there was neither beauty nor grandeur in those ridiculous cones, monuments to the stupid vanity of ancient potentates. And where now are the glorious remains of the Pharaohs? Their niches are empty, and flocks of tourists also moved by vanity sweat as they toil up the rocky piles for the satisfaction of being able to say, "I visited the Pyramids! I saw the tomb of Cheops." As if Cheops were a personage interesting and indispensable to modern education! And the Sphinx? Who, for heaven's sake, discovered the "enigma" in that stupid face? No. Give me the caryatids of the Erectheion and the noble silhouette of the Acropolis against the blue sky of Hellas.

The Greek royal family was also at Mena House. They lived simply, eating in the common dining room and taking their coffee in the hall; and one often saw the King returning from the city with a package under his arm. His brother and the princesses took their daily plunge in the swimming pool which was the hotel's chief attraction.

There, too, I met again the Greek Premier Tsouderos, whom I had known at Athens in 1924. We found him intelligent, well disposed, and open to the ideas we presented.

"We Balkan peoples," was our argument, "have always had delusions of grandeur—'Great Bulgaria,' 'Great Rumania,' 'Great Greece,' 'Great

Yugoslavia.' And now we're in the bottom of the abyss together. Isn't it time to realize that our sole chance of salvation lies in unity?"

But Tsouderos avoided a clear answer, and we knew he was afraid that his opposition would accuse him of treating with "the hereditary enemies." But we knew also that over there, under the German heel, was being forged a new solidarity of the Balkan peoples deeper and more genuine than any diplomatic document. And that this time the people will be heard—or victory will be in vain.

We were in Cairo when news came that the Germans had invaded Russia; news which astonished everyone but myself. Before leaving New York I had written at the request of the Overseas Agency an article on Russia saying in substance:

> "As soon as Hitler has finished his operations in the Balkans
> he will attack Russia, for that country has been and still is the
> principal object of his conquests, in spite of the pact of 1939."

I went on to state that the stubbornness and heroism of Russian resistance would astonish the world. The agency returned the article as fantastic and incredible. Now I had the satisfaction of seeing one part of my prophecy realized. And the second? Everyone around me looked for a swift and calamitous Russian defeat. Those who gave the Red army eight weeks were optimistic. I was almost the only one to believe not in an immediate Russian victory but in a savage resistance and a long war which would exhaust the Germans.

In Cairo we occupied ourselves with political conversations. Between engagements we had plenty of time, and I used it to study this country where eighteen million human beings were living in frightful misery for the benefit of the ten thousand exploiters who formed the aristocracy of beys and pashas, Albanian and Turkish in origin. Even the royal dynasty is Albanian. The agricultural workers get ten cents a day in American money—much less than the Hong Kong coolies. The ruling class is arrogant and exceptionally ignorant in spite of its French—the fashionable tongue in Egypt; it lives in sybaritic luxury and hoards wealth and power of which a modest share goes to some thousands of Greek, Italian, French and Levantine merchants. There are also a few British import-export firms which did good business before the war but are now in a state of progressive liquidation.

Thus Egyptian independence is of no use to the people, while on the other hand it terribly complicates the British defense of Suez and the Empire. For the Egyptian administration was clearly "fifth-column," sympathized with the Axis, and was impeding British defense. The Egyptian army command—the army is of doubtful quality—was spying for the Axis, as was proved in the case of the Chief of Staff. It required all the tact and nerve of the British to endure the situation. My Balkan blood revolted.

"Why in God's name do you tolerate this situation?" I asked Colonel J. of the British military intelligence.

"Oh, we're taking measures. But we hope to overcome all obstacles through patience."

"Don't you think your patience and your correctness toward all these guttersnipes will be interpreted as a sign of weakness?"

"Perhaps. But in the end they'll come to realize that we are the stronger."

"You talk as if you had fifteen years of war ahead of you!"

"Fifteen years? That's too long. But perhaps five; don't you think so?"

His calm exasperated me. I confess that for all my democratic ideas, or perhaps because of them, I would have used brute force. In London during the Iranian crisis several months later, I told Mr. and Mrs. Amery, who had honored me with their friendship, a story of Turkish wisdom which applies equally well to Egypt, Persia, and the Arab bandits:

Once upon a time in Istanbul the Sultan's son, having fallen in love with a young gypsy girl whom he met on his rambles, begged his father to give her to him as his wife.

The Sultan called in his aide-de-camp, an elegant and distinguished officer, and sent him to the girl's father, a blacksmith named Achmed—Achmed the Gypsy, despised by the faithful, who treated him as was fitting, like a mongrel dog.

"His Majesty, the Padishah," said the elegant officer, "may Allah prolong his days, has sent me to seek the hand of your gracious daughter for his beloved son Hamid. Would you consent to grant his request, Mr. Achmed?"

The Gypsy, unaccustomed to this gentlemanly address—especially the "Mr."—thought the officer was making fun of him. Enraged, he snatched up his hammer and hurled it at his tormentor.

"Get out of here if you don't want to be torn to pieces!" he shouted, and the officer, surprised and appalled, lost no time in suiting his action to Achmed's word. Returning to the palace he told his master that the Gypsy was unquestionably possessed, for he had threatened to kill him.

The Padishah, after a moment's thought, sent for the sergeant of the guard, Ibrahim, noted for his brutality. "Go to Achmed, the Gypsy," he ordered, "and bring me his daughter. He has dared to insult my envoy. Hurry up!"

In two minutes Ibrahim was there. "Are you that son of a bitch Achmed?"

"Yes, that's me," said the Gypsy, bowing humbly. The only answer was a rain of blows from the sergeant's horsewhip.

"I'll teach you how to treat the envoys of His Majesty the Sultan!"

Achmed neither wept nor cried out. He was used to the lash.

"May Allah bless our great Sultan who at last has had the sense to send me a man who knows how to talk to me, in place of that imbecile **who treated me like a gentleman. Take Fatima, and my thanks!"**

There were four of us—two Bulgarians and two Yugoslavs—on the voyage from Cairo across the Dark Continent, London-bound. Sometimes we had to wait as much as ten days in the heart of the jungle until places were available in a departing plane. And in those countries under British rule the food provided for the passengers of the air line was vile. For the British never complain, and the hotel-keepers take scandalous advantage of their patience.

The Hungarian proprietor of the hotel where we rested after the first leg of our long journey soon realized that his Balkan guests had none of the British tolerance. Paying dear, we demanded our due, and as if by magic we had fresh fish, lamb, cheese, and in sufficient quantity. Our British neighbors eagerly demanded to know how we managed to be so well treated.

"By showing a clenched fist to that Hungarian robber, who instead of being interned long ago as he deserved, steals legally from passing travelers," answered one of the Yugoslavs who was using the borrowed name of "Richardson." At dinner the next day a British officer suddenly pounded the table and sent the manager to the devil—and also got all that we had demanded. Thus we "Balkanized" a good Englishman and contributed to his well-being.

In the village beside the hotel—the country's commercial and transport center—there were a few shops kept by Greeks from Cyprus. In the local market were sold grain, a kind of millet, which formed the principal diet of the Negroes, a few Nile fish, skinny chickens, and sometimes goats, which represented opulence for these people. The father of a family will sell his daughter for three English pounds and buy himself a goat. For that reason he is delighted when his wife presents him with a daughter—she is prospective capital. Most of the natives are polygamous, even those who have been baptized, Catholics or Protestants. Some are hunters who go to the chase with spear and buckler, bringing back small game. There is bigger game in the surrounding forests; but also lions and panthers. During our stay one Negro served as breakfast for a lion which had ventured into the town.

Having learned that the Catholic bishop of the region was a Croat, we went to call on him. He received us with sincere delight and offered us excellent vermouth. In his large, airy apartment next to the church we sat for hours talking about Yugoslavia, for he was a great patriot and severely condemned the traitor Pavelich. He was heartily in favor of South Slav union, and prayed for a British victory.

"The more one lives among the English, the more one admires them," he said. "They're so correct. For example, I had a large number of Italian missionaries here, who were not interned but were moved away from this road, which is considered strategically important. Moreover, they were forbidden to leave the places where they are living without special permission from the military authorities. Naturally under those conditions they could no longer conduct their propaganda for the faith. And what do you think! The Anglican Bishop came to see me at once, to tell me that he had suspended all Anglican propaganda among the natives, because it seemed to him unfair to profit by the chance to proselytize under conditions so advantageous to himself.

"I confess I was deeply touched. Moreover, when I need anything that noble prelate is always at my service."

In the Belgian Congo we found a much more severe regime than that in the British colonies. Under the British the natives have a large measure of local autonomy. All British administrative measures must be sanctioned by the chiefs of the Negro tribes. The white who strikes a Negro is punishable by a fine of 100 pounds payable to the victim. Naturally everyone avoids violence, although the Negroes sometimes provoke the whites in the hope of getting what for them is a fantastic fortune.

In the Congo the Negroes have no such protection. Near Lebenga not long before our arrival a Belgian commissioner had been assassinated in revenge for the severity of the police. Lebenga has a bad reputation for other reasons. A case of "black water fever" had lately developed, followed by swift death. None the less we passed three agreeable days there, thanks to the honest and attentive Belgian couple who ran the small hotel. In a Negro village near which we went hunting there had been a recent case of cannibalism, according to the hotel-keeper and the chief of the airdrome. The victim was a member of an enemy tribe.

"What was done to the guilty tribesmen?" we asked.

"Three were arrested; but it's hard to get proof. No one 'knows' anything."

The humidity penetrated to our bones. Swift clouds charged with electricity raced just above the treetops. And three times we were obliged, after leaving the airdrome, to turn back, following the course of the Congo. On the fourth day the weather was still bad, but by common consent of crew and passengers we decided to leave. Below us as we flew a few hundred feet up, stretched forests and sinister swamps which would have swallowed us in case of accident. Then there were high mountains which seemed to be desert before we alighted in French West Africa, part of Free France, under the authority of General de Gaulle. The rain continued until our arrival at Lagos in Nigeria on the Atlantic Coast.

Nothing could be more desolate than this city of 150,000 inhabitants of whom only a thousand are white. Along the quays all day long promenade crowds of natives with strident voices and impudent smiles, casting arrogant glances at the whites. If you take a taxi the driver tries to charge you double the fixed price. If you tip Jean, who runs the hotel bar, he grimaces and declares, "Me civilized. Me speak French. Me run bar," and tries to short-change you.

We put up at a filthy hole known as the "Grand Hotel." The food was vile and people were crowded three in a room without even protection from the mosquitoes. The proprietress was an Italian whose son was in the service of Mussolini; but she called herself a Swiss from Lugano. The service was pitiable. But the English thought the place "Quite good."

One afternoon I was sitting sadly in the hall, sipping my third whisky, when someone tapped me on the shoulder.

"Well, old boy, it's you? Here? By what miracle?"

Before me in the flesh was M., a friend from the League of Nations, where for years he had represented a Paris paper.

"And you?" I answered, enchanted to find him in these regions of the damned.

"It's a long story. I fled from Paris leaving my family behind. I'm on my way to the Free French in the Near East. Under a false name, understand? Because of my family. Look, over there are some Belgian friends with whom I crossed Spain and Portugal. Come talk with them."

In occupied France, M. told me, people were dying of hunger, and at every step risked being shot. But that was better than unoccupied France. The people were holding firm. They detested the Germans and weren't afraid to show it. The collaborationists were a tiny minority, despised and hated by nine-tenths of the people. One breathed an atmosphere of revolt. But unoccupied France was ignoble. The speculation, the theft, the cynicism of the Petainists betrayed a vertical moral decline. Besides, there, too, one died of hunger, for the Nazis were masters quite as much as at Paris. But the bigwigs around the Marshal led a life of luxury and debauchery.

The vaunted regeneration consisted in plundering the country of all that remained after centuries of hard work. In this respect the government competed with the Nazis. It distributed money with a liberal hand, and gave speculators every possible advantage in spite of a façade of legislation which no one took seriously and which, so to say, followed the illicit commerce.

"And the Marshal?"

"Don't talk to me about that old scoundrel! When he got rid of Laval —for entirely personal reasons because Laval wanted all the power— he was popular for a few months. The people thought he was planning something and wanted to gain time. Now they have no more illusions. Their only hope is in a British victory—Russia wasn't in the war when I left—and they adore de Gaulle as the symbol of their liberation. The Marshal? Is it the first time in history that a marshal has turned traitor?"

"There was the Constable of Bourbon, Marshal of France, who betrayed Henry IV and went over to the enemy, the Emperor Charles."

"And Marmont who betrayed Napoleon."

"And Bazin who betrayed France in 1871."

After all, Petain has followed a long tradition and crowned a long list."

One of the Belgians told us, "In order to get away I paid 10,000 francs to a German officer for false papers. With the Nazis everything is for sale. I've never seen more shameless corruption. A friend of mine, by bribing a noncommissioned officer, got back his four requisitioned trucks, bought gas at German army depots, and secured a pass through the whole of Belgium."

Their escape across Spain was perilous. But everywhere the people had helped them. In spite of the famine, they shared their bread and olives—all they had—with the refugees. They detested the Franco regime, my friends said, and at the first opportunity would rise against it. The Franco police were hounding people trying to escape from German oppression, and anyone falling into their hands was as good as dead. People rarely emerge from Spanish prisons, where prisoners are fed almost nothing. "Two of my companions were taken," said M. "I've no hope of seeing them again. One is safe only when one has passed the Portuguese frontier."

He turned to me. "Let's not talk about it. . . . How about you? Tell me what on earth brings you here?"

"For a whole month I've been looking for a blonde Negress."

He laughed. "If I know you, that's what you've been doing all your life."

At last the American Clipper snatched us away from those desolate shores and two days later deposited us at Lisbon. What joy to be back in a free corner of Europe! To see a gay crowd on clean avenues well lighted at night! To listen to music on the terraces of crowded cafés.

To have everything—good coffee, good wine, good food and a comfortable room!

"Our country is against the Germans," said the Portuguese with whom we spoke. "We hope the British and the Russians will win. But we're weak, and we're afraid that in the end Hitler will occupy Portugal. The government too is afraid. That's why the newspapers are forbidden to attack Hitler. We believe that in his heart Salazar thinks as we do."

"Is he harsh?"

"Not too much so. There's nothing ferocious about his dictatorship. But the newspapers are empty because of the censorship, and no one reads them any more."

We were also told that Portugal was full of German spies, who had organized a fifth column, and that at any time the country might be taken from inside, without Hitler's sending in any troops.

Twenty-four hours more by plane and train brought us, in the blackout, to the Waterloo station. There we waited an hour for the taxi which took us to the Grosvenor Hotel.

I N EGYPT AND elsewhere I had often listened to the Berlin radio in various languages; skeptically, of course, yet I assumed there must be some truth in its description of London. "The famine in London has reached terrible proportions. In front of the bakeries the people wait in endless queues to receive a morsel of bread. . . . All traffic in the city is suspended because of the destruction."

The only queues I saw in London were those before the doors of the cinemas, waiting for seats at reduced prices. Bread was not rationed and traffic was normal. There was destruction, of course, but in the immensity of this huge city it was like scratches on an elephant's hide. Only part of the old city had been almost wiped out, to the satisfaction of my friend Harry, long the Reuter correspondent at Belgrade.

"Those old houses hadn't the slightest beauty and were rotten with the decay of centuries. They should have been torn down long ago. The Germans did it for us, and without casualties, for they bombed the city on Sunday when no one was there."

But there had been plenty of victims during the prolonged German "blitz," and everyone still talked about those tragic nights, and the superb courage of the people. "The police and firemen worked under the bombs with astounding calm," said a Bulgarian doctor who had been several years in London. "But they were, after all, doing their duty. What was even more admirable was to see women of all classes dash into burning houses, help to save the wounded, bind up their wounds, and give them tea often heated on the spot over the coals of their burned homes. One had to witness the bravery of this populace to understand what great virtues are hidden in the depths of the English soul. I assure you that never in my life have I seen a more striking and unselfconscious heroism than that of the English."

The Italians, said Montesquieu, were bad soldiers because their imagination was too vivid; they saw danger before it came. One might say that the English aren't afraid because they have no imagination and consequently don't see danger even when it is present. That's why they were so badly prepared for war. But "badly" is overstating. They weren't prepared at all, having for so long assumed that a few concessions would content Hitler—although the German gangster had long ago announced his intentions in his book.

"Never," declared Wickham Steed, the publicist who had constantly and vainly sounded the alarm, "has British foreign policy been more blind or pitiable than during the last twenty years. We are all to blame. Conservatives, Liberals, Labourites, all made the same tragic mistakes. Our diplomacy was especially bad." And he cited cases of incapacity, ignorance, and blindness which would have seemed to me incredible had I not already witnessed the same thing among British representatives in the Balkans.

"For example, in your country our diplomats believed King Boris. In Yugoslavia, Prince Paul, who was supposed to be an Anglophile. In Hungary, Regent Horthy. All three deceived them, and went over to the Axis. Only the Serbs resisted! Can you believe that a people as magnificent as ours has merited such a fate?"

We sat in his study. His secretary, a modest young girl, had just left. He posed that last question in a voice full of emotion and his pointed white beard, which gave him the look of a French chevalier of Richelieu's day, trembled.

"Oh no!" he answered his own question. "Did you notice that young girl who works for me? Nothing extraordinary, you'd say. A girl of the people, industrious and not very talkative. Nevertheless she is a heroine, sir, I assure you. When we were expecting a German invasion at any moment I was naturally deeply troubled. One day I confided my worries to her. I had found my answer to the question what I should do when the invasion began. And I said to her,

" 'Old as I am, I would rather go and die on a barricade, rifle in hand. The Germans know me too well as their enemy. They would be capable of torturing me. Well, don't you think it would be better to die fighting?' "

"She looked at me in astonishment. 'You've thought about that? I don't even think. Naturally I'd go and die on the barricades.' If you could have seen her eyes you'd have known that she was speaking the truth, with no trace of vanity. It was so simple for her! And there are millions like her in this country—men and women. Do they deserve to be so badly governed?"

"Surely you don't mean at present?" I countered.

"No. Churchill and a few others. But the civil servants!" And with a gesture of despair, "I can't talk about it. It's heartbreaking."

The civil servants of whom Mr. Steed spoke are for the most part very good folk. But they seem to have not the slightest idea that Britain is in the midst of the most formidable of wars—total war. They are conscientious in their bureaucratic work, but they haven't changed their methods and habits one iota. One might say they seem to think this is still the blessed epoch of Queen Victoria. They're never in a hurry. They arrive at their work at the usual time—around ten o'clock, take their lunch at one, return to the office around three, and never miss their five o'clock tea which, however, begins around four. At six they quit for the day. They have changed nothing since the "blitz." The week end remains sacred. And sports and hobbies. I believe that even if the Germans should invade, these people, behind the firing line or even among the grenades, would continue until the end to play baseball, tennis, Rugby or golf.

"Yes. They don't realize what total war means," said Harry. "And I'm afraid," he added, "that if ever the Germans try to land here they'll make it on a Saturday afternoon when this incorrigible island is reposing in the bosom of nature."

The beauty of the English countryside is moving; not only because there is nowhere to be found a green so vivid, but also because the houses in their simplicity and grace are so well suited to the sky and the climate. One senses that for the Englishman his home with its little garden represents the largest part of the universe. Above all I liked the ordinary English country where "everybody" lives, where there is nothing splendid or historic to attract the tourist, and where one can therefore penetrate to the very soul of old England which, having conquered half the world, has humanized itself and no longer desires anything but peace and quiet.

Forced to fight, nevertheless, it accepted war as a grim necessity, without hate or anger. But the enemy atrocities which astonished it at first began to arouse it. It adopted restrictions, scrupulously respected by almost every inhabitant. It subjected itself to a surprising voluntary discipline. The newspapers say that England needs vegetables, and immediately hundreds of thousands of families begin to pull up their arbors and plant vegetables in their place. It isn't necessary to threaten sanctions or work out plans. Any sensible rule is accepted without the need of pressure. Nowhere is there a people so easily governed.

London is not only the capital of the United Kingdom and the British Empire. It has also become the capital of Free Europe. Eight legal governments representing eight allies—Poland, Czechoslovakia, Yugoslavia, Greece, Belgium, Holland, Norway and Luxemburg—are in London with their sovereigns or Presidents, and enjoy there all their rights and prerogatives. Nor is this mere form. From London, Belgium governs the Congo. From London until March, 1942, the Low Countries administered their colonies, army, and navy in the East Indies. The Poles, Czechoslovaks, Yugoslavs and Greeks have their armies in England and the Near East. The Yugoslavs, moreover, maintain contact with General Draja Mikhailovich, who is continuing the war on Yugoslav soil. Most of the departments and ministries of these countries function normally—such as the ministries of foreign affairs and finances, propaganda or communications, for the larger part of their commercial fleets having escaped the aggressors, their ships fly their flags on all the seas. There are also the Free French, now the Fighting French, under General Charles de Gaulle, who refused to submit to the shame of capitulation and continued the war from the shores of England.

Among all of them I found friends and acquaintances. I met them in the restaurants of Soho, on Piccadilly, or in the hotels. I saw the Yugoslavs almost daily—without exception I had known them for years, and felt as if I were in Belgrade when among them. In the editorial offices of the French daily paper *France* I found Pierre Commert, Marius Moutet's oldest son, and other friends whom I had often seen in the cafés and editorial offices of Paris. Once more I called on Tsouderos, the Greek Prime Minister. Among the Czechoslovaks I had an interview with President Benes, and I often saw my friend Ripka, a member of the government, and the former Czech minister to Sofia, M. Maxa, President of the National Council.

With friendly teas and dinners, political conferences, memoranda to the British government, and short-wave broadcasts to Bulgaria over the BBC system, my time was fully occupied. The news from Bulgaria, with which our friends in the Near East had succeeded in re-establishing contact, was encouraging. The people detested the Germans; and the King and the government, even through the most atrocious repressions, were unable to control the situation. The official press of Sofia once more called me a traitor for refusing to approve the treason of Boris the Last.

When I arrived at the headquarters of Free France to meet General de Gaulle, I was much moved. Everyone, I think, feels somewhat orphaned without France. The course chosen by General de Gaulle promises a new dawn for the French spirit after a gloomy night. I found him a true officer in the best French tradition, direct, taciturn, energetic, with clear and honest eyes.

I cannot reveal what he said to me. He did me the honor to speak in confidence with a sincerity and precision which impose discretion upon me, for our conversation had to do with delicate military and political questions. But I left him with a renewed faith in the future of France, whose vivid and active symbol he is in character as well as in name.

To my great joy, a few days later I ran into my old friend Garreau. He had left Bangkok where he represented Vichy, to try to save Indo-China—and had joined de Gaulle after his mission had lost its meaning.

"You doubted me!" he said with friendly reproach. It was true. From

Hong Kong I had sent him a letter expressing my astonishment that he remained in Vichy's service. However, I had also expressed my certainty that we would find ourselves once more on the same side of the barricade.

From Garreau I learned what had happened to our mutual friends. Chataignaux, former secretary general of the presidency of the council under Blum, had become a Vichyist. Professor Moisset, former anti-German and friend of Clemenceau, who had published my lecture, *Hitler and the Slavs,* was now a member of the Darlan government.

"It's all to the good," Garreau observed, seeing my gesture of surprise. "France is being tested. The decay must be rooted out. But the behavior of the people is admirable. In France the Germans feel themselves on a stormy sea. Here comes a friend just arrived from there. I invited him for your sake."

The newcomer was a young man from the Ministry of Foreign Affairs —a fact which had enabled him to leave France legally by way of Lisbon.

"Vichy," he said, "has the support of speculators, poltroons and sellouts bought through the most cynical corruption. The officers and sailors especially get fantastic pay, while the rest of the nation is dying of hunger. At the first German defeat the country will rise up as one man. Then let the traitors beware! All the horrors of the great revolution will be surpassed; and it won't be too much. Under the superficial obedience, the spirit of 1793 is seething all over the country. All my life I've been a moderate. Well, at present I'm capable of shouting the *Carmagnole* and dancing around the guillotine. Ah, no! Those swine have passed all bounds."

"The Marshal too?"

"The Marshal above all. That deceitful, hypocritical old dodo is burned up by an ambition all the more dangerous for being senile. Through hate for the Republic he has betrayed France."

On October 19 the Berlin radio announced that my friend Matzankiev and I had been condemned to death by a Sofia court-martial. The Germans had jumped the gun. We were really condemned ten days later, on October 29. But the premature German announcement emphasized that the sentence was dictated by the Germans, and thus proved once more that Bulgaria was only another occupied country, forced to take orders from Hitler.

"Why don't the foreigners in London like us?" demanded a high British official whom I had invited to lunch in Soho. His question didn't surprise me; I had observed this dislike and given it thought.

"First of all, my friend, because you are so different from us. You live differently, you feel and act differently. You are a race apart, 'Islanders' who have isolated yourselves from Europe although you are separated from it only by the Channel."

"Thank God! Without the Channel we should already have shared the fate of the Continent."

"Perhaps, and perhaps not. The Channel has been your Maginot Line. You've regarded yourselves too long as protected from danger; that's why you've made so many mistakes in the recent past, between the two wars, and it's why you found yourself without sufficient military strength when danger came."

"Yes. We realize, although belatedly, that we were wrong. But we're doing our best to rectify our errors. And we treat foreigners very well."

"Undoubtedly. Sometimes too well, for there's no lack of questionable people who profit by your chivalrous tolerance. But the unfortunate thing is that you do it with an air of condescension, as if you were giving alms to beggars."

"But you're wrong! We haven't the slightest race feeling—at least toward Europeans."

"It's there, even if it isn't conscious. For that matter, in one form or another it exists among every people in the world. But there's an enormous difference between German racism, for example, and yours. Shall I tell you what it is?"

"Please do."

"Well then, the Germans say that they are the purest and most superior race in the world. But at heart they don't believe it. At heart they envy the French, the English, the Italians, and even the Russians. Their arrogance conceals an inferiority complex. Therefore they try to prove their superiority through hysteria and violence. But you English are good, tolerant, and polite to foreigners because you don't think it necessary to affirm your superiority. You simply never doubt it. You're so sure of it yourselves that you have no need to prove it."

My friend laughed heartily. "Perhaps you're right. But what conclusion do you draw from all that?"

"That one can live with you on this poor earth without any great mutual understanding, perhaps, and with no great mutual affection, but quite conveniently—which is impossible with the Germans."

"One more question: Do you yourself like us?" he inquired with a touch of malice.

"Frankly, no. But I respect you. I respect your spirit of liberty; your concern for justice; your institutions—above all your police tribunals. It's the first time in my life that I can go to the police without a mixed feeling of trouble and disgust. In England I pass through the door of a police station with actual pleasure. I have the feeling that I shall meet honest, understanding, well-disposed people ready to do me any service within their power. Yes, I respect you. Isn't that enough? Isn't it better than love, which often turns into an equally ardent hate? Besides, my impression is that you don't feel any particular need for our love."

And we shook hands as two good friends.

At tea in the home of Mme. A., on Eaton Square, the conversation drifted around to the same subject. Mme. A. is a cultivated English-woman of old stock, who knows Europe very well.

"There are a number of misunderstandings between us and the Continentals," she said. "You think us egoistic, cold, distant. That's because we're brought up not to be too demonstrative. We feel that truly great emotions are discreet, and perhaps for that reason all the more sincere and profound. For example, a very dear friend of mine was here a month ago, sitting in this same room with some other guests, when she was called to the telephone. After the conversation she took leave of us at once. It was still early, and I asked, 'Must you go so soon? Can't you stay a bit longer?'

" 'Impossible. I'm sorry.'

"And only when I had gone with her to the door did she whisper, 'John has just been killed.' John was her son, a twenty-year-old aviator. You would have called her a heartless mother; but I know how she adored her son. She'll weep for him in the room where he was born and grew up. But she'll never cry in public; first, to avoid making other people unhappy; second, because of the example—the country requires sacrifice.

"I showed you my son's room. It's my sanctuary. I have more than three hundred photographs of him at all ages. Well, you know he's in the Near East at present. If I lost him I should be desolate; my life would be finished. But no one would ever see me cry—not even my husband!"

London in the winter of 1941-42 was cold and rainy, and often the streets and the fields in the country were covered with a thick carpet of snow. One suffers from cold only in those countries where the climate is called mild! Most English houses are badly heated, but the English don't suffer. They are so firmly indoctrinated with the idea that England is never very cold that they don't even realize when they are freezing. Auto-suggestion and whisky take the place of central heating.

As I meditate on the future of this great nation, so humane and so free, it seems to me that its disappearance would be a world catastrophe. What Talleyrand said a century and a half ago is even truer today, "When the British Constitution goes under, the world will rock." Humanity would lose as much through Britain's fall as it would gain if Germany were suddenly annihilated. I don't believe it can fall. It will live on, having gathered together under the cover of its fog all the human values which are disappearing from Europe under the bloody boot of Germany.

It will live, but it will change profoundly. It will emerge once for all from its isolation, which no longer has anything splendid about it. Conserving the best of its traditions, it will break with those which are outmoded and keep it from marching in step with progress. Its youth, disciplined and ready for sacrifice, is already bitter against the ruling class. But don't think for a minute that it's a question of violent revolution. That of England will be made without violence. Indeed, it is already in the making. The enormous taxes demanded by the war are swallowing up most of the country's capital. And the gradual expropriation of the owning class is proceeding legally and without agitation.

Yes, the English revolution has already commenced. Already the palaces of the great lords have been turned over to government bureaus for war work. Already majestic parks have been converted into gardens and pastures. This revolution will have another curious result; Britain will be Europeanized. The Island will at last be united to the Continent; the mental barrier of the Channel will disappear. Hundreds of thousands of foreigners, military and civilian, who are at present living in England and helping in its defense, are contributing to that transformation by upsetting British habits, tastes, and prejudices.

Europe, on the other hand, will be drawn closer to England, for the Island has become the second fatherland and the great hope of all the subjugated peoples, represented there by their élite. These people will end by yielding to the profound charm of English life, as everyone does who has lived there long enough. Little by little they will discover England, by learning its language and soaking in its culture, by sharing its daily life. And they will find under the cold mask of the English gentleman the real man—loyal, often naïve, but generous.

"We've learned so much in this war," said an Oxford man who was beginning his career in the Ministry of Foreign Affairs. "We regarded the Poles, the Czechs, and the other small nations as obscure and almost barbarous little peoples. And we've found that they have solid virtues, and often know more than we do. We regarded Russia as our greatest enemy, and now realize that it has saved us."

But a Frenchman said to me, "Russia is saving us now, but we should have been lost without the British resistance which gave Russia as well as the United States time to prepare."

Without the will and determination of Winston Churchill, who inspired and eloquently expressed the British spirit after Dunkerque and who rejected the offers of Rudolf Hess, Russia would have been isolated and the United States reduced to impotence. Great Britain has placed humanity deeply in its debt.

THE EIGHTEENTH BIRTHDAY of King Peter II of Yugoslavia was celebrated by a reception in a private mansion in upper Grosvenor Street. The King and Queen Mother Marie of Yugoslavia expressed their wish to see me. I had not seen the Queen since her marriage twenty years before, when her youth had been so appealing. Now she was the modest mother of a family, who had suffered greatly. With charming simplicity and friendliness she talked to me about the late King Alexander.

"How often he spoke of you! I'm so glad you're safe and here with us. Peter, Mr. Todorov was a great friend of your father's."

The young King, lively, alert, and enthusiastic, spoke to me of his faith in Allied victory.

"We're going to win, aren't we? Yugoslavia will be born again, free and strong?"

"Yes, sire, but together with Bulgaria."

"Of course. We're all brothers."

The two young princes Tomislav and André were there too in their schoolboy dress, with short sleeves and tousled heads.

"Look at their ears," said their mother. "Do you remember their grandfather, the King of Rumania? They've inherited his ears."

From Belgrade as General Draja Mikhailovich's emissary to the Yugoslav government in London came my friend Dr. Mischa Seculich, who had managed to get to Turkey through Bulgaria with the aid of Bulgarian peasants. He had much to tell me about the man who was rapidly becoming the Yugoslav national hero; of his courage, energy, and uprightness.

"But surely you remember Mikhailovich," he said. "He was our military attaché at Sofia for some time."

I recalled him then. Someone had introduced him to me in a Belgrade restaurant, saying, "The Bulgarian government demanded his recall from Sofia because he talked openly about the need of union between the two countries."

The officer had smiled and his eyes twinkled behind his glasses.

"They're very sensitive on that subject in your country. The idea threw the government into panic while its popularity grew among the people and the army."

So that was the man who had raised the standard of revolt after Yugoslavia's tragic collapse! And the resistance he had organized inevitably followed the traditional Balkan form of guerrilla warfare carried on by *chetas* of *komitajis*. These modern *chetas,* of course, have not the slightest connection with the IMRO, whose gangsters are playing an ignoble role in the pay of the invader as members of the Bulgarian police and the Gestapo. Only the form of their organization and their methods of fighting follow the historic example of the old Macedonian revolutionary bands. In Macedonia itself, the people support Mikhailovich's *chetas* as they once supported the IMRO, and *chetniks* from that province are fighting side by side with other Yugoslavs for the same cause which inspired their forbears—freedom from their oppressors and the ideal of Slav democracy. In the mountains and forests—wherever they can find hiding places from which to attack the enemy, the invisible army of *chetniks* has girded itself for combat to the death.

The Serbs were the first to organize this warfare. I know some of their leaders. Ilya Birchanin, who lost his right arm at Kaimakchalan in 1916, who fought at Kumanovo in 1912, and who was a guerrilla as early as 1905 in the region of Skoplje, is once more fighting in the mountains. The old hero had been ready with his volunteers to aid our Peasant insurrection of 1925 which the Communists treacherously wrecked. In Bosnia, Doulé Dimitrievich, old and ill, is leading on horseback a large *cheta* of intrepid guerrillas. After the first World War, Dimitrievich became a lawyer; but before and during that war he was a *voivoda*.

The Serbs were the first. But the Croats and the Slovenes soon followed; then the Greeks; and at last the Bulgarians began to fill their own mountains, attacking railways, German supply depots, and even concentration camps and military objectives in the cities of Burgas and Plovdiv. The Montenegrins have reverted to the period of their struggles against the Turks; the Dalmatians and Croats have remembered the tradition of the *Uskoks,* the Greeks the methods of the *Kleftis,* the Serbs and Bulgarians of the *haiduks* and *chetniks*.

"Our *chetniks*," said Dr. Seculich, "endure the most painful privations without complaint. They move from one place to another with disconcerting rapidity. They attack unexpectedly and replenish their meager supplies of arms at the enemy's expense. The Germans, the Italians, Pavelich's *Ustashis* and the gendarmes of Nedich lose thousands of prisoners to them, with their rifles, machine guns, cannon and munitions."

"What do you do with the prisoners?"

"We often exchange them for wheat, gasoline or munitions. The exchange value of the Italians is lowest—one Fascist, one gallon of gas."

"Where are the *chetas*?" I asked.

"Everywhere and nowhere. One can travel hundreds of kilometers without seeing a single one. Then suddenly, as if by magic, rifle fire crackles from all over and the Germans and their allies fall wounded or killed by an invisible enemy. The Fascist monsters avenge themselves on the women and children; but they pay for their crimes. The *chetniks* destroy entire regiments. And so the Axis doesn't dare withdraw its troops. Several divisions which might have been used in Russia or elsewhere are needed to continue the war against the supposedly conquered Balkans."

"And do you think it can last?"

"Until victory if the Allies support the *chetniks* and send them airborne supplies. And on the day when the Allied armies come again, they will find an army of seasoned veterans eager to facilitate their job of cleaning out the Nazi and Fascist canaille. An army of 150,000 in Yugoslavia; and with the Bulgarians and Greeks perhaps 180,000—no inconsiderable force."

The sufferings of the Serbian people, as Dr. Seculich described them, were heartbreaking. Whole regions of Bosnia, he told me, had been depopulated by Pavelich's *Ustashis,* who had massacred all the Serbs except those able to escape to the mountains and join Mikhailovich's *chetas.* In Serbia the Nazis had found agents. General Milan Nedich had undertaken to apply the "new order" there, and had created a police force which was hounding the *chetniks.* But Mikhailovich's men eluded them, attacking unexpectedly, seizing arms, munitions, food, and retiring once more to their mountain fastnesses. In revenge for their frequent defeats the Germans were destroying towns and villages with dive bombers and artillery. In the city of Kragovevatz in Chumadia, the cradle of Serbian liberty, they had shot all the pupils of one high school, and all the professors. As they died the children had shouted, "We're not afraid to die; we're Serbs; long live liberty!"

"You see," remarked the Czechoslovak Minister Ripka one day at a dinner party, "we all make the mistake of failing to understand that this war is at bottom a great civil war. Every country has its pro- and anti-Hitlerites. You remember Masardjik, who was Krofta's secretary in the Ministry of Foreign Affairs? And Colonel Moravac whom you knew so well? They're both Nazis now! Whether out of spite or corruption I don't know; but they're our enemies, while you, a Bulgarian, have proved yourself our friend over and over again though your government is with Hitler. There are only two fronts and nothing, or almost nothing, between the two. And those fronts don't coincide with the frontiers between states. There's de Gaulle, and there's Laval. There's Quisling in Oslo and King Haakon here; Pavelich at Zagreb, and Croats in the Yugoslav government here. When our great allies understand this fact it will ease our task, for in the last analysis numbers and quality are on our side. The question is simply to organize and know how to utilize the enormous forces for democracy everywhere."

"Tell that, I beg you, to the British Foreign Office," was my answer.

Several days after the Japanese aggression I dined with Garreau, who had been appointed General de Gaulle's representative in Russia. "Come with me," he urged. "The General will make you a member of our mission, with the rank of military correspondent. You, who speak Russian and French equally well, can be very useful there." But I had promised my friends to work for a free Bulgaria and could not accept the invitation.

Garreau, who had been on special missions to Russia, Japan, Indo-China, and China, was an authority on Oriental questions. He told me how the Japanese had occupied Siam almost a year earlier with the complicity of the Siamese government.

"Did you warn the British?" I asked.

"Yes. I told the British Minister at Bangkok, but in spite of the proofs I gave him, he refused to believe me and gave full credence to the lying assurances of the Siamese."

Everywhere the same thing had happened! Even the Russians had been taken by surprise. They expected a German attack sooner or later, but refused to believe the British, who warned them of the day and even the hour when it would come—a record for their military intelligence. Because of this incredulity a large number of Soviet planes had been destroyed on the ground during the first hours of Hitler's offensive. "In the Orient the whole world knew of the Japanese plans," said Garreau, "except the people whose duty it was to know them."

"And what do you think will be the outcome?"

"It will depend on the duration of the war. Japanese industry is unequal to a long war. The Japanese cannot build enough merchant ships to provision so many far-flung expeditionary forces indefinitely. If the Allied fleets succeed in sinking a large part of their tonnage, their situation can become suddenly critical. That's why they don't attack Russia, whose position in the Far East makes their successes precarious. Since the Russians occupied Chan-cou-Feng after defeating the Japanese in 1938, their naval base at Posiet is protected, and its submarines are a very great menace to the Japanese. Imagine that fleet let loose on Japan's maritime routes!"

"But why haven't the Russians taken advantage of the situation to attack Japan?"

"Because they consider, and rightly, that their western front is more important. There is where the war will be won."

And his large eyes became dreamy as he remarked,

"What a passionately interesting epoch we are living in!"

Which was a point of view quite opposite to that of a Frenchwoman whom I had heard sighing, "When shall we be relieved at last of 'great events' and 'great men,' and allowed to return to our peaceful little daily lives with their simple, healthy joys?"

With Dr. Chubrilovich, a member of the Yugoslav government, I invited the Soviet ambassador, Ivan Maisky, and his councilor, N. Novikov, to dinner at a villa near London. Maisky is an old revolutionist who was a refugee in London before the first World War. Both in his appearance and his encyclopedic knowledge, he is the typical old Russian intellectual, and he talked politics, literature, art. Novikov is of the new school, a worker's son, and he talked chiefly about political and social questions. Both were proud of their country's exploits, but without fanfares. Maisky, who comes from Siberia, talked with feeling about his native land with its immense and scarcely tapped resources and its majestic rivers.

"Some day Siberia alone will be able to feed all Europe."

It was a very Russian remark. Russia is fighting for its existence, but that doesn't prevent the Russians from thinking on a world scale. "Feed all Europe." How much better than to plunder it as the Germans are doing! There lies the great difference between the Russian ideal, which continues to be universal, and the German ideal, which is to enslave humanity in order that a few thieves may fatten on the labor of the conquered peoples.

My old friend Gavrilovich, former Yugoslav Minister to Moscow, had arrived in London from Turkey. "I'm here," he told me, "to urge the British and Americans to do the impossible to help Russia. The Russians will win if they get the wherewithal. In Ankara, before the Germans invaded Russia, I warned the British and American ambassadors that the attack was imminent. They were skeptical, but at my insistence they notified their governments. I also urged that Britain and the United States immediately announce their solidarity with Russia when the war began and I was glad when they did so."

The Russian army, said Gavrilovich, was magnificent because "it's a people's army. The officers aren't a separate caste but like their men are children of the people. That makes for absolute solidarity and reciprocal confidence between the command and the soldiers."

"And what do you think of the government?" I inquired.

"Unquestionably it's severe. But I don't think it could be anything else in a country of so many different nationalities, especially with war threatening as it has for the past ten years."

"And Stalin?"

"With Stalin it was my privilege to talk for one whole night, until seven in the morning. In my opinion he's a great man, a great leader, and a great patriot although a sincere Communist. And he has a character of iron."

The different national groups in London were carrying on a diplomatic activity which was none the less important for being inconspicuous. The Europe of tomorrow—political and economic—was the object of studies and plans. Intrigues also flourished.

There was an Austrian intrigue aimed at restoration of the Austrian Empire under the Hapsburgs. The idea was rather popular among Anglo-Saxons. It is also very dangerous. The restoration of the Austrian Empire would mean in effect a renewal of the German menace the day after the war. It would permit the Germans to take refuge behind the Hapsburgs and thus escape the consequences of defeat. The intrigue is cleverly conducted. And up to date many actual Nazis who should have been interned have avoided internment by calling themselves Austrians. People are prone to forget that Austria was Germany's ally during the first World War, and that it was the Slavs who destroyed the Austrian Empire while the Germans of the Tyrol, Carinthia, and Burgenland defended it to the end. They tend to forget, too, that Hitler himself is Austrian, and so are the Sudeten Germans who voted en masse for Hitler in 1938.

Some of the Poles in London were intriguing more or less openly against Russia, and against General Wladyslaw Sikorski, who is wisely trying to reconcile Poland with the Soviet Union. Some former officials of the Baltic countries were in the intrigue. From this milieu came the impracticable plan for a Central European bloc with the thinly camouflaged purpose of creating a new *"cordon sanitaire"* against the Russians. And the English who were unofficially inspiring this plan are the same who applauded the treason of Munich and, having learned nothing, are still more afraid of Russia than of Germany.

There was also a Hungarian intrigue. The British Minister to Budapest counseled appeasement of Horthy and his medieval robbers even while Hungary was attacking Russia and massacring 100,000 Serbs in Voivodina. The Hungarian apologists are Professor McCarthy and the young Lord Rothermere who, with his father's millions, inherited his defeatist and Hungarophile sentiments.

Upon the tragic world-wide struggle for freedom these equivocal plots are stains which will disappear under the sun of victory.

And when victory comes, what is to be done with the nation which has committed and gloried in so many hideous crimes? I posed this question to my British acquaintances. And they answered, "Disarm them, re-educate them, pacify them while at the same time rendering them powerless in the future."

For the British, aside from the bombings which they are repaying in such overflowing measure, have not, thank God, suffered the outrageous treatment which Germany has inflicted on the vanquished nations. They are ready to forgive, as they forgave after that other war. Tomorrow they will no doubt be weeping again for the "poor Germans," as they wept yesterday for those "poor lambs" who had "suffered so much under the Treaty of Versailles"—which was never enforced—and the reparations—which they never paid.

Professor Seton Watson of Oxford is ready for a generous pardon. He told me so in his sad, monotonous voice. Naturally he is a fine man. But what right has any man to pardon crimes committed against others? Have not those others the right to be heard? May the victims not testify before tomorrow's tribunal? Russians, Poles, Czechoslovaks, Fighting French, Yugoslavs, Norwegians, Dutch and Belgians are saying, and with justification, "No! It is for us, the victims, to settle with the assassins. Not with our consent shall a Lloyd George tomorrow stay the hand of a Poincaré, or a Chamberlain brand as 'bloodthirsty' those people who wanted to defend Spain from German and Italian aggression or to prevent Czechoslovakia from being tossed into the maw of the German monster in a vain attempt to appease his insatiable appetite."

Such is the cry of the victimized peoples. Yet professors, parlor humanitarians, appeasers both sincere and suspect, attack Lord Vansittart when he dares to speak aloud the truth about Germany; not about naziism alone but about all Germany which voted freely for Hitler and brought him legally to power by a popular majority which has continued to grow ever since.

"But what would you do to German culture!" one of these "men of good will" exclaimed to me.

"I? Nothing. Ask the Germans, rather, what they themselves have done to it."

"What do you mean?"

"It's clear enough. They freely chose Hitler. Between *Faust* and *Mein Kampf* they chose the latter. Between Beethoven and Wagner, they chose the man who sang the atrociously cruel and bloody legends of the *Nibelungenring*. They have rejected Christianity in favor of the stupid and murderous gods of Valhalla."

"Perhaps they've gone mad, and need to be cared for and cured?"

"Madmen or mad dogs—I don't know. But they require unsentimental physicians. Let Stalin take care of them, for example. Don't repeat the stupid mistakes through which, after the last war, you yourselves set the stage for this one."

Such is the opinion of the conquered peoples; the cry which rises from millions of fresh graves to which millions more will be added before this war is ended. They hate, but without hate there is no real love. If one does not hate the executioner, it is because one does not sufficiently love his victim. And without the fecund hate which gives birth to fury on the battlefield there can be no victory.

A pilot in command of a fighter squadron said to me,

"The Poles under my command fight with the fury of the damned. They hurl themselves upon the German planes as if they had before them an enemy ten times stronger than themselves, and often die by crashing into them. Nothing I can do stops them. If I don't take them along on our patrol flights, they shed tears of rage. Their bravery is like that of madmen."

Yes, because they hate; because they see in the Germans the murderers of their families, the destroyers of their homes. Victory will come out of such feelings when they become the feelings of a majority in our camp. A British sergeant who came to my hotel to visit his friend the manager was introduced to me. He had escaped from a German prison camp and while we drank together he described his adventures, simply and without excitement, as if he spoke of ordinary things.

"It was near Dunkerque. I'd been wounded in the leg, and they took me along with a hundred others, wounded or stragglers. Not more than fifty survived. What happened to the others? The Germans killed them on the way, like animals, to amuse themselves. By chance they spared me but I saw my comrades fall as if they had been knocked out—stiff, dead. In the camp we were badly treated, especially in the matter of food. Without our packages from home we'd all be dead by this time. As soon as my wound healed I decided to escape with two friends, Scots like myself. Our comrades gave us part of the contents of their packages. Adding ours to that and rationing ourselves severely, we were able to reach Switzerland after several nights. After that we traveled on American passports and reached Lisbon without trouble."

"Did nothing happen to you in France and Spain?"

"Nothing. Only in France, in the railway carriages everyone, thinking we were Americans, asked us, 'When will the United States at last enter the war?' When we confidently answered, 'Soon,' there was general rejoicing. That's all."

"What do you think ought to be done to the Germans after the war, after the victory?" I asked. He shrugged his shoulders.

"Nothing special. Just apply their own methods to them. That'll be enough. Nothing more."

This one did not talk to me about German culture. He had tasted it.

The Bulgarian Minister to London, Nicholas Momtchilov, had resigned as soon as Bulgaria went over to the Axis. He had always been personally devoted to King Boris. Now he was very much depressed and anxious about Bulgaria's future.

"The most disgusting thing," he said, "is that the King lied to me up to the last minute. Three days before the German troops entered Bulgaria I received a dispatch from Sofia ordering me to inform the Foreign Office that the news of preparations for the entry was false and that Bulgaria would remain neutral. Imagine my situation when three days later the Germans occupied the country with the King's consent! Even now I'm actually ashamed to look an Englishman in the eye."

"Don't you think the King may have been sincere when he protested his good intentions, and that he may have yielded only to force?"

"I don't know. But I do know that every time I talked to him about Bulgaria's interest in remaining completely neutral or following Britain's advice, he couldn't conceal his spite. It seems to me he must have made his decision long ago."

"Then why, knowing your sentiments, didn't he recall you?"

"Because he wanted to have a man here who could deceive the British by repeating his lies in good faith."

I was reminded of Talleyrand's formula, "When you want to fool a foreign government, send it a man of good faith who is himself the dupe of your intentions."

The news from Bulgaria was at once tragic and encouraging. Tragic because of the numerous executions. In the trial against Dimitrov, six of our friends were condemned to death. His wife, however, was acquitted; her innocence was too evident even for judges commanded by the Gestapo. The editor of *Pladne,* which I had founded, the engineer Volkov and his brother who had once been my bodyguard, were condemned to death. More than 600 others were executed. In the concentration camps and prisons more than 1,200 peasants, workers, and intellectuals were condemned to die of privation and ill treatment.

On the other hand, the army obstinately refused to fight against Russia. In the occupied Serbian provinces, thanks to conscientious officers, there had been neither violence nor massacres—the Yugoslavs themselves loyally testified to that. But what rejoiced me most was that when Bulgarian soldiers were sent to fight Draja Mikhailovich many of them went over to him. This was confirmed by the American Minister to

[338]

Sofia upon his arrival at Istanbul after Boris had declared war on the United States and Great Britain. I was doubly pleased because for several months the main theme of my short-wave broadcasts to Bulgaria had been, "Go over with your weapons to the Serbian hero, Draja Mikhailovich!" In the mountains of the Balkans a firm solidarity was being forged between the "conquering" Bulgarians and the "conquered" Yugoslavs.

As for the Croats, their beloved leader, Dr. Machek, had been arrested and interned with thousands of his partisans. The Croat peasants were boycotting Zagreb and bringing it almost no food. Those near Mikhailovich's insurgents were informing them of every movement of the *Ustasha* bands. The regular Croat soldiers were avoiding encounters with the *chetniks* or surrendering without a fight. Here and there they too were deserting to the mountains and making war on Pavelich's gangsters, imposed on Croatia by Mussolini and Hitler. In Dalmatia the Fascists were shooting the Croats and the mountains were already full of partisans. My friend Ripka had been right—this is a great civil war.

All over the Balkans a fifth column of speculators, cowards, and paid agents had placed themselves at Hitler's disposal. And everywhere the people—above all the peasants—were rising up against him, uniting and fighting together for liberty. On the one side was the triumvirate, Boris, Nedich, Pavelich, on the other, the people.

Such is the psychological basis for the union of tomorrow. There, in perspective, is the ideal for which I have fought more than twenty-three years, the ideal for which Alexander Stamboliski and Alexander of Yugoslavia paid with their lives, on its way to realization not in the chancelleries but in life—in common misery, blood, and suffering.

About to take my leave of London, I made the rounds of my friends. The Gaviloviches, who had arrived at the end of December, would miss me most. They didn't want to go to America; life there was too good! They chose to "remain nearer to the fatherland and share the privations of the English who are fighting for us." Such were the reasons Mme. Gavrilovich gave me for preferring London to New York. But I had to carry out the plan made in Cairo—to organize the Bulgarians of America behind a free Bulgaria. And I was about to leave for Canada.

At the end of February, 1942, I boarded a large ship somewhere on the coast of Scotland. The Battle of the Atlantic was in full swing, and we had to sleep fully dressed and wear our life preservers constantly. The sea was rough, with waves like heaving mountains. The ships of our escort often disappeared, only to reappear on the foamy crest of a wave. But the passengers were gay and unafraid. They were youngsters of the British air corps, instructors and students, bound for the training fields of Canada.

We were on our way to America, and I was on the last leg of my journey around the world. At the thought of seeing New York again I was as moved as if I were going, after a long separation, to rejoin a beloved being.

The war goes on. It will be long. My adventures are not ended. I too shall continue to fight in the ways open to me. I am on the side where I know the hearts of my people to be. If barbarism and tyranny triumph, life will not be worth living. But if we win, tomorrow there will be a brotherhood of free Balkan peoples. In my heart I hear the voice of hope, and old Pashich's words, uttered so long ago, ring in my mind:

"The most important thing is that the peasants forget neither good nor evil. And they know how to wait. . . . The peasants plant the seed in the autumn and gather the harvest only the following summer. They are accustomed to wait for the harvest—and there shall be a harvest!"

THE END